WILDLIFE AND WESTERN HEROES

Alexander Phimister Proctor, Sculptor

WILDLIFE AND WESTERN HEROES

Alexander Phimister Proctor, Sculptor

[handwritten inscription:]
*For Howard Neville
With all best
wishes,
[signature]
Gifford Proctor*

Peter H. Hassrick

With contributions by Katharine C. Ebner, a memoir by
Phimister Proctor Church, and recollections by Gifford Proctor

Amon Carter Museum, Fort Worth, Texas
in association with Third Millennium Publishing, London

© Copyright text Amon Carter Museum, Fort Worth, Texas, 2003.
© Copyright all illustrations Amon Carter Museum, Fort Worth, Texas, 2003, unless otherwise noted.

Amon Carter Museum
3501 Camp Bowie Boulevard
Fort Worth, Texas 76107
www.cartermuseum.org

First published in 2003 by Third Millennium Publishing
An imprint of Third Millennium Information Limited
First Floor
2 Jubilee Place
London
SW3 3TQ
UK
www.tmiltd.com

ISBN: 1 903942 22 5

Will Gillham: Director of Publications
Miriam Hermann: Publications Assistant
Sarah Louise Kane, Polly Koch: Editors
Sarah Louise Kane, Mary Jane Crook: Proofreaders
Design by Anikst Design: James Warner
Produced by Third Millennium Publishing, an imprint of
Third Millennium Information Limited
Reprographics by News S.p.a., Italy
Printed and bound in Slovenia by Mladinska

Library of Congress Cataloging-in-Publication Data

Proctor, Alexander Phimister, 1860–1950.
  Wildlife and western heroes : Alexander Phimister Proctor, sculptor / essays and catalogue entries by Peter Hassrick with a memoir by Phimister Proctor Church and recollections by Gifford Proctor. — 1st ed.

    p. cm.
"The Amon Carter Museum, in conjunction with the Proctor Museum in Poulsbo, Washington, is presently organizing the first major exhibition of the sculpture of Alexander Phimister Proctor (1860–1950)." Includes bibliographical references and index.
  ISBN 1-903942-22-5 (Hardcover)
1. Proctor, Alexander Phimister, 1860–1950—Exhibitions.
2. Wildlife art—Exhibitions. 3. West (U.S.)—In art—Exhibitions.
I. Hassrick, Peter H. II. Amon Carter Museum of Western Art.
III. Proctor Museum. IV. Title.

  NB237.P74A4 2003
  730'.92—dc21

                        2003013800

CONTENTS

FOREWORD

The Amon Carter Museum is justly renowned for its important collection of sculpture by Frederic Remington (1861–1909) and Charles M. Russell (1864–1926). My own work on Russell's sculpture, which resulted in a study published by this museum in 1994, included an investigation of bronzes produced by other worthy American sculptors who were contemporaries of Remington and Russell. One of the most important of these was Alexander Phimister Proctor (1860–1950), whose small bronzes and magnificent monumental sculpture seemed sadly neglected. Happily, that historical deficiency has been redressed by this publication and the exhibition that accompanies it.

This project owes its inception to one man: Phimister Proctor Church, the artist's grandson, who provides a brief reminiscence in this volume. "Sandy" Church, as he is known by family and friends, has devoted his life to the investigation, collection, and appreciation of Alexander Phimister Proctor's art. It was Sandy Church who founded the A. Phimister Proctor Museum to showcase his grandfather's life and work. He engaged the services of Peter Hassrick to author the present volume—the first monograph on the artist's work—and he convinced all of us here at the museum to undertake the publication and mount a traveling exhibition. The results are as much a vindication of Sandy Church's devotion as they are a celebration of the artistic accomplishments of a grandfather who still very much lives in his grandson's memory. But Sandy himself would be quick to acknowledge—as we do here—the support and assistance of many other members of the extended Proctor family. They have all descended from the close-knit group, described in the following pages, who accompanied the peripatetic sculptor as he created his unforgettable monuments. One of the sculptor's sons, Gifford Proctor, is happily still with us and creating sculpture in his Connecticut studio. "The Great Proctor," as other family members like to call him, has also provided in these pages a wonderful recollection of an inspiration to mischief during his eventful childhood. Today the Proctor family is deeply committed to the achievements of their illustrious ancestor, but they also recall the selfless efforts of Proctor's devoted wife, Margaret, who was herself a sculptor. Mr. and Mrs. Proctor's admirable accomplishments are chronicled in the following pages.

As always, it has been a pleasure to work with Peter Hassrick, who began his museum career at this institution. Researching and presenting the life and work of a sculptor is a very difficult enterprise. To the many individuals who provided research information, and to the various lenders who have allowed us to borrow works for the exhibition, we offer our sincere gratitude. The exhibition will travel to the Buffalo Bill Historical Center in Cody, Wyoming, and we express our appreciation to Robert E. Shimp and other members of the staff for their participation and support. Finally, the Amon Carter Museum gratefully acknowledges support from the Proctor Foundation for the publication of this volume. For their support of the exhibition, we are deeply grateful to Mr. and Mrs. Sebert L. Pate, the Mary Potishman Lard Trust, and the Ruth and Vernon Taylor Foundation.

Rick Stewart
Director

April 2003

ACKNOWLEDGMENTS

It was with great excitement in 1998 that I accepted the invitation extended by Phimister Proctor Church to explore the possibilities of a full, critical treatment of his grandfather, the sculptor Alexander Phimister Proctor. "Sandy," as he is affectionately known, has been gathering materials on Proctor for many years. His enthusiasm for and dedication to the sculptor's art and legacy have involved everything from preserving the artist's archives and artworks to defending his creative integrity and establishing a small museum to house a wide variety of the artist's remarkable sculptures and paintings. Sandy has proved to be not simply a devoted namesake but also a serious student of the artist. I am privileged to know and to have worked with him and his family, especially his wife, Sally, and have been inspired by their resolve to accomplish something of merit with the subject.

To Sandy I owe the inspiration for this book. His unflagging moral and financial support (both personally and through the Proctor Foundation) moved the project forward over many years. His knowledge and perseverance account for much of its success. In addition, the trustees and staff of the A. Phimister Proctor Museum, especially Laura Proctor Ames, Jeff Oens, Carolyn McClurkan, and Kathy Engelstad, provided invaluable research assistance as well as vital work in organizing the artist's archives and collating and conserving the collections. Other members of the Proctor family were also generous with their assistance. I am especially appreciative of the infectious enthusiasm shown by the artist's son, Gifford Proctor, who aided the cause in many ways, and Gifford's daughter, Susan, as well.

Rick Stewart and the Amon Carter Museum staff are responsible for infusing the project with life. Rick saw immediate potential for both a book and an exhibition. He pressed for a full and substantial effort, regarding Proctor as an extraordinary artistic force in his time. There has not been a moment over the course of the project that Rick has not given completely of his encouragement and support. With a long and distinguished history of fostering scholarship in American art and bringing major art trends and expressions to public audiences, the Amon Carter Museum has once again proved its worth in sponsoring the work on such a heretofore unheralded artistic figure.

The museum's staff has also contributed much. Wendy Haynes, director of exhibitions at the Carter, ably guided the exhibition. Will Gillham, director of publications, and Miriam Hermann, publications assistant, labored over the catalogue, and the museum's library staff, especially Sam Duncan, provided valuable research assistance. To them all, I am profoundly grateful.

When I embarked on the Proctor project, I was a professor of art history and director of the Charles M. Russell Center for the Study of Art of the American West at the University of Oklahoma. That institution offered many welcome benefits in this pursuit of scholarship. The university art school's director, Andrew Phelan, promoted the project from the start. My assistant, Stephanie Rahill, was a great help. The art history department provided two most capable students to assist in the work, Jeff Cooper and K. C. Ebner. The latter rendered invaluable insight into the study, along with excellent organizational savvy, bright spirit, and gifted research and writing skills. I am especially indebted to K. C. for her genuine contribution to this book and the exhibition.

Much of the writing and research for this endeavor took place in Cody, Wyoming. The Buffalo Bill Historical Center and its library made me welcome, and in fact hosted me over one summer, affording me research facilities and support that were invaluable. Byron Price, until recently director of the Cody museum, was particularly gracious, as was the library staff: Frances Clymer, Nathan Bender, Mary Robinson, and Lynn Pitet. The museum's curator of art, Sarah Boehme, extended collegial cordiality and counsel that facilitated my work and enhanced my efforts considerably.

Acknowledgment must also go to the artist's two daughters, Hester Proctor and Nona Proctor Church, for preserving the legacy of their father over the years from 1950 (when the sculptor died) to the 1970s, when Sandy assumed the role of preserving their celebrated ancestor's legacy. It was Hester who got Vivian A. Paladin of the Montana Historical Society interested in Proctor and helped publish the first modern biographical account of the artist, an article by Paladin that appeared in *Montana, the Magazine of Western History* in 1964. Moreover, it was Hester who encouraged the University of Oklahoma Press to publish the artist's autobiography, *Sculptor in Buckskin*, in 1971.

Another individual who has worked diligently to preserve the memory of Proctor and to recognize his talent is Jeff Nelson, an independent scholar from Washington, D.C. Over the past decade or more Jeff has studied Proctor's role in decorating the Q Street Bridge in the nation's capital. His inquiry has lent much positive information and insight into the artist's life and creative genius.

Many major institutions across the country provided me with assistance, opening their collections for review and sharing their talented staffs with me. I extend my deep gratitude to the following institutions and personal and professional colleagues: Albright-Knox Art Gallery, Janice Lurie and Tara A. Riese; American Museum of Natural History, Lise Darst and Laila Williamson; Archives of American Art, Smithsonian Institution; Art Gallery of Ontario; The Art Institute of Chicago, Andrew Walker and Bart Ryckbosch; Baltimore Museum of Art, Sona Johnston; Bohemian Club, Peter Johnson Musto; Boone and Crockett Club, Jack Renault and George A. Bettas; Bronx Zoo Library, Steve Johnson and Diane Shapiro; Brooklyn Botanical Gardens, Robert T. Hyland; Brooklyn Museum of Art, Sarah Snook and Linda S. Ferber; Brookgreen Gardens, Robin Salmon; Buffalo

Bill Memorial Museum, Steve Friesen; Buffalo and Erie County Historical Society, Patricia M. Vigil; Century Club, Jonathan P. Harding; Chicago Historical Society, Rob Kent; Cleveland Museum of Art, Henry H. Hawley; Colorado Historical Society, Georgianna Contiguglia and Allis Sawyer; Conner-Rosenkranz, Janis Conner, Joel Rosenkranz, and Mark Ostrander; The Corcoran Gallery of Art, Marissa Keller; Dallas Historical Society, Ann Westerlin; Dallas Public Library; Dallas Southern Memorial Association, Mrs. Dewey D. Johnston and Nita Stover; Dayton Art Institute, Ena Murphy; Denver Art Museum, Ann Daley and Bridget M. O'Toole; Denver Public Library, Western History Department, Kay Wisnia; Des Moines Art Center, Jeff Fleming; Gerald Peters Gallery, Gerald Peters and Julie Schimmel; Genesee County Village and Museum, Matthew Moore; Gilcrease Museum, Anne Morand; Glenbow Museum, Kirstin Evenden; Grey Towers National Historic Landmark, Becky Philpot and Marie Chambers; Harry Ransom Humanities Research Center, University of Texas at Austin, Peter Mears and Tara Wenger; Harry S. Truman Library-Museum, Clay R. Banske; The Houghton Library, Harvard University, Theodore Roosevelt Collection, Wallace Dailey; Indianapolis Museum of Art, Harriet G. Warkel; James Graham & Sons, Cameron Shay and Meredith E. Miller; Jasper County Historical Society, Hanz J. Brosig; Lee Chapel and Museum, Washington and Lee University, Patricia A. Hobbs; Library of Congress; Mead Art Museum; The Metropolitan Museum of Art, Thayer Tolles; Monroe County Historical Society, Lynn W. Reaume; Musée des Sciences, Jérôme Tréguier; Nassau County Museum of Fine Art; National Academy of Design, David B. Dearinger and Margo L. Hensler; National Cowboy and Western Heritage Museum, Charles Rand; National Gallery of Canada, Charlie Hill; National Museum of Wildlife Art, Adam Harris; National Park Service, Long Distance Trails Office, Jere Krakow; National Sculpture Society, Gwen Peir; New York Public Library, Robert Sink; R. W. Norton Art Gallery, Jerry M. Bloomer; North Carolina Museum of Art, Michael Klauke; Oregon Historical Society, Marsha Matthews; Paine Art Center and Gardens; Parrish Art Museum, Novella Laspia; Pendleton Round-Up and Happy Canyon Hall of Fame, Robin Rew; Portland Art Museum, Debra Royer, Ann Eichelberg, and Margaret Bullock; Prospect Park Alliance, Julie Moffat; Rauner Special Collections Library, Dartmouth College, Jeanne W. Merrill; Rockwell Museum, Stuart Chase; C. M. Russell Museum, Nancy M. Wheeler and Elizabeth Dear; Saint-Gaudens National Historical Site, Henry J. Duffy; The Saint Louis Art Museum, Richardson Library; San Diego Museum of Art, David L. Kencik; Santa Barbara Museum of Art, Robert M. Henning Jr.; Sagamore Hill National Historical Site, Susan Sarna; Smithsonian American Art Museum, George Gurney; Southwest Museum, Kim Walters; State Historical Society of North Dakota, Mark J. Halvorson; Texas Memorial Museum, Sally Baulch-Rhoden; Texas State Historical Association, Ron Tyler and George Ward; Tutt Library, Colorado College, Ginny Keifer; Theodore Roosevelt National Historical Site, Katherine A. Hansen; Third Cavalry Museum, Scott Hamric; Toledo Museum of Art, Lee Mooney; University Gallery, University of Delaware, Janet Gardner Broske; University of Oregon Museum of Art, Jean Nattinger; Walters Art Gallery, William R. Johnston; Webb Institute, William G. Murray; West Point Museum, David M. Reel; Wichita Art Museum, Novelene Ross and Charles K. Steiner; Wichita High School East, Katie McHenry; William S. Hart Ranch, Zandra Stanley; Wilton Public Library; Woodrow Wilson House, Meg Nowack; Woolaroc Museum, Robert R. Lansdown and Linda Stone; Yellowstone National Park, Lee Whittlesey, and Susan Kraft.

In addition to those mentioned above, a host of individuals were helpful in this project. I gratefully acknowledge their contributions here and offer them my sincere thanks: Lowell E. Baire, Patricia Broder, Britt Brown, Scott Church, Adrienne Conzelman, Carolyn Cuskey, Betty Due, Paul Fees, Steve Good, Belle Clegg Hays, Lynn J. House, Harriet Kaye, Barbara Knight, Shirley A. Leckie, Barbara Lindauer, Rod Lister, Charles McGhee-Hassrick, Vern Milligan, Marcy Mongon, Paul Moore, Thomas Nygard, Thomas Petrie, Chris Polk, Jonathan Richards, Prudence Roberts, William Ruger Jr., Virgil Rupp, Richard J. Schwartz, Senator Alan K. Simpson, Michael Shapiro, Henry O. Smith III, Annette Stott, Jean True, and Mrs. Ray C. Westman.

Peter H. Hassrick

April 2003

"NEEDS MUST WHEN THE DEVIL DRIVES"

RECOLLECTIONS OF A SCULPTOR'S SON

There could be no doubt about it. The Devil made me do it, seducing me, Wee Mac, about five years old, to commit a crime for which, once discovered, hell would be raised.

All nine of the Proctor tribe had just left the Northwest and all the life that I had ever known, which was being among Indians, cowhands, round-ups, bucking contests and bulldoggings, camping, tents and tipis, the P Ranch, the Snake and Clearwater Rivers. We left behind Pendleton, Oregon, and Lewiston, Idaho, to end up in Los Altos, California.

To get her tribe from up there down to central California, Mody, my mother, had Dad and the two oldest sons, Alden and Phim, take off with full camp outfit in a huge, high-wheeled Cadillac Dad had bought from "Uncle Bill" Hanley of the P Ranch. The five of the rest of us and Mody took off by train, which for our delectation stopped at Shasta Springs where it was revealed to me, with disgust and regurgitating revulsion, that Shasta's "soda water" simply wasn't the anticipated sarsaparilla.

In Los Altos Dad had taken over a barn and converted it to a studio in which to enlarge and cast in plaster Denver's *Broncho Buster* with its frenzied horse. To get the necessary height for this enlargement, a section of the barn's bay-loft floor had to be done away with to open a space from the ground floor to the roof, which left a "balcony" of loft flooring that surrounded the enormous bucking horse and rider.

Apparently, in 1916 a five-year-old could still solo around Los Altos, for on this particular day I had moseyed down our pepper tree-lined street to a dirt farm road, paralleled on one side by the Southern Pacific's steam railroad tracks and on the other by an olive grove, and so on to Dad's barn studio. Having arrived, I soon found myself perched on the bay-loft balcony, high up behind the *Broncho Buster* and his mount, looking directly at the rider's back and, slightly lower, at the rump of his mount. It was up there—

out of sight of Dad and the enlargers, modelers, and caster below—that the Devil took possession of me.

What happened next took place before the development of the contemporary sculptor's modeling material called "plastaline," an oil-impregnated modeling clay. The *Broncho Buster* was being enlarged with the ancient material of water clay, some of which the Devil had placed in my hands. "Needs must when the Devil drives," and I was driven to fashion a small ball of this clay, which I tossed down onto the great rump of the broncho. Suddenly, in my head, this act became a threatening, appalling desecration for which, were I to be fingered as the perpetrator, scalping would be but the lesser of the evils I would suffer. The fear gripping my small gut demanded immediate, evasive action. I crept out of the studio, back past the olive grove and up the street to home, where I sought sanctuary and the security provided by Mody. I made it!

I only now realize I never told Dad of my treachery.

That was some eighty-six years ago. Now, going on ninety-one, I am aware of a growing admiration and wonderment for both Mody and Dad. I am increasingly impressed by Dad's creations, by the impressive quality of his brain's retention, by his animals' anatomies and movements, and by his sensitivity to their psyches. (At this moment I recall the dignity of his *Princeton Tiger.*)

But then it is not only the *quality* of his production that impresses me, but the *quantity,* the number of monumental equestrian statues he created, an achievement that could only have resulted from seemingly endless days spent in his studio. During our two years in Rome, *per esempio*, I recall (perhaps somewhat mistakenly) that he took only about two weeks off from a two-year routine of morning to supper time in his studio.

It is my conviction that he never would have achieved these objectives had he not had his "Margaret" as his companion. It was she who freed him from family and household cares, moving everyone and everything from one house and studio to another about every three years, who cared for him, encouraged him, loved him, and in every way freed him for his work, even making it possible for him occasionally to retreat into the wilds, hunting and fishing to restore his soul.

At this time in my life, I find myself astonished that I cannot recall ever being in conflict with Mody or Dad. Also, unbelievably, over the many years of closeness to them I never heard them raise their voices in tension toward one another, except this: Mody never learned to drive a car and never would, apparently as a result of Dad's early efforts at giving her driving instructions.

Now, finally, I recall receiving nothing but love and support from them, and these many years later harboring nothing but respect and admiration for each of them and for the inspiration of their lives.

Gifford Proctor
Wilton, Connecticut

November 2002

MY GRANDDAD, THE ARTIST

It may seem odd, but my principal passion in life developed after an encounter with an old man when I was five years old. This passion now borders on obsession, and the majority of my time is devoted to uncovering the many mysteries of my grandfather, Alexander Phimister Proctor.

I cannot count the number of times over the past forty years I have mentioned Granddad and, describing his various monumental statues throughout the United States, heard in reply, "I know that statue, it's great. You mean he did that?" This in turn has led to, "I thought Remington did that"; or, "You mean Russell didn't do that?" People are amazed when I tell them Granddad created twenty-seven works of monumental sculpture, while Frederic Remington did only one, and Charles M. Russell, none. The conversation has usually concluded with, "What was his name again?"

The name Alexander Phimister Proctor is well known in the art world, but largely unrecognized elsewhere. This will soon change. With the tireless support of my wife, Sally, I have traveled down a road of discovery, intrigue, and excitement that is hard to believe. The end results are this catalogue, authored by one of this country's most prominent scholars of western art, Peter Hassrick, and the exhibition, organized by the prestigious Amon Carter Museum in Fort Worth, Texas. Along the way, the A. Phimister Proctor Museum in Poulsbo, Washington, has been created, which today houses the most complete collection of art by any one sculptor in this country.

Where did this all begin? When I was born my parents named me Malcolm MacGregor Church. Where Malcolm came from I don't know, but MacGregor was the Proctor family Scottish clan. Some months later, my parents changed my name to Phimister Proctor Church. As I write this, I can't believe I never asked my mother about the change while she was alive. I documented so many facts and stories from her about her life and items related to the Proctor family, but I neglected to ask many questions about our immediate family and my own childhood.

Alexander Phimister Proctor with his daughter Nona Church's children: Sandy is on his lap. Left to right behind him: Peggy Ann, Campbell Scott, and Betty Jean.

A. Phimister Proctor Museum Archives, Poulsbo, Wash.

A sketch by Proctor of his honeymoon at Niagara Falls, 1893

A. Phimister Proctor Museum Archives, Poulsbo, Wash.

A silver bowl given to Sandy by his granddad, 1940

A. Phimister Proctor Museum Archives, Poulsbo, Wash.

I do know that my name change pleased Granddad a great deal. Shortly after my birth in 1937 he wrote a letter to my parents, having received news of his namesake from my Uncle Harvey. He referred to me by my nickname, Sandy, and wrote about his feelings and a silver bowl he intended to buy for me. I still have this bowl.

Harvey just told me that you had named my bully little pal after me—I didn't realize how pleased it would make me to hear you do it—It simply tickles me to death—Odd how the blessed little monkey took to me—he certainly pulled my heart right out of me—How I'd love to see him, as well as the rest of your lovely kiddies. None of the rest of them took to me that way. Someone said lately, looking at Sandy's picture, that he looked like me—he has something to live down poor kid…. Give my dearest love to yourselves & lovely kiddies, especially—Phimister Proctor Church. Lovingly Dad

Thus began a unique relationship between a boy and his granddad. It was five years later that my grandmother, Margaret Gerow, affectionately

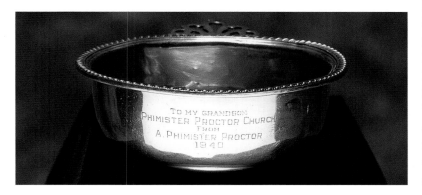

referred to by all as Mody, passed away. In addition to his lifelong devotion to art and to the wilderness, Granddad had an equally important love—Mody. I can imagine the void he must have felt when she died. Mody not only raised their eight children, but she was his most important art critic. He met her at the World's Columbian Exposition in Chicago in 1893. It was love at first sight. Shortly thereafter they were married, honeymooned at Niagara Falls, and left for Paris. She gave up her own promising career as an artist to be with Granddad and raise their children.

After Mody's death, Granddad moved in with us. My parents were struggling with financial problems brought on by the war, and they were trying to save their family business. My older brother and sisters were all off in school and involved with their lives. There seemed to be little family time for me. To cope with his loss, this gentle eighty-one-year-old man turned his attention to his namesake.

I recall the two of us walking through our backyard in Seattle to Lake Washington, our special place where we spent time together. He would have me gallop by him like a runaway stallion, and with his rope he would lasso my foot as I passed. He called his rope "old friend" and told me it had been by his side for forty years. He insisted I neigh like a wild horse, and we practiced making the right sound. On one trip to the lake he brought an old Indian warbonnet and peace pipe that had belonged to one of his models, Big Beaver. After putting on the bonnet, he did a war dance and had me follow along. The two of us chanted and danced around and around in a circle. We then sat cross-legged and pretended to smoke the pipe and pass it to each other in a ceremonial way. Today, these two artifacts are in the collection of the American Museum of Natural History in New York City, along with the rest of Granddad's Native American objects, which numbered around 125 items.

him ever saying that anyone was shot to death, but at the end of the story he gave me an old gun he found in that creek bed.

He also told me the story of the first Indians he saw in 1865, at the time he was my age. He talked about standing on a woodpile to peer across the landscape, trying to see who was visiting his house on the outskirts of town. As the group got closer, Granddad saw they were Indians on ponies. One of the Indians saw the curious little boy and let out a war cry in jest. Granddad almost fell off the woodpile scrambling to get away. He headed to the house running faster than he had ever run in his life.

Can you imagine the images that danced in my head and my dreams at night? While listening to "The Lone Ranger" on the radio, I knew that I had the real story of life in the Old West, as told to me by my Granddad.

Several years later, after he had moved out, Granddad visited us again while waiting to go on a bear hunt in southeastern Alaska. The wilderness and hunting in it were a large part of his life. He would get restless when fall came, packing up his art supplies and gun to head out on a sketching trip. The hunting provided food, along with models for studying the anatomy of animals for future sculpting jobs. His paintings were good, but his modeling was exceptional. During this visit I once again heard some wonderful stories, and he gave me two of his bronze statues, a bear cub and a stalking panther. He also gave me a pen-and-ink drawing of "Mountain Jim & Grizzly" inscribed, "To Sandy with love from Granddad. Feby. 14th 1945." This started my collection of Proctor art. (Incidentally, during this Alaska hunting trip Granddad bagged a bear seventy years to the day after he shot his first bear at Grand Lake, Colorado, at age sixteen.)

I find it fascinating that my great-grandfather, bringing up young Alexander Phimister Proctor in the rough frontier town of Denver in the 1870s, recognized Granddad's artistic talent and, by the time the boy was

Granddad was an excellent storyteller, weaving together facts and memories of frontier battles between Indians and cowboys. One story he told me was about a shoot-out between a posse and some outlaws. His words painted a vivid picture of the creek and surrounding countryside, describing how the posse had "got the drop" on the outlaws. I don't remember

"Mountain Jim & Grizzly". To Sandy with love from Grand dad. Feby 14th 1945.

thirteen, had secured art lessons for him. In Granddad's autobiography, *Sculptor in Buckskin* (1971), he grouses about these art lessons being on Saturdays and holidays: "This arrangement was not entirely to my liking because it interfered with baseball and rabbit hunting." As Granddad grew older, his father encouraged him to go to Europe; he even tried gold-mining in the hopes of striking it rich and having enough money to send his son to art school. At age twenty-four Granddad himself tried mining for a summer; but after failing to find gold he sold his homestead at Grand Lake to fund his studies at the National Academy of Design and the Art Students League in New York City.

In 1884, just prior to his studies in New York, a life-altering experience occurred while Granddad was on a six-month excursion through California. Setting out with his friend from Los Angeles, Alden Sampson, the two rode their horses to Yosemite Valley, sketching and hunting along the way. While camping in the valley, someone told them about cables that had been installed up the backside of Half Dome to help climbers reach the summit. The cables had been destroyed by a winter storm, and a Swiss team was being organized to replace them. Granddad couldn't understand why someone from the United States could not do the job, so he volunteered Alden and himself. On the way up Half Dome, Granddad used a rope to lasso each of the pegs that had previously been drilled into the face of the rock. After two days of dangerous climbing, the two had replaced all the broken cables with new ropes. It was at some point on this harrowing adventure that Proctor declared he would devote his life to art.

My mother, Nona Proctor Church, inherited Granddad's gift for storytelling and over the course of her life recounted many stories of having grown up the child of a passionately devoted artist. Her memories added remarkable dimension to Granddad's life and richly conveyed the connections he had to people and places. Mom remembered living in a tipi in 1914 on the Cheyenne Indian reservation while her father modeled Robert Little Wolf. Granddad greatly admired Indians, especially Laban Little Wolf, who was father of Robert and chief of the tribe. Laban possessed mutual respect for Granddad. In a secret ceremony, Granddad became a blood brother to Laban Little Wolf. His Indian name was Okomahkahchitah, meaning Large Coyote. What happened during that ceremony has remained a secret.

Mom also told of Slim Ridings, who lived with the Proctors in Pendleton, Oregon, while Granddad was modeling what became the *Broncho Buster* (now in Denver). The local sheriff, Til Taylor, arrested Slim for stealing horses. It was not the first time Slim had been in trouble with the law. The sheriff agreed to release Slim into Granddad's custody to complete his modeling for the statue. I have a letter from Slim, asking Granddad for bail, in which he wrote, "I don't know how those durn horses got in my corral, every time I pick up a rope there's a horse on the end of it." When Til Taylor was killed years later, Granddad created a monumental statue of him on his horse for the town of Pendleton.

Another of Proctor's models was Jackson Sundown, nephew of the famed Chief Joseph of the Nez Perce tribe. Sundown had escaped with a small band of his tribe across the Canadian border when the United States Cavalry captured Chief Joseph and his followers and sent them back to the reservation. Sundown later returned to the reservation, and he was one of Granddad's favorite subjects, posing for a small statue called the *Buffalo Hunt*. Granddad convinced him to come to his home in Los Angeles to complete the job. Upon arrival, Jackson Sundown decided the big city was too overwhelming and told Granddad he left his saddle on a fence and had to go home to get it. No amount of persuasion could get him to stay. One of the bronzes of the *Buffalo Hunt* has been on display for years at the Metropolitan Museum of Art.

At age ninety, Mom still remembered life with her father when she was only three years of age. Granddad kept animals on their farm in Bedford, New York, for study and sketching. On moonlit nights, he would wheel a caged panther out of the barn. The panther would scream, sending chills up the spines of the Proctor children. He also had an eagle, wolf, and other animals for modeling.

Over the past few years my wife and I have had many wonderful experiences on our journey to bring wider recognition to Alexander Phimister Proctor. We call this adventure "following in Granddad's footsteps." One of our most exciting discoveries was when we set out to find the place rendered in Proctor's 1909 painting of Yarrow Creek Basin in Waterton Park, Alberta. I found an article in *Outdoor Life* magazine, written in 1957, about the world-record bighorn sheep that Granddad bagged there. We took with us Granddad's daily diary of the trip and an article written by his sketching and hunting partner, George D. Pratt, that was published in the *Brooklyn Museum Quarterly* in March of 1914. After much inquiring in the town of Waterton Park, we not only found the location of the basin but the phone number of Andy Russell, a distant relation to Pratt. I called Andy and asked if I was speaking with Andy Russell. He responded, "If it ain't, then I must be dead." I told him who I was and why I was in Waterton Park. Twenty minutes later, Sally and I were on his front porch. Andy was eighty-five years old, and, needless to say, we heard many wonderful stories. From a hill at his summer home he pointed out the far mountains and location of Yarrow Creek Basin.

The next day I hiked up the basin, armed with a can of mace to protect me from bears. Instead of bears I found "No Trespassing" signs. The basin had been turned into an oil refinery. Not to be dissuaded, I continued up the basin on a gravel road. The refinery loomed ahead. Andy had told me about the side canyon and described the exact location of the bluff in the painting.

He confirmed that it was the same bluff where his father-in-law had packed out the bighorn sheep and almost lost his life. Beyond the foundry I located the side canyon, and, by lining up the cliffs with the painting, I was able to locate the old campsite, which had changed very little in the past ninety-two years. A chill scurried up my spine as I felt the presence of Granddad beside me. I thought of his group riding on horses and struggling up the valley on an old Indian trail. They enjoyed three weeks of camping, hunting, and sketching in untouched wilderness. I am sure Granddad would be distressed if he saw Yarrow Creek Basin today.

Granddad's friends were many, and most often the friendships were forged over his love of the wilderness. Gifford Pinchot, one of America's leading advocates of environmental conservation at the turn of the twentieth century, was one of his closest acquaintances. George Pratt, president of Standard Oil and founder of the Pratt Institute, was a benefactor and patron. President Theodore Roosevelt invited him to join the Boone and Crockett Club in 1893 and later commissioned him to create the buffalo heads that appear on the mantel of the State Dining Room at the White House. I suspect there are few people who have turned down invitations to lunch with a person destined to be president of the United States, yet Granddad declined Roosevelt's invitation, choosing instead to dine with his eighteen-year-old sweetheart. President Woodrow Wilson also invited Proctor to lunch to honor him, along with some other individuals, but having a previous commitment for a sketching and hunting trip, Granddad graciously declined. Toward the end of his life, he did wonder what changes might have happened in his life had he lunched with Roosevelt.

Many years later, as a young man out of college, I started to add to my collection of the two small bronzes Granddad had given me. It seemed every few years a statue would become available for purchase, and I would buy it, usually on time payments. I had the goal of owning every small bronze ever created by Granddad. As time passed, I expanded my purchases to paintings, etchings, and anything related to his art and life. At one point, a New York art dealer offered to sell me a Proctor oil painting. I thought it was too expensive. Sally took one look at it and said, "We have to own this." Thus, we have what I consider one of his most important oils.

Recently our collection of Proctor art took a major step forward. Upon her death, my mother gifted to Sally and me her collection of Granddad's art. Clearly, she was aware of my passion for Granddad and was comfortable leaving her collection in my care. I often wondered what the motive was for Granddad, with eight children, to leave all his bronzes and plasters to Mom. Was it because he had some premonition that I would follow through for him?

Sally and I struggled as to how best to use this collection. In 1997 we formed the A. Phimister Proctor Museum. Our collection includes twenty-two bronzes, eighty plasters, numerous watercolors, pencil sketches, modeling tools, dry-point etching plates and related etchings, Indian artifacts, a thirteen-foot-high Rough Rider statue in plaster, signed documents from Teddy Roosevelt and Robert E. Lee, Mody's wedding dress, important correspondence, and much more.

The publication of this book is a pivotal moment in my quest to spread the word about Alexander Phimister Proctor's life and art. With this exhibition and catalogue, Granddad's art will reach a wider audience. He deserves no less, and I am delighted to have been part of the journey.

Sandy Church
Bainbridge Island, Washington

November 2002

Thank Howard for the Great statue at Grand Lake

Phimister Proctor Church

1

ROCKY MOUNTAIN ROOTS

Unlike most romantics, whose lives (at least among the French) ran from emotive discontent to mordant resignation, Alexander Phimister Proctor shouldered through a long and rewarding life with a contagious sense of joy and good humor. He embraced adventure, both physical and intellectual, and was pushed by a creative muse to great accomplishments in art. As a sculptor he achieved remarkable heights that were at once tempered by a traditional Beaux-Arts aesthetic and expanded by a wonder for nature and the American frontier.

This is the story of Proctor's adventure in art, one that unfolded over a period of nearly seventy years. Recognized as the acknowledged leader among American animalier sculptors and as the nation's foremost creator of sculpted monuments on western themes, Proctor was raised to that lofty pedestal in equal measure by his peers and the public. His meteoric success was described by his early mentor, the painter J. Harrison Mills, in 1916:

> *A sculptor, now of national fame as among the foremost of his guild, gradu-ated from the chrysalis bed of the mining regions, where the cocoon of romance was spun about the vanishing life of the last frontier and came to the full metamorphosis of the acclaimed Academician in a time so brief that comprehension is staggered. No more phenomenal success, based on real achievement, is to be found in the annals of American Art since the days of Benjamin West; perhaps I should say—none to compare with it.*[1]

Compelled by a restless urge to seek new adventure and fresh inspiration, Proctor, with his indulgent family, led a peripatetic life. For this he blamed genetic predisposition as much as the appeal of novel geography or business opportunities, citing a "nomadic strain" that imbued his family with wander-lust and through his youth kept the Proctors "continually wandering."[2]

Proctor was born in Canada. The family Bible gives the town's name as Arkona, located about seventy-five miles east of Detroit in Lambton County, Ontario. He came into the world on September 27, 1860, the fourth child of Alexander Proctor of Scottish Highland descent and Tirzah Smith, who traced her family back to American Colonial days.[3] Of eleven children, he was the last to be born in Canada. Sometime before his sister Mary came along in 1862, the Proctors moved south to Michigan via covered wagon and quickly thereafter to Newton, Iowa, and then Des Moines. At the State Fair in Des Moines in 1869, the family heard Horace Greeley make one of his famous "Go west, young man" speeches, and they were soon off again, this time to Denver, in the shadow of the Rocky Mountains. Proctor's father moved to what the artist affectionately referred to as the "promised land" in mid-1871, and the rest of the family followed later that year. The senior Alexander established himself in the tailoring business, and the children enrolled in school. Because the family was not, as a later account gracefully put it, "overburdened with what are called 'this world's goods,'" young Proctor, or Phim as he was called, worked as a paperboy. His pals, who called him "Newsie," admired his "ardent spirit" but were mostly impressed by his ability to fend off nuisance dogs on his route. The accuracy and range of his rock-throwing abilities caused much envious chatter among their ranks.[4]

Proctor later wrote in an autobiographical sketch that he "began to draw as soon as [he] could hold a pencil," and much of his energy went to pursuing his artistic development.[5] Many of his boyhood chums, such as A. Wilbur Steele, later to become a noted Denver cartoonist, and Charles Partridge Adams, a landscape painter, were nascent artists as well. They sketched together, encouraged each other's efforts, and ventured together into the mountains in search of inspiration. Proctor also received encouragement from home. Despite its humble confines, the Proctor residence was hung with reproductions of European masterpieces, and Alexander Proctor, who read voraciously on the subject, shared his enthusiasm for the likes of Sir Edwin Landseer and Michelangelo with his promising young son. As the Dallas art critic John William Rogers said many years later, his father "liked to talk of them and perhaps that touched the boy's imagination," though obviously the young Proctor "had within himself an inclination for art which needed no external stimulus."[6]

In fact, according to Proctor's own telling, Alexander Proctor did much more than talk about art with his son. Recognizing a stirring talent, he dreamed aloud of the day when his son might have an opportunity to study art formally. He hoped the future might include classes not just in Denver, Chicago, or New York, but in Paris or even Rome. The artist would recall this later in his autobiography:

> *I can't remember a time when Father didn't have the idea that I should go to Rome or Paris to study art. He never failed to encourage me in my art studies. I never produced a drawing or a bit of modeling too bad for some word of encouragement from him. Father's reading in art literature was mostly about the Greeks and the Italians. His ideal sculptors were Phidias and Michelangelo, and he showed me pictures of their work. Raphael was the painter talked of most, though he liked best the works of the English animal painter Edwin Landseer, and our walls were hung with prints of the latter's paintings. They may have stirred my early interest in wild animals.[7]*

In an effort to secure the financial resources necessary for art studies in New York or Paris, Alexander Proctor filed a number of mining claims as did the young artist, and they worked some of them together. Although those efforts proved fruitless, father and son clearly formed a bond that had art as

Fig.1

its foundation. Proctor would later do the same thing, to more productive ends, with his own son Gifford.

J. Harrison Mills, Proctor's first serious art teacher, met the boy in 1874 when he was about fourteen, describing him as "a delicate lad—somewhat crippled by rheumatism, [and] handicapped by circumstance." From Mills' perspective, without the "devotion" of Proctor's mother, who with maternal "prescience saw and determined his future," the artist would not have developed. It was she who "obtained for him what seemed the best available instruction."[8] At thirteen Proctor had started drawing classes with an eccentric "Dutch artist"; he was set to making copies in pencil from reproductions of paintings—not, in Proctor's recollections, a terribly constructive means of advancing his art education.[9] The next year, seeking a more practical approach, young Proctor was apprenticed to Mills to learn the art and craft of wood engraving.

Mills and another artist, James M. Bagley, had set up engraving shops in Denver in the early 1870s. Mills and his wife had come to Colorado for her health. They originally settled in Grand County near Long's Peak, where he painted landscapes and portraits, and she taught school. When it became evident that northern Colorado's art patronage could not support their family, they moved south to Denver. Mills took a studio and established one of Denver's first, though short-lived, art schools, the Colorado Academy of Fine Arts in the Tabor Grand Opera House building. He also opened an engraving shop downtown on the top floor of the *Rocky Mountain News* building. There Proctor absorbed the rudiments of the engraver's art and much more.

Proctor attended public school through the eighth grade.[10] For the next ten years, until Mills moved to New York in 1885, Proctor worked with Mills, beginning as an office boy and advancing to a student and protégé.

Several things about Mills' studio and workshop as well as his philosophy of art impressed Proctor. For one thing, the studio attracted many "interesting characters" who led Proctor to reflect on the unique ambiance of the American West. James Baker, a trapper and guide who had worked for the American Fur Company and several independents from 1830 through the 1850s, once came to Mills' studio to sit for his portrait. Intrigued by Baker's stories and by the history of the region, Proctor wrote later that Baker "was colorful and authentic."[11] These two qualities would inform the artist's future work—not only the subjects he chose but the manner in which he elected to present his favorite themes.

As Proctor moved through his mid-teens (fig. 1), he and Mills discovered they shared a common outlook on the world: a profound personal identification with nature. Some of their appreciation for the outdoors came from a Thoreauvian need to be at one with a domain beyond civilization. In a complex set of associations, Proctor's own awareness of approaching manhood and his ability to survive in the wilds met the larger cultural imperative to resist a perceived feminization of society through masculine deeds. The backcountry of Colorado's expansive western mountains, a place of union with a pure world, became both a refuge for self-discovery and an escape from society's constraints.

Mills wrote and illustrated a story published in the September 1878 issue of *Scribner's Monthly*. "Hunting the Mule-Deer in Colorado" touted self-reliance, solitary encounters with the wilderness, survival techniques, the conservation of wild game, and fundamental lessons in the "art of woodcraft."[12] The account was partly autobiographical: one illustration pictured Mills suffering the agonies of a lost shot after his own buck fever allowed a deer to escape unharmed (fig. 2). The article argued that with care, patience, and determined effort, even a novice might achieve both a

Fig.2

A. P. Proctor
Grand Lake
Colo. 1881 — at old Wescot cabin — his hunting pony in middle distance.

Fig.3

union with nature and a full larder. In time, Mills wrote, a hunter might "in the future be able to set out on a trip through a few hundred miles of primitive wilderness in a buckskin suit of your own stitching, and carrying, for equipment and subsistence, your gun, three cartridges, a pinch of salt and a jack-knife…."[13]

Proctor already fit comfortably in Mills' mountain world. Since 1873 his family had owned property near Grand Lake on the west side of Colorado's Front Range; it was there that Proctor and his brother George learned to hunt and trap. As Mills noted with approval, in between art lessons and developing his own work as an engraver and painter, Proctor "betook himself to the really best possible school and with his rifle and prospecting tools, struck into the Northern range of the Rockies."[14] Proctor in turn admired Mills because "he believed in the naturalistic school…and felt strongly that an artist should live the life he intended to depict."[15] Proctor proved himself worthy of Mills' lessons in nature in his sixteenth year when, in a legendary test of his mettle and hunting skills, he shot and killed an elk and a grizzly bear in one day. Repeated hundreds of times over the ensuing years of Proctor's life, the story became something of a signature anecdote, a symbolic fixture for the artist's identity.[16] Like Mills' ideal hunter, Proctor soon donned his own buckskin suit and made lonely forays into the backcountry.

His friends at Grand Lake were kindred spirits like Mills, who hunted there in the 1870s, but also old-timers who regaled him with stories of wilder times in the West. Among his favorites was a crusty veteran named Judge J. L. Wescott; Proctor spent the summers between 1873 and 1885 near his cabin (fig. 3).[17] It was from Wescott and other Grand Lake characters like the guide Antelope Jack Warren or a cabin mate of Wescott's named "Old Avery" that Proctor learned the ways of the wilderness, fitting into his own persona many of the more romantic qualities of that way of life. Between

these characters and his father, who claimed serious proficiency with rod and rifle, Proctor enjoyed a rich reserve of advisors and kindred spirits. They were to him what the mountain man Jake Hoover had been to a youthful Charles Russell or the old Montana freighter had been to Frederic Remington: role models and muses guiding him to adulthood through an inculcation of nature's wisdom.

Beyond the sheer exhilaration of Grand Lake life for a young man at that time and the joy in being part of the backcountry world, Proctor had begun positioning himself in art history without really knowing it. Just as Russell's eleven years on the range and Remington's firsthand experiences with the U.S. military in the West would establish their personas as artists, so would Proctor's summers of hunting and exploring. Where Russell became "The Cowboy Artist," and Remington, "America's Man for the West," Proctor was on his way to becoming the nation's "Artist as Western Huntsman," one in a long line of such characters that had begun with the very first Anglo artists in the West, Titian Ramsay Peale and George Catlin. These two early-nineteenth-century painters of western life were celebrated as much for their heroic quests and monumental adventures as for their art. In the generation just before Proctor's, Albert Bierstadt had established a similar pattern with his epic trips west and the grand landscape paintings that followed, incorporating their heroic dimensions into his persona as an artist.[18] Mills' writings lauded Bierstadt for bringing "universal attention" to the West through works that were "'spectacular' to a wonderful degree," while Catlin—whose life and artistic pursuit, he said, "fired my young soul to emulation"—provided further inspiration.[19] Proctor began to construct for himself a similarly double-faceted life; as his hunting skills matured and his forays into the mountain wilds became more bold, so, too, did his adventures in art. Although the two pursuits would seem to be distinct exercises, Proctor

Fig.5

Fig.5
J. D. Howland (1842–1914)
Group of Buffalo on the Plains, 1883
Oil on canvas, 21⅛ x 30⅛ inches

Gerald Peters Gallery, Santa Fe, N. Mex.

Fig.6
Alexander Phimister Proctor
Buffalo, c. 1884
Oil on academy board, 13 x 16¼ inches

A. Phimister Proctor Museum, Poulsbo, Wash.
Photograph by Howard Giske

increasingly intertwined one experience with the other. Thus, while more and more at home in the wilderness, Proctor also worked hard to fit into the Denver art and cultural community. The *Rocky Mountain News*, in a lengthy report on activities at Grand Lake in 1881, reflected this duality. Even as the paper reported that the Proctor family was building a "commodious two-story frame dwelling" on their homestead adjacent to Wescott's land, and that Wescott himself, perhaps with the help of Proctor, had pulled no less than five thousand trout from the lake over the summer to satisfy restaurant appetites in such places as Empire, Idaho Springs, and Central City, it was giving a reserved, though encouraging, puff to an aspiring young painter from the area:

> The other day visitors were shown a beautiful oil painting of Grand Lake and the surrounding scenery. The artist is Mr. A. P. Proctor of Denver. The bold outlines of the rugged mountains and the delicate tints of the foliage and the shadows in the water give the highest evidence of genuine talent of no ordinary degree, especially when the age of the artist is taken into consideration....[20]

At the time of this article, Proctor had recently turned twenty-one. He undoubtedly took this painting with him to Denver when he left Grand Lake that fall.[21] By the following summer, Proctor had joined many other artists in support of what the *Denver Tribune* referred to as Mills' "Academy of Fine Arts." Proctor was presumed among "the artists of Denver" who "acting together have secured the entire 5th floor of the Tabor Grand Opera House Bldg. and will occupy it at once." The venture was patterned after the Crosby Opera House in Chicago, which had featured studio and exhibition spaces in its building and succeeded, until the fire of 1871, in providing a major art center for that city. Now Denver endeavored to match those efforts and to "open the eyes of the outside world as to Denver's taste and culture."[22]

It may have been at this time and place that Proctor and his friend and fellow painter, Charles Adams, opened a studio together. Adams had been a student of Denver's other art teacher, Helen Henderson Chain, who began offering painting classes out of her husband's shop, the Chain and Hardy Bookstore, in 1877. Her penchant for landscape painting took her and her classes into the mountains where they studied directly from nature.[23] In the previous year, she had been preparing herself and her students for a major exposition mounted by the Denver Mining Association, with leadership from H. A. W. Tabor and a group of the city's businessmen. The Mining and Industrial Exposition opened on Colorado Day, August 1, 1882, and Proctor joined many other local artists in filling the exposition's art gallery. His painting *Mountain Lion Drinking* received praise for its fidelity: "The wildness of the fierce brute is indicated in the glaring eye and in the ears, laid back with feline malignity as if even it would not do to assume an attitude of peace while drinking water from a mountain stream."[24]

A few of Proctor's early paintings have survived including *Self-Portrait* (fig. 4), depicting Proctor in soft earth tones as a determined, though pleasantly optimistic, character with a cheery countenance and piercing blue eyes. The broad-brimmed hat pushed back from his forehead suggests a confidence that would allow him to coexist comfortably both in the Rocky Mountain wilds and among the urbane pretensions of Denver's nascent art scene. Another painting by Proctor treats the same subject as *Group of Buffalo on the Plains* (fig. 5) by local painter J. D. Howland, which garnered the most attention among the exposition's presenters. Where Howland's defiant but weary bison bull faces off wolves in its final hour as if braced against the impending extinction of its whole species, Proctor's *Buffalo* (fig. 6) reflects slightly less overtly fatalistic sentiments even as it echoes the tonal harmonies and rich, somber palette of the Munich-trained Howland.

Fig.6

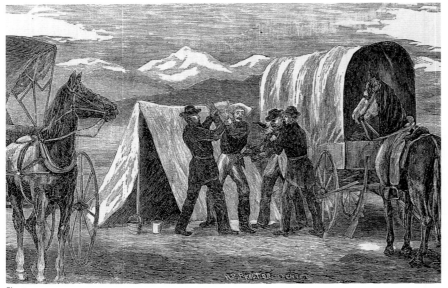

Fig.7

Fig.8

Chain, Mills, Proctor, Howland, and others of what were later termed Denver's "pioneer artists of the golden '80s" faced difficult circumstances. According to a biographical sketch on Chain that appeared in 1934, "the mining magnates" were "free spenders" in matters of opera and theatre, "but their ideas of art were peculiar."[25] Nonetheless, those peculiar fellows sponsored another Mining and Industrial Exposition in 1883. Proctor again participated, along with eighty-five other artists. His name appears beside those of Chain, Adams, and another of his close friends, Curtis Chamberlain. Proctor's painting, *A Winter Woodland Hunting Scene*, was praised for showing "some fine coloring."[26] Proctor and his father must have been pleased to find that someone had loaned an original painting by Landseer to the exhibition.

The year before, Proctor had received a lucrative illustration assignment: he was commissioned to produce thirty-two images that he was then to turn into wood engravings for a book by General David J. Cook, superintendent of the Rocky Mountain Detective Association. *Hands Up* was an autobiographical account of the famed sheriff's deeds in the service of Colorado justice. Proctor's crude paintings, which translated into even rougher engravings, fell short of expectations for either medium during that era. Nevertheless, spread over 285 pages of text, they evince a raw and brittle quality that reflects the tenor of Cook's life and writing style (fig. 7). Adams must have been envious of Proctor's success because he soon began engraving lessons with Bagley, Mills' partner and another Denver teacher.

The Denver art writer Roberta Balfour, recalling the early contributions to the local cultural scene made by Adams, Chamberlain, and Proctor, said in 1903 that as "young lads" they were all studying along similar lines. "Wood engraving and out-of-door sketching was what they began at. But the wildlife on the mountains" exerted an undiminishing pull. They longed to paint and "study things as they really were."[27] Proctor and Adams continued to retain their joint studio on the top floor of the Tabor Opera House and, during the hunting season, they spent time together in the mountains. A photograph from 1883 documents their hunting success even though the outing was described as a "sketching trip in the Flat Top Mountains" (fig. 8). As a Colorado newspaper reported on September 27, "Charles Adams, of Denver, an artist friend of Pheme [*sic*] Proctor, has been spending a week in Grand Lake making sketches. Yesterday he and Pheme started to Egeria Park on a sketching tour."[28]

The same paper announced early the next year that Proctor's work was bringing him "to the front as an artist. His 'Deserted' is now upon exhibition in Chain and Hardy's window.... It is a beautiful piece of work in an entirely new line for Denver. We hope it will meet with the recognition it deserves."[29] The painting is now lost, so there is no way to know exactly what aesthetic innovations Proctor brought to the canvas. Proctor was not around to read the review. He had no sooner returned from his trek with Adams than a wealthy New York artist friend, Alden Sampson, whose acquaintance he had made at Grand Lake some years earlier, tempted him into an even bolder adventure. They had traveled and camped together before, when they took a hunting and sketching trip through the Ute country of western Colorado and the White River reservation in 1879. Now Sampson was proposing a six-month junket through California with the promise of a visit to Los Angeles, Yosemite, and San Francisco. Since Sampson was probably settling most of the expenses, Proctor could not refuse the invitation. A chapter in Proctor's autobiography recounts their many adventures, including an unprotected climb up Yosemite's Half Dome during which Proctor's skill with a lasso enabled them to reach and reset a fallen climbing cable. That harrowing escapade took two days and, he later recalled, signaled his entry into manhood: "I had decided long before to be an artist; there was no other profession for me. Those hours of anxiety and danger crystallized in my mind the goals toward which I would direct my life."[30]

Fig.9

In addition to the encouragement Proctor had received from his parents, several fellow artists had urged him to expand his artistic horizons by taking up study in New York or even in Europe. Frederick Dellenbaugh, a Paris- and Munich-trained artist who had accompanied Major John Wesley Powell through the Grand Canyon in the early 1870s, settled for a while in Denver. He told Proctor that his painting efforts deserved more sophisticated guidance than he could hope for in the Rocky Mountain West. Dellenbaugh had been exhibiting paintings of western subjects with some success at the National Academy of Design in New York since 1880. According to Proctor, Dellenbaugh saw "some shadow of hope" in the young man's work, which gave Proctor a motivation to strive further. The painter David McClusky, who taught at New York's Art Students League, arrived in Denver around 1880 to teach art classes and establish an art society. Working with him in the evenings, Proctor drew from plaster casts and listened attentively to McClusky's stories about New York art schools and what might be learned there.[31]

But perhaps the main impetus for Proctor to consider leaving his beloved West for the somber corridors of some distant art academy was Mills' decision to return to New York in 1885. His wife's health had improved over the years since they came west for Colorado's salubrious climate. Now he was ready to reenter the New York art world and in the process provided Proctor with a familiar connection.

Before heading east, though, Proctor needed to deal with some logistical problems and say farewell to the Colorado backcountry. The logistics primarily concerned financial realities. The Proctors were not well-off (most reports suggest in fact that they were quite poor) and had no money available to support art school in the East. Neither Proctor nor his father had struck it rich digging for gold, and the young artist's sales generated modest rewards, only enough to sustain day-to-day life in Denver. But a savvy move that Proctor had made earlier held the answer. He had taken a homestead at Grand Lake, and when a friend, the Reverend Bayard Craig, offered to purchase it, the deal enabled Proctor to make his farewells and move east.[32]

During the fall of 1885, he returned to the Flat Top Mountains in far northwestern Colorado. There he spent several months alone communing with, and living off, nature's bounty. The inscription on a photograph he took of himself and his camp underscores the self-sustaining aspect of his wilderness adventure (fig. 9):

Route County, Colo
I was alone in the camp
3 months. 1885
Lived on venison, mountain sheep, bear and elk meat.
Had an Indian scare in or near this camp – Saw no Indians myself [33]

His list of prey suggests that his venture into the wilds was less transcendental than transgressive. Yet he hunted animals not strictly for sport but for food and for artistic inspiration as well. He sketched them in many poses to be used later in his paintings.

When Proctor embarked on his journey east later that fall, he was headed to New York to train as a painter. Thoughts about a future as a sculptor had not yet entered his mind, though his dream was to advance in a career as an artist. The *Rocky Mountain News*, eight years later, contrasted his old world with that new purpose:

In his mountain home he became adept in all that makes the successful hunter and mountaineer, in all the art of packing, camping or riding he wore a reputation with the best. He delighted in the sublime beauty of the highest and wildest recesses of the Rockies, and shut away from the great world, the expectation that he would become an artist, and a great one, became the unuttered but undying purpose of his life.[34]

BECOMING A SCULPTOR

Soon after Mills' arrival in the East, he received a letter from his enthusiastic protégé and, before long, Proctor joined him in Manhattan.[1] Proctor settled in Mills' studio initially, at least until he could find satisfactory and inexpensive quarters of his own. The next thing he did "was to swarm up to the menagery [*sic*] to see the wild animals." He obtained a special permit and began immediately to sketch the animals in pencil, moving among the zoo's two hundred cages. "It was difficult to work at the menagerie during the day time," he wrote, "so I used to get up at 5:00, get a hasty simple breakfast and be back at the lions, or some other building in the winter or in summer wherever any animal was that I wanted to draw."[2] He had soon established good working relations with the chief keeper, William Snyder, and when Proctor later began to model as well as draw, Snyder allowed him to store his easels and models in his office.

Proctor started classes at the National Academy of Design in the fall of 1885. As with all new students, he was required to take drawing from the antique. His instructor, Lemuel Everett Wilmarth, had been Jean-Léon Gérôme's first American pupil, and he assiduously imparted the French master's dicta regarding the probity of drawing. Concisely summarized, Gérôme's teachings were to "draw the model exactly, after disposing it artistically."[3] For Wilmarth, the maxim related to all branches of art, and a student with no grounding in drawing was not going to achieve success in any other medium. About 140 students attended these classes, from which eighty would be selected to advance to life drawing. Proctor reported that Wilmarth was exceedingly demanding and that his own "rough-and-ready work did not quite accord with [Wilmarth's] smooth, painstaking style and refined tastes." Thus Proctor made only gradual headway, especially since his preference for sketching at the menagerie diverted his attentions. "If I had taken Mr. Wilmarth's advice," he continued, "I'd have made more

Fig.10

progress, but in those days I didn't care quite enough for painstaking drawing." Yet Proctor, who was also serious and hard-working, did conclude that he "gradually earned his respect." Whether he subsequently won a seat in Wilmarth's life class is not known. He did attend classes in perspective with Frederick Dietman, which were offered twice a month, and apparently felt that he profited from those.[4]

Wilmarth allowed his better pupils to paint at the same time they attended his drawing classes. Apparently Proctor continued his painting with or without Wilmarth's encouragement, and in May 1886 he boasted that he had exhibited an "elk picture" (fig. 10) that attracted "considerable attention and much favorable comment."[5] He sold it to his artist friend Sampson, who may have liked the painting or simply acquired it to help his colleague financially.[6]

In the fall of 1886, Proctor switched schools. He signed up for antique drawing under James Carroll Beckwith at New York's Art Students League. It was there, he reported, that he "really began to learn how to draw."[7] He also watched more senior artists at work, especially at the menagerie, where Frederick S. Church often sketched, studying the wild animals for what Proctor called "his charming fanciful pictures."[8] But another influence soon emerged that would ultimately have a more far-reaching and profound impact on Proctor's life and career: he began to take serious notice of sculpture. Mills attributes Proctor's shift from a focus on painting to his attendance at an exhibition of bronzes by the French animalier master sculptor Antoine-Louis Barye presented in the galleries of the American Art Association in 1889. At this moment, according to Mills, Proctor experienced an epiphany and "was fired with sudden recognition of his natural medium." Once he had "found himself," Proctor began immediately on his first wax sculpture:

He went straight off to his den with some wax and began an antelope. With delight he saw its graceful body and slender limbs growing under his hand. The wax was hard but the heat of his enthusiasm warmed it; lest the wax chill in his absence, he left it by the radiator when he had to leave the house. The fiend below, as in all apartments, turned on a flush of steam—when he came back the antelope was on the run—the soul of it gone to its native plains. He recalled, with fierce incantation, as it cooled, it grew more beautiful than before.[9]

Barye had died in 1875, yet in France as well as in the United States he was held in high esteem. *Harper's Monthly* featured his monumental accomplishments in its September 1885 issue. Proctor had no doubt read the lengthy tribute by Theodore Child, which asserted that "such realism in the sculpture of animals, such forcible and passionate rendering of life and movement," had rarely been seen even by Proctor's generation. Child commended Barye for the way in which he "boldly and simply took nature for his model and guide," bringing to sculpture the same passion that Théodore Géricault had achieved in his paintings of nature.[10] Barye's fame and the fact that he had served for over thirty years as a professor of drawing at the Paris zoo may well have influenced Proctor's early studies among the barred cages of New York's menagerie. Barye's devotion to precise realism and a fidelity of line, combined with romantic themes of wild nature, had obvious aesthetic and practical appeal for Proctor.

Proctor's other New York mentor in sculpture had a penchant less for romantic drama than for purely American themes. John Rogers was an immensely popular genre sculptor, and Proctor encountered him at the height of his public acclaim. Proctor first noticed a particularly dynamic plaster group by Rogers, *The Bugle Call*, in 1886 at the National Academy of Design's annual exhibition. It showed a Civil War cavalryman about to mount a rearing horse. Despite the fact that the critics disparaged the work as trite and compositionally unbalanced, Proctor was intrigued. He had always liked military themes in art, and as a schoolboy, according to one account, he "would fill his slate with crudely drawn battle pictures." Like Remington, he too had pored over art prints and periodicals that featured the battle paintings of French artists Alphonse de Neuville and Édouard Détaille, expressing particular admiration for the "dash, freedom, and courage" with which de Neuville treated his subjects.[11] Thus the Rogers work caught his attention. He took the initiative to meet the older artist and for a while became Rogers' one (and evidently only) pupil.[12] As Proctor frequented Rogers' home and studio, he learned the essence of the sculptural idea as well as the practical matters of handling clay and building effective armatures. It was Rogers who, through his encouragement and personal involvement, started Proctor on his first successful sculpture, *Fawn* (plate 3, p. 98).[13]

Proctor's recognition as an artist and his turn toward sculpture came more gradually than Mills later reported. A letter from Proctor to Reverend Craig, written in the late 1880s or early 1890s, speaks of the hardships he was experiencing as he attempted to break into the art world in the years that followed his formal schooling. Yet, in spite of these privations, Proctor proclaimed, "I would rather be hungry and paint than be a millionaire and be compelled to lay down the brush."[14] To that end he maintained an impressive schedule of study and work. He continued to visit the menagerie in the early morning, availed himself of classes at the Art Students League in the late morning, and with Rogers' encouragement was soon modeling in the afternoon. His oil paintings started appearing at the National Academy of Design in 1888 and would be exhibited there again the following year and in 1895 as well. Proctor also enjoyed working in watercolors and found an outlet for this medium at exhibitions of the American Water Color Society.[15] He

began to expand his network of friends, potential patrons, and supporters. Especially important to him was a contact he made in the late 1880s with art dealer N. E. Montross of New York, who sold at least one of Proctor's paintings in 1890 and would become Proctor's primary dealer. Proctor valued both his professional association and his counsel in art matters.[16]

During this time Proctor typically spent his summers away from New York, largely in the mountains of the West. A Chicago newspaper in 1893 discussed these respites from his labors:

> *Housed in the narrow walls of schools and studios, the old yearning for the mountains would sweep over him with almost irresistible power, and every summer found him again in the saddle, among the mountain fastnesses of Colorado, California, and British Columbia, followed by a pack mule or two and some faithful dogs, finding invaluable help in the study of animals at long range in the use of the binocular telescope. Last year, from his boat, Mr. Proctor lassoed a full-grown deer in Puget Sound, and kept the beautiful creature until he made several studies in clay from life.*[17]

In New York Proctor often felt as caged as the animals in the menagerie. He shared the need periodically to refresh himself in the wilds with other American artists of his day. Rufus Zogbaum lived among various Montana cowboys in the mid-eighties, returning to New York with stories and illustrations of the western drovers' colorful lives. Proctor must have seen his depictions of that "picturesque, hardy lot of fellows" in the pages of *Harper's Monthly*. He would also have watched the rise of Remington, whose illustrations in *Harper's Weekly, Outing,* and *Century Magazine* brought to life the ranching and hunting escapades of Theodore Roosevelt and the sun-baked Arizona campaigning of the U.S. cavalry in search of Geronimo.[18] But while these other artists sought to document (and romanticize) men on the western frontier, Proctor mined a different theme. It was not entirely novel—Mills had explored it to some degree in his paintings and illustrations, and the New York sculptor Edward Kemeys had clearly staked out the territory—but it had been treated less often than other subjects in American art. The theme was animals in the western wilds, and Proctor began to chase it with the same stealth and determination that he employed in the hunt itself. He knew intuitively that firsthand exposure to animals in the wilds would be crucial to his success in developing his eye and his work.

The study of animals involved a spectrum of methodological knowledge gathering. The French had developed a means of working with animal models that stood at one extreme. Claiming to "live in the midst of the life which they paint," artists like Luigi Chialiva painted animals posed in natural light but conveniently separated from the painter by a wall of windows.[19] Those of more robust constitution, like the Fontainebleau painter Rosa Bonheur, ventured into the roads and pastures to sketch domesticated animals, and even into the nearby woods for an occasional drawing of a deer. But for the most part, artists who wished to render wild animals had to rely on the zoos. Perhaps because of Kemeys' familiarity with animals in the wilds—he had traveled widely in the West in 1873—his renditions were recognized as being a step above the norm. The critic Julian Hawthorne observed in 1884 that Kemeys' sculptures invoked in the viewer a "feeling that he has learned much more of the [animals'] characteristics and genius than if he had been standing in front of the same animals' cages at the Zoölogical Gardens."[20] Kemeys had no formal training, however, and Proctor was determined that he would correct that deficiency, hoping to bring personal knowledge to bear on the process of making his art, as Kemeys had done, but with more formal skill. In his work, he would reintroduce the wilds into

the caged animals he was forced to use as models in New York and convincingly render them in those he actually captured out-of-doors. Without his trips of renewal, though, Proctor feared losing credibility and connectivity. He understood that his inspiration came as much from his oneness with the western wilderness as from the artistic muse.

Early in the game, Proctor even transformed his work space into a place of adventure and potential peril. His autobiography is filled with accounts of hair-raising escapes that range from dodging charging elephants to fending off crazed thoroughbreds. The episodes invariably occurred either in the studio or in specially assigned artist spaces at the stables or at the zoo. Perhaps the most famous story concerned one of his first sculptures, *Panther* (plate 5, p. 103) and the dangers surrounding its conception. While in Colorado during a backcountry trip in the mid-1880s, Proctor had shot a cougar and made sketches of it for future reference. He supplemented those drawings by sketching one of the panthers at New York's menagerie, just a few blocks north of his 55th Street apartment and the Art Students League. One day while doing this, he turned his back on a big cat named Satan. Before he knew it, the panther had stretched out a paw and clawed the back of Proctor's neck and shoulder (fig. 11). It was, according to an inscription on one of several drawings Proctor made of the bloody incident, a "subject to remember Black Panther reaching for my juglor [*sic*]."[21] Countering the common view of artists' studios as feminized spaces, Proctor took great pains to prove that his was not.[22] In or out of New York, Proctor's world in those days was emphatically masculine.

Yet despite this rather transparent insistence on his own masculinity, Proctor's first significant sculpture and the work that would propel him into the limelight showed a fundamentally different side of his nature. Proctor later credited Rogers with pushing him to sculpt his first version of *Fawn*,

Fig.11

based on a newborn white-tailed deer at the menagerie that Snyder allowed him to approach and use as a model. It was small and helpless and dependent, starkly different from Proctor's self-image, yet in its fledgling state, the fawn, like Proctor, was also just beginning a new life. This attentive, patient, and nonthreatening model provided a balance to other works, like *Panther*, that Proctor was conceiving at the same time. The "infinite pains," as one critic put it years later, that he took with the tiny sculptural production came not from physical injury but from "the sheer love of it," the fundamental hope that, like his art, if properly nourished and nurtured, the fawn might grow to its full potential and promise.[23] *Fawn* has the familial spirit of the genre groups that Rogers sculpted, which were often laden with moral lessons meant to uplift the public conscience even as their crisply smooth surfaces enhanced a general appreciation for sculpture as an art form. These sentiments appealed to Proctor's gentler side, and the rewards soon proved their merit.

The artist Dellenbaugh, who had known Proctor in Denver and encouraged his interest in New York study, saw a plaster cast of *Fawn* in Proctor's studio. He was so impressed with its delicate form and sensitive treatment that he offered to get it shown at the Century Club where he was a member. It turned out to be an auspicious venue. Frank D. Millet saw it there and went on to meet the artist. Later, when Millet was placed in charge of the decorations for the grounds of the World's Columbian Exposition in Chicago, he remembered that fragile fawn and the engaging young man who produced it. In the fall of 1891, as Proctor returned to Snohomish, Washington (where his family had moved from Denver), following a hunting trip in the Cascade Mountains, he received a telegram from Millet inviting him to be part of a team of artists who would provide monumental plaster staff (plaster and hemp) sculptures for the fair's elaborate promenades. After negotiations in Chicago, Proctor accepted the assignment to decorate

the end posts of the fair's bridges with heroic-sized animals from America's western wilds. He would join Kemeys in that effort but would also work side by side with the nation's most esteemed sculptors and their assistants. It was, in his estimation at least, all thanks to *Fawn*, with its wobbly legs and uncertain future. Reaching out at the right time and place, it had claimed for the young artist what he would term "my first big commission."[24]

Proctor's hard work as a painter had paid off as well, and his network of potential patrons grew. When Dellenbaugh arranged for the plaster model of Proctor's *Fawn* to be displayed at the Century Club, the invitation included the artist's presence at the opening of the club's annual member showing. There Proctor met a host of new contacts and future friends. At the same time, paintings that he had completed in the early 1890s began to win more than ordinary praise. A watercolor of a panther shown in the American Water Color Society's annual exhibition in 1892 had, according to one paper, been the "sensation of the season"; another report said the work had excited such a "favorable comment" that it attracted the buyer William T. Evans, one of the nation's most highly regarded and vigorous collectors of American art.[25] Moreover, an oil painting titled *On Guard* (now lost) had been hung at the Society of American Artists' exhibition in 1892. It was "received with enthusiasm by gallery haunters" and was purchased by New York's Governor Roswell P. Flower.[26]

Art aficionados recognized the Society of American Artists as the ascendant power among national art organizations at the end of the nineteenth century. Its membership covered a broad mix of the most distinguished painters and sculptors of the day. Their painting styles represented the lessons of Munich and Paris about equally, and they preached and practiced artistic tenets that conformed to a set of agreed maxims: that artworks should project a "partial illusion of reality that stops short of mere imitation," express a system

Fig.12

of harmonious values, and credit the "vital importance of good drawing and modelling." These standards prevailed, according to the writer George Parsons Lathrop, regardless of artistic scope, "realistic, impressionist, fanciful, or ideal," and so long as they sprang "from a purely graphic (not literary) motive…, [conveyed] some direct original insight into the subject…and [were] carried out according to some one of the generally recognized standards of skilful [sic] technique."[27] Proctor's work fit these requirements well: his eye was for the graphic, he had intimate knowledge of the animals he portrayed, and he had trained diligently with Beckwith and others to hone his techniques. His painting style, which mixed vigorous brushwork in the manner of the Munich school with the light, harmonized palette of the French school, placed him well within the ranks of New York's up-and-coming artists. Because his sculpture was inspired by the French, with his obvious indebtedness to Barye and his followers apparent in every manipulation of the wax and every push of the clay, Proctor would be regarded as one of New York's "exponents of the modern tendency." In hopes of building "up a great national art," practitioners were called upon to exercise spontaneity in their creative lives, an immediacy tailored for Proctor's approach:

> [I]nstead of moulding all their observation of real things to some preconceived model of what a picture or a sculpture should be, [artists should] hold themselves more in readiness to respond sensitively to any phase of nature, animate or inanimate, which may appeal to them as curious, beautiful, interesting or inspiring, and to reproduce it in such manner as will give the most of life and truth vividly, dexterously, and harmoniously.[28]

This spontaneity found expression in Proctor's work for the World's Columbian Exposition. Expositions like this began in London in 1851,

designed as venues for promoting nationalistic sentiments, and Chicago proved to be no different.[29] This made Proctor, a student of the new American art and an advocate for the West's native animals, a logical choice. The original commission was for six animals to adorn the bridges over the lagoons. By January 1, 1893, four months before the fair was to open, Proctor had completed two polar bears, two jaguars "in full action, with extended muscles," two elk, and a couple of moose (fig. 12). They were all judged "strong and purposeful to a remarkable degree." Artist and historian Lorado Taft wrote that "few things in the entire exposition were more interesting or impressive than those great motionless creatures, the native American animals as sculpted by Proctor and Kemeys."[30]

Once the initial commission was complete, Millet returned to Proctor with a further request. Now he asked the Colorado artist to create two equestrian sculptures, one of a cowboy and the other of an Indian. For the cowboy group alone, Proctor protested, he would need at least a year. But Millet was persuasive and in a hurry and Proctor completed the first of the two pieces in six weeks.[31] The Indian plaster was ready for the fair's opening on May 1, 1893.

Proctor used the Chicago zoo to model his animals in combination with sketches from his fieldwork. He had shot and then drawn many elk and one cougar. Hunting moose and polar bears was not part of his experience, however, so the zoo had to suffice. For the cowboy and Indian, ample sources were close at hand: camped just outside the exposition gates were William F. Cody and his Wild West troupe. Cody graciously offered performers from his show as models for the artist. The cowboy who posed (his identity is unknown) appeared to have been cooperative. The Indian model, Kills-Him-Twice, proved less so. Though "fierce and majestic," according to Proctor, he was also petulant and impatient. The artist ended up using the Sioux Chief Red Cloud's son, Jack, instead.

Fig.13

Once the fair opened and a few of the cowboys had been given an opportunity to visit the grounds, Proctor found he had another problem. On May 26 a Chicago newspaper reported that a group of Wild West show cowboys had been seen gathered around Proctor's *Cowboy* (fig. 13) "having all kinds of fun criticizing the rider's seat in the saddle and the 'help! help!' way in which the alleged cowboy was hanging on to the reins." The article went on to tell how the cowboys planned to sneak onto the fairgrounds and push the statue into the adjoining lagoon until Buffalo Bill learned of the plot and came to the rescue. He called the cowboys together and advised them to mute their art criticism, since "it was considered fashionable and perfectly correct to call things by their proper names on the other side of the Missouri, but on this side a man had to be quite a graceful liar to be in good standing in society." After this, he let them know that he would take it personally if the statue were molested. The scheme dissolved in grumbles.[32]

Obviously, one of the maxims for Lathrop's New York artists—holding to a graphic rather than literary motive—had been lost on at least one element of the lay audience: the cowboys wanted literal transcriptions of nature and not artistic interpretations. Worse, by reducing the matter to regional differences of East vs. West, Buffalo Bill suggested that Proctor had abandoned his Colorado roots with their ties to realistic portrayal and joined the affected ranks of eastern dilettantes. But Proctor had actually been proved correct: to do the job right, he would have needed far more time and better assistants. A later review of both the *Cowboy* and the *Indian* by Halsey C. Ives, who was in charge of fine arts at the exposition, referred specifically to these issues:

It seems at first curious that a sculptor so familiar with animals should have made such bad horses, but the truth about this is that these statues were made in great haste, and the sculptor himself did not have time to make the horses, but left this work to his assistants almost entirely. The figures, on the contrary, are his own.... On the whole, these groups are exceedingly interesting. Such work marks Mr. Proctor as one of the rising sculptors of the day—one who is capable of doing very great work indeed.[33]

The *Cowboy* was Proctor's first equestrian statue. It was also the first sculptural depiction of a cowboy in the history of American art. Its companion work, the *Indian* (fig. 14), was deemed more successful, though it was neither as original a composition nor was it the first of its kind. Although the model, Jack Red Cloud, had been the genuine living article, the pose of the statue

Fig.14

derived from an uncredited illustration in the Wild West show program, and the *Indian* was not the only Indian equestrian monument on the grounds of the fair. Cyrus Dallin's *Signal of Peace* (fig. 15), a heroic-sized bronze, was displayed in the Fine Arts Pavilion, winning praise from the critic William Coffin as "one of the best things shown by the Americans." But Proctor's big plaster did not go unnoticed. Among the dozens of monumental outdoor decorations, Proctor's was judged by one writer "by far the most striking of all these impressive figures."[34] Many of those who saw *Indian* felt it represented the passing of the Indian or at least the pacification of a once formidable and resistant foe.

The two sculptures comprised a celebration of the past. With their white plaster images reflected in the lagoon and silhouetted in front of the only avant-garde structure at the fair, Louis Sullivan's Transportation Building, they provided a brilliant emblem of loss and change. Like the Indian, the cowboy in 1893 was seen as a dying breed. Both figures and several of the species of large animals with which Proctor and Kemeys had decorated the bridges, as well as the frontier itself, had been proclaimed that year by historian Frederick Jackson Turner as prime players in the closing scene of a grand American epoch. For that reason Proctor and Kemeys, as two men close to the West in their lives and art, were singled out among a legion of sculptors to eulogize a region, its people and their culture, and even nature itself. As one writer penned after seeing the works of Proctor at the fair, "He is a Western man and he naturally seizes Western types, because, after all, the West is nearer to nature than we of the East can ever be."[35]

For the most part, the sculptors at the fair—more than thirty were hired to do the job—chose (or had chosen for them) figures of peace, progress, and plenty as their subjects. Daniel Chester French and his assistant Edward Potter designed an elaborate *Quadriga* to represent national

Fig.15

Fig.16

Fig.16
Philip Martiny's group for the central
façade of the Agricultural Building at
the World's Columbian Exposition,
Chicago, 1893
From *Harper's New Monthly* magazine,
May 1893

Fig.17
The "Hunter's Cabin" at the World's
Columbian Exposition, Chicago, 1893
From Halsey C. Ives, *The Dream City, A
Portfolio of Photographic Views of the
World's Columbian Exposition* (1893)

growth and expansion, while Philip Martiny's symbol of prosperity that topped the Agricultural Building featured an elaborately draped young woman leading two garlanded oxen and other domestic animals into a future of promise and abundance (fig. 16). The woman represented nature, but a harnessed variety—nature in the service of civilization, rather than the wild nature of the West, left for dead by Proctor's generation.

On an island in the lagoon, connected to the massive Beaux-Arts buildings by a bridge decorated with two of Proctor's guardian elks, stood a small, rustic log structure (fig. 17). Called the "Hunter's Cabin," it served as headquarters for an organization that sought to do something about nature's perceived demise. Known as the Boone and Crockett Club, the group had emerged in New York in 1887 as a reaction to reports of the threatened extinction of American large game animals following their mindless exploitation by meat and hide hunters. It represented not just an attempt to reverse declining game populations but a whole gestalt championing nature's survival and male relevance. The club's sentiments were summarized by one of its leading members, Theodore Roosevelt, who wrote in his book *The Wilderness Hunter* in 1893:

> *In hunting, the finding and killing of the game is after all but a part of the whole. The free, self-reliant, adventurous life, with its rugged and stalwart democracy; the wild surroundings, the grand beauty of the scenery, the chance to study the ways and habits of the woodland creatures—all these unite to give to the career of the wilderness hunter its peculiar charm. The chase is among the best of all national pastimes; it cultivates that vigorous manliness for the lack of which in a nation, as in an individual, the possession of no other qualities can possibly atone.*[36]

Proctor was inducted into the club that year. Although not the first artist to join, (Albert Bierstadt was a charter member), he proved a loyal and zealous cadet. He welcomed the opportunity to address the increasing feminization of American culture (most of the animals he depicted at the fair, for example, were male) and to resist the threatening encroachment of civilization on wilderness areas. Although Proctor and Kemeys were praised with all the other sculptors for their work's harmonious alliance with the Beaux-Arts architectural grandiosities that surrounded them, the two men's contributions stood somewhat apart. While the writer J. H. Gest observed that none of the sculptors, among the dozens who participated, was "capable of modeling merely detached statues," in spirit and philosophical slant, the animal plasters did stand alone.[37]

Fig.17

This does not mean that Proctor attempted to separate himself from the other artists, painters, architects, or sculptors. A photograph of his compatriots (fig. 18) shows Proctor very much in their midst. He received and welcomed advice and criticism from fellow artists, especially comments from Augustus Saint-Gaudens, Olin Warner, and J. Alden Weir. "It was a wonderful experience for me to be associated with such leaders in American art and to have the benefit of their criticism," he later reflected.[38] Proctor was fully a part of the exposition, with its attempted reification of the American dream through architecture, landscaping, and the greatest number of public sculptures ever assembled. As art critic William Howe Downes wrote ten years later, here began "our American rebirth in sculpture."[39] Indeed, it was enough to inspire poet Katherine Lee Bates to write "America the Beautiful." J. P. Morgan's comment on the French art displayed in the Palace of Fine Arts, that it must have been "picked by a committee of chambermaids," underscored the sense of liberation from European models.[40] Twenty-seven million visitors were proof of the art's allure.

The impact of the World's Columbian Exposition was far-reaching, not only for American cultural history but also for individual artists like Proctor. It set the stage for the continued assertion of traditional (some would say retrograde) aesthetic principles over the next two generations. Gest wrote:

The beauty of grand buildings harmoniously grouped in Jackson Park, the charm of decorative sculpture, the richness of public places and avenues abounding with statuary, create an unsuppressible longing that something of this, apparently so permanent, yet really so temporary, may remain as a lasting impression upon our people.[41]

Much to the chagrin of some modernist thinkers like Louis Sullivan, who would lament that the "damage wrought by the World's Fair,... penetrated deep into the constitution of the American mind..., [and] will last for half a century," Gest's projections were correct.[42] For Proctor the fair provided a springboard for his career. It put money in his pocket, gave him enough credibility as an aspiring artist to enable him to win the hand of a fellow sculptor at the fair, Margaret Gerow, and afforded him an opportunity to further his studies in Europe. The painter Gari Melchers persuaded Proctor that Paris would make a wonderful honeymoon spot and its ateliers were the proper environment for improving his skills. On October 27, 1893, as plans were being made to ship the *Cowboy* and the *Indian* to Denver for display in the city park, Proctor and his bride boarded the *City of Paris* to sail across the Atlantic.[43]

Ten years later, Balfour would note Proctor's promise at this time:

The cowboy, puma and Indian, treated as Proctor treated them, were new subjects for the art critics. 'Ere the world's fair ended it was authoritatively announced and generally conceded that Proctor was the greatest of young American sculptors.[44]

He was about to get even better.

Fig.18

Chicago Fair Artists, 1893
Proctor is in the front row wearing the
light-colored coat. Also shown are the
sculptors Edward Potter (top row, far
left), Daniel Chester French (directly in
front of Potter), Frederick MacMonnies
(middle row with his hand on his
jacket lapel), and Karl Bitter (bearded
man, with left hand raised, to
MacMonnies' left)

A. Phimister Proctor Museum Archives,
Poulsbo, Wash.

Fig.18

3

ON TO FRANCE

In his 1893 article on the New York art scene, George Parsons Lathrop concluded that art students had enough resources in Manhattan to "nearly complete their education."[1] Yet Proctor knew that he needed some additional instruction. Moreover, he longed for an opportunity to broaden his exposure, to see European museums and art treasures, and to avail himself of the formal lessons of the Beaux-Arts tradition. Once he arrived in Paris in the fall of 1893, he and his new bride, Margaret, embarked on a cultural learning spree. Margaret was already fluent in French, but Proctor was not, so he enrolled immediately in language classes. They visited every museum in the area, and then Proctor, "eager to learn French methods in sculpture," began classes at the Académie Julian.[2] He was bent on furthering his career as an animalier artist, focusing especially on the medium of sculpture so as to build on the successes he had enjoyed during his time in Chicago.

Paris, rather than Rome, had been a conscious choice for Proctor. In selecting the French art capital, he was following in the footsteps of his favorite American sculptor, Augustus Saint-Gaudens. Although Saint-Gaudens had spent time as a student in Rome, his tenure there was brief and followed three years of study in Paris at the atelier of François Jouffroy (Proctor was his first American student). Saint-Gaudens had returned to America with a style that mixed neo-Florentine elegance with the selective, formal realism taught by the Paris academicians. To these he added what art historian H. W. Janson has referred to as a "mythic 'native American' quality."[3] Proctor was prepared to explore both formal realism and that mythic quality in his own works, with the immediate goal of improving his technical skills.

Proctor and his wife had been in Paris only a few weeks when he entered into his financial ledger for the trip the purchase of two bronzes by Antoine-Louis Barye: *Rabbit* for $12.50 and *Elephant* for $50. Given an entry a few days earlier for general art supplies that included nine pounds of modeling wax for $11.25, it is obvious that the Barye pieces were as much studio models as household decorations. Proctor's classes cost $12.50 per month, and he spent an extra $2 to obtain a pass for the Jardin des Plantes, the Paris zoo. His tuition got him into the sculpture class of Denys Pierre Puech, a recent recipient of the prestigious Chevalier medal of the Legion of Honor who was, like Saint-Gaudens, a past pupil of Jouffroy's. Puech was not an animalier sculptor, but as a teacher of the French technique of making studies from life, he proved to be superb. Proctor later remembered that Puech's "ability in modeling, as revealed in his criticism of our figures, was amazing."[4] Proctor also studied independently under the somewhat older but equally celebrated French master Jean-Antoine Injalbert. Proctor and Puech remained in contact with one another over the years. Injalbert's relationship with Proctor was more ephemeral, but his American student later recalled a comment that had gratified him and elevated his hopes: on seeing one of Proctor's works, Injalbert was reported to have heartened the young sculptor with the words "Continue, my child. It is good."[5] It was just what Proctor wanted to hear.

The time Proctor had left after sculpture and language classes, and trips to the Paris zoo, was spent on his own work. He had brought several sculptures with him from Chicago, including his *Panther* and the first version of his *Fawn*. These he perfected and subsequently cast, the former in bronze and the latter in plaster. He also worked up in wax a second version of the *Fawn* (plate 6, p. 107), which he had started in Chicago several months earlier. This, too, he cast in plaster. The two works that carried the most French flavor, though, were his gaunt yet amusing *Dog with Bone* (plate 9, p. 117) and a portrait of a local boxer (now lost). The latter won for him the sculpture competition at the Académie Julian in 1894, indicating the seriousness with which Proctor approached his studies.

It is not known if Proctor intended to stay at the Académie Julian long enough to gain entry to the ultimate art education establishment in France, the École des Beaux-Arts. After success in the Académie's competition, another year of work would likely have seen him achieve that goal. As it turned out, however, after classes ended for the summer of 1894, Proctor's life and career veered homeward. To escape Paris for the summer, the newlyweds had chosen a popular vacation spot near Illier, southwest of Paris, but no sooner had they settled into the rustic country life than a cablegram arrived from New York. It was an invitation from Saint-Gaudens to take on the modeling of the horse for a monument to the flamboyant Civil War general John A. Logan that was slated for one of Chicago's public parks. It was a rare opportunity, and Proctor elected to continue his lessons in the French method indirectly, under the great Saint-Gaudens.

For the next year, Proctor worked with the American master, first in Windsor, Vermont, at his New England home and studio, where the *Logan Monument* (plate 7, p. 108) took shape, and later in New York City on a similar assignment to produce the original horse model for the *Sherman Monument* (plate 8, p. 112). Theirs was a collaborative effort in which Proctor and Saint-Gaudens jointly selected the models and worked out the poses. The overall invention of the two works fell to Saint-Gaudens' genius, but Proctor's role was undeniably more than that of a mere assistant. Dominant in American art in the mid-1890s, Saint-Gaudens was often forced by his crowded schedule and numerous commissions to delegate responsibilities. Proctor, who was content just working beside the master, bore a heavy burden of responsibility. Modeling the two horses was no small matter, and Saint-Gaudens recalled Proctor from France only after making several futile attempts to find a sculptor at home suitable for the task. He was greatly pleased with Proctor's participation, even though he did make changes in the two models that Proctor supplied. Not only did the two horses satisfy the master, but the experience, in Proctor's mind, was "one of the most valuable parts of his formative work."[6]

In appreciation of Proctor's assistance, Saint-Gaudens gave his protégé a Mannlicher rifle upon his completion of the Sherman horse model in 1895. Proctor had admired a 7mm Mannlicher belonging to a fellow Boone and Crockett Club member, and when Saint-Gaudens learned this and the fact that the younger man could not afford such a weapon, he purchased one for Proctor. He also took steps to ensure Proctor resumed his interrupted studies abroad, only this time on more auspicious terms.

Back during the World's Columbian Exposition, several art cognoscenti had written on the need for art scholarships to enable the most praiseworthy American students to study abroad. For example, in an 1893 essay Sadakichi Hartmann called for a set of "National Prizes" to provide an allowance for the most promising of the country's young talent to visit Europe and "broaden their views and perfect their technique."[7] The American sculptor William Henry Rinehart, who died in 1874, had already left funds in his will for such purposes. Operated by a board of Baltimore art patrons, including W. T. Walters and D. C. Gilmore, and under the auspices of the Peabody Institute of that city, the Rinehart Scholarships were inaugurated in 1895. Proctor's friends from his Chicago years, Daniel Chester French, Charles F. McKim, Edwin H. Blashfield, and Saint-Gaudens, served as advisors, and, at Saint-Gaudens' urging, the board made Proctor a recipient of the first award. The scholarship carried a stipend of $1,000 annually over a four-year tenure.[8] Proctor welcomed the chance to return to France, having heard tales of woe from some of his young colleagues who had tried to make a go of it in the art market on their own. Hermon Atkins MacNeil, for example, who decided to stay in Chicago after his successful association with the fair, had "almost starved to death."[9] He later became the second Rinehart Scholar, studying in Rome from 1896 to 1900. Saint-Gaudens considered both Proctor and MacNeil to be "advanced students," each of whom has "shown that he will undoubtedly make a thorough life work of his art."[10] In both cases Saint-Gaudens' confidence proved to be justified.

Before leaving again for Paris in the fall of 1896, Proctor went west once more to Montana, this time with his new Mannlicher rifle and an old lawyer friend, Henry Stimpson. The purpose was to set their sights on some mountain sheep. While the hunt did not pay off, Proctor's sketching did. He stopped for a while on the Blackfeet reservation and made studies of two young men as well as a sketch for a small equestrian sculpture of an Indian soldier.

Back in Paris, Proctor returned to his routine of classes at the Académie Julian and visits to the Jardin des Plantes. He also rented a studio and began work on the *Indian Warrior* (plate 12, p. 122) from his Blackfeet sketch that would become his diploma piece for the Rinehart Scholarship. At the zoo he sketched alongside George Gardet, France's leading animalier sculptor—Gardet had been crowned the successor to Barye in 1887 when he exhibited a bronze of a panther and a python in mortal combat. Proctor was impressed with Gardet's technical precision and modeling skills. Proctor also befriended a host of American artists during those Paris years. Bela Pratt and his wife were next-door neighbors, and the Proctors socialized with Solon Borglum and his French bride, Emma Vignal. Borglum was taking Puech's life class at the Académie Julian, just as Proctor had done earlier. When Saint-Gaudens moved to Paris in 1897, he and the painter George de Forest Brush often visited together with the Proctors.

During the summer of 1897, the Proctors moved out of Paris to be close to the Brushes at Marlotte Montigny, near Fontainebleau. The next summer they abandoned their Paris studios again, but this time they headed for the shore at Boulogne-sur-Mer. Their friend the writer Mary Mears recalled over forty years later that she, too, was part of that halcyon time:

At Mr. Saint-Gaudens' suggestion, my sister [Helen Mears] and I joined him and his son Homer, Mr. A. P. Proctor, the animal sculptor, and his beautiful young wife and infant daughter, Mr. and Mrs. George de Forest Brush and all the young Brushes at Boulogne-sur-Mer. Of that wonderful vacation the most I recall are hours spent in the sharp sunlight of the beach, now listening to Mr. Proctor's stories of the wild life in the western mountains of the United States,—stories in which the tenderness of the artist triumphed over the instinct of the hunter,—again following some theory Mr. Brush was developing on the technique of painting.[11]

In describing Proctor as a combined wilderness hunter, raconteur, and artist, Mears accurately identified the qualities that distinguished Proctor in his own mind (and in the public's perception) from others around him. He sold himself not simply as a sculptor of developing talent but as a man of uncommon experience. It was not just that he knew how to express himself in the plastic arts. He also had something significant to say that was based on real, worldly interactions. This immediacy was common to other artists of the day. Both Remington and Russell owed part of their successes to their real-life experiences in the West. The French master sculptor Emmanuel Frémiet saw a similar edge in Solon Borglum because of his life in the West. "You are lucky, sir," he told Borglum. "Many young men go to art school, and come out polished with nothing to say. You lived, you had something to say, then you studied art."[12]

Proctor had also formulated a message before going to France to gain the technical facility to articulate it. In fact, Proctor had more than one idea he wanted to express. One idea had to do with the West and its people. To that end Proctor conceived his *Indian Warrior* as a tribute to the martial prowess and resolute fortitude of the Plains Indians. Although never enlarged to monumental scale, the *Indian Warrior* was nonetheless heroic in psychological dimension.

Another idea had to do with his personal, quasi-political message about American animals and nature. By the late 1890s, he had produced at least eight finished animal sculptures beyond the works in plaster for the Chicago fair. They ranged in theme and psychological nuance from idealizing the weak and tentative steps of a newborn in *Fawn* and the curiosity of young animals in *Cub Bear and Rabbit* (plate 10, p. 119) to commemorating the relentless pursuit of the hunter in *Panther* (plate 5, p. 103). With Proctor, nature was expressed in the bodies of those wild beasts, and the native American animals he consistently chose to portray represented quintessentially national qualities.[13] Thus one of Proctor's prime goals was to foster a zeal for the preservation of America's wildlife that was born of reverence for the traditional belief in America as a place of pristine beauty. He was able to do this, as Mears suggested, by adopting a style that balanced the tender side of the artist with the more visceral side of the hunter.

In many ways Proctor was following the tradition of earlier Romantic painters in both France and America. His animals, like the birds and beasts of John James Audubon, were invariably identified with the artist in a personal way: Proctor's *Panther* stalked prey just as the artist himself had done. Proctor's animals, as with those of Landseer, his father's favorite painter, often reflected the popular Romantic view that nature ultimately triumphs over human aspirations. Although contemporary critics would regard Proctor in time as the "antithesis" of Landseer, averring that he allowed "no human element to enter into [his] beasts," his animal sculptures did retain powerful associations with the artist and with a broader humanity.[14]

Back in 1851 Audubon had affirmed the connection between the panther and America's primitive sanctuary. The cougar, as he referred to the cat, was to be found only "in the very wildest parts of the country."[15] Audubon then proceeded to paint not one but two images of the illusive

Fig.19
John James Audubon (1785–1851)
The Cougar, Female and Young.
Lithograph, 10 x 7 inches
From John James Audubon and John
Bachman, *The Quadrupeds of North America*
(1851–1854)

Amon Carter Museum Library, Fort Worth, Tex.

Fig.20
Edward Kemeys (1843–1907)
The Jaguar Lovers, 1888
Bronze, 14⅝ x 30 x 17 inches

The Corcoran Gallery of Art, Washington, D.C.

Fig.19

hunter, *The Cougar, Male* and *The Cougar, Female and Young* (fig. 19). This presentation of a family of wild animals surviving by partnership, wit, and what Audubon called "noiseless stealth" suggested a sense of continuity in nature. Kemeys explored similar ideas in 1888 with his two bronzes *Cougar and Young* and *The Jaguar Lovers* (fig. 20). Proctor's *Panther*, by comparison, was different: it evinced a solitary presence, more of a testament to the lone figure in nature, to the Darwinian idea of nature as struggle, and to the fatalist expectation that such beautiful treasures of the American wilds might not survive. What would cause its demise was the very thing that Proctor resisted with the predominantly masculine side of his personality by escaping into the wilderness himself—civilization.

Proctor's animal sculptures were often seen as antimodernist statements.[16] In their emphasis on the wildness of nature, they appeared antithetical when set beside the works of some of his favorite artists such as Frederick S. Church. Indebted to the English Aesthetic Movement, paintings by Church like *Knowledge Is Power* (fig. 21) retreated from the realities of an industrial world but in a direction opposite to that chosen by Proctor. In Church's work the woman, emblematic of intellectual control, personal charm, and pervasive love, dominates nature with calm resourcefulness. For men like Proctor and Roosevelt, that control of nature was merely a transference of the feminine's real subversion of those pure, time-honored masculine instincts that had governed the wilds for as long as most could remember. Paintings like Church's thus provided a convincing demonstration of the dangers that civilization posed for nature in the wilds. Proctor fought against these imagined subversions whether they emanated from the industrial might of a growing nation or from the intellectual and emotional cunning of a feminized world.

Proctor's swaggering *Buffalo* (plate 16, p. 131), a bronze casting of which he sent back to New York in 1898 for display in the third annual exhibition of the National Sculpture Society, demonstrates the conviction with which he viewed nature's resilience.[17] Although the bison on the North American continent had been regarded as essentially doomed for over a decade, Proctor's bull stands resolutely defiant of his fate. With head lowered in a position of defensive power, this wooly monarch braces himself before the forces ranged against him. Nothing would tame this vital symbol of unspoiled nature.

In September 1898 Lorado Taft published an article specifically devoted to Proctor as a rising star. It appeared in *Brush and Pencil,* a magazine that featured American art. According to Taft, Proctor enjoyed genuine popularity: his "quiet geniality and modest air" had won him many friends at home and abroad. His wife and their daughter, Hester, shared his joy of life (fig. 22). He was seen as "one of the most promising of America's younger sculptors." To Taft's eye, Proctor's *Puma* (plate 15, p. 128), commissioned for Prospect Park in Brooklyn, seemed a bit eccentric in its pose but was praiseworthy for its originality. The *Indian Warrior,* though, received Taft's unreserved commendation. The two works had been submitted as an ensemble to the Paris Salon that year where they won a gold medal for sculpture. Award in hand, the Proctors returned to America just as Taft's article in *Brush and Pencil* appeared on the newsstands.[18]

As it turned out, Proctor's American stay was again only a brief one. Hardly had his family settled in New York when he received a major commission that would require their return to Paris: he was asked to be a member of the sculpture jury for the 1900 Paris Universal Exposition and to create the *Quadriga* that would crown the United States Pavilion. These were two tremendous honors, and he promptly accepted the invitation. After returning to Paris, Proctor rented a large studio on Rue Boileau. There, through the winter of 1899–1900, he modeled a monumental tribute to the mandates for American expansion proclaimed by the William McKinley administration.

Fig.21

Fig.22

Fig.21
Frederick Stuart Church (1842–1924)
Knowledge Is Power, 1889
Oil on canvas, 20⅛ x 36 inches
Grand Rapids History & Special Collections Center, Archives, Grand Rapids Public Library, Grand Rapids, Mich.

Fig.22
Proctor and his wife, Margaret, with their daughter Hester, 1897
A. Phimister Proctor Museum Archives, Poulsbo, Wash.

Fig.23
Proctor's *Liberty on the Chariot of Progress* on the United States Pavilion at the Paris Universal Exposition, Paris, 1900
A. Phimister Proctor Museum Archives, Poulsbo, Wash.

Drawn by four leaping horses, the chariot of progress was driven by a winged, gossamer-clad Liberty (fig. 23). At Saint-Gaudens' suggestion, Proctor turned the female figure's design and execution over to a fellow American, Caroline Peddle. When Saint-Gaudens saw the work, he wrote to their mutual friend, the sculptor Helen Mears, "Miss Peddle's 'America' for Proctor's chariot, although somewhat amateurish in parts of its treatment is really large and fine in gesture and conception and quite personal and original." The multifigure triumphal group would be gilded and rest atop the pavilion's neoclassical dome designed to resemble something built for the Roman Empire.[19]

While he was working on the *Quadriga,* Proctor's ambition and the bitter chill of the Paris winter almost got the better of him. A friend and neighbor, Vance Thompson, told the readers of the *Saturday Evening Post* how he helped save the sculpture on one freezing night:

Fig.23

Rue Boileau; a large studio—large enough to wheel a coach-and-six in; a glass roof and a glass north wall through which the winter wanders in at will; in the center of the studio a huge plaster chariot; near by, mounted on their scaffoldings, four ramping plaster horses—five times larger than life. Two French stoves of the biggest sort—and they are not very big—are blazing their best, while a heart-broken boy…is shoveling in unlimited coal. Still it is cold—freezing cold. The plaster hide of the ramping horses is crinkling into all kinds of queer patterns. And it is midnight.

Even as the bells of Notre Dame of Auteuil tell the hour the door opens, and a bearded sculptor and his assistants come rushing in with armfuls of blankets and quilts, overcoats and furs, and they wrap up the ramping horses as though they were croupy babies. All the while the chariot is freezing on its wheels. The sculptor sees a crack running up its carved front. He dashes back to his house, reappears with the drawing-room rugs and the baby's *pelisse. He takes off his coat and wraps it around the chilled tail of a rearing charger. Always the little French stoves are blazing away and the heart-broken boy shovels in coal. Out of doors it grows colder and all the cold night air sifts into the glass-roofed studio.*

It was one o'clock—by the bell of Notre Dame—when the man who writes these true words was startled out of his bed by a mighty clanging at his door-bell. He opened: "A note from Monsieur Proctor, sir—it's a matter of life and death." And the man who writes these true words read:

"For Heaven's sake send me all your blankets and coats and rugs and furs— the horses are freezing to death. Proctor."

And the man who writes these true words sent them, and for the rest of the night he slept on the kitchen stove and dreamed fitfully of art. Rome was saved by geese; I like to think that I saved the quadriga—chariot, horses and all—that is to look riverward from the United States building during the Exposition of 1900.[20]

Proctor showed his *Panther,* among other bronzes, in the Grand Palais, where the United States Paintings Exposition was housed. Across the room hung Brush's circular neo-Renaissance portrait of his family, *Mother and Child,* which he had painted a couple of summers before when the Proctors were his neighbors at Marlotte Montigny. Saint-Gaudens had remarked then that the painting was a "stimulating thing...the composition is fine and...it is so splendidly drawn."[21] In an adjoining gallery was *Young Mother,* a delicate portrait of Margaret Proctor with a child, which had been sculpted by her closest friend, Bessie Potter Vonnoh. Compared to these portrayals

of familial sentiment, especially maternity, Proctor's wild cougar stood apart in spirit and purpose, distinct in fact from most of the American works at the Grand Palais.

The *Quadriga* is what brought him the most critical attention, exposing a substantial paradox since the sculpture spoke to ideologies of progress that he strongly opposed in his usual work. Of course, in taking on the job of sculpting the *Quadriga,* he was forced to accept the agenda of the McKinley administration as articulated by U.S. Commissioner Ferdinand Peck and his appointed director of fine arts, John Britton Cauldwell. Those two gentlemen had decided to champion the cause of American polity and to assert its cultural equality with, if not superiority over, that of the European nations. The more formal and classically derivative its pavilion and the accompanying decorations were, the more likely it would be that other nations would take the United States seriously. In 1898 the art critic Hartmann called on people not to "be too hard on the American sculptors as they accommodated to national priorities and tastes." Sculpture, he said, was driven essentially by commercial need, first because it was an extremely expensive medium and second, because "only decorative work and portrait statues are in demand, which, superintended [as they are] by architects, politicians and other lay committees, do not permit a free unfolding of art."[22] Another American critic, Georgia Fraser, who watched Proctor as he labored over the complex and massive *Quadriga,* praised its "spirited conception" but spoke candidly about the creative challenge that it entailed:

It is about as difficult to imbue a quadriga with so-called originality as it would be to do the same by an arc de triomphe. But it is not futility of conception, but futility of composition and treatment, that constitutes originality in art; and it is certain that Mr. Proctor's treatment of his subject will add greatly to the dignity and beauty of the United States building. For such a work no better man could have been selected.[23]

Proctor recognized the need to conform to the standard demands of his profession. He knew how things worked and in fact had already begun to maneuver at home, trying to pull strings so that he might win government support for some of his projects. Back in the summer of 1897, Proctor had heard rumors that Congress intended to commission statues of American wild animals. He wrote to his friend Roosevelt, then assistant secretary of the navy, and asked how he might become involved with the project. Roosevelt advised Proctor to take direct action:

I like that buffalo bull [plate 16] of yours very much indeed. Do you know any Congressmen? If so, it would be well worth while writing him about it. I will mention that in these matters it is particularly good to have the Congressman from somewhere in the West, and if you can pose as a "splendid specimen of our native raw (and finished) material" from the boundless Pacific slope, it will help things materially.[24]

Nothing is known to have come of this. However, Roosevelt and Proctor were clearly simpatico. Not only did Roosevelt admire Proctor's work, especially the *Buffalo*, but they both also shared a sense of the West as essentially "finished." Proctor's animals were to be tributes to endangered "wild beasts," as Roosevelt termed them. Proctor was determined to learn how to position himself in the official game of state patronage so that he might further explicate his message.

Proctor's role in the Paris Universal Exposition proved to be critical for his future. Along with other American sculptors, including George Barnard, Richard Brooks, and Charles Grafly, he won gold medals. Of the seventy American sculptures among the 1,546 (mostly French) works listed in the exposition catalogue, Proctor showed more than any other artist. His two bronze-colored plaster *Pumas* decorated the exposition's main entrance on the Place de la Concorde. Scattered among the United States galleries of the Grand Palais were his *Panther, Indian Warrior, Fawn, Elk* (plate 17, p. 133) and *Dog with Bone*. The plaster maquette for Saint-Gaudens' *General Sherman* was displayed as well, winning a medal of honor along with much stir in the press. Proctor's horse in the monument was celebrated for its truth of purpose: "It is a real horse," claimed Taft, "not one of those bulky, pneumatic-tire creatures which are the traditional war-horses of art."[25]

Proctor came away from the Paris Universal Exposition a fully developed sculptor. The express purpose of the American participation there had been to expose the "American School" of art to world view and raise awareness of national trends at home and abroad. Thompson, in an article on Proctor that appeared in the *Philadelphia Post*, attested to the sculptor's accomplishment in that regard: "Of all the American sculptors, I think Mr. Proctor deserves most of America.... His sculptures all speak of that great West from which he came; they are Indians, elk, panthers, bronchos—they are the West."[26] Proctor had made his point and his mark.

4

THE NATURALIST-HUNTER
AND THE SCULPTOR

The Proctors were welcomed back to the United States in the fall of 1900. They soon settled in Palisades, New York, across from Dobbs Ferry. Their old friend Mary Lawrence Tonetti, one of Margaret's cronies from their Chicago days and a coworker with Proctor on Saint-Gaudens' *General Sherman*, offered the young transients a comfortable house in her family compound called Sneden's Landing. The Proctors were the first of many distinguished cohorts to rent what was known as the Ding Dong House. The Tonettis built Proctor a studio behind the house, so that from his back door he had immediate access to his work and from the front porch he and Margaret had a magnificent view of the Hudson River.[1]

Proctor also maintained a studio in the city at 13 East 30th Street. He split his week between the two work spaces and soon began to solicit business among new and old acquaintances. In December 1900 he wrote to his Boone and Crockett Club friend Gifford Pinchot that the promised casting of the *Panther* had inexplicably been delayed in Paris. "I have trouble always in getting bronzes from those Frenchmen," he apologized.[2] Then he went on to tell Pinchot that John La Farge had mentioned possibly commissioning an animal relief for the Pinchot house. Not one but several works would result from that lead: a large bronze overmantel, *Moose Family* (plate 19, p. 136), for a house that Pinchot was building in Washington, D.C., and a series of eight animal medallions on shield-shaped plaques. The latter would one day decorate Pinchot's dining room.

The 30th Street studio could accommodate larger requests, the most important of which came from Karl Bitter, who was in charge of sculpture decorations on the exteriors of buildings being planned for the Pan-American Exposition in Buffalo, New York, the following year (1901). Bitter had been impressed with Proctor's *Quadriga* in Paris and sought his permission to have it brought to Buffalo to be part of the embellishments for

Fig.24

Fig.24
View of plaster/staff model for Proctor's
monumental plaster *Agriculture*

A. Phimister Proctor Museum Archives, Poulsbo, Wash.

Fig.25
Horatio Walker (1858–1938)
*Labour aux premières lueurs du jour/
Ploughing—The First Gleam at Dawn,* 1900
Oil on canvas, 60⅛ x 76⅞ inches

Musée national des beaux-arts du Québec 34.530
Photograph by Jean-Guy Kérouac

the Ethnological Building. The art critic Charles Caffin had been rather displeased with the *Quadriga* in Paris because, he later said, it "was dwarfed by the structure" of the United States Pavilion. In Buffalo, however, it showed up well because it joined other sculptures on the building instead of being what Caffin called a "single emphatic note, for which purpose it was too slight in composition, unduly stringy and deficient in cohesion."[3]

While generally solicitous of Proctor's vision as a sculptor, Caffin did make the observation that Proctor focused more on naturalist concerns than on sculptural precepts. The pumas he had done for Prospect Park possessed a sense of monumentality and sculptural presence, but in Caffin's estimation Proctor's other work did not—with one exception. Proctor's monumental plaster group titled *Agriculture* (fig. 24), which also decorated the grounds in Buffalo, celebrated the dignity and force of manual labor and the earthy richness of farm life in a way that resonated with Caffin's taste. Here, he claimed, was a "remarkable example of the force of realism, when governed by the sculptural intention." By contrasting the brute power of the straining beasts with the focused determination of the man and boy, Proctor had achieved an effective balance of movements within a simple but fundamental narrative. Unlike Daniel Chester French's allegorical *Farmer* sculpted for the Chicago fair, Proctor's figures were real men of the soil. It complemented a large painting by his Canadian friend Horatio Walker, which also hung at the exposition that year: *Ploughing—The First Gleam at Dawn* (fig. 25). Indeed, Caffin described the painting as if it were a companion piece to Proctor's, noting how it evoked "times of spaciousness and simplicity, when we fancy that man's strength was in closest affinity with nature's; times of wholesomeness and poise of mind and body, when man lived by nature's rule and labor was loving."[4] Both the painting and the plaster were reminiscent of the rustic tributes in paint produced by the French

Barbizon master Jean-François Millet. Proctor knew Millet's work from his years in France, and he had seen Walker's canvas several times, including at the annual exhibition of the National Academy of Design in 1901. Although similar in theme to Millet's peasant scenes, the Walker and Proctor works had shifted the mood from a melancholy typical of the Frenchman's tableaus to a stance in which, as a Canadian critic pointed out, optimism reigned and the toiler "feels joy and purpose in his work."[5]

Proctor was well represented at the Pan-American Exposition; in addition to the two plaster monuments, he exhibited three watercolors and nine small sculptures. The catalogue for the Fine Arts Exhibition noted that

Fig.25

THE NATURALIST-HUNTER AND THE SCULPTOR

Proctor was already a medal winner at both the Chicago and the Paris world's fairs. The catalogue also listed him as a member of several professional art organizations, including the National Sculpture Society, the Society of American Artists, the American Water Color Society, and the Architectural League of New York.[6]

Being on the jury for the Pan-American Exposition made him ineligible for any medals in Buffalo, but Proctor was about to add another feather to his cap. In 1901 the members of the National Academy of Design elected Proctor as an associate member; his friend Robert Vonnoh submitted a portrait of the sculptor (plate 1) shortly thereafter, thus formally qualifying him for the honor. That same year Proctor began to exhibit sculpture at the National Academy, starting with a single submission, a casting of *Elk* (plate 17, p. 133). Again, Proctor demonstrated that what Caffin referred to as "man's strength…in closest affinity with nature's" meant for him not toiling on the earth but rather a direct association with the animals that wandered the wilds. *Elk* was a reassertion of his mission as an animalier sculptor. That it garnered for him the honor of adding "ANA" after his name simply strengthened his resolve to stake his reputation there.

Animal sculptors did not always enjoy equal stature with other sculptors. Daniel Chester French often found himself defending his associate and collaborator, the animal sculptor Edward Potter. As French's biographer, Adeline Adams, noted, his "wrath was justly aroused by any slurring mention of an 'animal sculptor' as less the artist than is the sculptor of the human form."[7] Despite acclaim from as far afield as Seattle, where a newspaper declared, "there are few Americans who enjoy greater distinction in the world of art," Proctor still faced a pervasive discrimination.[8] He also confronted stiff competition within his selected genre. Both Potter and Edward Kemeys already enjoyed distinguished national reputations as American animalier sculptors, and several younger artists were ascending to prominence, including Anna Hyatt Huntington, Frederick G. R. Roth, Arthur Putnam, and Charles M. Russell. Of these, Kemeys held the highest position. Articles by and about him abounded at the time, proclaiming him "the Barye of the western continent" and a practitioner of an especially "robust picturesqueness and intense Americanism."[9] But like Huntington, Putnam, and Russell, Kemeys was also entirely self-taught. Thus Proctor in his formal, academic approach to preparing himself for his career differed markedly from most of his associates. He admired Kemeys and went out of his way to befriend him, but despite their apparent common interests and background, Kemeys remained aloof from his younger associate even as he charmed audiences with his animal sculptures and tales of Indian lore.

Proctor at first gave Kemeys' coolness a charitable reading. When he first met the older artist in 1893 at the Chicago fair, Kemeys had, in Proctor's words, been "very cordial and helpful," adding, "Kemeys had hunted buffaloes on the plains and was full of interesting stories so we had things in common." Yet he noticed a "little strangeness or aloofness in his attitude" toward him, which he explained away as a trait born of the "lonesome life of the hunter." A cousin of Kemeys, however, later explained to Proctor that it was nothing more than professional jealousy that kept Kemeys from warmer relations with Proctor. This became clear after the cousin had seen Kemeys' animals in Chicago:

> [He] congratulated Kemeys on his sculpture and said to him that it must be a great satisfaction to be doing such large statues and receiving appreciation of the public. Then the [cousin] said that a shadow came over Kemeys' face and he said—yes, yes, but there is a young man just arrived here…[10]

Fig.26

Proctor realized that lack of confidence and not a clash of personality had caused the rift.

Like Kemeys, Proctor cultivated the image of a sculptor whose hunting skills equaled those of his art. To that end Proctor practiced marksmanship with the same concentration that he gave to his art. "The sculptor is a crack shot with both rifle and revolver," wrote one newspaper in 1901.[11] And the journalist Henry J. Allen once quoted Proctor as saying that the marksmanship that required "steady hand and unerring eye" was linked directly to his success as a sculptor.[12] It also made him a formidable hunter. In the spring of 1902, Proctor's name appeared in several newspapers after he killed a massive bull moose in Canada. So spectacular was the trophy that it was mounted and put on display in New York's American Museum of Natural History. The *New York World* speculated that it was not only the "biggest moose ever brought to New York" but "probably the largest ever killed." And in the same breath, the reporter noted that Proctor was working on a series of animal sculptures for the homes of Cornelius Vanderbilt Jr. and J. Pierpont Morgan.[13]

For both Proctor and his public, then, hunting and sculpting were inextricably and logically intertwined. They were complementary disciplines. Proctor was not some weekender happy to take potshots at the occasional mallard that happened to take refuge on the local pond. He was a real hunter, with unflinching nerves and steady hands. The coordination between his eye and his trigger finger showed the same precision as his hand and eye when modeling clay. His .44-70 Sharps or the Mannlicher were for him master tools similar in power and effect to the sculptor's tools he wielded when creating his clay models and plaster maquettes. While he savored the pursuit and kill with an unwavering passion, he spent equal energy bringing animals back to life through his art. His trophies were not simply glass-eyed mounts like the one displayed in New York or the furred remains of some

great beast rolled out on the oak floor of the library. His trophies took the shape of the animals themselves, like *Moose* (plate 26, p. 150), posed in symbolic triumph at their most memorable and glorious moments.

When the Canadian woods or the Colorado Rockies were lacking in subjects, Proctor turned back to the New York City zoo for inspiration and, now that he had achieved a certain level of success, for patronage as well. Even before leaving Paris, Proctor had solidified connections with the New York Zoological Society that would lead in the next decade to a series of commissions. The first came when the city opened its new Zoological Park on November 8, 1899. The largest and most modern of the structures was the Reptile House. Fashioned by architect C. Grant la Farge as a long, low white sandstone building, it featured decorations by Proctor. The artist had used the Chicago fair's Fishery Building as a model to produce what New York's *Evening Post* reported as an assemblage of "turtles, lizards, frogs and 'crawling creeping things' of diverse sorts…grouped and interlaced in wild profusion."[14]

Other artists also participated in decorating the buildings of the Zoological Park. Eli Harvey and Charles R. Knight provided architectural embellishments for the Lion House and the north end of the Elephant House, but Proctor secured the largest share of the work. After finishing the Reptile House decorations, he took on the Aquatic Bird House, the Antelope House, the Primate House, and the south end of the Elephant House (fig. 26). As architectural details, Proctor's limestone animals and birds provided great pleasure for zoo visitors. The zoo's director, William Hornaday, who disliked Harvey's overcrowded designs, was ecstatic over Proctor's elegant, solitary figures. He even allowed Proctor to borrow certain animals from the zoo as models; they were transported in cages to his studio in Palisades, where the artist could work undisturbed by visitors.[15]

Fig. 27

Proctor exhibited the plaster maquette for the pediment of the Primate House (fig. 27) in 1902 at the annual exhibition of the National Academy of Design. A portrait of an orangutan, it was singled out for special notice by the critic Harrison N. Howard.[16] By then the commissions of the New York Zoological Society, particularly the orangutan and monkeys, had brought Proctor to the attention of the New York public.[17] People especially enjoyed watching Proctor work, and in the spring of 1903 he received an invitation to join a group of artists and naturalists that included Ernest Thompson Seton, Carl Rungius, Daniel C. Beard, and Harvey to advise the society on the design of a special viewable studio for artists to use. So solicitous was Hornaday about the fraternity of artists he had gathered that a room, twenty-one by twenty-six feet, half of which comprised a cage for the models, was constructed and opened in July. Most of the credit went to Seton and Hornaday, but Proctor played an important part in the project and benefited materially from the result.[18]

Until that point, Proctor and others worked in the public corridors of the various animal houses, arranging themselves before the cages with easels or modeling stands. Proctor, who was working on a commission of two heroic-sized lions to guard the entrance of the Frick Building in Pittsburgh, positioned himself before the cage of a lion named Dewey. The head of the lion that Proctor eventually produced was regarded as "especially fine," and the full-sized model that resided in his studio was considered "expressive of immense dignity and grandeur."[19]

Proctor's analytical approach to observing his models garnered for him a reputation "as a thoroughly scientific student of animal life." He was known to study dissected animals at the American Museum of Natural History and to dissect them himself on his own hunting expeditions. These investigations greatly enhanced his ability to extract the wild essence from caged beasts. Moreover, Proctor proved to be proficient at getting the most

Fig.28
One of Proctor's two bronze lions on
the Frick Building, Pittsburgh,
Pennsylvania

A. Phimister Proctor Museum Archives,
Poulsbo, Wash.

Fig.29
Newspaper photograph of Proctor
modeling *Lions* for the McKinley
monument, 1906

A. Phimister Proctor Museum Archives,
Poulsbo, Wash.
Reproduction photograph by Howard Giske

Fig.28

from the beasts even behind bars. The lion Dewey, it was claimed, had been
"trained" by Proctor. The sculptor somehow combined pole-prodding with
an "ability to make Dewey understand that he didn't in the least fear him" to
get the lion to pose cooperatively and in the "correct attitude" for hours at
a time.[20] The resulting *Seated Lions* sit formally, like bearded Edwardian gentlemen cloaked in the prosperous aura of America's industrial Golden Age (fig.
28). They convey a complacent dignity and aloof rectitude, qualities that
Henry Clay Frick no doubt wished to impress his visitors with as they entered
his $2 million building. All this led Taft to suggest that Proctor, like MacNeil,
"threatened to become…almost too clever to be convincingly savage."[21]

In 1903 Proctor wrote his old Denver artist friend Chamberlain,
expressing pleasure and surprise that his *Indian* and *Cowboy* were still to be
seen in Denver's city park. He told Chamberlain how Roosevelt, now president,
had praised them a decade earlier when he visited the artist's Chicago studio.
To Chamberlain's suggestion that perhaps Proctor could have them
reworked and made into permanent monuments, the sculptor showed interest
but little hope: "It would give me a lot of pleasure to do them. I am afraid
Denver would think the price too high." But he concluded that the city "is of
sufficient importance now to begin to think of the artistic things."[22]

Still, Denver would wait over fifteen years before fitting her native
son's sculpture into the community's "artistic things." In the meantime
another western city was ready to avail itself of Proctor's talents—Saint Louis.
Karl Bitter, now head of sculptural decoration at the Louisiana Purchase
Exposition, contacted Proctor about creating a pair of gilded copper griffins
for the Fine Arts Palace (plate 20, p. 139) and a plaster staff monument to the
explorer who "discovered" the upper Mississippi in 1673, Louis Joliet. Bitter
called for a "broad, catholic spirit" in the sculptures of the latest world's fair, one
in which "historical records and poetic symbolism play an equal part."[23]

MODEL OF McKINLEY MONUMENT LION.

A. P. PROCTOR MODELING THE LION.

Fig.29

Proctor's *Louis Joliet* stood on the left flank of the Plaza of Saint Louis, the entrance concourse to the exposition grounds. It faced a similar monument by Potter, *Hernando de Soto*, across a broad grassy expanse. Proctor's work feels, in comparison, a little inert. Joliet sits upright with his right arm rather lifelessly hanging at his side. His shoulders are thrust slightly back, as if the explorer were awed by his first sight of the mighty watercourse. Although critics referred to it as an "ideal equestrian statue" and "a splendid example of realism in art," Potter's more flamboyant exercise somewhat overshadowed its companion. As one overly exuberant writer wrote, "in conception, pose, modeling and execution" Potter's De Soto "was rightly regarded as one of the greatest works of art shown in 1904."[24]

By now Proctor and Potter, both recognized as animalier sculptors able to conceive fully heroic equestrian monuments, were becoming rivals. Potter, who trained in Paris at the same time that Proctor worked with Saint-Gaudens, had pulled many commissions out from under Proctor in the ensuing years. One art historian contends that Proctor's *Joliet* was modified in design "to complement" Potter's *De Soto*. Be that as it may—and there is no evidence to support that notion—the two works faced off across the concourse, each seeking a place in history. In the spirit of Bitter's call for "historical record," however, Proctor at least fell a bit short; his explorer, mounted on a fully caparisoned Morgan horse, had actually traveled by canoe.[25]

On May 12, 1904, Jonathan S. Hartley (who had probably taught Proctor at the Art Students League and whose heroic-sized plaster of Saint Louis' founder, Pierre Laclede, also appeared at the exposition) sent Proctor a card. It congratulated him on having been elected to full membership in the National Academy of Design the night before, adding in a postscript, "you got a very high vote." Proctor was now officially an artist among America's highest ranks. And those ranks, at least among the nation's art cognoscenti

in 1904, were lofty ones indeed. While the artists of the Old World were, as A. A. Howard put it, "floundering about in a chaos of new ideas and methods that as yet have not given evidence of their adaptability to the requirements of art," the "sculptors of the United States are the most original in the world."[26]

Buoyed by such an association, Proctor won numerous important commissions for animal work over the next several years. The *Lions* (plate 23, p. 145) for the McKinley monument, begun in 1903, earned perhaps the most widespread recognition. Yet part of the public appeal of animal sculpture may have been its newness in America, and there was some question about how long its popularity would last. The artist, interviewed around 1906 when he was in the final stages of completing the giant sleeping lions for the McKinley project (fig. 29), expressed the following about the recent interest in animals:

It is only about 10 years now that wild animals have been a fashion in art. No one quite knows how it came about, but it was probably the animal books that gave an impetus to it. People began to be interested in animals, and then they began to want pictures of animals and animals done in marble and bronze. The rage will probably not last as it is at present, but for the main part, the wild animal has come to stay.[27]

Popularity led to intensified competition. Proctor sought the commission to sculpt the lions on the front porch of the J. P. Morgan Library in 1903, but McKim gave the job to Potter instead. Proctor wrote Pinchot about the loss, suggesting that the architect's decision had been based on financial considerations: "Potter took them for a heap less money than I wanted to do them for. They wanted a masterpiece, by lowest bidder."[28] But Potter's sketch may have been more pleasing to McKim. Proctor did not always have the most effective presentation. For example, in 1906 Proctor troubled his old and infirm mentor, Saint-Gaudens, for a critique of a lion sketch he was preparing for some unidentified job (possibly the New York Public Library). Saint-Gaudens returned the sketch and followed it up with his comments:

I think it is excellent as all your work is. I only feel that for architectural work it should be more in planes, more formal. I do not know why I say that to you, as you say the same thing yourself in your letter.

You will forgive me for speaking just as frankly as I always have about your work, and as I wish people to do with me. I think you have not insisted enough on the nobility and force and power of the manes of the lion and have perhaps insisted a little too much on the ape-like character (that is putting it rather strong) of the face. Some of the photographs of those British lions in that famous book on animals that I have, show they can have a nobility which is extraordinary. This one looks a little too much like the lions in the menagerie and distinctly the head does not bear the importance to the rest of the body— the overpowering importance—that one generally feels with a lion....[29]

Proctor's response, quoted here in full, captures the essence of the artistic challenge, the business realities, and the physical commitment involved in a monument project, as well as the profound respect and the personal bond that existed between him and Saint-Gaudens:

Dear Mr. Saint-Gaudens,
I want to thank you most sincerely for your letter & criticism of small model I sent you. It seems like old times to get one from the shoulder from you. I have missed them more than I can tell—One is not apt to forget your criticizing. It is like giving the edge of a door a fast push with ones nose in the dark. They tell, & that is what I want—your letter was forwarded to me by my wife & I send clippings from her letter—in regard to head of lion. I told her

you would see it at first glance. I was not quite so severe on myself however. I did not then see the ape likeness, probably will though when next I see the lion—while working I always wonder what you would say about the thing I am doing. I always try to keep before my mind those fine qualities, nobleness, dignity & simplicity. As I look over my goods, however, I see so little of it. I wonder what I was thinking of when doing them. I try to make careful studies from life & then, if I can, put in the artistic qualities. The sketch I sent you was in first stage, & not complete as I told you. It was, as you say, a menagerie lion & my live model was not a good one. Will hunt up a first class model when I get at it again. If it had not been for the wife I would not have sent that sketch. I thought from your letters that others had sent in finished studies. I thought it strange that I had not heard of it since now. Carriere [architect John Carrère] & [architect Thomas] Hastings had given me cause to hope that I might get the commission. Tho, as I said before they have not promised it to me—I think I know the kind of lion you would like to see in front of the library—I also know how terribly difficult it will be to get those fine qualities. The image in mind is one thing, but accomplished in marble as bronze is another we all know. I think the pose of the lion I sent you is the finest one he takes, it gives me a fine sensation. I must get it some day. As soon as I am through with the McKinley lions, I would like to make a good model of lion in that same pose, & try to give it the qualities you mention. They cannot be insisted upon too much. I will then have no excuses to submit. I should like to know what book of photographs of lions etc. it is that you speak of—will get it—Mr. Carriere [sic] was here yesterday, & seemed pleased with the two lions now in place & which I am working on. The lion I had for model was all mane, & I have had the worst job of my life trying to do it. Have not succeeded with a single lock as yet. I hope the marble will hold out long enough for me to get something out of it. I would give a great deal for your criticism on these lions, before it is too late—I shall hope to get some of the finer qualities in the next lions, that may be lacking in these.

I had intended to make this letter as short as possible so as not to worry you too much, but have not succeeded very well. Have tried to bother you as little as possible of late years.

Thanking you again for your letter & frank criticism & promise of good word.

Sincerely yours,
A. P. Proctor

Mr. Augustus Saint Gaudens
Windsor Vt.

I plied the hammer from early morn till six this eve, & am tired in the hands, as you may imagine I enjoy it very much.[30]

In the coming year, Saint-Gaudens would die, and Proctor would lose out to Potter again, for the lions on the porch of the New York Public Library. His deep respect for his mentor, however, remained, and he kept a photograph of Saint-Gaudens in the studio at Indian Hills, his sixty-acre farm near Bedford, in Westchester County, New York. (Proctor called Indian Hill "my ranch," boasting that at the highest point of land it commanded a view all the way to the Rocky Mountains.) He later told the master's surviving son, Homer, that "I am continually looking at it, & saying to myself while working, 'I wonder what the Saint would think of that?'"[31] Those qualities of nobleness, dignity, and simplicity advocated by Saint-Gaudens continued to define Proctor's artistic vision. He also respected the precise drawing and meticulous finish of George de Forest Brush, who spent the winter of 1907–1908 with the Proctors at Indian Hill painting their children.[32]

Though Proctor's animalier work provided part of his bread and butter, he was less successful in those years at winning commissions for large equestrian monuments. Opportunities were constantly coming forward, but on numerous occasions he competed in vain. In one early instance involving a monument to General George B. McClellan, he lacked the time to focus on producing a sketch; he was given only fourteen days, with the result that the horse and rider ended up out of scale. He lamented in a letter to Pinchot that he had mistakenly "[t]rusted a hastily made working scale rather than my judgment." He went on to assure his friend that "barring that mistake, very easily rectified with a little time, I could have taken that rag off the bush. Am sure I can do a better equestrian statue than any fellow in that mess."[33]

He also failed in the competition to produce a George Washington monument for the University of Washington in 1906, which Saint-Gaudens had encouraged him to pursue. He lost out for internal political reasons on a portrait statue of Nathan Hale for Yale University that Pinchot wanted him to sculpt in 1907. And he was especially disappointed to miss the chance to create a heroic equestrian bronze of General George Armstrong Custer in 1908. "I am not interested in doing statues of an ordinary individual," he had confessed to Pinchot in a letter of 1907, "but I am tremendously interested in the fighting animal, man or beast."[34] The Custer statue would have fit that definition of his goals, but politics and time limitations of a different sort played a role in his defeat.

In June 1907 the Michigan legislature had appropriated $25,000 for a bronze monument to Custer to be erected in the town of Monroe. Governor Fred Warner appointed a special commission to select a sculptor in concert with the general's widow, Elizabeth. She and the commission's chairman, Colonel George G. Briggs of Grand Rapids, contacted several sculptors, including the two brothers Solon and Gutzon Borglum, Potter, Henry Shrady,

Fig.30

Henry Bush-Brown, and Proctor. Mrs. Custer visited Indian Hill in November 1907 and met Proctor, inviting him to submit a sketch for the committee's review. Proctor quickly set to work, intent not only on producing the preliminary model (fig. 30) but also on gathering forces to promote his cause. He let Pinchot know what he was pursuing, which resulted in an impassioned letter of support from the U.S. Forest Service chief. Pinchot pointed to the fact that Proctor's family had once lived in Michigan and that the artist's "intimate, first-hand knowledge of Western life, through many years of the kind of life of which you have told me so often as having been lived by the General and yourself during many years in the West, gives him a special fitness for the task."[35]

Other testimonials arrived on Mrs. Custer's desk as well. Loyall Farragut, son of the famous Civil War admiral whose portrait monument in New York had started the careers of Saint-Gaudens and Stanford White, sent a note of endorsement. Proctor, he said, was "a conscientious, painstaking and modest man and he will do his work well. No one excels him in animals (horses etc), but he is an all around good sculptor. He has lived a good deal in the West and his heart would be in the subject!" Remembering that Proctor had yet to produce a bronze equestrian monument, and endeavoring to associate Proctor with his prime mentor, Farragut wrote a follow-up letter to Mrs. Custer a few days later:

I know most of the principal sculptors, French, Borglum, etc. in the most friendly way and am aware of their good work but I have the feeling that Proctor would make a great reputation for himself if he had the appointment—just as St. Gaudens did with the "Farragut" which is undoubtedly that piece that commenced his reputation.[36]

Others came forward on Proctor's behalf, but none more convincingly than his old friend Henry Stimpson, now the U.S. Attorney for the Southern Division of New York, who wrote in early 1908:

I stopped at Proctor's studio this morning and saw his model for the statue of the General. I cannot refrain from telling you [how] much I liked it. It (the figure) seemed to me to mingle the dash of the cavalryman with the stern spirit that carried through the Civil War. While the horse seemed to me to be the very best of Proctor's many fine horses. I have no business to volunteer my views to you on [a] subject as to which you are so much a better judge, but you know my weakness for the cavalry and for the West and this model seemed to breathe so the spirit of both that I felt I must tell you how it hit me. The way in which that figure sits his horse and the way his head is set on his shoulders is enough to make every Wolverine sit up in his saddle and fairly tingle for the first note of the charge.[37]

Proctor in the meantime embarked on a vigorous correspondence with Mrs. Custer. In one letter he told her that the original composition had changed within the first several weeks. The horse's pose, adapted from the initial sketch for the *Joliet* monument, was retained, but the general had dropped his waving right arm and now rode with his hat at his side (fig. 31). Many generals had fought in the Civil War (the period that the committee wanted commemorated), but Proctor flattered the widow, contending that there was only *one* General Custer: "His statue should be distinctive, dignified and dashing & one seeing it at a distance, who knew anything about him, should say, that must be General Custer."[38]

Despite Proctor's best efforts, the project did not come his way. Briggs persuaded Mrs. Custer that the figure's presence should be one of "repose" rather than the dash that Proctor proposed. An equestrian in repose, he argued, "will become alive to those who behold it and in their imaginations not only will action be suggested but there will be the added vision of a great soldier...."[39] Briggs was impressed by Proctor's "kindly nature and happy disposition" but, along with the committee, ultimately

Fig.30
Proctor's preliminary model for *Custer*, 1907

A. Phimister Proctor Museum Archives, Poulsbo, Wash.

Fig.31
Proctor's plaster sketch for *Custer*, 1907

A. Phimister Proctor Museum Archives, Poulsbo, Wash.

Fig.31

chose Potter for the task. Mrs. Custer preferred Proctor's model but was said to have been impressed by Potter's request to visit and examine the site on which the monument would stand.[40] That and the stolid, inert "repose" of Potter's composition garnered the endorsement of Briggs and his old soldier cronies on the committee.

Proctor later put on a good face for Mrs. Custer. He graciously told her that she had made a valid decision with Potter. Even so, Proctor's confidence was shaken. Viewing this loss as something of an omen, he wrote to Pinchot in March 1908:

I have come to the conclusion that I must change my methods in regard to getting work. Have had the old fashioned notion that the commissions should come to me. Of course I'd starve rather than get work as some are doing, but I intend doing what I can in a decent way—a sculptor without fortune must have commissions in order to show what he can do. I'm getting scared that I won't leave as much good work behind as I had hoped—I don't intend to turn out any thing less than the best.[41]

Proctor was also concerned for his family. He and Margaret now had five children to feed and educate as well as a farm to manage. For the time being, he would have to set aside his dream of an equestrian monument and focus on his animal work. He must therefore have been reassured to read in an article commemorating Saint-Gaudens' influence on the nation's art that "statuettes of animals" were considered "the most wholly satisfactory American work [that] has been done" and that Proctor's bronzes were every bit as "perfect as anything Barye ever did."[42]

To take advantage of the current taste for small animal bronzes and other works in a similar scale, Proctor opened discussions with the New York dealer N. E. Montross to plan a major exhibition. The show, which took place just before Christmas 1908, included 169 original sculptures, paintings, and drawings and sixteen photographs of completed monuments (fig. 32). Of Proctor's friends, Alden Sampson provided twenty paintings and watercolors, and Pinchot loaned nine animal relief sculptures. "Have got to whoop things up," the artist told Pinchot in a letter announcing the coming retrospective.[43] By this Proctor probably meant that he needed all the publicity he could get. The newspapers responded accordingly. The *New York Evening Telegram* proclaimed the works to be "fine" and "simple," with the "sculptor having avoided the temptation to introduce more than the essentials." A review in *The Craftsman* magazine also spoke to those same qualities, describing Proctor's bronzes in ways that mirrored Saint-Gaudens' definition of ideal sculpture. "Proctor's animals seem alive and unsentimental," the reviewer asserted, which was understandable since "the sculptor knows animals intimately." Proctor was also seen as addressing a full range of emotions in his work, from rage to humor, always expressing "things simply, with dignity, [and] with incisive intelligence. Apart from his great gift of understanding, it is undoubtedly these qualities of simplicity, accuracy and intelligence" which had allowed Proctor to succeed.[44] Finally, the critic Mary Fanton Roberts, writing under the pen name of Giles Edgerton a few months before the show opened, found an appealing American quality in Proctor's work. Such homemade expressions of truth and beauty, Roberts wrote, "could only be the product of an American art" based on "frankness, honesty and force."[45]

By the end of the decade, Proctor was spending more and more time in his MacDougal Alley studio in New York City. The family ultimately sold Indian Hill and moved to Stanford, Connecticut, so that he would be within commuting distance of Manhattan. The shift seemed to accelerate his career, and by late 1909 he had begun to attract large commissions (albeit

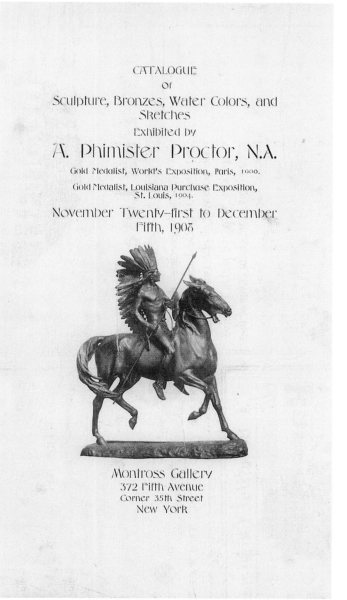

CATALOGUE
OF
Sculpture, Bronzes, Water Colors, and
Sketches
Exhibited by

A. Phimister Proctor, N.A.

Gold Medalist, World's Exposition, Paris, 1900.

Gold Medalist, Louisiana Purchase Exposition,
St. Louis, 1904.

November Twenty-first to December
Fifth, 1903

Montross Gallery
372 Fifth Avenue
Corner 35th Street
New York

Fig.32

not equestrian monuments), like the two *Tiger Couchant* bronzes (plate 32, p. 163) for Princeton University's Nassau Hall and another set of tigers for the Sixteenth Street Bridge in Washington, D.C. (plate 30, p. 158). Smaller works proved to be lucrative as well, such as the high-relief multiple-edition plaque *Head of Brown Bear* (plate 27, p. 153) for the Boone and Crockett Club (he was a member of the club's executive committee at this time) and single private jobs like the *Moose Family* for Pinchot. He also fell back on portrait work, producing several circular reliefs of friends like Secretary of the Interior James Rudolph Garfield and members of the Pinchot family.

In a real sense Proctor as an animalier had shaped the art of American sculpture during the first decade of the twentieth century. Fashioned from what Royal Cortissoz, the traditionalist art critic for the *New York Tribune*, would refer to as a "new ideal" in art, "our latter-day scientific dispensation," Proctor had ushered American art into what was emphatically regarded as "the age of the animal sculptor." He had carried forward the notion originated by Barye that "substituted truth for convention," touching the world with his combination of astute "anatomizing" and natural mystery. To Cortissoz's way of thinking, the vitality, variety, and truthfulness of Proctor's animals, avoiding as they did sentimentality and sensationalism, defined a movement in American sculpture that boded well for the decades to follow. He was the "exemplar of modern realism" in America, this man who was by turn "the naturalist-hunter and the sculptor."[46]

5

THE WEST AS MUSE

As the first decade of the twentieth century came to a close, Proctor began to search out new territory both for patronage and for artistic inspiration. With Saint-Gaudens gone, he could no longer rely on a mentor to push potential commissions his way or to speak in his favor, so competing with Daniel Chester French's protégés became even more difficult than before. The commission to model the lions for the portico of the New York Public Library provided an onerous example. Proctor had worked with the library's architects, John Carrère and Thomas Hastings, on the McKinley monument and felt that this successful association might increase his chances on this new commission. But sadly, he wrote Pinchot, "Carrère and Hasting[s] do not seem to be so much in my favor now, since French has taken the place of St Gaudens on the Advisory Committee."[1] When French's ambitious assistant Potter won the commission, Proctor's fears were confirmed. Proctor was given a token job, that of sculpting the lion heads for the keystones over the windows on the library's first floor.

In his search for expanded horizons, Proctor soon made contact with the Canadian art community. He had known several of its leading figures for some years, including painters Horatio Walker and Edmund Morris. In 1908 a small group of painters that had grown disaffected with the Ontario Society of Artists formed the Canadian Art Club in Toronto. Proctor received an invitation to exhibit with them in 1909. They liked him and his work, and they needed a sculptor on their rolls. Proctor had already exhibited with both Walker and Morris, most notably at the Pan-American Exposition in Buffalo, where the two Canadian painters had gone home with special commendations. Now, in 1909, Proctor's name was formally added to the art club's membership roster (fig. 33), and he sent a dozen bronzes and six watercolors to Toronto for their spring exhibition.

As one reviewer suggested after visiting the 1909 exhibition, it was a proud moment for Canadians to see a new artist joining their ranks, who

Fig.33

was "practically unequalled in his own particular line in this country." Viewers savored not simply the "careful and conscientious" workmanship and the "industry and faithfulness to detail," but a less tangible quality as well, that "finer something" that "makes of a man an artist."[2] The National Gallery of Art in Ottawa affirmed Proctor's stature in the art world by purchasing a casting of the large version of his *Indian Warrior* (plate 12, p.122) that year.

One of the most appealing aspects of Proctor's association with the Canadian Art Club was the renewal of his friendship with Morris. The two had probably known each other since the early 1890s when Morris studied with William Merritt Chase and Kenyon Cox at the Art Students League in New York. Morris was also in Paris at the Académie Julian in 1893, the same time that Proctor was in France. But the more compelling connection between the two was their preference for western subject matter. Since 1907 Morris had been seriously involved in a project to record the likenesses of western native peoples, and he and Proctor painted together among the Blackfeet Indians in Alberta in the fall of 1909. The two shared a true affection for the West.[3] Proctor continued to exhibit with Morris in the Canadian Art Club for five years until Morris died.[4]

Another chapter in Proctor's outreach efforts involved his return to the western states below the Canadian border. Although he chose to spend the late fall of the years 1909–1914 hunting and sketching among the mountains of either British Columbia or Alberta (fig. 34), in matters of art, his western thrust took him further south. Mary Fanton Roberts, writing as Giles Edgerton, had pointed out in 1908 that America's unique place in art history was being written at the time by the nation's sculptors. Among the most important elements of an art with a true "national expression" was the inspiration found in what she called "the great new-old West."[5] So it began to occur to Proctor that he should expend some energy in harnessing not only its subjects but its audience as well.

In the early fall of 1909, Proctor wrote to an old school chum from Denver, Irving Hale. Hale was by then a prosperous businessman, managing the Denver offices of the General Electric Company. Proctor asked him if Denver might be interested in hosting an exhibition of his bronzes. Hale responded enthusiastically, saying that he had discussed the idea with Charles Partridge Adams and they both agreed that the timing was good and Proctor's work worthy of celebration.[6] It is not known if such an exhibition took place, but in the exchange of letters, Proctor realized that he enjoyed quite a favorable reputation in Colorado. As a result he took his personal connection one step further, asking Hale in December if he would write a letter on his behalf to William F. Slocum, president of Colorado College in Colorado Springs. Slocum was chairman of a committee charged with finding a sculptor for a proposed monument to that city's founder, General William

Fig.34

Fig.35
Proctor's *Indian Warrior* at the Portland Art
Association, Portland, 1916

Portland Art Museum Archive, Portland, Ore.

Fig.36
Proctor's round relief of a bearded man in
plaster (Charles Erskine Scott Wood)

A. Phimister Proctor Museum, Poulsbo, Wash.
Photograph by Howard Giske

J. Palmer. Hale did, suggesting that Proctor, as a homegrown talent and a master sculptor, was the natural choice. He pointed out to Slocum that, even though Proctor had not won the Custer monument job, the general's widow had favored his model above all others and in fact had recommended Proctor to the committee in Monroe.

Proctor unfortunately did not get the Palmer commission either. It took the Colorado Springs group twenty years to raise sufficient funds, and by then Proctor had moved on to other projects.[7] Nonetheless, Proctor had begun to rally support in Denver. The *Denver Post,* on learning that Proctor was interested in the Palmer monument, crowed that "a Denver boy who has become a whole-world man is the great sculptor whom Colorado wants to honor by securing him the commission...." The newspaper confirmed his friends' effectiveness in pressing Proctor's cause by reporting that Slocum was said to be in full agreement.[8]

Another market Proctor began to pursue was that of the Pacific Northwest. He had family in the Seattle area whom he tried to visit once a year or so, often following his annual hunt.[9] In order to spur enthusiasm for his work in Seattle, Proctor made several judicious gifts. The *Seattle Post-Intelligencer* in October 1909 announced, under the headline "Sculptor Makes Gift," Proctor's contribution to the Washington State Art Association. In another instance, catalogued among the recent gifts to a planned museum of arts and sciences were two mastodon tusks; a plaster cast of the *Apollo Belvedere;* a pair of Egyptian mummies; a bushel of dusty, stuffed fish and birds of the region; and three freshly burnished bronzes by Proctor. These consisted of the *Elk,* the *Buffalo*, and the *Indian Warrior*; they were probably purchased by the Proctor family and given in the artist's name.[10]

Proctor did some portrait work in Seattle as well and eventually sold some bronzes there. But it was in Portland that he enjoyed his most notable

Fig.35

Fig.36

success. In 1911 the Portland Art Association hosted an exhibition of Proctor's sculpture along with works by the late Olin Warner. The exhibition was organized by the Portland Art Museum's curator, Henrietta Failing, and one of the prominent founders of the association, Colonel Charles Erskine Scott Wood. The two worked hand in hand for years to create an atmosphere for art appreciation in Portland, and Proctor would play a vital role in those developments. Wood in particular pushed the cultural scene forward. Raised in Baltimore, he was a graduate of West Point. A gifted artist, he had studied drawing and painting under Robert W. Weir at the Military Academy. After military service, which included a stint in the West during the Nez Perce campaigns of the 1870s, Wood attended law school at Columbia University. In New York he met and befriended a wide range of artists including Saint-Gaudens, Brush, Warner, and the Impressionist painter Childe Hassam. Wood moved to Portland in 1884 and established a law practice there. Because of his devotion to art, he helped found the Portland Art Association, the parent organization for a new art museum that was established eight years later.

As an institution mandated to teach and inspire an interest in art, the museum originally collected and exhibited plaster casts of Greek and Roman statuary along with photographic reproductions of famous paintings by Rembrandt and others. Wood insisted, however, that the museum should also strive to obtain original artworks, and to that end he encouraged artists to visit his city and to paint and sculpt there. Hassam went west in 1904 and again in 1909. On the latter trip, he painted with Wood in eastern Oregon; here he produced a celebrated series of paintings, one of which became the first original work to enter the museum's collection.[11] The first original bronze acquired by the museum was Proctor's *Indian Warrior*, purchased by subscription from the 1911 exhibition that Wood helped

organize. As other original works began to grace the galleries, Wood's vision for the museum gradually became a reality (fig. 35).

Proctor's exhibition was still on view at the museum when he visited Portland in December. It comprised fifty watercolors and a "fascinating group of little bronzes" that caught the attention of the city's art critic. The *Silver King* (plate 25, p. 148) attracted most of the attention because of its spirited display and the interesting story that Proctor relayed about his related Texas coast fishing trip. The *Indian Warrior*, though, was more important for Proctor's immediate mission. He was pleased to read that "the group proves that the artist is not alone the master of animal life but is equal to the more difficult problems of the human figure." The *Indian Warrior* was not simply skillfully handled but conveyed "a quality of picturesqueness, of atmosphere, that is peculiar to the artist's work." Those were welcome remarks for the artist, who offered a flattering response. "Art appreciation here," he replied, "is keener and more discriminating than in any other Western city that I have ever visited." Not wanting to dampen enthusiasm in his old hometown, however, he tempered his next statement somewhat: "Of course, I like Denver, for I lived there during my boyhood, but Portland is different. It has the breadth and breeziness of the West with the taste and culture of the East,… a rare combination."[12] So cultured was Portland, in fact, that Proctor established a temporary studio in the city where prominent citizens like Wood could sit for their portraits (fig. 36). Over two brief stays there in 1910 and 1911, Proctor executed at least eight portraits in bas-relief. "They are in great demand," observed the local paper, "and command a high figure." They were also, for this newly itinerant artist, his bread and butter.

Sometime in late 1909, Hornaday of the Zoological Society sent around to Proctor's New York studio one of the scions of the New York art

Fig.37

Fig.38

scene, George D. Pratt. Hornaday had been impressed by a record-sized bighorn ram's head that Proctor had brought home as a trophy from Yarrow Creek Basin, Waterton Park, but Pratt's enthusiasm extended to the sculptures that were also displayed in the MacDougal Alley studio. He proceeded to purchase several bronzes for himself and later bought another set of ten works for the Brooklyn Museum of Art. He and Proctor became close friends and frequent hunting companions, tramping into the Canadian Rockies in 1910, 1912, and 1913.[13] On Pratt's advice his brother Herbert, who was chairman of the board of Standard Oil Company, bought a four-foot enlargement in bronze of Proctor's *Buffalo* (plate 16, p.131) and commissioned two monumental bronze tigers for his Glen Cove, Long Island, mansion (fig. 37). A few years later, Pratt would orchestrate a commission for a marble high-relief of a lion, also for the Brooklyn Museum of Art (fig. 38), and two reclining marble lions for the front porch of the Pratt Institute.

With these big cat pieces and his mammoth Q Street Bridge *Buffalo* (plate 34, p. 166) for Washington, D.C., of 1913, Proctor was increasingly regarded as the master of American animaliers. Much of his success relied on his French-taught elegance of line, as seen in the contours of the Pratt mansion tigers. With architectural embellishments, the balance and proportion of the works are determined to a large degree by the sculptures' positioning in relation to the building. Thus the massive heads and shoulders of the tigers offset the wings of Pratt's Glen Cove house, with the lower hindquarters serving as a visual transition. But Proctor still gave priority to the animals' anatomy rather than stylized abstract notions of composition. The sculptor Walter Winans had written in 1913 about the importance of anatomy, calling it one of the essential elements of the medium. "You have to know anatomy…in order to put in the planes right," he noted.[14] To develop a knowledge of anatomy, artists could either work at the zoo, where the impa-

tient models might not feel like cooperating, or in the field, where dissection allowed the interior musculature to be carefully studied and replicated. It was his outdoor work with his hunting knife that set Proctor apart from others. In some circles such quasi-scientific investigation was regarded as the "dynamo of a movement that may electrify American art," forming "an effective protest against the imitation of the prim casts of the antique, and the servile copying of a degenerate art of lands beyond the sea"—meaning Europe.[15] So not only did Proctor's sculpture help showcase American art museums, as it had done in Portland, but it also energized the nation's art, guarding it against new and, for many, unwelcome foreign trends.

In October 1913 Proctor's primary foundry at the time, the Gorham Company, presented a large, comprehensive exhibition of the sculptor's work at its New York gallery. Promoted as an exhibition of bronzes and plaster models, it also included an array of watercolors that, according to critic William B. McCormick, were unequaled since the days of the late Winslow Homer (fig. 39). The paintings amazed and delighted visitors, he said, with their "virile realism, dramatic power and superb technical accomplishment." Those same qualities applied to the bronzes as well. The works were cited for their avoidance of artistic convention and their association with nature's innocence.[16] But other critics were not so sanguine. Proctor's natural bent did not always connote good art. Charles H. Caffin, writing for the *New York American,* hinted that Proctor's affinity with nature, though it "has always kindled his ardor as an artist, has at times submerged the artist in the naturalist." For Caffin, Proctor's dissecting skills and shunning of convention pointed to something other than pure art. They pointed to an oversensitive awareness of client demand, which Caffin felt might too often determine Proctor's focus. Washington's Q Street Bridge *Buffalo,* for example, succumbed too much to the naturalistic preferences of the public, while the *Buffalo* succeeded as art,

Fig.39

being both "impressive" and "expressive." While McCormick had seen what the literati of the day called "the elemental things" in Proctor's art, Caffin had not. For him the sculptures seemed to lack the power of "essentials." The works that McCormick felt suffered from pretension and aesthetic convention, like Proctor's *Lions* panel (plate 33, p. 165), were the same ones that Caffin separated out as achieving an effective balance between the "artistic and naturalistic." McCormick saw *Lions* as suffering from ingenuousness, while Caffin touted it as almost the only work in the show with "a durable aesthetic value."[17]

This tension between the aesthetic and the naturalistic seemed not to bother Proctor. For example, in 1914 he showed a group of lion works in an exhibition at the American Museum of Natural History, joining sculptor-naturalists like James L. Clark and Carl E. Akeley and wildlife painters like Charles A. Corwin.[18] At the same time, he presented his Q Street Bridge *Buffalo* (the sculpture that Caffin deemed least artistic of all his work) at the National Academy of Design, where it was highlighted as an important "modern addition to the repertory of art."[19]

In the spring of 1914, Proctor decided to return to the West once more, but instead of seeking patrons to impress or wild animals to sketch or shoot, he went in search of fresh themes. As he did on his trip in 1895 to the Blackfeet reservation, Proctor went to Montana to find models for sculptures of Indians and cowboys. He also wanted to give Margaret a summer without the children while he himself recovered from the pressures of competition and overwork, so he told Pinchot that the two of them would be gone possibly as long as three months, time enough to get his "tripe straightened out."[20] (His stomach problems would develop into full-blown ulcers within a few years.) His primary motive, however, remained reacquainting himself with the West and its people. Almost twenty years had passed since he fingered the clay for the first sketches he made of his *Indian Warrior*. Now he had an

idea for a sequel: a small bronze of a mounted Indian in flight. To find the right model, Proctor spent time among the Northern Cheyenne in Montana, befriending the Laban Little Wolf family. After several months of working with their son, Robert, he completed a plaster maquette for what would become his bronze *Pursued* (plate 38, p. 178).

With its dynamic motion and the complexly configured pose of the warrior twisting to face a different direction from the horse's charge, *Pursued* resembled Remington's sculpture *Cheyenne* of 1903. Yet Proctor's work had none of the threatening gesture or grimacing savagery found in the Remington bronze. And although the fleeing Indian image brimmed with portent, the Proctor bronze that resulted later that year deliberately avoided the sentimental message of stoic defeat manifest in the sloping shoulders and drooping braids of James Earle Fraser's *The End of the Trail* then taking shape in that artist's MacDougal Alley studio.

At the end of the summer, Margaret returned to Connecticut while Proctor headed further west. His target, after a stopover in Portland to see friends and patrons, was the Pendleton Round-Up. There he intended to revive another theme from some twenty years before: the cowboy. His spirits were so rejuvenated by the rodeo and the warm welcome he received from the townspeople, he soon persuaded Margaret and the children to move west to Oregon. Margaret rented out Proctor's New York studio and sold their house in New Rochelle, where they had been settled for a couple of years. The whole troop then happily set out for their new home in eastern Oregon.

Proctor's tribute to the American cowboy emerged from that fall's work at the Round-Up. The *Buckaroo* (plate 35, p. 170) was conceived from the start as something monumental. Proctor was familiar with other work by fellow artists that used the forward leap of a bucking horse as a motif. Remington's *Outlaw* of 1906 was the most widely known, although Proctor

Fig.40
Charles M. Russell (1864–1926)
A Bronc Twister [Bucking Broncho], 1911
Bronze, 17 ¾ x 14 ⅜ x 11 ⅜ inches
Amon Carter Museum, Fort Worth, Tex.

Fig.41
W. Herbert Dunton (1878–1936)
*Phantom shapes of men and animals were
shooting from the dust in every direction
as though hurled by an explosion*
Illustration in *Scribner's*, April 1914
Amon Carter Museum Library, Fort Worth, Tex.

Fig.42
Proctor's *Buffalo* at the Panama-Pacific
Exposition, San Francisco, 1915
From *Sculpture and Mural Decorations
for the Panama-Pacific Exposition* (1915)

Fig.41

Fig.40

would have seen Joseph L. Mora's *Fanning a Twister* at the 1914 National Academy of Design annual exhibition and may have come across Russell's 1911 *A Bronc Twister [Bucking Broncho]* (fig. 40) in the galleries of the Theodore B. Starr Company on Fifth Avenue in New York. Remington and Russell had also produced paintings on this theme, and the pose likewise appeared widely in the public literature of the day, such as W. Herbert Dunton's illustrated story in *Scribner's* about Wyoming's Cheyenne Frontier Days rodeo (fig. 41).[21]

Each of these artists strove to capture the sheer excitement of the contest between man and wild horse: "The *thrill* is the thing," Dunton exclaimed about his own rendition.[22] Yet the sculptors also had an individual artistry distinguishing their bronze action works. The modeling in Mora's and Russell's works sets them apart, especially the vigorous surface dynamic added to the already convulsive thrusts and the tangle of limbs. But both were small in scale, physically and conceptually. Remington's *Outlaw* more closely paralleled Proctor's rendition. Not only did its crisply delineated forms, polished finish, and deftly managed composition have a hint of formality, but its proportions went beyond its tabletop size—there was grandeur inherent in its expression. Proctor built on similar attributes, designing a work that retained the fundamental thrill and the requisite expression of action but that never lost its sense of dignity or its beauty as a decorative piece. In *Buckaroo* Proctor was continuing to strive for the ideals that Saint-Gaudens had so firmly ingrained in him: nobility of character, dignity of expression, and simplicity of design. There is a rough elegance to Proctor's cowboy and bucker, and stated tensions exist between the controlled, idealized form and the explosive, kinetic action. In that totality of statement, Proctor achieved a unique and powerful result.

Proctor was not the only one to regard the *Buckaroo* as an expression of monumental potential. The people in Pendleton, Seattle, and Portland who saw the first twenty-eight-inch plaster recognized immediately that its universal appeal demanded a heroic measure. Pendleton and Portland

Fig.42

newspapers responded to this public reaction, reporting that the sculpture did not just document an ordinary rodeo event but "virtually breathes the spirit of Pendleton's famous epic drama."[23] This was obviously no commonplace event, and a tabletop bronze, while nice, would be hard-pressed to symbolize the "epic" dimension of the Round-Up.

The *Buckaroo*, sadly, never became an Oregon monument, despite considerable public enthusiasm. Proctor would have to wait until 1920, when the City of Denver adopted the bronze for a monument, the *Broncho Buster* (plate 41, p. 190), which was placed in the city's new Civic Center. But still this small version of the work garnered more than modest fame for Proctor. When he was persuaded by supporters in Oregon to send a casting south in 1915 to help decorate that state's pavilion at the Panama-Pacific Exposition in San Francisco, it brought such warm recognition to the artist and his family among Oregonians that the Proctors decided to remain in eastern Oregon and southern Idaho for the next three winters. Proctor even took a homestead in Harney County, Oregon, in 1915, hoping with those 120 acres to establish himself as a rancher as well as an artist.

Despite his distance from the pressures of New York, and the friendly regard in which he and his family now lived, Proctor's health remained shaky. His "tripe" problem did not mend itself and in December 1916 he wrote Pinchot that "you nearly lost me the other day." A hemorrhaging ulcer had sent him to bed with a milk diet and a prescription for surgery at the Mayo Clinic later that winter. Yet in the same letter to Pinchot, he also spoke in hopeful and self-assured terms about his art. He had just completed the finished model for his latest piece, *Buffalo Hunt* (plate 40, p. 186), and felt truly elated over the accomplishment. The day he had fallen ill, "nearly bleeding to death internally," so severely that it was "just luck" that he "didn't hit the high trail," he also somehow felt ebullient because his buffalo group was "all but finished and [was,] even if I'd hiked out, the best work of my life." He continued, "It seems to me, I have caught some of the things I've been striving for all my life." Though he expressed doubt about the extent of his intellectual capacity and bemoaned the fact that his artistic development had progressed only "slowly, so slowly," he held out great hope for his present and future work. With improved health and a little encouragement, he contended, "I'll really do something good, never felt so sure of myself as now, and never enjoyed my work more."[24]

Just a year earlier, Proctor had won a gold medal for his sculptures at the Panama-Pacific Exposition in San Francisco. His plaster, the full heroic-sized *Buffalo* that had been used in 1914 for casting the Q Street Bridge *Buffalo* in Washington, had guarded the Fine Arts Colonnade (fig. 42). His works' "strength and originality" were enough to excite one critic into calculating that they had "attracted more attention than perhaps any other group of objects of statuary on the Exposition grounds."[25] And just a few months before that, a Portland writer, grandly dismissing the efforts of Solon Borglum, Frederic Remington, and Charles M. Russell, estimated that Proctor with his *Buckaroo* was literally responsible for "putting the cowboy on the art map."[26] Even so, it was *Buffalo Hunt* that most bolstered his pride at the time. As with the *Buckaroo*, it possessed the formal qualities of balanced masses, graceful momentum, economy of line, and dynamic but noble presence.

After Proctor recovered from his hospital stay at the Mayo Clinic in the spring of 1917, he and Margaret stopped in Denver on their way home. William F. Cody had just died, and Proctor's confidence had grown large enough for him to say "yes" when invited by the Buffalo Bill Memorial Association to consider designing a monument to the western hero. Roosevelt, who served as honorary vice president of the association, called Cody "an American of Americans" who embodied "those traits of courage, strength, and self-reliant hardihood which are vital to the well-being of the nation."[27] He recommended Proctor for the commission, and Proctor made

Fig.43

Fig.44

Fig.43
Proctor's drawing of *William F. Cody*, 1917, in the *Denver Rocky Mountain News*, 27 May 1917

A. Phimister Proctor Museum Archives, Poulsbo, Wash.
Photograph by Howard Giske

Fig.44
Proctor's wax sketch for *Lewis and Clark*, 1916

A. Phimister Proctor Museum Archives, Poulsbo, Wash.

a quick, though totally unoriginal, sketch of what he and the committee proposed for the monument. It appeared in the *Rocky Mountain News* on May 27, 1917 (fig. 43), with the note that Proctor would "probably…make the statue of William F. Cody, which will be put over the grave of the dead scout." Proctor was also quoted by the *Denver Post* as saying that Cody symbolized "all pioneers," and, although he had been a "showman in the end" and a darling of Europe, he deserved a great memorial as "one of our real scouts."[28] The full concept of the proposed monument, estimated to cost $500,000, appeared the next year as an illustration in Wilbur Fiske Stone's *History of Colorado*; but this was as close to reality as the concept ever came. Proctor's ideas were worked up into a plaster model (now lost), but World War I interfered with fund-raising and the grand scheme was postponed indefinitely. Perhaps it was just as well, given the committee's desire to have Proctor merely replicate in three dimensions an image of Cody that had appeared ad nauseam in his Wild West show programs and posters since at least 1893.

Just before Proctor went to Denver, while he was still convalescing in Rochester, the Art Institute of Chicago held a sizable retrospective exhibition of his sculpture and watercolors. Forty-four bronzes and plasters filled one gallery, surrounded by landscape paintings that the *Chicago Tribune* regarded as "unostentatious" but "effective" background for the statuary.[29] Although reviews of his various shows generally stressed Proctor's skills as a sculptor, disregarding the paintings, the artist usually included more than one medium in his exhibitions. It was as if he, too, saw the paintings as an adjunct to the sculpture, a necessary part of a larger ensemble. A reviewer for the *Christian Science Monitor* spoke of this larger reality of Proctor's art:

Proctor's small bronzes depict western motives with knowledge as his early residence in Colorado, and his subsequent sojourns among the Indians and ranchmen in Oregon and Washington have enabled him to reflect convincingly the action of western animals and characters. No one imagines his animals are made in Boston from photographs. They come from an experience that knows how animals run, wild horses buck, careless cowboys retain their saddles, young bears walk and mounted Indians turn sharp corners in mountain passes when pursued.[30]

The impression given by one reviewer of the Chicago show was that viewers would find themselves "surrounded by diminutive representatives of animal creation." The works were "small" even though an "infinite degree of spirit and action [was] crowded into their tiny bodies."[31] Much to Proctor's relief, however, he was about to begin scaling up his art. Three patrons came forward at about the same time to transform a creator of animalier statuettes into a sculptor of monuments in bronze. One patron was an old friend, Proctor's hunting partner George Pratt; another was the wealthy Portland timber baron Joseph N. Teal; and the third was the City of Denver in the person of its visionary mayor, Robert Speer.

Late in his stay in Oregon, Proctor had worked up a wax sketch of a possible monument to Lewis and Clark (fig. 44). He told Pinchot about it in a letter in early 1916, saying that it represented the explorers at the time they descended the Columbia River. He may have heard of efforts by the Society of Montana Pioneers to raise money for such a monument a few years earlier; Charles M. Russell had contributed a design but nothing had come of the idea beyond that.[32] "I don't know of a single monument to those gentlemen," he remarked to Pinchot, "and it seems to me, there are few more deserving of one than they."[33] Proctor felt that Oregon patrons or institutions might be interested. If so, he would be ready.

The one Oregon patron who came forward, however, wanted

Fig.46

Fig.45

instead to celebrate the pioneers who came west in the 1840s and 1850s. Teal contacted Proctor in January 1917, and after initial discussions Proctor told Pinchot that "their ideas of pioneers here are a little different from ours in the East."[34] Nevertheless, from the day the pioneer monument was publicly announced a few weeks prior to Proctor's letter, the concept was destined to find its inspiration in a very eastern prototype. Teal viewed the Oregon pioneers as the western counterparts of America's first English and Dutch settlers, and he wanted Saint-Gaudens' tribute to those colonial fathers, *The Puritan* (fig. 45), a statue in Springfield, Massachusetts, to provide the compositional template for Proctor's work. To ensure that the theme of resolute, determined, and principled Anglo pioneers reached future generations, Teal negotiated to give the finished monument to the University of Oregon in Eugene.[35]

Proctor's first task was to find an appropriate model. Remembering an old trapper named Jess Craven whom he had met in Pendleton a couple of years before, he tracked Craven down and retained him for the job. He worked over the summer with Craven on the initial sketches in Lewiston, then continued that winter in Los Altos, California, with Craven and his wife following him south. Craven may well have reminded Proctor of the frontier type developed by Remington in his illustrations for Francis Parkman's 1892 edition of *The Oregon Trail*. Remington's *Emigrant* (fig. 46) had captured (in rather less than heroic terms) the essential character of the Oregon pioneer that Parkman had remembered meeting on the road west in 1846.[36]

In early versions of the *Pioneer*, the figure carried a rifle over his right shoulder, but in the finished monument, the rifle hangs off the man's left shoulder as he strides forward. Unlike Saint-Gaudens' *Puritan*, the man in Proctor's *Pioneer* (fig. 47) expresses earthly wariness rather than the austere severity of spiritual determination. Without the drama of the cloak over the *Puritan*'s shoulders, the *Pioneer* seems more human. The monument, sited

Fig.47

among giant redwoods, is shrouded by nature. Frederick V. Holman, president of the Oregon Historical Society, who spoke at the sculpture's dedication in 1919, praised Proctor and his "genius" in perpetuating the fundamental qualities of the early white Oregonian settlers. These were masculine "Anglo-Saxon qualities" he contended, including "courage…determination…instincts and…high ideals." The bronze was also, in Holman's mind, a symbol of the fight just won against the Germans.[37]

The two Colorado monuments were confirmed in September 1917 after a meeting between Proctor and Denver's Mayor Speer, who was in the midst of developing the city's new downtown Civic Center. The *Rocky Mountain News* that month reported that "it is believed that certain Denver persons have followed Mayor Speer's suggestion that for the bestowal of gifts the city should have appropriate sculptural adornment."[38] Put more simply, the mayor wanted sculptural monuments but not at taxpayers' expense, which meant launching a plan called "Give While You Live" that appealed to well-heeled citizens to make public art possible.[39] In less than a year, he had succeeded in lining up donors for Proctor's proposed monuments of a "Broncho Buster" and an "Indian." Two Denver millers, John K. Mullen and Stephen Knight, were announced as contributing the money necessary to produce the monuments, which they hoped would be in place by the spring of 1919.[40]

A month after meeting with Speer in September, Proctor wrote Pinchot exuberantly:

I have received commission for two Equestrian statues, an Indian Scout and the Buckaroo, heroic size for Denver—isn't this bully…. Wasn't it fine to get two equestrian statues in one day, when I'd been trying all my life for one & couldn't make the riffle—am just getting things in shape now to go to work.[41]

By September the next year, Proctor had finished the first monumental plaster (fig. 48) and sent it east to the Gorham Company in Providence. The large bronze *Broncho Buster* arrived in Denver in time for Christmas 1919, although it was not dedicated until December 1, 1920.[42] As part of Mayor Speer's City Beautiful campaign, Proctor's first monumental equestrian bronze became, according to official Denver parlance at least, "the spoke of the most effective city plan in America."[43]

Proctor worked on his "Indian Scout," later titled *On the War Trail* (plate 43, p. 196), simultaneously with the *Broncho Buster*. While the *Broncho Buster* essentially involved pointing up from the *Buckaroo* statuette, the Indian work was a totally new conception. Over the years Proctor employed two Indian models for this work: Jackson Sundown, the champion Nez Perce bronc rider, and Big Beaver, or "Red Belt," a colorful Blackfoot Indian who lived and traveled with the artist and his family in California and New York. The sculpture was modeled to maquette size, approximately four feet high, then Proctor took it back east to the grand studio that he and Sampson had built in 1914 at 168 East 51st Street. Proctor had rented his part of the studio to Frederick MacMonnies while he lived in the West, but he now resettled into the space to manage the enlargement process.

Realizing, as he said to one Portland reporter, that when a sculptor finds a good Indian model, especially "a chisel-featured one" like Big Beaver, he had "better keep him," Proctor took special pains to accommodate his model's needs. Big Beaver was "quite wild and wooly," Proctor noted, "but lots of fun" as well.[44] The Blackfeet worked long, hard hours, posing also for a fountain figure, *Indian Drinking* (see fig. 50), commissioned by George Pratt, and for the *Bear Hunter*, a work that was never cast in bronze, though the striding human figure was finished in plaster to life size. Big Beaver added life and color to Proctor's New York studio, but also critiqued the

Fig.49

sculptor's efforts and may even have assisted Proctor's Japanese associate, Gozo Kawamura, who supervised the pointing-up process (fig. 49). The bronze monument was cast by Roman Bronze Works and set on its granite pedestal next to the *Broncho Buster* in May 1922. Over the years Proctor cast twenty-inch and forty-inch bronze reductions of *On the War Trail* with the Gorham Company, Roman Bronze Works, and L. Petermann, a Brussels foundry.

George de Forest Brush visited Proctor in his 51st Street studio in late 1919 and probably watched Big Beaver as he posed for Pratt's commission (fig. 50).[45] Brush himself had explored similar ideas in paint thirty-five years earlier in a series of exquisite works including *The Indian and the Lily* (fig. 51). Brush's influence, with his idealized interpretation of native people literally in touch with nature's beauties and cycles, had held remarkably broad sway over several of his fellow artists into the twenties. The Taos painter E. Irving Couse explored this theme in numerous works, and in 1913 Cyrus Dallin had executed a successful monumental interpretation, *Indian Drinking*, for the Robbins Memorial Park in Arlington, Massachusetts. Praised for its emotion and its advocacy of a greater sensitivity toward nature, reductions of that work (fig. 52) were available in the marketplace as Proctor began formulating his own treatment.[46]

Once embarked on his Pratt commission, Proctor worked on several alternate poses and compositions. One early sketch included a horse waiting behind the hunter, and Big Beaver struck one pose with his knee in the air and the bow and arrows held horizontally. Proctor's final rendition (see fig. 50) had the nearly nude figure sitting astride a boulder with his right hand reaching for the water. Compared to the Dallin pose, Big Beaver's posture in Proctor's work is less downcast, less humbled, and his legs gripping the rock suggest a firm union with earth as well as a graceful connection

Fig.50

Fig.51

with water. When the plaster was finished in May 1920, Proctor and Pratt hosted a reception in New York. The *New York Times* seized on the "beauty of muscular energy" captured by the sculptor and the subtle coordination of physical and spiritual gesture. "It is rare," the reviewer concluded, "for an artist provided with the incorrigible picturesqueness of an Indian subject to reject easy indulgence of that picturesqueness in favor of organic energy and an intellectual conception."[47] The drama and symbolism that had so impressed Oregon critics who saw the *Indian Warrior* earlier in the decade were now considered passé. Emotional response and aesthetic conceptualization instead were in demand.

Pratt donated the finished bronze monument to the New York Historical Association for the Lake George Battleground Park at Saratoga Springs, north of Albany. Pratt, who was serving at the time as state conservation commissioner, selected the site and attended the dedication in September 1921. The statue, though not an equestrian piece, measured nine feet high and weighed 1,800 pounds. It had taken two years to make, and, though purporting to pay tribute to the Seneca Indians of upstate New York, it was promoted as featuring a "genuine Indian brought…from the western reservations to pose."[48] Thanks to Pratt and Proctor, Big Beaver was now known from Montana and Colorado to New York and the Adirondacks.

Fig.52

6

BEAUTY IN HISTORY

Once the Denver monuments were underway and the publicity about them began to spread nationally, Proctor's prospects improved. Officials in other cities, wishing to follow Mayor Speer's success and build on the dream that theirs "should be the most beautiful city in America," encouraged their citizens to consider funding embellishments for their parks and campuses.[1] Portland came forward in the person of Dr. Waldo Coe to commission an equestrian monument to Theodore Roosevelt in the late spring of 1920. Proctor was thrilled to be chosen for this project since his personal regard for Roosevelt ran deep and this would be the first such tribute announced since Roosevelt's death in 1919.

An authoritative article appeared on Proctor in the September 1920 issue of *Scribner's Monthly* just as the sculptor was starting to model the first Roosevelt sketch. Written by the illustrator and critic Ernest Clifford Peixotto, the article focused primarily on Proctor as an animal sculptor. Peixotto marched out the old platitudes about Proctor's figures carrying forward Barye's legacy, as well as the scientific and experiential base of Proctor's production. He spoke, as others had, of "a fundamental feeling of vivid actuality" that infused the animal bronzes. They existed "without a trace of transcendentalism," and they manifested a "realism untempered by the beauty of creative art." But Peixotto also argued that the appeal of Proctor's works, including the two Denver monuments mentioned near the end of his story, was primarily to an uninitiated male population defined as "[t]he big audience that he commands among red-blooded men, hunters, sportsmen, lovers of the out-of-doors, who understand nothing of the superlative technical qualities of his art but are carried away by its reality."[2] This was a man's art, and one not intended for a particularly discriminating group of men at that.

Peixotto's pointing to Proctor as a man's artist helped to justify Coe's choice of sculptor for the Roosevelt statue. Proctor was pleased that Coe wanted an equestrian monument rather than a symbolic animal, as had been required

Fig.53

for the McKinley monument. There was a good deal of pressure from various quarters in New York, especially from Carl E. Akeley at the American Museum of Natural History, to have Roosevelt represented as a lion, and Proctor and Akeley had disagreed publicly on the matter.[3] For Proctor, who had at last tasted success with the two Denver equestrian commissions, to have acquiesced to Akeley's perspective would have been an unacceptable step backward. It would have meant returning to the natural history mentality when the artistic muse that he had long defined for himself had only recently emerged.

If, as Peixotto asserted, Proctor's audience comprised men of little understanding in matters of art, then the sculptor confronted an additional challenge. The Roosevelt group would have to speak both to art principles and the obvious macho aura of the man to be eulogized. Thus Proctor, instead of giving the figure the swagger of his Custer sketch, sought a more cerebral and reflective approach, one that echoed the words of a Canadian critic, W. H. de B. Nelson, in 1915:

There is nothing dramatic in his work, whether it be a mounted cowboy or an Indian in his warpaint; Proctor never wanders out of his way to compose some striking effect calculated to cause a sensation by making appeal to those who judge good art by its daring departure from accepted canons of sculptural taste.[4]

By mid-December 1920, Proctor had decided on the pose for *Theodore Roosevelt* (plate 44, p. 200) and wrote Pinchot from his Palo Alto studio:

I expect to make small working model, about 4 feet high & take it to N. Y. late in winter & get criticisms from T. R.'s friends. I hope you will be the first to show up—I want to make this statue my best so far.[5]

Proctor's "best" would be a work of containment. He hoped to represent Roosevelt as a vital force but not a theatrical figure. The former president was not to be an actor in bronze playing out a dramatic scene from his historic past. Rather, Proctor intended to express reserve and latent energy that would, he hoped, befit those proper "canons of sculptural taste." Roosevelt's own words, quoted by the Portland writer Fred Lockley, defined Proctor's intentions with the monument:

The only safety in our American life lies in spurning the accidental distinctions which sunder one from another and in paying homage to each man only because of what he essentially is, in stripping off the husk of occupation, of position, of accident, until the soul stands forth revealed and we know the man only because of his worth as a man."[6]

Perhaps Proctor had recalled what Briggs had advised Mrs. Custer about the latent power of repose in sculptural work. Or perhaps it was a natural progression for the artist from the cowboy action sculpture in Denver to a more thoughtful, even transcendental, treatment of the Spanish-American War leader. "[I] decided if possible to show the rider and horse in repose," he told reporters at the statue's dedication in November 1922. The horse is "ready for instant action," and Roosevelt is very much "in control," but the outward presence of the two is one of reserved, though potent, equilibrium.[7]

The *Portland Journal* in November 1922 ran a photograph of Margaret (fig. 53), who managed all of Proctor's business affairs as well as family matters, when she and her husband were guests of the Teal family at the time of the unveiling of the Roosevelt sculpture. Teal, who had commissioned Proctor to sculpt the *Pioneer* for the university campus in Eugene, probably introduced Proctor to the former senator from that city, R. A. Booth. The senator remembered Proctor, and in the summer of 1920, developed with him a concept for another equestrian monument, a frontier minister on horseback.

Booth and Proctor were seeking a western equivalent to a monument being sculpted by New York artist H. Augustus Lukeman for Washington, D.C. *Francis Asbury* (fig. 54) immortalized the father of all-American circuit riders, an itinerant Methodist Episcopal pastor of late eighteenth-century New England. Like Potter, Lukeman had been a protégé of French's, learning

Fig.54

from that master how to give mass to drapery and how to add mystery to figures by downplaying details and obscuring facial features. Asbury's cloak collar and broad-brimmed hat effectively shroud the minister's face. The twist of the horse's head and the clutching of the Bible to the rider's chest provide a feeling of self-absorbed spiritual inwardness.

Proctor's rendition of the western *Circuit Rider* (plate 45, p. 205) is more individualized, a depiction of the patron's own father, Robert Booth. By deliberately removing the hat from the rider to reveal the man's face and expression of concentration, Proctor enhanced the narrative force of the work. Although not entirely in vogue in the early 1920s, an emphasis on the underlying story was at least still tolerated in traditional American monumental sculpture. Adeline Adams, writing for the National Sculpture Society at the time, contended that story line as well as content were vital for public equestrian monuments. The people for whom the statues were intended, she stressed, expected to share in a story, a "something doing," and not strictly in some ideational intellectualized message that "the solemn critic,… thirsting for pure abstraction,… beats everybody into" accepting as the exclusive province of art.[8]

In American art the lines between modernist and conventional traditions were beginning to harden. Proctor, who in 1921 had been unanimously elected to life membership in the Beaux Arts Club of New York, clearly and unequivocally made his stand with the representational ranks.[9] He wanted his monuments to be publicly accessible both physically and intellectually. He had told Lockley, "[M]y theory is that a statue should be where it can be seen by the passing throng all day long," seen *and* understood.[10] The *Circuit Rider* would enjoy plenty of public attention in front of Oregon's state capitol building in Salem.

Coe, Teal, and Booth were all men willing to invest their financial resources in the cultural community of the Pacific Northwest. Proctor, who

Fig.55

Fig.56

continued to frequent Oregon over the years, refuted Peixotto's contention when he spoke of Portland in particular as a center for the region's art:

Easterners, who have never been west, think of the West as a country of Indians and cowboys, where there is no such thing as culture, nor any appreciation of art. That their conception is utterly without foundation goes without saying. Take for example, Portland. You will find few cities in which there is greater appreciation of art.[11]

He then went on to mention not only the city's large bronze monuments but over twenty portraits in the round and in relief that he had done for patrons of that city over the previous decade.[12]

It was in fact Proctor's stunning bas-relief portrait of his friend and eastern Oregon host William Hanley (fig. 55) that led to the Roosevelt commission. Coe had seen the Hanley portrait, produced when the Proctors spent the summer of 1915 on Hanley's famous "P" Ranch south of Pendleton, in Proctor's New York studio five years later. Based on his favorable reaction to the likeness, he decided on the spot to give the Roosevelt commission to Proctor.[13] Working from photographs (fig. 56) and personal sittings, Proctor avoided Hanley's most familiar pose capped in a wide-brimmed black Stetson and chose instead to portray him in his role as an orator. Hanley's nickname was "the sage of Harney County." A droll and highly amusing raconteur, he loved to think of himself as the Northwest's equivalent of his friend Will Rogers. Robust, genial, chivalrous, gracious, and as broadly ambitious and humane as his ample girth, Hanley was one of the greatest ranchers in Oregon history. In Proctor's portrait Hanley's gentle face and piercing stare reveal a complexity of character, as does the contrast between his barrel chest that grounds him in the frame and the unkempt silver locks that fly freely behind his head.[14]

Proctor once said that portrait work in bas-relief was the most difficult sculpture he knew.[15] Many times he would take a period of years to capture a proper likeness. His portrait of his closest friend, Pinchot, took fourteen years to complete. He began work on two portraits in early 1902, one of Pinchot and another of his father. The son's portrait was sent to the foundry and cast in 1916, but the father's was never finished, nor was an interim effort at a portrait of Pinchot's mother. Proctor could somehow never bring the last two likenesses to a satisfactory point.

Proctor moved his studios in 1921, taking over one end of the large Aerodynamics Laboratory at Stanford University. The university's president, Ray Lyman Wilbur, made the building available and even accommodated Proctor's needs by installing a skylight. Proctor enjoyed the new space, although he had trouble on campus with the college boys harassing his Indian model, Big Beaver.

At this time he was showing smaller sculptures on both coasts. The Babcock Gallery in New York exhibited five of his animal bronzes along with works on a similar theme by five other New York animalier sculptors: Anna V. Hyatt, Grace M. Johnson, Albert Laessle, Frederick G. Roth, and Charles Cary Rumsey.[16] (Rumsey had purchased one of Proctor's *Panthers.*) On the West Coast, Proctor had several plasters and bronzes in the Bohemian Club's annual art exhibition in San Francisco. According to newspaper accounts, the most impressive of these was the four-foot plaster maquette for the Roosevelt monument. Also included were a bas-relief portrait of Margaret and a plaster bust titled *Cow Girl,* which the *San Francisco Chronicle* observed had attracted especially "favorable criticism."[17] This tribute to the female side of the Pendleton Round-Up scene was a change for Proctor. It may have been a portrait of one of the Thompson sisters, Helen or Thelma, who served as Round-Up queens in 1921 and 1922, or one of the

Fig. 57
Pendleton Round-Up Cowgirls, c. 1922

Howdyshell Photos/Matt Johnson

Fig.58
Proctor's living room and gallery in his
Los Angeles house, 1923–1925

Alexander Phimister Proctor papers 1924–1950,
Archives of American Art, Smithsonian
Institution, Washington, D.C.

Fig.57

women horse-bucking contestants who thrilled the crowds with their daring feats of wild riding (fig. 57). Proctor clearly envisioned this statue or something larger decorating some city landscape. He included in his speech before the San Jose branch of the American League of Penwomen in December 1922 a "tribute to the ability of women in the arts," urging the promotion of "great women as well as great men" to "be recognized by the erection of statues." Perhaps he hoped his *Cow Girl* would appeal to them, but there is no record of the plaster even surviving, much less being cast or enlarged.[18]

In January 1923 Proctor notified Pinchot that he was thinking of moving to Los Angeles. He was slated for a big exhibition there at the Stendahl Gallery in the Ambassador Hotel; Charles M. Russell had recently

enjoyed a successful showing at the gallery, and Proctor wanted a turn.[19] "I am going to pack my car with plaster casts & move down to Los Angeles for an exhibition—Am thinking of moving there. Will have a studio there anyway & see if I can make enough to keep the wolf from the door."[20] The exhibition proved to be at least a moderate success financially, and the critical notice was gratifying: the *Los Angeles Times* termed the thirty works "impressive," and as if prompted by the words of Saint-Gaudens himself, "at once fine, noble, simple and sincere."[21] Proctor also met the art community, introduced by the painter James Swinnerton as "the most modest famous person we have ever met."[22] First impressions felt good and before long the Proctors were residents of Los Angeles, with a big house at 8224 Sunset Boulevard. A spacious room on the main floor served as an area to display his sculptures (fig. 58) and he began making plans for a studio behind the house. Various motion picture luminaries soon found his sculptures worth adding to their collections, including Charlie Chaplin, Cecil B. DeMille, Pola Negri, and William S. Hart.[23] They saw in Proctor's sculpture aspects of their own work in cinema—"strength and delicacy, power and refinement, classic poise with modern freedom."[24]

As he had in Portland, Seattle, Denver, and probably Palo Alto, too, Proctor began to characterize this new city as on the cultural cutting edge. By the fall of 1923, he was telling those whose egos might be flattered that nature had "selected two great centers for art when the world was in the making—Athens and Los Angeles."[25] With such words Proctor was being both gracious and mercenary, hoping that his comments might fall on the right ears and result in commissions for one or more of the city's parks. In the same letter to Pinchot in which he told his friend that he might be moving to Los Angeles, Proctor had also confided that he was beginning to get hungry for a fresh challenge, a large new work. Although, he said, "pictures of my

Fig.58

Fig.59

Fig.60

'Circuit Rider' are going over the country & something may come of it and the T.R.—Have not had a new commission for 2 years now."[26] The proclaimed Athens of the West, however, would not come through for Proctor. He secured one commission for a hefty and engaging bust portrait of Frank Wiggins, a man who had been secretary of the Los Angeles Chamber of Commerce. But that was the extent of his southern California monuments. Proctor stayed in Los Angeles, however, for the people—the City of Angels was replete with available models. "Los Angeles is the best home city for a sculptor of western subjects," he told the *Los Angeles Times* art critic Arthur Miller in 1931. "Every time I go on the street I see real frontiersman and real Indians of the finest types."[27]

A wealthy Kansas City miller named Howard Vanderslice had purchased a casting of Proctor's recently remodeled *Panther* at the Stendahl Gallery. In talking with Proctor at the gallery, Vanderslice learned that the artist had long hoped to sculpt a memorial to the pioneer women of the West. Vanderslice seized on the opportunity to venerate his own mother and the legions of Kansas pioneers who had helped to people his state, and eventually the artist and patron struck a deal. Los Angeles, at least through the creative stages of the project, became home to the enterprise.

In his autobiography Proctor stressed that the concept for what would become the *Pioneer Mother* (plate 47, p. 210) was entirely his own; he had it fully in his head before meeting the patron, so the invention rested squarely with him.[28] Even the title was proprietary material in his mind. In June 1923 he wrote to Pinchot:

A man in middle west wants to give a group to his city, price is $40,000.00…
The subject is the pioneer mother—I don't want the name to get out. The chief art connoisseurs here say that it will be the best group in America.

Anyway, my heart & soul are in it, & if I can pull it off, I will be pretty well satisfied that my life has not been spent in vain—There are a couple of dozen more subjects in my head that I want to do before I hit the long trail but I want to do this group, which is my tribute to the women who gave themselves & lives to the making of this great West & this whole country in fact.[29]

Although Proctor's vision for this tribute was his own (he was increasingly inclusive of women in his work at this time), the typology involved and the composition for the work trace their roots to the mid-nineteenth century. The Missouri artist George Caleb Bingham had explored the theme of American migration to the wilderness in his 1852 painting *Daniel Boone Escorting Settlers Through the Cumberland Gap* (fig. 59). That work, widely distributed as an engraving, helped to "sanctify" Anglo settlement in the West. Similar morally laden pictorial tropes with biblical allusions to Moses or the Holy Family found expression in the next generation, such as Emmanuel Leutze's flamboyant *Westward the Course of Empire Takes Its Way* of 1861. In both cases the artists used the Madonna figure and its associations with purity, righteousness, and the divinity of motherhood to justify and promote the United States' doctrine of Manifest Destiny. Proctor composed his most ambitious monument in the spirit of these earlier masterworks, carrying their complex symbols forward several generations.

One of the most talked-about works of Proctor's own time, Solon Borglum's monumental staff *The American Pioneer, A Reverie* (fig. 60), shown at the Panama-Pacific Exposition in 1915, expressed similar sentiments regarding the nation's destiny. But the work was all about men, as was Proctor's own *Pioneer* (see fig. 47). Proctor had to look further back to time-honored icons if he was to construct what he thought would be his "best group in America."[30] Others later concurred in his estimation of the sculpture's

Fig.61

importance. Lorado Taft would write to the Proctors shortly before its dedication that "I think it is to be the masterpiece."[31]

In fact, Proctor's seminal *Pioneer Mother* created such a sensation that, even before its November 1927 dedication in Kansas City, others were enthusiastically beginning to pursue similar tributes to the women of the western trails. The Oklahoma oilman Ernest W. Marland initiated a national sculpture competition for the ideal pioneer woman. A dozen sculptors submitted models, and those subsequently toured the country in a madcap plebiscite that gathered a reported 750,000 votes and catapulted a little-known English sculptor, Bryant Baker, into fame. Enlarged to heroic size in 1927 for the lawn of Marland's Ponca City estate, Baker's *Pioneer Woman* (fig. 61) with her set jaw, rapt focus, and ambitious stride could have made an appropriate companion for Proctor's later Oregon *Pioneer.* The difference between Marland's project and Proctor's Kansas City group came down to gender predominance. Even though Proctor spoke of celebrating the frontier woman, of seeing to it that she was "given the honor due her," in his group she is surrounded by men, protected and escorted to her destination.[32] In contrast, Marland's dozen artists were instructed to present the woman solo. In the one work in which a man appears, John Gregory's *Pioneer Woman* (1926, Woolaroc Museum, Bartlesville, Okla.), he lies dead and she takes his rifle from his limp hand.

Thus Proctor's *Pioneer Mother,* carrying a baby with the young father marching beside her, was not so much about mothers as about families. It reflected Proctor's closeness to his own household. By this time the Proctor children numbered eight, and the family comprised a remarkably affectionate and close-knit unit. Most of the Proctors were fluent in French, they each had artistic skills of various sorts, and they lived cosmopolitan lives but were equally happy in a tipi or out camping in the mountains. A photographer

from Portland, Mary Briggs, was approached by an Ohio art collector, Edwin Shaw, in 1923 when he was preparing a book on American artists and wanted a photograph to use with his entry on Proctor. She responded with the requested picture (fig. 62) as well as additional insights. To appreciate the artist, she contended, one had to know the whole clan and the "charm and radiant spirit one finds in every member of the family." She went on, "It would be worth a trip to California just to see that beautiful family! To live in such a lovely home atmosphere as theirs is a real experience. One seldom sees such wonderful devotion as they bear toward one another."[33]

In the mid-1920s the whole family lived in California. Hester, Alden, and Phim attended Stanford, which as Proctor told Pinchot, "costs a heap less than in the East." When Proctor was based in Palo Alto, everyone lived at home. Once he and Margaret moved to Los Angeles, the children began to slip away. Hester moved to San Francisco, Phim remained in Palo Alto, and Alden eventually moved east.[34]

Proctor continued to exhibit his works in both New York and Los Angeles. He was represented in a large exhibition of American sculpture sponsored by the National Sculpture Society in 1923; the show was mounted in the galleries and gardens of New York's Hispanic Society on 155th Street. He also exhibited with three other West Coast artists at the Los Angeles Museum during the winter of 1923 and 1924.[35]

A critique of the Los Angeles exhibition lamented that none of Proctor's works could be experienced locally as monuments. Earlier that year Proctor had told the *Evening Herald* that he would help the city develop a program for enhancing the city's parks, and the paper concurred that "he would be most fitted to aid in the work of erecting monuments here that would tell the story of the country."[36] Proctor's ulterior motive, of course, was to see some of his own work commissioned for that purpose. When this did not happen, with

Fig.62
Mary Briggs
Portrait of Alexander Proctor,
December 1921

Collection of the Akron Art Museum, Bequest
of Edwin C. Shaw
Reproduction photograph by Joseph Levack

Fig.62

the exception of the Wiggins portrait, Proctor once again became restless. Offering the excuse that his *Pioneer Mother* could not be enlarged from the maquette size to full monumental scale in his Los Angeles studio—even though he had working with him Robert Paine, one of the country's preeminent enlargers— Proctor announced in 1925 that he would return to New York. But when he found that the costs of living and working in New York would leave him little or no profit, Margaret suggested he take the *Pioneer Mother* and other large pieces then in production to Italy. After some checking, they decided to move everything, including the five children still living at home, to Rome where Proctor arranged for a studio at the American Academy.[37]

Proctor's old friend Charles Follen McKim had founded the American Academy in Rome. One of McKim's partners, William Mitchell Kendall, was its director, and he secured a special work place for Proctor and made other arrangements for the sculptor's stay, which was originally planned for one year and then extended into two. The academy was designed for young artists to hone their skills and, according to the critic Royal Cortissoz in 1923, to help them achieve creative restraint by living among inspiring examples of aesthetic balance and "good taste." For Cortissoz the academy was a sanctuary for the "believer in the gospel of beauty," and students "will be led by the masters of Rome to a new sense of law and order, to a new sense of grandeur, of line and mass, of discreet detail, and, especially, of style and beauty."[38] In other words, it was to be a temple of learning buttressed by tradition. Proctor, who at sixty-six was a senior fellow, enthusiastically lent his voice to the choir to whom Cortissoz was preaching. A review of Proctor's work in the Los Angeles Museum exhibition confirmed that Proctor's style had altered little and that his artistic vision had remained solidly focused over the two decades since Cortissoz had affectionately labeled him a "modern realist" back in 1909. Although they now referred to him as a "post" realist, his goals had changed very little:

The sculptor may be ranked among the realists in that he follows nature very closely in all his forms, but he is also a post, in that all his figures have a touch of idealism, something of an added grace that was not inherent in the model but came from the enraptured soul of the sculptor. Proctor is not a modernist, in the usual sense, neither is he a classic interpreter. We may perhaps say that he has always marched steadily forward in the middle of the road.[39]

Proctor and Cortissoz shared a resistance to modernism. They both felt, as Cortissoz had articulated in 1923, that art was governed by "certain fundamental laws" reliant upon "a sane vision of nature and an honest craftsmanship." They distrusted modernism because it was untested and because it seemed to "repudiate" what they felt to be art's primary function, "the creation of beauty." Modern art was rife with foreign influences (Cortissoz called it "Ellis Island art") and represented everything that true art should not. It was "crude, crotchety, tasteless, abounding in arrogant assertion, making a fetish of ugliness and, above all else, rife in ignorance of the technical amenities."[40] These were convictions that Proctor embraced for the rest of his life.

Just before sailing on the steamship *Cono Verde* on October 10, 1925, Proctor watched a film made about him by the Metropolitan Museum of Art in New York. Called *The Making of a Statue*, it documented the incredibly complex and laborious efforts required to produce the *Theodore Roosevelt* monument three years earlier. It also documented the sculptor's dedication to formality, ideal form, and technical expertise. Proctor referred to the film as "an educational picture," one that he hoped would carry his message of art's essence and function to wider audiences than would see the monuments in Oregon and North Dakota.[41]

Once the Proctors settled into the American Academy scene, the sculptor set to work on his *Pioneer Mother* group and a number of other large pieces he had shipped ahead. By the spring of 1926, he had completed his *Indian Girl* (plate 46, p. 208), which, he reported with pleasure, "has had a great deal of praise from both Italians and Americans, especially members of the faculty of the Am. Academy. This for a nude figure means a lot I think."[42] Its ideal grace and elegant poise fit well with the art philosophy of those who worked around him.

His *Pioneer Mother* also received accolades. "This makes a westerner feel good," he remarked. The faculty called him "Professor," and the Fine Art School's director, Frank P. Fairbanks, encouraged his participation in the academy's activities. What amused and pleased Proctor the most was "the excitement within my family over art." As he recounted, each of the children was studying art at the British Academy:

Ona & Jean are painting in watercolors & with a fine Italian artist, Bill is studying etching & drawing. Gifford is modeling and working in oils. Joanne is working in all these mediums nearly—They all have made wonderful improvement, I am simply amazed at it. It shows what an art atmosphere will do. I feel sure tho that "Dad" has made more progress than any of them. There was an[d] is large need for it tho. Glad I'm not too old to learn. I never have worked any harder than I've been doing here. Am doing etching[,] studying Roman history, and Italian, besides 7 to 9 hours in studio.[43]

Fairbanks produced a large neo-Renaissance fantasy in oil showing the Proctor clan assembled around the *Pioneer Mother,* which has been hoisted majestically onto a canopied stage (plate 2, p. 90). Bill, in a jaunty black Stetson, watches Gifford sketch as Proctor stands on a ladder, as if serving metaphorically as the connection between the lofty ideals of high art and their aspirants. Margaret, wearing the dress of her own making that was used by the *Pioneer Mother* model, is surrounded by two of her daughters, Jean and Joanne.

In the fall of 1927, Proctor returned to the United States briefly, traveling to Kansas City to dedicate the *Pioneer Mother*. A crowd of five thousand looked on as the mother and her weary entourage appeared from beneath a canvas veil on a crisp November day. Proctor read in the next morning's *Kansas City Star* that this was "the greatest thing Kansas City and the West could have. It gives us more with one look than all the books and stories of the settling of the prairies." He must have particularly savored the words of one visitor that "this is the only kind of statuary worth a damn."[44] Buoyed by such comments, he went on to Saint Louis and the City Art Museum, which at that time owned three of his sculptures. When a reporter from the *Post Dispatch* invited his comments on modern art, the answer was predictable. Proctor wrinkled his nose and responded, "I think it's hellish!" With wishful optimism he also projected a reversal of trends. "People will go back to the love of beauty," he said, reminding readers of the wonders to be seen in classical and Renaissance art.[45]

Proctor also spent time that fall with a lawyer, Burt Brown Barker of Montclair, New Jersey. A benefactor of the University of Oregon, Barker wished to explore an ideal of frontier motherhood different from that revealed in Proctor's hugely popular Kansas City monument. Wanting to perpetuate an image of the frontier woman in repose, peacefully resting in her later years after the struggles of pioneering were passed, Barker commissioned from Proctor another western monument to women. It was a challenging but rewarding new project for Proctor.

The family left Europe in early 1927 and moved to Wilton, Connecticut. Proctor promptly reconnected with the New York art scene. Although his primary energies were focused on Barker's project, the *Oregon Pioneer Woman*, he also sculpted a magnificent bas-relief fireplace surround in marble for one of George Pratt's Long Island homes. And he exhibited in

Plate 2

Plate 2
F. P. Fairbanks (1875–1939)
*Proctor (and Family) at Work on
Pioneer Mother,* 1928
Oil on canvas, 126 x 78 inches

Courtesy of Jonathan Fairbanks Richards
and Claudia Jessup
Photograph by Herb Lotz

New York at the Grand Central Art Galleries and in the Whitney Museum of American Art's opening exhibition, both in November 1931.[46]

Proctor also accepted a small but deeply personal commission to produce a memorial portrait plaque for General Hale, his dear friend from Denver. In early 1931 he received a letter from W. C. Brown of Denver enlisting his "cooperation as a sculptor" to design "something which will be a credit to the subject." Several of Hale's friends had wanted to erect a life-sized bronze portrait at the intersection of 16th Street and 16th Avenue, but the "business depression" was such that they despaired of raising sufficient funds.[47] Their next best effort was to commission an inscribed plaque to be permanently installed in the Colorado state capitol building. Hale had been an important civic leader for the city, managing the General Electric Company's branch there for years and being responsible for installing the first electric car system in Denver in 1889. He had also garnered considerable fame as the leader of the first Colorado regiment of Spanish-American War volunteers. Proctor visited Denver with his son Gifford in August 1931 to secure photographs, ultimately selecting one showing Hale in the Philippine campaign.[48] The Hale portrait in low relief was also used for a bronze plaque in Cullum Hall at the United States Military Academy at West Point, where he had been a member of the Class of 1884.

Proctor's visit to Denver was part of a long western tour in 1931. He stopped in Wichita to dedicate his *McKnight Memorial Fountain* (plate 51, p. 222) in September but spent most of the summer on various Indian reservations from Oklahoma to Montana. He had received special permission to work with Gifford among the Southern Cheyenne, Sioux, Crow, and Blackfeet.[49] Proctor's intentions were to mentor his son and make small models of Indian subjects for etchings. At Pine Ridge they were joined by retired Army Major General Hugh Lenox Scott, who had served in the Plains territory during the 1880s and 1890s. He had been put in charge of investigating the Ghost Dance disturbances in 1890, producing one of the few thoughtful reviews of that situation and an unbiased assessment of the Indian prophet Wovoka's vision.[50] Scott and Proctor would work together to help bring some financial relief to the Sioux in advance of John Collier's 1934 Great Depression programs.

Trips such as this reinforced Proctor's devotion to the empirical relationship between artist and subject. Because sculpture was an especially tactile medium, and the West with its powerful spaces and fascinating people encompassed such engagingly sensate experiences, the artist's reliance on, and replication of, observable things was crucial. In Wichita, Proctor told a reporter with tongue in cheek but in basic honesty that "I am a native of the West and I like to portray things there which are real. And I don't like to make a statue of an angel. In other words I like to make the things that are; not things that ain't."[51] About a month later, he repeated that message to another reporter, only this time with a slightly stronger emphasis on the cognitive base to his art: "The only way to thoroughly understand your subject is to look at your work with the same viewpoint as your subject, and this requires much time spent in living with them."[52] But what he was about to learn, or actually relearn, was that to understand the subject, the sculptor must also understand and accede to the viewpoint of the *patron*.

7

THE AYES OF TEXAS

In Wilton, a community that Proctor would call home for the next half dozen years or more, he could relax somewhat, holding no particular expectations that he would find patrons there. Although he retained partial tenancy with Alden Sampson in the large studio at 168 East 51st Street in New York, he also had a sizable red barn converted to a work space in Wilton and spent much of his time with his family and various projects in the semirural setting they came to know as his Chestnut Hill studio. The Proctors enjoyed Wilton, and the town's citizens, realizing that they harbored an extraordinary talent in their midst, bloomed with pride over the association. In 1934, one local art writer, S. Clarke Keeler, proclaimed Proctor not just "probably the greatest sculptor of heroic equestrian statues in America," but in fact "one of the world's greatest living sculptors" altogether. Proctor had told the reporter that, although he lived in the East, his ambition had long been the joining of art and western history in an unbroken thread of remembrance. It had been "to glorify the West as he knew it as a boy."[1]

Yet along the way, as Keeler observed, Proctor had also seized opportunities, and the sculpture that he saw in Proctor's studio was a case in point. Proctor was just putting the finishing touches on the plaster for a double equestrian monument to the Confederacy's General Robert E. Lee. There was nothing western about the subject, and little from his childhood connected Proctor to the South. But he had seen the commission as a grand accomplishment, a work nearly as complex as his Kansas City *Pioneer Mother* and perhaps even more sophisticated. And it did make some local connections. A Yale divinity student served as the model for the general, and a local woman, Mrs. John Erskine, loaned her horse "Uncle Sam" to stand in for the historic Traveler. Futhermore, the spirit of Proctor's *General Robert E. Lee* (plate 54, p. 230) was reminiscent of Saint-Gaudens' studies for the Robert Gould Shaw memorial in Boston and some of the Civil War genre sculptures that John Rogers, the New Canaan artist and one of Proctor's early mentors, had produced back when Proctor was still a boy in Colorado.[2]

Part of the complexity of the Lee statue had to do with the physical scale of the work and the number of figures. Countless artists and critics would observe that, with its double-mounted composition, the work was unique in the history of sculpture.[3] In addition, the artist's masterful revelation of the compositional connection between the figures underscored the work's complexity. A true connoisseur of the harmonious line, the balance of juxtaposed masses, and the interplay of physical and emotional tensions, Proctor reached a level of consummate achievement in this group. "This makes twice that you have made masterpieces within the last few years," wrote Lorado Taft, his friend and fellow sculptor. "I do not know anyone else who can touch you in this line of work."[4] Proctor had indeed claimed a dominant position.

Another sentence in Taft's letter spoke of the complexity, or what the artist might have regarded as perplexity, of that work when Taft alluded to his indirect involvement in the commission. "I had a little to do with it," he confessed, though "I recommended you earnestly to those Dallas ladies."[5] Those ladies would prove to be one of Proctor's greatest challenges.

Over the last productive years of Proctor's artistic career, from the early 1930s to the mid-1940s, Texas patrons would provide the primary sponsorship for his art. Sometimes profoundly inspiring, but just as often fickle and feckless, they helped shape his art and his reputation, keeping his career buoyant, while at the same time they exasperated him professionally and personally to the point of physical and emotional exhaustion. Although those Texans offered promise to an aging master, who in his seventh decade produced two of his life's finest achievements, they also squeezed his self-confidence to a point of near strangulation and, in one instance, almost ruined him financially.

The first of his great Texas monuments resulted from a letter Proctor received in 1931 from Mrs. R. V. Rogers representing the Dallas branch of the Southern Women's Memorial Association. She asked him to consider being the artist for a monument to General Lee that they hoped to situate in the city's Oak Lawn Park. While outside the normal purview of Proctor's vision, this significant work promised a fresh challenge as well as welcome remuneration. Yet over the course of many months, although Proctor produced several sketches, none of them proved satisfactory to the committee in charge of the project. No matter how much he read about and reflected on Lee, and no matter what adjustments he made to the model, the resulting studies would not suffice. In 1932 he traveled to Dallas to lecture on art and to present his latest sketch.[6] The latter was rejected again, and Proctor's speech was dismissed as trivial next to the ladies' lofty notion of Southern history.

Eventually the committee accepted one of Proctor's models, but then they overwhelmed him with so many contractual obfuscations that he dropped the project. A year later he vented to his friend Pinchot:

Monkeying around with that ---- committee of women for the Lee Memorial cost me a lot of money and I never got a cent out of it. Knowing how difficult women committees are I kept out of it for two years, then I fell and fell so hard it kind of knocked all the enthusiasm out of [me for] big statues. They liked my model but imposed such restrictions I had to give up the contract. This thing of having to submit to a ------ committee not one of whom knows anything about sculpture—I'm tired of it.[7]

Afterward, he literally could not work at all. Nearly half a year later, he complained to Pinchot again, still in a state of confused depression:

Fig.63

I had a devil of a time with that Southern Womens Memorial Sty. over Lee. Got so disgusted I chucked everything & haven't done any work since—Just can't get my self to do a thing. Don't know whether I'll be able to pull my self out or not—First time in my life I've loafed with pleasure.[8]

Eventually the boredom of loafing and Margaret's pressure led him to swallow his pride, readjust his model, and swing into line with the requirements of the memorial association. Mrs. Rogers and her group's formidable bargaining almost sunk the career of the normally plucky veteran sculptor.

The Lee monument was ultimately an overwhelming success, and as a result several other Texas commissions came Proctor's way. The Texas State Board of Control and the Federal Centennial Commission granted Proctor the task of executing a memorial to James W. Fannin and his ill-fated troops at the battle of Goliad. Many, including the *Dallas News*, were pleased with the prospect. Despite the fact that, according to the paper, "only $25,000 was allotted to this project," Proctor could "be counted on to produce a lasting work of art with this limited sum."[9] Proctor, however, was not so sure, and within a couple of months he had eased himself out of the job.

Another project in Austin seemed more promising. In 1938 the University of Texas folklorist J. Frank Dobie wrote to Proctor inviting him to submit a sketch for a monument to the state's legendary mustangs. A Texas oilman, Ralph Ogden, was prepared to put up $60,000 for the work, and Dobie had been given the assignment of selecting an artist. Dobie was much impressed by Proctor's Lee monument in Dallas. Once he saw Proctor's initial mustang sketch and got confirmation from Ogden, he gave the job to him with no further ado.

Ogden and Dobie gave Proctor full reign in matters of design and execution. The provisions of the contract, too, were straightforward and reasonable. And unlike the Goliad monument, sufficient money had been promised to do the work right. Unfortunately, the patron did not live up to his promises. Ogden missed payments with enough regularity to severely compromise Proctor's efforts. Dobie served as intermediary and was effective to a certain degree. But a major payment to Gorham, the foundry selected to cast the final bronze statue, was delayed in early 1941, putting the project on hold for five years, until World War II was over.[10] By then Ogden had died, as had Margaret, and Proctor's spirits had sorely declined, along with his fortunes (the contract did not call for paying the bulk of the compensation until the bronze was completed). "We have been living on our fat for a couple of years," he wrote Dobie in 1942, "& may have to continue till we go on relief."[11]

Several other circumstances also worked to dampen Proctor's normally sunny outlook. For one, he felt that Texas had snubbed him socially. Several of the Dallas ladies had looked down on him as a "damn Yankee," he told Dobie, and the Tom East family, his hosts at the King Ranch where he made the sketches for his mustang group, had ignored him. The Proctors were made to feel socially inferior, the victims of a Texas "caste system," he contended. Worse, Ogden had treated him like a pest, refusing to answer his letters or acknowledge his pleas for professional accountability and contractual adherence.[12] Then, when *Mustangs* (plate 55, p. 234) was dedicated in 1948, the art faculty at the University of Texas was less than complimentary. In late 1947 a bitter Proctor wrote Dobie about what he envisioned his role to be in the unveiling ceremonies:

All that is expected of the sculptor is that he looks pretty. That's all I'm good for on an occasion like an unveiling. The fact is, the sculptor doesn't cut much ice. The donor is the main guy. News papers & public are as one in that. If the public likes a statue, they write to the chap who put up the money.

Fig.64

The sculptor, he was paid to do the job—Vanderslice, who gave me the Kansas City "Pioneer Mother" got letters from nearly all over the world. I don't remember getting any—That is right in a way, for any body, according to the popular idea, can do a statue, but only a few will cough up the dough.[13]

In the end, though, Proctor felt vindicated. His *Mustangs*, all ten tons of it, won high praise from many quarters. Frank Langston of the *Dallas Daily Times Herald* told how Proctor, forced to overcome all manner of discouraging circumstances, had produced something unique, "the only work of its kind in the United States, perhaps in the world."[14] And contrary to Proctor's own expectations, many people wrote to offer their compliments and encouragement. The painter John Young-Hunter echoed Langston's remarks. "No one else in the world I realized could have done that group," he wrote in 1948. A fellow sculptor, Malvina Hoffman, pointed out Proctor's bravery. "What courage you must have to tackle so many of them in a bunch," she commented.[15]

In fact, so encouraged was Proctor by the response to his *Mustangs*, he began to experience a late rejuvenation as a sculptor. "My mind has so filled with wild compositions of late, it would take another lifetime to do them all," he told Dobie in the fall of 1947. "I seem to crave savage action, and nothing else."[16] He said he might need a nurse to prop him up, but even thus hampered, he was ready to take on another monument. Dobie had just such a project, a companion piece for the *Mustangs*. He "expressed hope" to the *Austin American* in early June 1948 "that the mustang statue will soon be joined by a monument to the longhorns."[17] Three weeks later, he wrote with confidence to Proctor telling him that he had three or four potential patrons lined up, along with possible financial assistance from the State of Texas: "I think it would be as easy to raise $125,000 as to raise $75,000. There ought to be an impressive group of steers, and I think that the cowboy ought to be

with them."[18] Dobie sent Proctor a set of photographs of longhorns, and the sculptor began investing them with the wild energy he felt compelled to convey. Before long, a sketch model had emerged (fig. 63), and over the next several weeks it was perfected. "I feel that this group will be as interesting as the mustangs," he confided to Dobie in late July. "I'm having a lot of fun with the group, even if nothing comes of it.... It seems to me we could put the group over for $100,000.... There is one cowboy on his horse, 5 steers and one dogie in the group now."[19] Even though both Dobie and Proctor's family rejoiced in the artist's renewed vigor, the longhorn project languished. Mostly it was delayed because Dobie unexpectedly could not pin down a donor. Proctor worried with the model over the next several months, eventually casting it in plaster. But the piece never developed to the working model stage, and the two friends, although they exchanged letters with regularity, gradually refrained from mentioning it.

Aside from a large, decorative medallion of an Indian warrior, which he produced in 1949 for the Medallic Society, the longhorns were Proctor's last effort at serious artistic conceptualization. In the same way Remington's last sculptural work, *The Stampede* (fig. 64), failed to come to fruition in his lifetime. Cast after he died, Remington's crush of running steers tends to focus on the cowboy, who rides high above the mass and gives the impression of being at least somewhat in control of the onrushing beasts. Proctor's version suggests a final engagement with destiny of a slightly different sort, as the longhorns crest a hill and lunge downward into an unknown space. Proctor, in his craving for savage action, perhaps envisioned a more calamitous conclusion.

Proctor played with one other complex action composition, an Indian group, very late in his life. A long letter to Dobie explained his creative burst:

Since Margaret went, I haven't been able to settle on anything I wanted to do except hunting bears. The moment I stepped into our big studio here & with every thing to work with, I had a "brain storm." A composition of a band of Indians on the rampage on horseback flashed into my brain— Suddenly I knew what I wanted to do—Injuns in action.

I immediately began the group—4 savages on ponies, mustangs tearing with weapons set, right into battle. You would have thought I was a 20 year old idiot—In such a hurry I hated to quit to eat or write. When light was good, I worked till 6-7 oclock-

I suppose this is second childhood enthusiasm but it's such fun. I was afraid after 5 years without modeling I wouldn't be steady enough at 87 years to do the stuff. I find that my hand has its six shooters steady & I have more patience to do details than I ever had—Probably my work isn't as good as I think it is. But gosh it's fun.[20]

Two years later he was still playing with the idea and hoping to interest the Oklahoma oilman Thomas Gilcrease in sponsoring an enlargement of the idea for his "Indian Museum." Proctor was now eighty-nine years old and as enthusiastic and ambitiously visionary as ever:

The figures mounted are only about a foot high but I'm giving 'em all I've got in me. I hope some day to make 'em more'n life size—I am all out to give the U.S. the best Indian group in the country. I have simply got to do it. Seems to me I'm doing as good work anyway as I ever did and perhaps better—Seems to me I'm holding up in good shape. Anyway I can carry my models to a better technical finish then ever. Just listen to the old codger boast.[21]

Those rampaging Indians, however, were never taken beyond the sketch stage. Proctor left the plaster at the Bohemian Club, where he stayed from time to time in his advanced years and where he had been made an honorary member in 1944. Later, because the plaster model was so fragile, it was cast in bronze.

Alexander Phimister Proctor died on September 4, 1950, just days short of his ninetieth birthday. He had been living in Palo Alto with his eldest daughter, Hester, for the previous six years. The local newspaper acknowledged his passing the next day, saying that although he had "left uncompleted a group of five Indians on horseback," he had remained "active in his studio until a few weeks before his death."[22] Appropriately, he had just been awarded recognition as the "Man of the Year" by the Camp Fire Club of America.

And so the world was left to remember Proctor through his art as a man who had lived joyously in the wilds and had in turn brought the wilds to life. Proctor had been a warm and modest man, unusually observant yet with few pretensions, artistic or otherwise. He was dedicated, throughout a career that spanned sixty years, to creating simple, noble, and honest evocations of life. His was a legacy to a grand vision of western American history and an unaffected, though romantically driven, response to nature.

A NOTE ON THE CATALOGUE

The subjects in this catalogue are arranged by modeling date. Those works known to have been modeled in a particular year (1897, for example) precede those believed to have been modeled in that year (c. 1897). Possible modeling dates are superceded by probable ones, as in the case of *Charging Elephant*. Those objects modeled in the same year are arranged alphabetically by title.

Titles of works are from the official copyright record. In the few instances when a copyright record was not available, the title given is the one used in the *first* recorded exhibition literature. Entries authored by Katharine C. Ebner bear her initials at the end (KCE).

Each subject entry is divided into eight fields of information:

Variant title(s): If known, variant titles associated with a particular piece are listed.
Date(s): The modeling date refers to the creation of the clay or plaster model for the bronze subject. The casting date refers to the particular cast featured.
Medium: All sculptures are in bronze, unless otherwise noted.
Dimensions: Measurements for objects reproduced as plates are provided as length followed by width followed by height. For monumental works, no dimensions are provided.
Markings: Only those markings inscribed in the base of the work, as opposed to those that appear on plaques or separate bases, are included.
Copyright information: When known, copyright dates are given. In most cases, copyright records for the sculptures prove useful in determining titles (both main and variant) and sequence.
Exhibited: Only those exhibitions dating from Proctor's lifetime are listed. Information includes title of exhibition (where available), exhibition venue, and exhibition date.
Other known versions: Distinctions are made between large and small versions; mediums, when different from the featured cast, are identified. If other versions are known to exist but have yet to be located, such is noted.

Variant titles: *Fawn (First Model);*
The Fawn's First Step; First Step
Modeled, 1887
Bronze, 9 x 3¾ x 6¾ inches
Markings: "FIRST MODEL FINISHED
BY A PHIMISTER PROCTOR 1888
GORHAM CO. FOUNDERS/QUG"
Copyright: By A. Phimister Proctor
under No. G23532 on June 4, 1892;
reregistered by Nona Proctor Church
under No. H53321 on July 15, 1973

The R. W. Norton Art Gallery, Shreveport, La.
(acquired 1946, gift of Richard W. Norton Jr.)

Plate 3 Fawn (first model)

It seems appropriate that this exquisite rendition of new life should be the first sculpture in Proctor's oeuvre. As with the newborn white-tailed deer that is portrayed, the artist, too, was taking his first steps away from painting and toward sculpture. Proctor credited this move first to his acquaintance with the influential sculptor John Rogers, who encouraged him to begin modeling and taught him how to make armatures and handle clay, and second to a chance encounter with a newborn fawn at the menagerie in New York. Enchanted with the baby deer, Proctor entered the fawn's paddock to befriend the creature:

Sensing a friendly presence, the trembling little thing came close and tried to reach me. Opening the paddock, I went in and gently patted her. She snuggled close and rubbed me with her dainty muzzle. I sat on my sketching stool and stayed with the baby for some time, studying her young form. Suddenly the idea flashed through my mind that I would make a model of her in wax.

Hurrying back to my studio, I made a small armature. For a support for the body I used a small piece of wood and then securely fastened wires to it for legs and neck. Over all, the model was but seven inches high. Then I made a small stand high enough to work at while sitting down.

So equipped, I went back to the menagerie and set up my equipment. The little fawn watched what I was doing, brushed against me, and sniffed at my ears. I had to be careful to keep her from pushing over and breaking the model. When I wanted her to pose, I'd take the little animal and stand her the way I wanted, either placing her legs in the proper position or turning her head. I had to do most of the work sitting down, both because of the size of the paddock and because my model was so small I could not see much when I stood up. Since the light was not always right, I often had to do my work after feeling the fawn. The fawn was most co-operative. The only distraction was curious people who stopped to watch.[1]

Proctor had this premier effort cast in plaster and showed it to his colleagues at the National Academy of Design. Most of his fellow students frowned on the enterprise, considering his delicate modeling a waste of time and energy. But a few artists looked upon his accomplishment with approval. One, according to Proctor, arranged to have a photograph of the work illustrated in *Harper's Weekly,* while another, the Denver artist Frederick Dellenbaugh, used his influence to have the *Fawn* shown in New York's Century Club.[2] The latter venue provided a turning point in the young artist's career. It was there that the small plaster attracted the attention of Frank D. Millet, who was in charge of sculpture decorations for the World's Columbian Exposition. Taken with its charm, sentiment, and the powerful statement it made about the fragility of nature, Millet invited the young Colorado artist to join Edward Kemeys in producing animal statues to ornament the bridges over the fairground lagoons and canals. It proved to be Proctor's first major commission and catapulted the artist into the limelight.[3]

In January 1893, the *Chicago Sunday Inter Ocean* took notice of Proctor. It commented on many aspects of his life and work, but praised in particular the two animal sculptures he displayed in his studio on the exposition grounds, a panther and a fawn. "The panther [see plate 5]," the article observed, "is an excellent example of the forceful power of his creations while the shivering fawn overtaken by a storm shows the keen and sensitive perception of the sculptor."[4] Proctor often played those two counterbalancing forces of nature against one another in his work. Here the powerful and the meek were presented together.

Proctor exhibited bronze castings of the *Fawn* in many of his major shows throughout the years. Well into the 1920s, the story of that small sculpture and its formative role in determining Proctor's future course would be reported in news accounts.[5] With its tentative pose, the *Fawn* formed an apt metaphor for the artist's own initial steps into a new medium and gradual emergence as an artistic personality.

Exhibited: Century Club, New York, 1887; Panama-Pacific Exposition, San Francisco, 1915; *Twenty-ninth Annual Exhibition of American Oil Paintings and Sculpture,* Art Institute of Chicago, Chicago, 1916; *Contemporary American Sculpture,* Buffalo Fine Arts Academy, Albright Art Gallery, Buffalo, N.Y., 1916; *Small Bronzes by A. Phimister Proctor,* Art Institute of Chicago, Chicago, 1917; *Works in Sculpture by A. Phimister Proctor,* Corcoran Gallery of Art, Washington, D.C., 1918; *Bronzes from the Collection of Simon Casady,* Des Moines Association of Fine Arts, Des Moines, Iowa, 1929

Other known versions: A. Phimister Proctor Museum, Poulsbo, Wash. (Gorham cast bronze pattern)

Variant titles: None recorded
Modeled, c. 1891; cast, 1893
Bronze, 10½ x 5¼ x 7¾ inches
Markings: "PROCTOR 92/Cast by the
Henry-Bonnard Bronze Co./New York 1893"
Copyright: By Nona Proctor Church under
No. H55362 on December 15, 1973

A. Phimister Proctor Museum, Poulsbo, Wash.
(on loan from Phimister Proctor Church)
Photograph by Howard Giske

Plate 4 Polar Bear

According to Proctor, he arrived in Chicago to begin his commission with the World's Columbian Exposition on his thirty-first birthday, September 27, 1891. His primary assignment was to produce large staff animal decorations for the bridges over the lagoons and canals around which the monumental buildings of the fair were situated. In all he estimated that he produced or collaborated on thirty-five heroic-sized animal sculptures and two full equestrian works.[1]

One of the Chicago newspapers that took special notice of art activities at the exposition observed in early January 1893 that Proctor spent many of his days studying animals at the zoological garden in Lincoln Park. "Local visitors at the fair will undoubtedly recognize ... the counterfeit presentments of some old acquaintances on guard at many bridges of the 'Little Venice.'"[2]

One of the animals at the zoo that Proctor visited early on was the polar bear, a behemoth that inspired his first sculpture for the fair. Perhaps he chose it because its white coat translated so effectively into plaster. Or perhaps it was simply that the polar bear was one of the few native large animals that Proctor had never seen before. In any event, he produced two versions of the arctic bruin, one with its head up and extended forward, sniffing the wind (fig. 65), and one with its head down as if scanning the immediate foreground. It was the latter pose that Proctor selected to work on first, necessitating many repeat visits to the zoo:

At the Chicago Zoo I made a small model, about ten inches high. I brought it to the studio, where my assistants and I began copying it full size. Again and again I returned to the zoo with the little model to improve on details. By the

time the small model was finished, the men had carried work on the big one as far as they could. Meanwhile, I began work on the jaguar so that the men would have something to do while I finished the big model of the bear.[3]

Proctor was seen as "one of the youngest and most gifted of the noble band of American sculptors" who worked for the exposition. Comparing him to Antoine-Louis Barye, observers of his work noted that while Proctor "lacked the finish of the master," he modeled his bears "con amore" and brought "a certain perfect naturalness, which perhaps even Barye's great art could hardly compass."[4]

Proctor's *Polar Bears* are admittedly somewhat static. But the fair required sculptures that would serve essentially as "architectural finish," avoiding any presentation that might be viewed as threatening. Even "violent action" was not allowed. According to one source, "the sculptor was ... debarred from representing his animals in combat or in any of the natural fierce movements."[5] Proctor conformed to these rules, even restricting the head-down version to the confines of its squared off, rectilinear base. Proctor also displayed four works at the exposition as part of the *Sculptors of the United States* exhibition.[6] Two of these were small plaster companion studies of his *Polar Bears*.

According to Proctor family history, Augustus Saint-Gaudens, who was an admiring advisor to Proctor, asked if he could make two castings of the head-down *Polar Bear*. The young protégé was quick to agree. Saint-Gaudens later referred to it as Proctor's "bully little bear" that would remain with him "wherever I fix my tent."[7] He took one of the castings for his personal collection and presented the second as a gift

to another artist, Margaret Gerow, around the time that she married Proctor. That sculpture — modeled, as they said, "con amore" — thus helped to cement a relationship that lasted throughout all three artists' lifetimes. In fact it was while Proctor was working on his first large *Polar Bear* that he met Gerow, then an assistant to Lorado Taft, whose studio adjoined his. Because *Polar Bear* was the first work of Proctor's that Margaret saw, she cherished her casting of it all her life. Saint-Gaudens' bronze was later destroyed in a studio fire. Margaret's was exhibited from time to time with other works by Proctor, but was never offered for sale and apparently never replicated. It always served as something of a special memento of their first months together as a couple. It was passed down in the family through their first child, Hester.

Exhibited: *Sculptors of the United States*, World's Columbian Exposition, Chicago, 1893; *A. Phimister Proctor*, Montross Gallery, New York, 1908; *Second Annual Exhibition*, Canadian Art Club, Toronto, 1909; *Exhibition of Bronzes and Plaster Models by A. Phimister Proctor*, The Gorham Company, New York, 1913 (listed as "loaned by Mrs. Proctor not for sale")

Other known versions: None

Fig.65
One of Proctor's *Polar Bears* at the
World's Columbian Exposition,
Chicago, 1893
From *The World's Columbian Exposition
Reproduced* (1894)

Fig.65

Variant titles: *Fate; Panther—Fate;*
Stalking Panther; Charging Panther;
Prowling Panther; Panther Charging;
Stalking Cat; Large Stalking Panther
Modeled, 1891–1893; remodeled,
1922–1923
Bronze, 37¼ x 6½ x 9¾ inches
Markings: "A. Phimister Proctor/
1891–1892" and "COPYRIGHT"
Copyright: By A. Phimister Proctor under
No. 23939 on April 17, 1897; reregistered
by Nona Proctor Church as *Large Stalking*
Panther under No. H55768 on June 12, 1973

The Corcoran Gallery of Art, Washington, D.C.
(Bequest of James Parmelee)

Plate 5 Panther

In several respects Proctor's bronze statue of the *Panther*
must be regarded as a fundamentally autobiographical work
of art. The most obviously self-revealing element is its theme
of the hunter in nature. Nothing was more basic to Proctor's
identity than his role as a hunter—a man in union with
nature and its patterns of survival. Whenever the artist was
interviewed or had an opportunity to speak about himself in
public, he invariably began and ended his delivery with stories
of his prowess with a rifle and his adventure on the hunt.
When he provided a four-page handwritten biographical
sketch for his friend and fellow artist Edmund Morris in 1909,
Proctor filled one full page with his hunting exploits.[1] The
Panther thus not only demonstrated the sculptor's prowess
with his medium, but also reinforced the self-image he
wished to leave with his patrons. When critics described this
work, they were in effect providing a portrait of the sculptor.
The *Palo Alto Times* in 1922 characterized the bronze as "a fine
study of action," embodying "an amazing sense of power ...
stealthiness ... and forcefulness ... expressed with genuine
feeling and capacity."[2] By process of association, Proctor was
regarded, too, as strong, shrewd, and assertive.

Those who acquired the *Panther* often identified with it
as well. In Theodore Roosevelt's autobiography, the former
president used a reproduction of the *Panther* as the lead illustration for the chapter on his youth and early manhood, "The
Vigor of Life." Roosevelt had received a cast of the statue as a
gift from his "Tennis Cabinet" on March 1, 1909, just three
days before he left office.[3] The thirty men who made that presentation and whose names are engraved around the base of
Roosevelt's casting must have felt that it epitomized the president as a man of bold and powerful determination.

Although most castings of this bronze are marked with
the date 1891, Proctor began conceptualizing the work several years earlier. He made his first studies of a panther during a
six-week hunting trip and "sketching vacation" to the Flat
Tops in the northwestern corner of Colorado in 1887. After
shooting a western cougar, "a beauty of a cat" as he called it,
Proctor spent the remainder of the day sketching it.[4] Those
drawings then went east with him to New York where, under
the tutelage of the sculptor John Rogers, he began modeling;
one of his initial experiments in clay involved the form of a
stalking panther. He expanded on his field studies by dissecting alley cats and by observing "two beautiful specimens" of
cougars at the New York menagerie, especially a female
named Grace. Of particular importance for him was capturing the cat's sense of motion and latent energy. To accomplish this he developed a special method of freezing action:

Once while I was standing between two buildings, I looked
up just in time to see a boy dash from behind one building
to the other with arms and legs extended. Applying this
experience to the study of animals, I found that I could get
an action picture by closing my eyes, opening them for a
split second, and then shutting them again. I practiced this
exercise until I arrived at the point where I could retain the
picture long enough to do a rough sketch. It was in this
manner that I made the sketches for my panther.[5]

This was an important discovery for the artist. At the same
time, Thomas Eakins was teaching at the Art Students League
and touting his explorations into stop-action photography as
advanced by the photographer Eadweard Muybridge.

Fig.66

Proctor's observational skills, and his interest in dissecting animals to study musculature both in the field and in the studio, coincided with Eakins' lessons, establishing not only a modus operandi but Proctor's seriousness as a student of animal life and form. When one of the cougars died at the local menagerie, he even took pains to dissect it and, using facilities at the American Museum of Natural History, to take plaster casts of important anatomical details.[6]

Proctor began the wax model for *Panther* in his New York studio on West 55th Street. He called it *Fate,* and some early exhibitions of the work referred to it by that title. In his autobiography Proctor indicated that the Panther was not finished and cast in bronze until after he and his wife, Margaret, had settled in Paris late in 1893. However, Proctor exhibited four sculptures including one titled *Panther* that was described as a bronze at the World's Columbian Exposition in Chicago earlier that year. Moreover, Chicago's *Inter Ocean* on January 1, 1893, commented on Proctor's "panther recently completed in bronze" as being "an excellent example of the forceful power of his creation."[7] In any event, the three-foot plaster model was taken to Paris for further work. Eventually a new plaster was made, resulting in another bronze that pleased both Proctors immensely.

The panther had also provided early inspiration to Cyrus Dallin, another western sculptor. But Dallin's *Algerian Panther* (fig. 66) was copied from Antoine-Louis Barye's *Panther of Tunis* (1840) and cast in terra-cotta. Its reclining pose, while alert, gave the impression of a work copied in a museum gallery (the Museum of Fine Arts in Boston, to be specific), rather than developed from firsthand acquaintance with big cats in nature. Dallin's first effort was thus rather inert by comparison with Proctor's.

More dramatic were several variations on the crouching panther theme by Edward Kemeys in the 1880s. Proctor knew of two, one in New York's Central Park and the other decorating one of the bridges at the World's Columbian Exposition in Chicago (fig. 67). Kemeys had been, like Proctor, an observer of animals in the wild. His panthers are the embodiment of kinetic force but they are coiled, ready to spring, whereas Proctor's cat moves, stealthily and purposefully, toward some phantom prey.

All three artists viewed the cougar as a quintessentially American subject. They sought to express nationalistic sentiment through these feline symbols of America, poised to prevail in the world with power, stealth, and cunning. Cougars were also emblems of resistance against a disappearing wilderness. Even as early as the mid-nineteenth century, John James Audubon was lamenting the loss of big cats in the eastern United States. The cougar, he wrote in 1851, "has been nearly exterminated in all our Atlantic States."[8] By Proctor's era the West was the last, though increasingly vulnerable, sanctuary for these icons of wild nature.

The *Panther* met with sustained popularity through most of Proctor's long career. Typical of the critical acclaim that greeted the work were the comments of a reviewer in 1911:

> ... [H]is "Charging Panther," gripping the earth in its stride, determination in its cruel jowl, fury in its swinging tail, and in its taut muscles, the clear proclamation of an irresistible leap. It does not require much effort of the imagination to see the long grasses part before the brute's advance, and all around you are aware of the hot sun and the smell of the woods.

His animals are all like this. He gets their gait, the rippling of their skin, the tense direction of their ears, and the palpitation of their snuffing nostrils. Also he gets their grace and beauty, the charm that makes them worthwhile even to the beholder who has never slain anything more ferocious than a rabbit.[9]

Proctor had it cast by many foundries, sometimes in the sand-cast method. In the early 1920s, after reading further praise from the critics for the work's "admirable craftsmanship," "fine study of action," and "genuine feeling and capacity," Proctor remodeled the sculpture to a smaller size.[10] He had made changes to the original *Panther* before, "studying it and improving on it all these years."[11] The reduced size of the 1922 bronze was seen as the final improvement, but it was also intended to expand the market for the work.

Exhibited: *Sculptors of the United States*, World's Columbian Exposition, Chicago, 1893; *Sixteenth Annual Exhibition of the Society of American Artists*, New York, 1894; *Exhibition des Beaux-Arts*, Paris Universal Exposition, Paris, 1900; *Exhibition of Fine Arts,* Pan-American Exposition, Buffalo, N.Y., 1901; Century Club, New York, 1902; Louisiana Purchase Exposition, Saint Louis, 1904; *A. Phimister Proctor*, Montross Gallery, New York, 1908 (two versions); *Second Annual Exhibition*, Canadian Art Club, Toronto, 1909; *Canadian Art Club Exhibition*, Art Association of Montreal, Montreal, 1910; Washington State Art Association, Seattle, 1915; *Small Bronzes by A. Phimister Proctor*, Art Institute of Chicago, Chicago, 1917; *Works in Sculpture by A. Phimister Proctor*, Corcoran Gallery of Art, Washington, D.C., 1918; *A. Phimister Proctor,* Montross Gallery, New York, 1922; *A. Phimister Proctor*, Stendahl Art

Fig.66
Cyrus Dallin (1861–1944)
Algerian Panther, 1880
Terra-cotta, painted brown,
16¾ x 5⅛ x 8¾ inches

Fig.67
Edward Kemeys (1843–1907)
Panther at the World's Columbian
Exposition, Chicago, 1893
From *The World's Columbian Exposition
Reproduced* (1894)

Gallery, Los Angeles, 1923; *Bronzes from the Collection of Simon Casady*, Des Moines Association of Fine Arts, Des Moines, Iowa, 1929; Inaugural exhibition, Whitney Museum of American Art, New York, 1931

Other known versions: Campbell Scott Church III, Seattle (gift of the artist); Metropolitan Museum of Art, New York (gift of William Cullen Bryant Fellows and Maria DeWitt Jesup Fund, 1994); Thomas A. Petrie, Denver; Sagamore Hill National Historic Site, National Park Service, Oyster Bay, N.Y. (Theodore Roosevelt estate); Belle Clegg Hays, Compton, Calif. (inherited c. 1950); Parrish Art Museum, Southampton, N.Y. (gift of Don Orlando Cord, 1956); Harry Ransom Humanities Research Center, University of Texas, Austin (bequest of J. Frank Dobie, c. 1964); Gilcrease Museum, Tulsa, Okla. (gift of Thomas Gilcrease, 1955); National Gallery of Canada, Ottawa (acquired, 1909); Montreal Museum of Fine Arts, Montreal (bequest of Sir Edward W. Beatty, 1945); R. W. Norton Art Gallery, Shreveport, La. (gift of Richard W. Norton, 1946); Gerald Cooper, Holland, Mich.; A. Phimister Proctor Museum, Poulsbo, Wash.; Henry O. Smith III, New York

Fig.67

Variant Titles: *Young Fawn; Fawn
(Second Model); Fawn (New Model);
Mule Deer*
Modeled, 1892
Bronze, 8¼ x 2¾ x 6⅝ inches
Markings: "A.P. Proctor/1893"
Copyright: By A. Phimister Proctor in
1895 (according to markings on a
casting in the Metropolitan Museum of
Art collection); may also be the sculpture
titled *Fawn* registered in the name of
the Gorham Company under No.
K99515 on November 25, 1915

Brooklyn Museum of Art. 13.1089.
Gift of George D. Pratt

Plate 6 Fawn (second model)

When the Proctors moved to Paris in the fall of 1893, they took with them a wax model of the artist's popular little statue, *Fawn*. It was packed carefully among Margaret's clothing and survived the voyage well. Using it as a starting point, Proctor proceeded to model a second version of this sleek, delicate form. This time the fawn was presented on an oblong rather than a rectangular base with its ears laid back along its neck, the tail timidly tucked further between its legs, and the head posed to reach out in a more searching gesture. With these changes, Proctor achieved both an enhanced sense of drama and a more elegant contour. While the first version seemed to show a halting, timorous beginning, the new interpretation afforded a sense of grace and movement.

These two statues were often displayed together during Proctor's life and may have been seen as a sequential pair — the first a reflection of anticipated action and the second the gentle beginning of movement. In fact, there are suggestions that the artist was experimenting with companion works well before he reached France.

Proctor reportedly produced a clay model of a deer while visiting his brother, J. L. Boyle, in Snohomish, Washington, in 1891. He took this model to New York where, according to a later newspaper account, its popularity caused it to "outshine his record as a painter," and he was soon recognized for "the brilliancy of his work as a sculptor."[1] This may have been the origin of the second version of the fawn, but more likely it was a totally independent work that simply demonstrated his affection for deer as a subject, an idea supported by the *Chicago Sunday Inter Ocean's* story telling how Proctor actually "lassoed a full-grown deer in Puget Sound, and kept the beautiful creature until he had made several studies in clay from

life."[2] The *Rocky Mountain News* in 1893 observed that before he left for Paris, Proctor was working on a "small model of two fawns, 'The Orphans.'" The article went on to say that "so tender, graceful, touching and beautiful" was the pair "that those of his friends who have been permitted to see them are unmeasured in their praise. They will be cast in bronze in Paris the coming winter."[3]

As both sculptures have used the same title since their creation, it is difficult to determine which of the two is meant by the exhibition listing of *Fawn*. The artist referred to the later version simply as "the second fawn," and facts suggest that it was finished in clay and cast in plaster in Paris in 1893.[4] We have assumed, however, it was this later version that Proctor exhibited most widely and that was part of the group of bronzes that won a gold medal at the Paris Universal Exposition in 1900.

Twelve years later, a casting of the little figure found its way into the collection of the Metropolitan Museum of Art, New York. The chairman of the trustees' committee on sculpture, Daniel Chester French, recommended its acquisition, and the museum purchased the *Fawn* directly from the artist in 1912.[5]

Exhibited: *Exhibition des Beaux-Arts*, Paris Universal Exposition, Paris, 1900 (gold medal); *Exhibition of Fine Arts*, Pan-American Exposition, Buffalo, N.Y., 1901; *A. Phimister Proctor*, Montross Gallery, New York, 1908; *Second Annual Exhibition*, Canadian Art Club, Toronto, 1909; *Sculptures by Olin Warner and A. Phimister Proctor*, Portland Art Association, Portland, Ore., 1911; *A. Phimister Proctor*, Montross Gallery, New York, 1912; *Exhibition of Sculpture*, Montross Gallery, New York, 1912; *Sixth Annual Exhibition*,

Canadian Art Club, Toronto, 1913; *Twenty-second Annual Exhibition of the Society of Washington Artists*, Seattle, 1913; *Exhibition of Bronzes and Plaster Models by A. Phimister Proctor*, The Gorham Company, New York, 1913; *Small Bronzes by A. Phimister Proctor*, Art Institute of Chicago, Chicago, 1917; *Works in Sculpture by A. Phimister Proctor*, Corcoran Gallery of Art, Washington, D.C., 1918; *Painters and Sculptors of Animal Life*, Babcock Gallery, New York, 1920; *A. Phimister Proctor*, Stendahl Art Gallery, Los Angeles, 1923.

Other known versions: Mead Museum of Art, Amherst College, Amherst, Mass. (Gorham casting, gift of George D. Pratt, in 1932); Metropolitan Museum of Art, New York (Rogers Fund Purchase, 1912).

Variant titles: *General John Logan
Monument*
Modeled, 1894–1895; dedicated, 1897
Bronze, monumental sculpture
Markings: "AUGUSTUS.SAINT-GAUDENS
MDCCCXCVII/The Henry-Bonnard bronze
Co Founders New York 1897"
Copyright: None recorded
Grant Park, Chicago

Photograph from the Chicago Historical Society
Photograph by J. Sherwin Murphy

Plate 7 Logan Monument

Without a doubt one of the most exciting moments in Proctor's fledgling artistic career must have been the day in the early summer of 1894 when a telegram from Augustus Saint-Gaudens arrived on his doorstep. The Proctors were summering in Brittany at the time, having escaped the heat and bad water of Paris. Saint-Gaudens' telegram was to the point: "Will you come to New York to do the model of the horse for my equestrian statue of General Logan, for Chicago?"[1] This was a great honor for Proctor, so he and his wife packed immediately and were soon on their way back to America.

Proctor had known Saint-Gaudens for at least a couple of years. The master had visited the young sculptor's studio on several occasions during his work on the World's Columbian Exposition in Chicago and, as Proctor later recalled, "encouraged me a great deal."[2] Now he wanted Proctor to assist with the horse for a monument to the famous Civil War general John A. Logan. Proctor, already known for his ability to render animal forms, was a logical choice.

The *Logan Monument* would become one of the best-known public sculptures in the city of Chicago. When Logan died in 1886, he was serving his third term as United States senator for Illinois. Deeming him worthy of special recognition, the state legislature appropriated $50,000 for a proper commemorative sculpture, an amount matched by an equal share from private subscriptions; the City of Chicago donated an impressive site and $14,000 for a foundation and base. Saint-Gaudens was invited to submit a model that in 1894 garnered him the commission.[3]

Proctor later mentioned that Saint-Gaudens had retained "several" other sculptors to model the general's horse before Proctor received his invitation to participate, but who they were or how many efforts were made prior to Proctor's arrival are not known.

Once Proctor arrived in New York, he checked in with Saint-Gaudens at his famous studio on 36th Street. They both agreed that the New York studio was too crowded and busy for Proctor to do his part of the work, so he and Margaret moved north to Saint-Gaudens' home and studio near Windsor, Vermont. They chose a Logan family horse as the model, a stallion named Privatel that was owned by Logan's son. Work progressed well and the two sculptors collaborated effectively; every couple of weeks, Saint-Gaudens came to Vermont to critique Proctor's efforts while Proctor made his own suggestions. The final twenty-four-inch maquette, for example, shows the horse's head bowed down and turned to the left, a significant change that Proctor introduced and that Saint-Gaudens happily accepted. It balanced the rather exaggerated, groping step of the horse's right leg and the flamboyant gesture of the mounted general.

Proctor's model was completed by the spring of 1895. Nonetheless, numerous delays had built up by that time. For example, Privatel fell ill with pneumonia in March 1895 and Saint-Gaudens had to respond to Logan's angry son.[4] The widow was distraught that the process was taking so long, as were the committee members from Chicago who thought Saint-Gaudens was neglecting their project. In late May 1895, John R. Walsh, treasurer of the state legislature's committee, wrote Saint-Gaudens that "we ought to know when the work is likely to be completed or else you should refund the money paid and let us deal with some other sculptor."[5]

Problems continued to plague the project. One had to do with Saint-Gaudens' son Homer, who many years later told the following story:

Fig.68
Emmanuel Frémiet (1824–1910)
Joan of Arc, 1872–1874
Place des Pyramides, Paris
From Robert Rosenblum and H. W. Janson,
19th Century Art (1984)
Photograph by H. W. Janson

Fig.68

*It came about through my pet goat. The "Logan" horse
had been modeled for my father in Cornish; and, after its
completion, stood in modeling wax in the studio barn,
waiting to be cast in plaster previous to enlargement.
During that summer I had brought to delightful perfection
a new game with my goat. First I would induce him to butt
and then, stepping aside, take joy in his bewildered
plunge past me. What could be more natural than that,
one noon hour, while the studio was deserted, I should
play this trick directly before the stand on which was
mounted the Logan model.*

*The result is obvious. When the goat made his dive
and I dodged, he drove his horns with a crash against the
pedestal. For a second of horror the horse rocked to and
fro. But as it did not fall, I never imagined future conse-
quences and, boy-like, soon forgot the incident. The horse
was cast and the pointing up carried on by hand for over
two months, until at last both my father and Mr. Proctor,
who was directing the work, began to notice that the rear
of the animal appeared strangely askew. Careful measurements were taken, with only too disastrous proof. The
large model had to be torn down and the small model
remade in clay at the loss of a summer's work.*[6]

Vast amounts of reworking were later required in the New York
studio as well. That and the laboriously antiquated methods of
pointing up the figures to monumental scale resulted in further delays to the program. In March 1896 Saint-Gaudens
advised Proctor that the "big horse" had finally been pointed
up.[7] Proctor then modeled the saddle and saddle covering, at
which point his work was completed. But it was nearly a full

year before Saint-Gaudens contracted with the Henry-Bonnard Bronze Company to cast the monumental equestrian statue and not until July 22, 1897, was the work finally dedicated.[8]

The city made a gala event out of the unveiling, once the day finally arrived. A public holiday was declared, the city was elaborately decorated, and even the long-suffering family was pleased. In a letter to Saint-Gaudens, Logan's widow confessed her "sincere pleasure," and told the sculptor "its wonderful conception, marvelous imagery and artistic execution delight me beyond measure." Moreover, she wrote, "I hope you have forgiven all my impatience and criticism and let me feel that in trying to gratify me you attained your eminent success."[9] Despite her expression of satisfaction, Mrs. Logan was soon negotiating with another sculptor, Franklin Simmons, to produce a substantially less exuberant equestrian monument to her late husband for Logan Circle in Washington, D.C. That work was dedicated in 1901.

Saint-Gaudens and Proctor had endeavored to capture the true grandiloquence of General Logan. Logan had volunteered for the Mexican War and later distinguished himself during the Civil War under General Ulysses S. Grant at the Battle of Vicksburg. The scene immortalized in the monument occurred during the Battle of Atlanta when James B. McPherson was killed and Logan assumed command of his troop, which was on the verge of retreat. As the soldiers around him were "wavering and turning to run," Logan grabbed the flag and, riding out in front to face a formidable Confederate cavalry charge, shouted, "Them fellers in gray is ridin' to their graves!" Saint-Gaudens commented later that he had tried his best to "impart to the statue the spirit" expressed "by those words."[10]

Although Proctor played an instrumental role in the monument's ultimate achievement, others were also important in helping Saint-Gaudens. The plinth was designed by McKim, Mead and White, and the site was planned by Chicago architect Daniel H. Burnham. Additionally two of Proctor's fellow sculptors, Annette Johnson and Mary Lawrence, worked in New York on the figure of Logan with Saint-Gaudens.

Saint-Gaudens is said to have admired the French sculptor Emmanuel Frémiet, especially his monument to Joan of Arc in the Place des Pyramides in Paris. Frémiet portrayed her with an arm reaching high and holding a banner atop a prancing horse (fig. 68). That work, in turn, owes a debt to Verrocchio's *Colleoni Monument* in Venice and marks a return to Renaissance conceptions of ideal form. Unlike Joan of Arc's horse, though, Proctor's steed does not "prance with elegant restraint."[11] Reflecting his fiery rider, the Logan horse paws the air in anticipation of a valorous countercharge. It was a powerful gesture, one that recognized the spirited bravery that had preserved the Union.

Exhibited: None known

Other known versions: None

Variant titles: *General Sherman; Horse*
Modeled, 1892–1895; cast, 1901; dedicated, 1903
Gilded bronze, monumental sculpture
Markings: "AUGUSTUS SAINT GAUDENS
MCMIII"
Copyright: By Augustus Saint-Gaudens as *General
Sherman* under No. 5290 on February 2, 1892; by
Augustus Saint-Gaudens as *Horse* under No.
60319 on December 26, 1894
Grand Army Plaza, New York

Photograph courtesy U.S. Department of the Interior,
National Park Service, Saint-Gaudens National Historic
Site, Cornish, N.H.
Photograph by Kevin Daley

Plate 8 Sherman Monument

On February 2, 1892, Augustus Saint-Gaudens, America's lead-ing sculptor at that time, copyrighted a design for a statue of the legendary General William Tecumseh Sherman. Nearly three years later, on December 26, 1894, he copyrighted an attendant work, the design for a statue he titled simply *Horse*. These two figures, along with an elegant rendition of a laurel-crowned *Victory*, comprised the high point of the sculp-tor's remarkable career and his last monumental work.

Because Saint-Gaudens suffered from health problems, and given the complexity and significance of the *Sherman Monument*, he engaged as many as twenty different assis-tants over the years of its development. Frederick MacMonnies helped Saint-Gaudens for a while as his lead assistant. As that relationship deteriorated, James Earle Fraser replaced MacMonnies. Others who helped included Saint-Gaudens' brother Louis, Philip Martiny, Adolph Weinman, Mary Lawrence, Bela Lyon Pratt, Annette Johnson, Helen Mears, and Henry Hering.[1]

Of Saint-Gaudens' assistants in this project, Proctor was probably the most independent. No sooner had he completed his work on the horse and saddle for the *Logan Monument* (see plate 7) than Saint-Gaudens set him to the task of modeling a suitable mount for General Sherman. To accomplish that, the Proctors left New Hampshire and moved to New York, renting an apartment and securing a studio on West 51st Street.[2] Presumably the work on Sherman's horse spanned the spring and early summer of 1895. Proctor reported that by August 1, 1895, he had completed the model and turned it over to Saint-Gaudens for his final touches and for pointing up.[3]

Saint-Gaudens had accepted the Sherman commission in the spring of 1891. He began putting clay on armatures the

following year. For a likeness of the general, he relied on a life-time portrait that he had made in 1888 (the Metropolitan Museum of Art in New York has a casting made posthumously). In selecting the proper horse for this equestrian monument, Saint-Gaudens and Proctor considered a variety of options. According to Proctor:

> *General Logan had been a flamboyant figure, and his statue
> had required a picturesque horse. Sherman, on the other
> hand, was a campaigner, and he required a plain, more
> serviceable mount. A horse show was being held in New
> York at the time, and we haunted the place looking for a
> suitable model. Though there were plenty of beautiful
> horses, none was quite right. One that I particularly liked
> we finally eliminated because he was a bit too showy.
> Moreover, the owner said that he would be delighted to
> let us use the animal as a model — for a fee of fifteen
> hundred dollars![4]*

Their mutual choice was a veteran jumper from Long Island named Ontario. The owner graciously loaned the horse, and they boarded him at Dorlan's Riding Academy on 59th and Central Park, close to where the statue would one day stand. Frederic Remington, who was reporting on the New York Horse Show in the fall of 1895, noted this selection, writing in *Harper's Weekly* that Ontario, a "gallant old" horse, was "to be immortalized by the master, for Mr. St. Gaudens has used the grand old fellow as a model in his statue of General Sherman."[5]

Like Ontario, the pose that Proctor and Saint-Gaudens used was less showy and more traditional. Drawing on the Renaissance for inspiration, they turned to the horse in

Fig.69
Andrea del Verrocchio (c. 1435–1488)
Colleoni Monument, 1483–1488
Bronze, monumental sculpture
Campo SS. Giovanni e Paolo, Venice
From H. W. Janson, *History of Art* (1967)

Alinari Picture Library

Fig.70
Sketch of the *Colleoni Monument*
horse in Proctor's notebook

A. Phimister Proctor Museum Archives,
Poulsbo, Wash.
Photograph by Howard Giske

Fig.69

Andrea del Verrocchio's *Colleoni Monument* in Venice (fig. 69). But Proctor thought the position of the legs on Colleoni's steed was "impossible for a horse to take," and he made a sketch of the classic work in his address book, noting that shortcoming (fig. 70). After watching Ontario, Proctor solved the problem by repositioning the horse's legs into their natural placement for a slow trot. Even with that modification, though, critics identified the work with Verrocchio's masterpiece. The *New York Tribune* noted at the time of the monument's dedication in 1903 that "it is no exaggeration to say that Mr. St. Gaudens' Sherman is to be grouped with ... those of the Renaissance masters." The writer cited Verrocchio's *Colleoni Monument* as the primary influence, more so than Emmanuel Frémiet's *Joan of Arc*, a work considered "clever, but not lofty" like the Renaissance model.[6]

As much as Saint-Gaudens' *Sherman Monument* benefited from historical antecedents, it also profited greatly from modern developments. The process of pointing up the work went far more smoothly than it had for the *Logan Monument,* thanks to the use of a special mechanical enlargement device designed by one of Saint-Gaudens' assistants, Robert Treat Paine. That same sculptor and his system assisted Proctor in later years with several of his monuments, including the *Pioneer, Broncho Buster* (see plate 41), and *Pioneer Mother* (see plate 47).[7]

Prior to casting the monument in bronze or increasing it to heroic size, Saint-Gaudens exhibited his Sherman sculpture in several important venues. It attracted attention in the Paris Salon of 1899 (without the *Victory*) and at the Paris Universal Exposition of 1900. Following some slight modifications, it was shown full-sized at the Pan-American Exposition of 1901 in

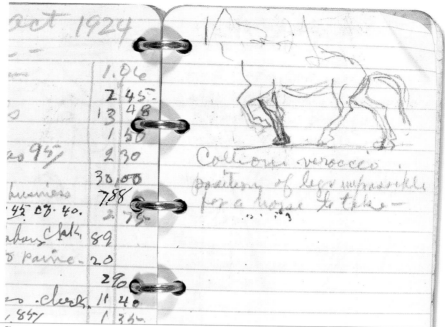

Fig. 70

Buffalo, New York.[8] It was from this plaster model that Thiébault Frères in Paris cast the final bronze that same year. The plaster horse's head remains, having survived a tragic fire that destroyed Saint-Gaudens' New Hampshire studio in 1904.

Saint-Gaudens originally wanted the monument placed on Riverside Drive in front of Grant's Tomb. The Sherman family objected, and the corner of 59th and Fifth Avenue known as Grand Army Plaza was selected as the alternative. It was a main entrance to Central Park. The pedestal and the monument's setting were designed in collaboration with Proctor's old friend Charles Follen McKim of McKim, Mead and White. In that location the monument attracted wide popular attention.

One bit of public scrutiny focused on the quality of the general's horse. In the spring of 1908, a controversy arose in the papers. As the *Philadelphia Inquirer* put it: "Old soldiers are complaining that the horse in the famous statue doesn't come up to their ideas."[9] The *New York Evening Post,* quoting a mounted policeman whose beat included the Grand Army Plaza, reported that "a man who called himself a cavalry officer fell over this statue the other day, and then wrote a letter to the papers saying that they had Sherman mounted on a plug." Proctor and Saint-Gaudens had deliberately chosen a serviceable mount, not too showy or flamboyant, but Ontario was hardly a plug. Indeed the policeman had exclaimed, "Now you take this from me: that animal is a grand good one…. He's all right — a typical, well-bred saddle horse." The *Post* then included the comments of a celebrated judge of horseflesh, James Trevelyan Hyde:

As horse lovers should know, the horse in the Sherman statue is a reproduction of Ontario, a noted prize winner a dozen years ago. James Trevelyan Hyde, for many years secretary of the National Horse Show and judge at many similar shows throughout the country, vigorously denied to-day that Ontario was in any sense a "plug."

"Ontario was one of the best-known jumpers in the horse shows of this country," said Mr. Hyde, "and was very far from a plug. He had good shoulders, and, while he was inclined to coarseness, was an excellent type of horse. He was a fine, big, strong animal, with plenty of substance, and he was a frequent prizewinner. To call him a plug is absurd. I'm not always so certain of the equine judgment of army officers."[10]

The critical assessment of the *Sherman Monument* as an ensemble was more to the point. In the unity of forms was found Saint-Gaudens' true genius. A few months before the "plug" controversy erupted, the *New York Times* had written:

Despite the obvious fault of permitting the charger's head to compete in interest with the rider, who seems crouched behind a bulwark when viewed from the front, this equestrian statue must nevertheless be ranked with the most notable achievements in equestrian sculpture produced in modern times.[11]

The *Sherman Monument,* as much a memorial to Saint-Gaudens as to Sherman, could be fairly claimed as "his masterpiece, and [as] … one of the noblest achievements of modern sculpture."[12] For Proctor to have been involved in such a significant way reflects positively on his stature and his place in American art. In later years, when asked about his role, Proctor tended to diminish his contribution. *The Century-Association Year-Book* for 1951–1952, published shortly after Proctor's death, recounted the following story:

For a long time word went around in the studios that he did the horse General Sherman rides in the Plaza. Some Centurions charged him with this one day. He said no, he didn't do the large horse, from which the bronze was cast; he did the study on a much smaller scale from which the large model was taken.[13]

Yet despite the smallness of Proctor's study, the scale of his contribution in the endeavor remains significant, as does the level of his partnership in the monument's success.

Exhibited: Paris Salon, Paris, 1899; *Exhibition des Beaux-Arts,* Paris Universal Exposition, Paris, 1900; *Exhibition of Fine Arts,* Pan-American Exposition, Buffalo, N.Y., 1901

Other known versions: Saint-Gaudens National Historic Site, Cornish, N.H. (plaster model of the horse's head and neck)

Variant titles: *Dog; Dog Gnawing a Bone; Dog and Bone*
Modeled, 1893; cast, 1893
Markings: None
Bronze, 8¼ x 5⅛ x 7½ inches
Copyright: By A. Phimister Proctor
under No. G56964 on December 7, 1894

North Carolina Museum of Art, Raleigh
Gift of Mrs. Arthur W. Levy

Fig.71
Marie-Rosalie Bonheur (1822–1899)
Barbaro après la chasse, c. 1900
Oil on canvas, 38 x 51¼ inches

Philadelphia Museum of Art: Gift of John G.
Johnson for the W. P. Wilstach Collection, 1900

Plate 9 Dog with Bone

Following his success at the World's Columbian Exposition in 1893, Proctor and his new bride, Margaret, spent almost a full year in Paris. There Proctor studied with Denys Puech at the Académie Julian, frequented the menagerie at the Jardin des Plantes, and became acquainted with French life. Since his primary purpose was to learn something of French sculpture methods and to develop his skills as an animalier sculptor, he could not take time to explore French peasant life, popular with American artists abroad at the time. Nonetheless, he came close to the French lower class in his sculptural interpretation of a dog that wandered hungry through his neighborhood.

Proctor had been using a Parisian alley cat to help with the finishing touches of his *Panther* (see plate 5), so it was a natural step to persuade a neighbor to loan him his skinny hound as a model. For Proctor, the image of the dog gnawing on a bone provided a metaphor for the marginal levels of survival in many quarters of Paris.

There is every indication that Proctor, unlike his mentor Augustus Saint-Gaudens, was fond of the French people. He and his bride enjoyed themselves immensely while in Paris and later when they toured Brittany and stayed for some weeks in a peasant's cottage in Illier. Thus it is unlikely that *Dog with Bone* was intended as satirical commentary. More likely it was a simple, honest effort at capturing an unrehearsed moment. The poverty revealed here, evoking the tenuous existence of many Parisians, might just mirror the state of a young struggling artist who must live hand to mouth. Proctor would also have found something appealingly modern about extracting artistic matter from the streets rather than following his normal routine of visiting the zoo for subjects. Here was the romance of the prosaic rather than the monumental statement of national ideals.

Proctor finished the model for *Dog with Bone* in Paris over the winter of 1894. He and Margaret worked together to cast it in plaster, and they were so pleased with the results, they soon had it cast in bronze.[1] It was copyrighted the next year and found its way into many of the artist's exhibitions in subsequent years.

Through the sweeping elegance of its line and the dramatic tension established between the dog and his meager meal, Proctor brought beauty to modern reality. In most instances when dogs appeared in American sculpture, they did so as companions to humans; John Quincy Adams Ward's *Indian Hunter* of 1864 is an example. Proctor's presentation instead focused on the dog's determination, despite its neglect, if not mistreatment. In a similar way, Rosa Bonheur's painting *Barbaro après la chasse* (fig. 71) generated sympathy for the pictured hunting dog, returned from the day's toils and tied up with a leash so short that the dog cannot lie down. The empty collar beside it may suggest the further loss of a comrade. As Bonheur commented in a letter to her cousin Georges Lagrolet in 1894, "[I] unfortunately find that the human race in general is not as worthy as the animals."[2] Proctor might well have agreed with her.

Exhibited: *Seventeenth Annual Exhibition of the Society of American Artists*, New York, 1895; *Exhibition des Beaux-Arts*, Paris Universal Exposition, Paris, 1900 (gold medal); *A. Phimister Proctor*, Montross Gallery, New York, 1908; *Second Annual Exhibition*, Canadian Art Club, Toronto, 1909; *Canadian Art Club Exhibition*, Art Association of Montreal, Montreal, 1910; *Sculptures by Olin Warner and A. Phimister Proctor*, Portland Art Association, Portland, Ore., 1911; *Contemporary American Sculpture*, Buffalo Fine Arts

Academy, Albright Art Gallery, Buffalo, N.Y., 1916; *Twenty-ninth Exhibition of American Oil Paintings and Sculpture*, Art Institute of Chicago, Chicago, 1916; *Small Bronzes by A. Phimister Proctor*, Art Institute of Chicago, Chicago, 1917; *Works in Sculpture by A. Phimister Proctor*, Corcoran Gallery of Art, Washington, D.C., 1918

Other known versions: Brooklyn Museum of Art, Brooklyn, N.Y. (gift of George D. Pratt, 1912); A. Phimister Proctor Museum, Poulsbo, Wash.

Fig.71

Variant titles: *Bear Cub and Rabbit; Cub and Rabbit; Small Bear and Rabbit*
Modeled, c. 1894; cast initially, c. 1894
Bronze, 3³⁄₁₆ x 2⅜ x 4⅜ inches
Markings: "A. Phimister/Proctor/COP RT 95/GORHAM CO. FOUNDERS QDO"
Copyright: By A. Phimister Proctor under No. G23532 on April 29, 1895; reregistered by Nona Proctor Church as *Bear Cub and Rabbit* under No. H53329 on July 15, 1973

San Diego Museum of Art (bequest of Mrs. Henry A. Everett)

Fig.72
Edwin Willard Deming (1860–1942)
Mutual Surprise, 1907
Bronze, 9⅝ x 3⅜ x 7⅞ inches

National Museum of Wildlife Art, Jackson, Wyo.

Plate 10 Cub Bear and Rabbit

Proctor was known for his sense of humor and an ability to reveal his own foibles through his stories. In the mid-1890s, at an early period in his career when he was endeavoring to assimilate many disparate styles and themes, he elected to sculpt this tiny tribute to the innocence of youth. He pulled the subject in all its charm and engaging cleverness from his imagination, as if preparing in wax some previously unrecorded episode from *Aesop's Fables* or Rudyard Kipling's *Jungle Book,* which was fresh off the presses at the time *Cub Bear and Rabbit* was first modeled. Yet unlike Kipling, with his "man cub" Mowgli who was raised by an old brown bear, or Aesop's typically paired animal antagonists, Proctor intended no overt moralizing with his bear cub and rabbit. They are more a refreshing expression of juvenile naiveté, capturing a moment gently charged by mutual reactions of astonishment and wonder.

The intimate scale of this work and its playful spirit suggest that it may have been a diversion from the extremely serious monumental horse that Proctor was sculpting for Augustus Saint-Gaudens at the time. Certainly nothing would present more of a counterpoint to General Logan's heroic steed: one appealed to the grand and bombastic, while the other retreated into a smaller, lightly inquisitive realm.

This work was likely conceived after Proctor returned to New York from Paris in the spring of 1894.¹ Yet it may have been inspired much earlier. When he first moved to New York in 1887, Proctor's studio adjoined that of Edwin W. Deming, who was noted for his paintings of the West. Many of Deming's paintings served as illustrations for children's books, and they often paired animals, juxtaposing them in nature as friends, or foes, or merely as sharing a common environment.² Years later his anecdotal and light-hearted

bronze *Mutual Surprise* (fig. 72) would seem to echo Proctor's earlier image of the unexpected encounter that was inspired perhaps by Deming's own work.

William Holbrook Beard was also living in New York when Proctor arrived there as a young student in 1887. Probably the most famous artist of animals in America during the late nineteenth century, Beard was known to anthropomorphize his animals, investing his paintings with highly elaborate human detail and complex social messages. Of greater interest to Proctor would have been Beard's equation of animals with humor. The art critic James Jackson Jarves wrote that Beard possessed "an exquisite sense of the ludicrous and sensuous," adding, "he paints not merely jokes, but ideas vital with merry thought and healthful absurdity...."³ Beard's humor would have appealed to Proctor, who loved a good jest.

As with many of his other works, Proctor appears to have been innovative with his *Cub Bear and Rabbit.* He enlarged the work in the early 1920s, replacing the rabbit with a frog, and he also produced at least one of the small bear cubs without the rabbit or frog for his grandson Phimister Proctor Church. At the 1918 solo exhibition of Proctor's sculpture at the Corcoran Gallery of Art in Washington, D.C., he exhibited both the *Bear Cub* (see plate 28, presumably the version without the rabbit) and the *Cub Bear and Rabbit.* These two and the later version with the frog appear to have been grouped under the original 1895 copyright for *Cub Bear and Rabbit.*

Exhibited: *A. Phimister Proctor,* Montross Gallery, New York, 1908 (both *Bear Cub and Rabbit,* no. 22, and *Bear Cub,* no. 23); *Second Annual Exhibition,* Canadian Art Club, Toronto, 1909 (both versions as above); *Canadian Art Club Exhibition,* Art

Association of Montreal, Montreal, 1910 (both versions as above); *Sculptures by Olin Warner and A. Phimister Proctor,* Portland Art Association, Portland, Ore., 1911; *Exhibition of Bronzes and Plaster Models by A. Phimister Proctor,* The Gorham Company, New York, 1913 *(Bear Cub); Small Bronzes by A. Phimister Proctor,* Art Institute of Chicago, Chicago, 1917 (*Bear Cub and Rabbit,* no. 3, and *Bear Cub,* no. 4); *Works in Sculpture by A. Phimister Proctor,* Corcoran Gallery of Art, Washington, D.C., 1918 (*Bear Cub,* no. 14, and *Bear Cub and Rabbit,* no. 15)

Other known versions: R. W. Norton Art Gallery, Shreveport, La. (gift of Mrs. Richard W. Norton, 1946); Phimister Proctor Church, Poulsbo, Wash. (bear without rabbit, gift of the artist)

Fig.72

Fig.73
Frederic Remington (1861–1909)
*Types of Saddle Horses: A Weight
Carrier; Park-Hack; Ladies Saddler;
A Smooth Trot*, c. 1892
Gouache on paper, 20½ x 29 inches

Amon Carter Museum, Fort Worth, Tex.
Bequest of Paul Mellon

Fig.73

Variant titles: *Bronze Horse; Stallion;*
Arabian Stallion
Modeled, 1895; cast initially, 1895
Bronze, 12 x 3¼ x 11¾ inches
Markings: "A. PHIMISTER PROCTOR"
Copyright: By A. Phimister Proctor
under No. G63381 on December 14, 1895
Location unknown

Plate 11 Arab Stallion

Working with Augustus Saint-Gaudens on the horses for the Logan and Sherman monuments gave Proctor an opportunity to study and render equine anatomy. When Saint-Gaudens first met his protégé-to-be in 1893, Proctor was already a recognized horseman. As the *Rocky Mountain News* that year reported, "In his mountain home [of Colorado] he became an adept in all that makes the successful hunter and mountaineer, in all the art of packing, camping or riding he wore a reputation with the best."[1] Proctor had bought, sold, ridden, tended and depended on horses for many years before coming into the studio. Now his job was to portray them in heroic scale, investing them with qualities that matched the personal characteristics of their celebrated riders.

So accomplished was Proctor at this task that owners began requesting portrait models of their favorite mounts. One day while he was working on the Sherman horse in his West 51st Street studio, a friend introduced him to a New York lawyer who sought not a portrait of himself but rather of his prized horses. As Proctor later told it:

Dixon, a lover of good horses, owned an Arab stallion,
which had been bred in the stables of the czar of Russia
and had on his neck the czar's brand, a crown. Dixon com-
missioned me to do a portrait model of the horse and was
so pleased with the small statuette that he gave me per-
mission to have bronze casts made for sale, besides paying
me a fee of five hundred dollars.[2]

Over the past decade or more, Frederic Remington had established a set of characteristics for western horses that reflected both their native environments and the personalities of

their riders: certain "types" of mount reflected particular categories of men and regions of the frontier.[3] Remington later expanded his definitions to include eastern and European horses as well. The wash drawing *Types of Saddle Horses* (fig. 73), a testament to the artist's acute powers of observation, not only is exceptionally simple as a drawing, but also provides an associative connection between each type of horse and its human counterpart.[4] Thus, one is a "Ladies Saddler" and another is designated "A Weight Carrier."

Arab Stallion, Proctor's portrait of Dixon's regal horse, may also have served in some sense as a likeness of the horse's owner. The "thoroughbred," as Proctor described the stallion model, stands with his head down, mouth agape, focused forward, and pulling at his bit. His contours are elegant. He exudes power and a certain restless disposition, qualities that may well have reflected Dixon's character as a New York attorney.

Portraits of horses owned by America's social elite became regular commodities in the early decades of the twentieth century. Charles Cary Rumsey, a sculptor who shared the affluent and ebullient lifestyle of Long Island's upper crust, produced a number of these sculptural alter egos. He portrayed America's most famous polo player of the era, Thomas Hitchcock Jr., with a bronze likeness of his favorite pony. And he immortalized many of Harry Payne Whitney's fabled racehorses in bronze, as well as Bouger Red, the favorite horse of Rumsey's wife, Mary, daughter of the tycoon Edward H. Harriman.[5] Although both the Gorham Company and Jno. Williams Bronze Foundry cast bronzes from Proctor's models, examples of this particular portrait are exceedingly rare. The only recorded casting, which belonged

to the Diamond M Museum in Snyder, Texas, was lost when that institution closed in the early 1990s.

Exhibited: *Exhibition of Fine Arts*, Pan-American Exposition, Buffalo, N.Y., 1901; Louisiana Purchase Exposition, Saint Louis, 1904; *A. Phimister Proctor*, Montross Gallery, New York, 1908; *Exhibition of Bronzes and Plaster Models by A. Phimister Proctor,* The Gorham Company, New York, 1913; *Small Bronzes by A. Phimister Proctor,* Art Institute of Chicago, Chicago, 1917; *Works in Sculpture by A. Phimister Proctor*, Corcoran Gallery of Art, Washington, D.C., 1918; *A. Phimister Proctor*, Stendahl Art Gallery, Los Angeles, 1923

Other known versions: None

Variant titles: *Indian Chief; Indian on Horseback; Indian Warrior on Horseback; Indian on Horse*
Modeled, 1898; cast initially, 1900–1902
Bronze, 31½ x 10 x 39½ inches
Markings: "A PHIMISTER PROCTOR/ 1898/GOLD MEDAL PARIS EXPOSITION/1900"
Copyright: By Alexander Phimister Proctor under No. G19847 on March 17, 1899

Amon Carter Museum, Fort Worth, Tex.
Purchase with funds provided by the Council of the Amon Carter Museum

Plate 12 Indian Warrior

Fig.74

During much of 1895, Proctor worked with Augustus Saint-Gaudens on the horse for the General William Tecumseh Sherman monument in New York. In the process and with the master's encouragement, Proctor ventured to expand the scope of his own work by attempting, on a studied and formal basis, to combine man and animal in one work. Following Saint-Gaudens' lead, that initial group was an equestrian statue, but Proctor's statue portrayed an Indian military leader rather than, like Saint-Gaudens', a famous vanquisher of native peoples.

Proctor was not only endeavoring to make his own statement about great military figures in the history of the American West, but also trying to improve on a subject with which he had experimented two years earlier. As part of his commission for the Chicago World's Columbian Exposition in 1893, he had produced a large, rather mournfully bellicose sculpture in staff showing a mounted Indian warrior twisted to the left and scanning the horizon. Generally referred to by the artist and others as the *Indian Scout* (fig. 74), this tensely searching work had received mixed reviews. The *Chicago Daily Record* claimed that while the horse was something of an embarrassment, having been "done by inferior assistants of Proctor," the Indian figure proved to be "one of the very best pieces of sculptural work on the grounds."[1] Such praise was enough to convince Proctor that the subject might be worthy of further development.

Because the Chicago horse had suffered understandable criticism, Proctor chose to improve on that element first. He employed a fine model owned by a New York lawyer friend named Dixon. It was not, according to Proctor, a "thorough-bred," but even so the animal suggested elegance, fleetness, and dignity, characteristics that the artist wished to confer on

the steed that would carry his Indian general.

Proctor was so proud of the horse that he later, on at least one occasion, presented it without the rider, submitting it in 1904 as his diploma work for admission as an academician at the National Academy of Design. The academy members apparently hoped that the sculptor would supply them later with "a more representative work," presumably one with a human figure, but Proctor was satisfied with the vigor and drama of the horse alone and never took steps to replace it.[2]

For his Indian model, Proctor went farther afield than Dixon's New York stables, traveling all the way to the Blackfeet reservation in Montana. There, after hunting for several weeks in the area that would become Glacier National Park, Proctor said he "began a small model of an Indian warrior."[3] Among the studies that he completed at that time were two portraits of Blackfeet men, *Aims Back* (fig. 75) and *Weasel Head* (fig. 76). Twenty years later both profile portraits would be separately copyrighted and exhibited as independent works, but in 1895 they were physiognomic studies only. Although Proctor probably did anatomical studies of Blackfeet men as well, unfortunately none of those survive. *Weasel Head* was ultimately selected as the portrait to be immortalized in Proctor's bronze *Indian Warrior*. "I was glad," he later wrote, "that I had modeled my Indian from a real one, since Indians' anatomy is somewhat different from that of the white man."[4]

When Proctor was awarded the Rinehart Scholarship to continue his studies abroad in 1896, part of the work he undertook to fulfill his obligation was the completion of his *Indian Warrior* group. His autobiography suggests that the small version of the work may have been completed in New York, but he waited until returning to Paris to enlarge it. By

1898 castings of the large and small versions were available in bronze. One of the large bronzes, measuring over three feet high, was sent to America as his submission for the Rinehart Prix de Paris Collection; it was lost in shipment and had to be replaced later.[5] Another casting found an enthusiastic audience at the 1898 Paris Salon, and by 1899 the bronzes were circulating in America. The *Chicago Evening Post* described the statue on display at a private residence in that city:

> It represents a fine specimen of savage manhood, mounted on a magnificent horse and clad only in breechclout, moccasins and war bonnet. The superb lay of this feather headdress, and even the turn of the warrior's braided locks, play their part in the composition.... Unlike the usual Indian pony, it is as noble a charger as that modeled by the same hand for St. Gaudens' Logan, now on our lake front.[6]

For much of the nineteenth century, Indians had been perceived as noble, just as was Proctor's warrior. The Baltimore painter and western adventurer Alfred Jacob Miller studied Indians and their horses near the Rocky Mountains in 1837. A later studio work, *Snake Indians*, anticipated Proctor's composition with remarkable similitude (fig. 77). As if speaking to Proctor himself, Miller wrote the following prescient words of advice:

> American sculptors travel thousands of miles to study Greek statues in the Vatican at Rome, seemingly unaware that in their own country there exists a race of men equal in form and grace (if not superior) to the finest beau ideal ever dreamed of by the Greeks. And it does seem a little extraordinary that up to this time (as far as I am aware)

Fig.74
Proctor's *Indian Scout* in front of the
Transportation Building at the World's
Columbian Exposition, 1893
Photograph from the Chicago Historical Society

Fig.75
Alexander Phimister Proctor
Aims Back, 1895
Bronze, 5¾ x 6⅜ inches
Gilcrease Museum, Tulsa, Okla.

Fig.76
Alexander Phimister Proctor
Weasel Head, 1895
Bronze, 5⅜ x 7½ inches
Gilcrease Museum, Tulsa, Okla.

Fig.75

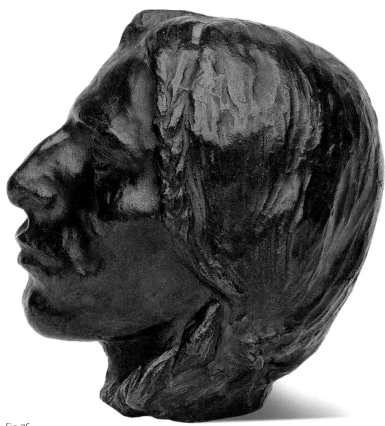

Fig.76

Fig.77

Fig.77
Alfred Jacob Miller (1810–1874)
Snake Indians, 1858–1860
Watercolor, 9⅜ x 13¾ inches
The Walters Art Museum, Baltimore

not a single sculptor has thought it worth his while to make a journey among these Indians, who are now sojourning on the Western side of the Rocky Mountains, and are rapidly passing away. Most unquestionably, that sculptor who travels here, —and models from what he sees (supposing him to have equal power and genius), will far excel any other who merely depends upon his own conception of what it ought to be.[7]

Like Miller, but nearly half a century later, Proctor was searching for that same beau ideal of the American West. He was joined in that effort by his friend and fellow artist George de Forest Brush. The Crow Indians, rather than the Blackfeet, interested Brush, and he saw and painted them as classical icons. "Their constant light exercise, frequent steam-baths, and freedom from over work," he observed in 1885, "develop the body in a manner only equaled, I must believe, by the Greek."[8] Proctor's chief was every bit as idealized as the riders on the Parthenon friezes or the stalwart and proud warriors in Brush's paintings.

In early castings of Proctor's *Indian Warrior,* the man carried a shield on his left arm, but by the turn of the century the shield had disappeared, leaving the warrior's lithe body more exposed to view. The *Indian Warrior* won a gold medal for sculpture at the Paris Universal Exposition in 1900. It went on to form the core of American sculpture collections in museums across the continent, from the Brooklyn Museum of Art and the National Gallery of Canada in Ottawa to the Amon Carter Museum in Fort Worth and the Portland Art Museum in Oregon. When patrons of the Portland museum gave a casting of the *Indian Warrior* to its permanent collection in 1911, it was the museum's first American sculpture.

It was a first for Proctor as well, evidence that his fame did not rest solely on his skill as an animalier.

The group proves that the artist is not alone master of animal life but is equal to the more difficult problem of the human figure. The chief in war paint and feathers is mounted on an eager, pawing horse, the dignity and poise of the warrior contrasting vividly with the impatience of the animal, who frets at the restraint of the rein. Both figures show skillful handling and a thorough knowledge of structure as well as conveying [the] quality of the picturesque, of atmosphere, that is peculiar to the artist's work.[9]

According to one source, published around 1915, the bronze castings of *Indian Warrior* were available exclusively through Tiffany & Co. in New York. But, as the article continued, it will eventually be "enlarged to heroic size and will adorn the public park of some one of our large cities."[10] This hope, unfortunately, was never realized.

Exhibited: Paris Salon, Paris, 1897; *Exhibition des Beaux-Arts,* Paris Universal Exposition, Paris, 1900; *Exhibition of Fine Arts,* Pan-American Exposition, Buffalo, N.Y., 1901; Century Club, New York, 1901; Louisiana Purchase Exposition, Saint Louis, 1904; *A. Phimister Proctor,* Montross Gallery, New York, 1908; *Second Annual Exhibition*, Canadian Art Club, Toronto, 1909; *Canadian Art Club Exhibition*, Art Association of Montreal, Montreal, 1910; *Sculptures by Olin Warner and A. Phimister Proctor,* Portland Art Association, Portland, Ore., 1911; *Exhibition of Sculpture*, Montross Gallery, New York, 1912; *Exhibition of Bronzes and Plaster Models by A. Phimister Proctor,* The Gorham Company, New York, 1913; Panama-Pacific Exposition, San Francisco, 1915; *Contemporary American Sculpture,* Buffalo Fine Arts Academy, Albright Art Gallery, Buffalo, N.Y., 1916; *Twenty-ninth Annual Exhibition of American Oil Paintings and Sculpture*, Art Institute of Chicago, Chicago, 1916; *Small Bronzes by A. Phimister Proctor,* Art Institute of Chicago, Chicago, 1917 (both sizes); *Works in Sculpture by A. Phimister Proctor*, Corcoran Gallery of Art, Washington, D.C., 1918 (both sizes); Annual exhibition, National Sculpture Society, New York, 1923 (small size)

Other known versions: *Small version*: Brooklyn Museum of Art, Brooklyn, N.Y. (gift of George D. Pratt, 1912); William B. Ruger, Newport, N.H.; American Airlines, Dallas/Ft. Worth (gift of C. R. Smith); Woolaroc Museum, Bartlesville, Okla. (gift of the Frank Phillips Foundation, Inc., 1930). *Large version*: Portland Art Museum, Portland, Ore. (gift of Mrs. A. L. Mills, Mrs. T. H. Bartlett, Henrietta E. Failing, Mary F. Failing, Mrs. H. C. Cabell, C. E. Adams, John C. Ainsworth, William D. Cartwright and T. B. Wilcox, 1911); Gilcrease Museum, Tulsa, Okla. (gift of Thomas Gilcrease); National Gallery of Canada, Ottawa (acquired 1909); Wilton Public Library, Wilton, Conn. (gift of the artist, c. 1948); Corcoran Gallery of Art, Washington, D.C. (acquired 1918); R. W. Norton Art Gallery, Shreveport, La. (gift of Mrs. Richard W. Norton, 1947); Belle Clegg Hays, Compton, Calif. (acquired from her father, A. E. Clegg, c. 1950)

Variant titles: None recorded
Modeled, c. 1895; cast initially, c. 1899
Bronze, 10⅛ x 3¼ x 10½ inches
Markings: "PHIMISTER PROCTOR/
1899/COPY/RIGHT/PATTERN"
Copyright: None recorded in Proctor's
lifetime; by Nona Proctor Church under
No. H5570 on December 14, 1973

Betty Due, Seattle
Photograph by Howard Giske

Fig.78
Frederic Remington (1861–1909)
*Transport, The First Horse in America to
Jump Six Feet,* 1893
Oil on canvas, 27⅛ x 40 inches

George F. Harding Collection, 1982.797
The Art Institute of Chicago

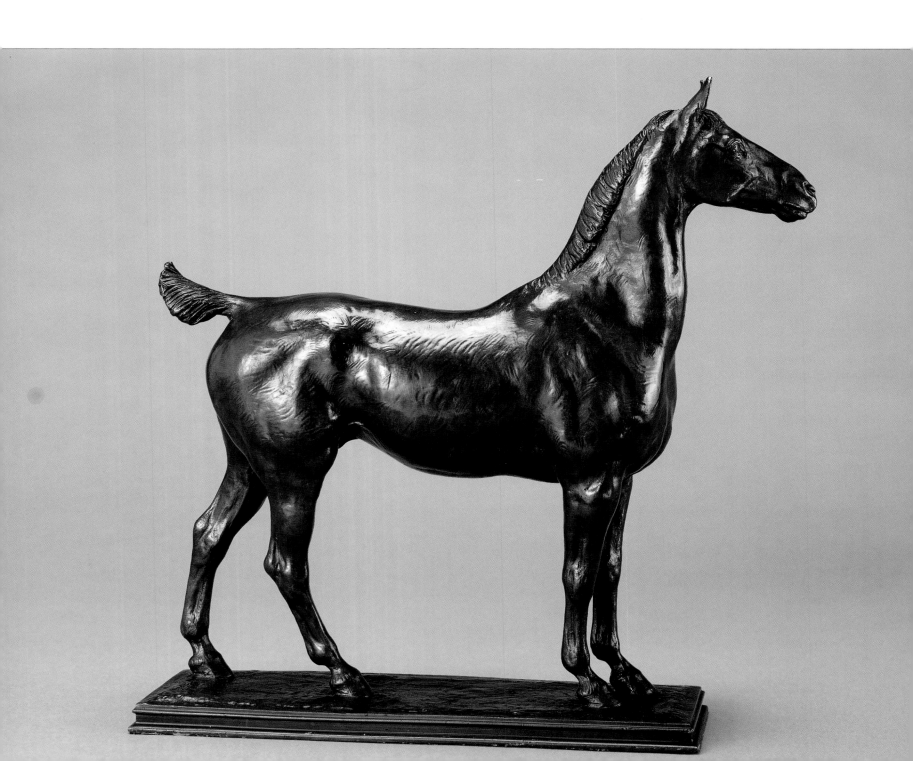

Fig.78

Plate 13 American Horse

Frederic Remington visited the New York Horse Show in 1895, and when he later wrote his article for *Harper's Weekly*, "Getting Horses in Horse-Show Form," he waxed eloquent about one handsome veteran in particular. The horse's name was Ontario, a "gallant" old hunter who had claimed the attention of many horse-savvy observers. When he was, according to Remington, "brought out and put over the rails for the education of some visitors," he did it "in his old workman like manner despite his lost eye and his years."[1]

Remington not only painted Ontario's portrait, showing him clearing the rail before a small yet admiring group of onlookers (fig. 78), but identified with the great hunter in personal terms.[2] The man who wanted his epitaph to read "He Knew the Horse" fantasized that "if my soul should ever transmigrate into a horse, let it be into a grand hunter's body" like Ontario's. Here before him stood a quintessential form: "unbroken to harness, arched in the loin, high withers running far back, lean shoulders extended and playing like a pugilist's arm, neck supple and far from the hand, tail set high and quarters as large as a freight car...."[3] Such a horse, Remington felt, would be an ideal subject for an artist.

In fact, as Remington went on to note, Ontario was about "to be immortalized by the master, for Mr. St. Gaudens has used the grand old fellow as a model in his statue of General Sherman."[4] What Remington did not say, and perhaps did not know, was that Proctor rather than Augustus Saint-Gaudens had been placed in charge of making the model of Sherman's steed. It was Proctor who faced the challenge of portraying Ontario and fitting the horse's powerful contours to Sherman's sturdy form, that of an indefatigable campaigner. Proctor described Ontario as comparatively "plain" and "serviceable" — a perfect mount for the no-nonsense vanquisher of the South.[5]

The bronze *American Horse* is thought to have been cast from one of the models of Ontario that Proctor made in 1895. Although the final pose for Saint-Gaudens' Sherman monument was considerably altered from this model, Proctor kept it. He probably had it cast in bronze during the winter of 1899 when he and his wife, Margaret, were briefly in New York between their lengthy stints in France. The first records of its exhibition appear in 1901, after the Proctors had resettled in New York. The artist showed the bronze that year at both New York's Century Club and at the Pan-American Exposition in Buffalo. It remained a staple on his exhibition checklist for nearly twenty years.

Exhibited: Century Club, New York, 1901; *Exhibition of Fine Arts,* Pan-American Exposition, Buffalo, N.Y., 1901; *A. Phimister Proctor*, Montross Gallery, New York, 1908; *Exhibition of Bronzes and Plaster Models by A. Phimister Proctor*, The Gorham Company, New York, 1913; Panama-Pacific Exposition, San Francisco, 1915; *Twenty-ninth Annual Exhibition of American Oil Paintings and Sculpture,* Art Institute of Chicago, Chicago, 1916; *Small Bronzes by A. Phimister Proctor*, Art Institute of Chicago, Chicago, 1917; *Works in Sculpture by A. Phimister Proctor*, Corcoran Gallery of Art, Washington, D.C., 1918; *Paintings and Sculpture by Four Artists of Taos*, Art Institute of Chicago, Chicago, 1919

Other known versions: None

Plate 14 *Puma*

Variant titles: *Standing Puma*

Modeled, 1897; cast initially, 1897
(one of two monuments)

Bronze, 12 x 3¾ x 5¾ inches

Markings: None

Copyright: By Alexander Phimister Proctor
under No. G12626 on February 16, 1899

North Carolina Museum of Art, Raleigh
Purchased with funds from the Mary Duke Biddle
Gallery for the Blind

Plate 15 *Pair of Pumas*

Variant titles: *Panthers*

Modeled, 1896; cast, 1897

Bronze, monumental sculpture

Markings: None

Copyright: None recorded

Prospect Park, Brooklyn, New York

Vintage photograph
A. Phimister Proctor Museum Archives, Poulsbo,
Wash.

Fig.79
Plaster working model for Proctor's
Puma No. 1, c. 1899

Alexander Phimister Proctor papers 1908–1949,
Archives of American Art, Smithsonian
Institution, Washington, D.C.

Fig.80
Proctor with plaster *Puma* created for
the World's Columbian Exposition,
Chicago, 1893

A. Phimister Proctor Museum Archives,
Poulsbo, Wash.

Plates 14, 15 Puma (Nos. 1 and 2)

Fig.79

Fig.80

As a result of his close association with many of the architects at the Chicago World's Columbian Exposition in 1893, Proctor enjoyed several profitable referrals in his early career. Among those was a pair of pumas for the south entrance to Prospect Park in Brooklyn. The commission came from a recommendation by Stanford White, who had designed two massive pedestals for the park and suggested that Proctor would be a suitable choice for fashioning a sculptural cap. Proctor's idea for pumas was welcomed, and he went on to produce two of the park's most dramatic artistic embellishments.

At the time of the commission, Proctor had just been awarded the Rinehart Scholarship for continued study abroad. He persuaded the scholarship committee to allow him to use some of his time for fulfilling this important commission. Thus his second stay in Paris, from the fall of 1896 through the summer of 1898, was spent in good part on the heroic-sized cats. Proctor wrote early on that most of his mornings were spent studying pumas at the menagerie at the Jardin des Plantes, and, following classes at the Académie Julian, he would devote his afternoons to working on either his *Indian Warrior* (see plate 12) or the large pumas. Both of the monumental cats were eventually cast in bronze in Paris and shipped to Brooklyn.[1]

In 1899 Proctor copyrighted two small bronzes made from the maquettes for the Prospect Park monuments. They were titled *Puma No. 1* (fig. 79) and *Puma No. 2*. As with the park bronzes, the stances of the two smaller works were slightly different. Although both cats stand upright, with their heads erect and their tails keenly swishing behind, *Puma No. 1* depicts a male with ears laid back and his right front leg forward while *Puma No. 2* portrays a female with ears perked up and her left foreleg in front. One of these bronzes (it is not known exactly which) was exhibited at the

Paris Universal Exposition of 1900 along with the *Indian Warrior*. Together, the group won a gold medal.

Proctor claimed the inspiration and models for the two sculptures came from studies he made at the Paris zoo in 1896 and 1897. But the stylized form of the two cats is reminiscent of Egyptian stone sculpture that Proctor had admired as a student in New York's Metropolitan Museum of Art.[2] Proctor could also not have missed the article on his fellow artist Edward Kemeys that appeared in the July 1895 issue of *McClure's Magazine*. The interview between Kemeys and Hamlin Garland made clear Kemeys' devotion to the western wilds and to animal sculpture, revealing him as a genuine kindred spirit with Proctor. One of Kemeys' sketches of a puma in clay, *An American Panther*, appeared as an illustration in the article.[3] Though somewhat more naturalistic in pose than Proctor's *Puma*, the Kemeys model must have served in part as a conceptual pattern for the younger sculptor.

According to several sources, Kemeys and Proctor had collaborated in 1893 on another pair of panthers, two large statues in staff for the Chicago fair.[4] A photograph of Proctor with one of the monumental cats, however, suggests that most of the effort came from Proctor (fig. 80). One observer of the plaster cats in Chicago felt that they exuded a special energy and were "strong and purposeful to a remarkable degree."[5] Another, remarking on Proctor's debt to Antoine-Louis Barye and Eugène Delacroix, felt he had not given "as careful a finish" to these pumas as to "some of [his] other work," preferring to distinguish himself from "other brothers of his craft" by using "masses rather than details in producing effect and expression."[6]

Certainly Proctor's time at the Jardin des Plantes and his several years of academic training in Paris allowed him to achieve more anatomical exactitude and elegance of design

in the Brooklyn versions of the pumas. The art critic Charles H. Caffin, writing for the *New York American* in 1913, assessed the Brooklyn pumas as perhaps "the most statuesque pieces" that Proctor had created up until then.[7] Sleek and noble, these two pumas have been arrested in a moment of defiant confrontation with some unseen force. Perhaps their superior air reflected Proctor's own sense of nature's primacy. These stately feline sentinels, regarding the city and its inhabitants before them, assert nature's power and ultimate invincibility.[8]

Exhibited: Paris Salon, Paris, 1897; *Exhibition des Beaux-Arts*, Paris Universal Exposition, 1900; *Exhibition of Fine Arts*, Pan-American Exposition, Buffalo, N.Y., 1901; Louisiana Purchase Exposition, Saint Louis, 1904; *A. Phimister Proctor*, Montross Gallery, New York, 1908 (both versions); *A Collection of Small Bronzes Lent by the National Sculpture Society*, Buffalo Fine Arts Academy, Albright Art Gallery, Buffalo, N.Y., 1909; *Second Annual Exhibition*, Canadian Art Club, Toronto, 1909; *Canadian Art Club Exhibition*, Art Association of Montreal, Montreal, 1910; *Sculptures by Olin Warner and A. Phimister Proctor*, Portland Art Association, Portland, Ore., 1911; *Exhibition of Bronzes and Plaster Models by A. Phimister Proctor*, The Gorham Company, New York, 1913 (both versions); *Works in Sculpture by A. Phimister Proctor*, Corcoran Gallery of Art, Washington, D.C., 1918; Winter exhibition, National Academy of Design, New York, 1919; *Painters and Sculptors of Animal Life*, Babcock Gallery, New York, 1920[9]

Other known versions: Gifford Proctor, Wilton, Conn.; Glenbow Museum, Calgary, Alberta (acquired 1962); Brooklyn Museum of Art, Brooklyn, N.Y. (gift of George D. Pratt, 1912); National Gallery of Canada, Ottawa (acquired 1909)

Variant titles: *Charging Bison;*
American Bison; Bison Bull; Buffalo
(Head Down); Bison
Modeled, c. 1897; cast initially, 1897
Bronze, 16½ x 8¾ x 12½ inches
Markings: "A. PHIMISTER PROCTOR
1897/COPY RT 97"
Copyright: By A. Phimister Proctor under
No. G52974 on September 22, 1897

The Walters Art Museum, Baltimore
(gift of Henry Walters, 1897)

Plate 16 Buffalo

Fig.81

In the spring of 1898, when the Proctors were living just outside Paris, the artist exhibited the *Buffalo* at the National Sculpture Society's *Third Annual Exhibition.* The bronze had been copyrighted in 1897 and may have been among the "several smaller pieces" that Proctor had "turned over for casting to a man who learned the art of chiseling bronzes in the studio of the sculptor Antoine Barye."[1] Proctor had met the French animalier sculptor George Gardet that year and worked with him at the Paris zoo, the Jardin des Plantes. Gardet, generally considered the successor to Barye, had recently been conferred the Chevalier medal of the Legion of Honor and carried substantial weight in the Parisian art community. To work with him would have been considered a great honor. Proctor, many thousands of miles from his beloved western prairies, possibly modeled the *Buffalo* during one of those collegial sessions at the Paris zoo. Gardet had earned considerable fame with his monumental bison sculpture that decorated the entrance to the Musée des Sciences in Laval.[2]

The artist, critic, and historian of American sculpture Lorado Taft used an illustration of the *Buffalo* in an article on Proctor that filled the pages of *Brush and Pencil* in September 1898. Taft claimed that Proctor, "one of the most promising of America's young sculptors," had learned much in Paris, especially from what Proctor himself referred to as the "artistic atmosphere."[3] But Taft also credited the World's Columbian Exposition in Chicago as crucial to Proctor's development. It was there that Proctor in 1893 had watched Edward Kemeys sculpt his monumental bison (fig. 81) for the grounds of the Chicago fair. Proctor greatly admired the self-taught Kemeys, who had "hunted buffaloes on the plains and was full of interesting stories."[4] Despite the fact that William Hornaday and

other naturalists had predicted the extinction of the species only a few years before, Kemeys' powerfully naturalistic buffaloes were symbols of continuance and persistence. In their inexorable, plodding march, they reflected the indomitable force of nature.

Proctor's *Buffalo* expresses those sentiments even more boldly. The thrust of his legs, the prominent exaggeration of his hump, the swagger of the lifted tail, and the bowed, almost threatening downward sweep of the bull bison's head all combine to project an image of virility and determined self-preservation. Five years after the Wisconsin historian Frederick Jackson Turner had announced the demise of the western frontier, Proctor revived the strongest of all the western symbols as an oppositional statement of hope for the region.

Around 1910 Proctor reworked the *Buffalo*, tripling its size and altering many of its details (fig. 82): he relaxed the arch of the bull's tail, reduced the forward extension of the hump, shortened the stride, softened the treatment of the hair, and separated the left foreleg from the buffalo's beard. Only one casting is known to have been made of this version. It was acquired by Herbert L. Pratt for the garden of his Glen Cove, Long Island, mansion.[5] An inscription on the base indicates that Proctor copyrighted this enlarged version in 1911, but no corresponding records exist in the U.S. Copyright Office today.

Exhibited: *Third Exhibition of the National Sculpture Society*, New York, 1898; Century Club, New York, 1901; *Exhibition of Fine Arts*, Pan-American Exposition, Buffalo, N.Y., 1901; Annual exhibition, National Academy of Design, New York, 1902; *A. Phimister Proctor*, Montross Gallery, New York, 1908; *A Collection of Small Bronzes Lent by the National Sculpture Society*, Buffalo Fine Arts Academy, Albright Art Gallery, Buffalo, N.Y., 1909; *Canadian Art Club Exhibition*, Art Association of Montreal, Montreal, 1910; *Sculptures by Olin Warner and A. Phimister Proctor*, Portland Art Association, Portland, Ore., 1911; *Fifth Annual Exhibition*, Canadian Art Club, Toronto, 1912; *Sixth Annual Exhibition*, Canadian Art Club, Toronto, 1913; *Exhibition of Bronzes and Plaster Models by A. Phimister Proctor*, The Gorham Company, New York, 1913; *Twenty-ninth Annual Exhibition of Oil Paintings and Sculpture*, Art Institute of Chicago, Chicago, 1914; Washington State Art Association, Seattle, 1915; *Contemporary American Sculpture*, Buffalo Fine Arts Academy, Albright Art Gallery, Buffalo, N.Y., 1916; *Small Bronzes by A. Phimister Proctor*, Art Institute of Chicago, Chicago, 1917; *Works in Sculpture by A. Phimister Proctor*, Corcoran Gallery of Art, Washington, D.C., 1918; *Painters and Sculptors of Animal Life*, Babcock Gallery, New York, 1920; *Bronzes from the Collection of Simon Casady*, Des Moines Association of Fine Arts, Des Moines, Iowa, 1929

Other known versions: Glenbow Museum, Calgary, Alberta (acquired 1955); A. Phimister Proctor Museum, Poulsbo, Wash. (gift of Phimister Proctor Church); Paine Art Center & Gardens, Oshkosh, Wisc. (acquired 1949); Henry O. Smith III, New York. *Large version*: National Museum of Wildlife Art, Jackson, Wyo.

Fig.81
Edward Kemeys (1843–1907)
Bronze bison in Humboldt Park, Chicago,
1893 (installed 1911)
From James L. Riedy, *Chicago Sculpture*
(1981)

Fig.82
Alexander Phimister Proctor
Buffalo, 1911
Bronze, 37 x 57 x 29 inches

National Museum of Wildlife Art, Jackson, Wyo.

Fig.82

Fig.83
Proctor's *Elk* at the World's Columbian
Exposition, Chicago, 1893

A. Phimister Proctor Museum Archives,
Poulsbo, Wash.

Variant titles: *The Challenge; Elk-Challenge;*
The Challenge-Elk; American Elk
Modeled, c. 1899, cast, 1899
Bronze, 16⅛ (base) x 4⅛ x 15¾ inches
Markings: "A.P PROCTOR/COPY RT
1899/POMPEIAN BRONZE WORKS N.Y."
Copyright: By Alexander Phimister Proctor
as *Elk* under No. G28272 on February 4,
1909, and by Mrs. A. Phimister Proctor as
The Challenge under No. G42236 on
November 21, 1912; reregistered by Nona
Proctor Church as *Elk* under No. H53327 on
July 15, 1973

A. Phimister Proctor Museum, Poulsbo, Wash.
Photograph by Howard Giske

Plate 17 Elk

Fig.83

Like many of Proctor's small animal bronzes, this work was inspired by one of his contributions to the World's Columbian Exposition of 1893 in Chicago.[1] Among the many monumental plaster sculptures he created in 1892 for the Chicago fair was a pair of majestic bull elk considered by promoters of the extravaganza to be "remarkable for the lifelike alertness ... attitude and ... truth to nature."[2] As many as ten elk, heads held high, crowned by twelve-point racks of antlers, may have graced the fair: four on pedestals in the Grand Plaza just in front of the giant Administration Building and alongside Frederick MacMonnies' extravagant *Columbian Fountain,* and two more on a bridge that crossed to the Wooded Island (fig. 83). They were all said to possess "stately grandeur" and to enhance "the charm of their surroundings."[3] Proctor made the bodies of the two "Watchful Elk," as they were called, identical. Only the neck and head of each were slightly different, with one turning to the left and the other to the right. "With heads raised, and nervous alertness and attention expressed in every graceful line," Proctor declared, they "are placed at intervals along the lagoon in attitudes as watchful as though they gazed upon the purple heights of the familiar mountains."[4]

In 1892 Proctor was invited by Theodore Roosevelt to become a member of the Boone and Crockett Club on the basis of his distinguished record as a sportsman and big game hunter, as well as his philosophy in matters of conservation. Another reason was his skill as a delineator of animal form, evident in the powerful renditions of American wildlife that he was producing for the exposition grounds. But he also may have been invited because Roosevelt liked to hear Proctor replicate the elk's bugle. "Roosevelt often delighted in hearing him give the elk call," reported the *Christian Science Monitor* many years later. "Proctor was the only man he had ever known who

could give it the correct note and the proper flection."[5]

Proctor would later refer to his exposition artworks as "youthful mistakes," telling reporters that he was grateful that they had been "destroyed in good time ... [and] swept away" so they would "not remain to haunt him."[6] And yet those early efforts were the genesis of many of his later successes. The *Elk* is a good example: it is probably a reworked small version of the Chicago fair *Elk.* Georgia Fraser saw the small plaster when she visited Proctor's studio on Rue Boileau in Paris in late 1899 or early 1900. Despite the "loss of its horn *en voyage,*" she wrote, the sculpture embodied a "beautiful creature" that was remarkable in the "dignity" of its pose.[7] The plaster was repaired and exhibited in the Paris Universal Exposition in 1900 as *Le Défi-l'élan (Elk-Challenge).* Although no records exist, inscriptions on known bronzes of this subject suggest that it had been copyrighted in 1899 before the artist returned to Paris to help with decorations for the United States Pavilion at the 1900 exposition. Changing the 1893 version, he extended the animal's two right legs and pushed the head forward to convey the idea of a bugling bull. These changes greatly increased the dynamic quality of the work.

Proctor, whose technique and style were now maturing, returned to America in late 1900 and prepared the *Elk-Challenge* for exhibition in 1901 at the National Academy of Design in New York.[8] Representing his premier exposure at the academy as a sculptor, the *Elk-Challenge* was the only artwork he submitted that year. He also showed the work, very possibly still as a plaster, at the 1901 Pan-American Exposition in Buffalo, where the catalogue listed it as *The Challenge-Elk* and noted that this work, along with several others that were part of Proctor's display, had garnered him a gold medal at the Paris exposition the year before.[9]

In Buffalo, *The Challenge-Elk* was displayed along with Frederick Roth's bronze *Elephant and Trainer* and Frederic Remington's *The Broncho Buster.* Both of those artworks treated the theme of nature relinquishing its power to man's dominance, though Remington's sculpture, like Proctor's, also carried a larger message about the West as a stage for that struggle. Proctor, however, seems to have wanted to send a different message. His *Elk* is triumphant in its stance and in the power of its forward thrust. It bows neither to man nor to fellow beast.

Exhibited: *Exhibition des Beaux-Arts*, Paris Universal Exposition, Paris, 1900 (gold medal); *Exhibition of Fine Arts*, Pan-American Exposition, Buffalo, N.Y., 1901; *Annual exhibition*, National Academy of Design, New York, 1902; *A. Phimister Proctor*, Montross Gallery, New York, 1908; *Third Annual Exhibition*, Canadian Art Club, Toronto, 1910; *Canadian Art Club Exhibition*, Art Association of Montreal, Montreal, 1910; *Sculptures by Olin Warner and A. Phimister Proctor*, Portland Art Association, Portland, Ore., 1911; *Exhibition of Bronzes and Plaster Models by A. Phimister Proctor*, The Gorham Company, New York, 1913; *Contemporary American Sculpture*, Buffalo Fine Arts Academy, Albright Art Gallery, Buffalo, N.Y., 1916; *Twenty-ninth Annual Exhibition of American Oil Paintings and Sculpture*, Art Institute of Chicago, Chicago, 1916; *Small Bronzes by A. Phimister Proctor*, Art Institute of Chicago, Chicago, 1917; *Works in Sculpture by A. Phimister Proctor*, Corcoran Gallery of Art, Washington, D.C., 1918; *A. Phimister Proctor*, Montross Gallery, New York, 1922

Other known versions: A. Phimister Proctor Museum, Poulsbo, Wash. (Gorham cast bronze pattern); Brooklyn Museum of Art, Brooklyn, New York (gift of George D. Pratt, 1912)

Variant titles: *Elephant; Elephant Trumpeting; African Elephant; Elephant Charging*

Modeled, possibly 1888 but probably 1902 or after; cast initially, c. 1908

Bronze, 11 x 3¾ x 11¼ inches

Markings: "COPY RT.08/A.PHIMISTER PROCTOR"

Copyright: By Alexander Phimister Proctor under No. G28384 on February 16, 1909

Brookgreen Gardens, Pawleys Island, S.C. (placed in gardens 1936)

Plate 18 Charging Elephant

The elephant was not among the many species that Proctor was familiar with in his Rocky Mountain youth. He knew them from books, of course, but it was not until he visited the New York menagerie and the American Museum of Natural History that he viewed the world's largest land mammal as suitable subject matter for his art.

During Proctor's second year as a student in New York, he tried modeling one of the zoo's elephants. The keeper, Bill Snyder, who had provided assistance to the young artist since he first began frequenting the park a year earlier, allowed Proctor to enter the elephant's cage, but only if staff accompanied him. On one occasion, according to Proctor's own account, Snyder had to leave momentarily. Somehow the artist startled one of the behemoths, and the animal went into a rage, threw its trunk into the air, and "let out a steamboat scream" right in Proctor's face that, he recalled, "nearly blew my head off."[1] Proctor survived the elephant's fit of temper and later made a sketch of the episode. According to his autobiography, he retained that model for about a decade, when it was cast in 1908 and copyrighted a year later.[2] As a bronze it appeared on public view in New York in 1908 at both the National Academy of Design and the Century Club. Critics praised it as representative of Proctor's ability to render bulky mass and fleet lightness simultaneously, and to contrast in his work the ferocity of the mighty and the fragility of the meek, the latter referring to his celebrated *Fawn* (see plate 3).[3] A writer for *Vanity Fair* offered an especially perceptive comment about Proctor's elephant and the artist's ability to individualize his animal portraits: "For him, each animal he models has a separate life and character."[4]

A 1902 article in the *New York Herald*, titled "Wild Animals at the Zoo Are Patient Models," contained several illustrations of artists at work in the city menagerie. Proctor is shown crafting a model of his favorite lion, Dewey, while others sketch or paint. Another photograph shows a keeper posing an elephant with its trunk raised and mouth agape while an artist makes notations in a sketchbook.[5] The article may have reminded Proctor of his elephant sketch and encouraged him to work it up as a finished bronze to be exhibited and sold.

As part of his studio décor, Proctor proudly included a casting of Antoine-Louis Barye's *African Elephant* (fig. 84). He had purchased it shortly after his arrival in Paris as a student in December 1893.[6] Barye captured the elephant in an almost humorous, dancing trot with a curious extension of its tail. Proctor's interpretation, in contrast, shows defiance and aggression. As a critic observed after seeing the bronze in an exhibition of contemporary American sculpture at the Albright Gallery in Buffalo, Proctor's elephant is a "wonderful study" of "trumpeting anger and ferocity."[7] The beast's bellicose blast may still have echoed in Proctor's ears from his early encounter.

Exhibited: Winter exhibition, National Academy of Design, New York, 1908; Century Club, New York, 1908; *A. Phimister Proctor*, Montross Gallery, New York, 1908; *Second Annual Exhibition*, Canadian Art Club, Toronto, 1909; *Canadian Art Club Exhibition*, Art Association of Montreal, Montreal, 1910; *Sculptures by Olin Warner and A. Phimister Proctor*, Portland Art Association, Portland, Ore., 1911; *Exhibition of Bronzes and Plaster Models by A. Phimister Proctor*, The Gorham Company, New York, 1913; Panama-Pacific Exposition, San Francisco, 1915; *Contemporary American Sculpture*, Buffalo Fine Arts Academy, Albright Art Gallery, Buffalo, N.Y., 1916; *Twenty-ninth Annual Exhibition of American Oil Paintings and Sculpture*, Art Institute of Chicago, Chicago, 1916; *Small Bronzes by A. Phimister Proctor*, Art Institute of Chicago, Chicago, 1917; *Works in Sculpture by A. Phimister Proctor*, Corcoran Gallery of Art, Washington, D.C., 1918

Other known versions: Henry O. Smith III, New York; Brooklyn Museum of Art, Brooklyn, N.Y. (gift of George D. Pratt, 1912)

Fig.84
Antoine-Louis Barye (1795–1875)
African Elephant
Bronze, 7 x 6½ x 3 inches

A. Phimister Proctor Museum, Poulsbo, Wash.
Photograph by Howard Giske

Fig.84

Variant titles: *Moose Relief; Bull Moose,*
Cow and Calf
Modeled, 1902–1906; cast initially, 1906
Bronze, 60 x 36 inches
Markings: "A. PHIMISTER PROCTOR 1906"
Copyright: None recorded

Grey Towers National Historic Landmark, Milford, Pa.
On extended loan from the Gifford Pinchot family

Plate 19 Moose Family

Proctor and Gifford Pinchot met in New York during the artist's student days in the late 1880s. Gifford was a promising young forester who would become America's leading proponent of utilitarian conservation. They became fast personal friends as well as celebrated advocates in the cause of championing nature's preservation. As fellow members of the Boone and Crockett Club, they shared philosophical attitudes that included a special affection for hunting and fishing as well as for the wild animals of America.

In the later 1890s, Pinchot, who came from a well-to-do family with homes in New York and Washington, D.C., purchased a casting of Proctor's *Panther* (see plate 5). Pinchot and his father then encouraged Proctor to devise other artistic schemes that might be used as decoration for their houses. Accordingly, in 1902 Proctor attempted to sell the Pinchots on the idea of commissioning a "full size vigorous bull buffalo head, carved in *dark wood*" to hang above one of the family fireplaces.[1] Pinchot's father was not enamored of the buffalo proposition, so Proctor came up with a second proposal a few months later. This time he suggested a bas-relief overmantel of a moose family. Proctor had just returned from a successful moose hunt in Canada and was currently showing off a record trophy bull—a true "monster" as the *New York World* reported—at the American Museum of Natural History. After first wounding the bull, Proctor had been charged by the animal and "came very near being made a bas-relief" himself, according to the paper.[2] The Pinchot commission would feature that bull.

The original concept articulated by Proctor was a split panel with a cow and calf on the right and the bull on the left.[3] Pinchot left the design to Proctor, "You will undoubtedly know the best about the group for the mantelpiece," he

replied to his friend.[4] What Pinchot did not realize, however, was that Proctor's schedule was so crowded that the moose commission would be set aside for almost a full year. In April 1903, twelve months after first approving the concept, Pinchot was perhaps not entirely satisfied to receive a letter from Proctor: "I am not going to disappoint you anymore about the moose relief. We go to country [Indian Hill] Tuesday & I will go right at it, & finish it, have finished up horns for the model I am to use. I don't think there will be anymore delay."[5]

But Proctor was overly optimistic. As the summer progressed, he labored and fussed over the composition. "I've chased the young moose all over the lot," he complained to Pinchot in June. "He's been everywhere except in the sky, & he is liable to wind up there if he is not satisfied where he is now."[6] It languished over the winter while the sculptor worked out problems with his wax supply, and it took many more months after that to perfect the *Moose Family* in plaster. Then, in early September 1904, when he had it cast in bronze and "tried to color it," he "made a failure of it" and had to start back with the finished wax.[7] Finally in November the plaster was sent at last to Jno. Williams Bronze Foundry of New York, who had bid to cast it in bronze for $85. When Proctor then asked if he might exhibit the finished work at the annual shows of both the Century Club and the National Academy of Design, Pinchot's consent was forthcoming, but probably only for the plaster, not the bronze.[8]

Evidently the *Moose Family* was a big hit once it found a home in Pinchot's Washington, D.C., living room. At Pinchot's request, Proctor made a second bronze casting for his friend's sister, Nettie, in 1906.[9] Over the ensuing few years, Proctor exhibited the plaster but always on the condition that it not

be replicated. Pinchot wanted his moose, long awaited, for himself and his family alone.

Exhibited: Annual exhibition, National Academy of Design, New York, 1905 (plaster); Century Club, New York, 1905 (plaster); *A. Phimister Proctor*, Montross Gallery, New York, 1908; *Exhibition of Bronzes and Plaster Models by A. Phimister Proctor*, The Gorham Company, New York, 1913 (plaster)

Other known versions: Present whereabouts of second casting unknown

Variant titles: None recorded
Modeled, 1903; set in place, 1904
Gilded sheet copper, 50⅞ x 21⅛ x 57⅛
inches
Markings: None
Copyright: None recorded

The Saint Louis Art Museum, Saint Louis
Vintage photograph A. Phimister Proctor
Museum Archives, Poulsbo, Wash.
Reproduction photograph by Howard Giske

Fig.85
View of the north façade of the Saint
Louis Art Museum, showing one of
Proctor's *Griffins* at upper right

The Saint Louis Art Museum
Photograph by Cervin Robinson, 1987

Plate 20 Griffins

On March 29, 1903, the *Denver Post* ran a special feature article on Proctor under the headline "Proctor's Inspiration Was Born in the West." The writer, Roberta Balfour, suggested that while Proctor had gone on to international fame, his creative spark had originally been ignited in the West. Colorado was his muse, she wrote, and though retained to work on projects far removed from the Rockies, his heart lay "among the forests and cliffs" of that state.[1]

The reality, however, was that Proctor's life and focus were often directed elsewhere. He mentioned in a letter published that spring by the Denver paper that he would relish the opportunity to sculpt a heroic-sized cowboy and Indian, but he knew Denver was not quite ready to make such a commitment to public art. At the time, Proctor had a wife, three children, and a French nanny to support. He had to look elsewhere for patronage, and as he did, the themes of his art were far from western. The *Denver Post* noted that his current labors included some monumental lions for the Frick Building in Pittsburgh (see fig. 28) and a recent commission for the Louisiana Purchase Exposition in Saint Louis, the latter said to "consist of figures for the frieze of the permanent Art Building."[2]

Actually, what Proctor had been invited to contribute to Saint Louis was a monumental plaster of the explorer Louis Joliet and two large finials for the Fine Arts Building, a structure that would ultimately become the Saint Louis Art Museum. These would take the form of mythological griffins, to be placed above the north entrance of the museum (fig. 85). In this project he worked with the building's architect, Cass Gilbert, and the exposition's director of sculpture, Karl Bitter.

Gilbert had produced a richly elegant, though reserved Beaux-Arts building that he called a "free treatment of the Renaissance Style" patterned after the Greco-Roman tradition.[3] In addition to beautifully arched windows and Ionic and Corinthian columns, the building was decorated with medallions bearing portraits of world-famous artists, most of them classical or Renaissance masters. George T. Brewster and Orazio Piccirilli sculpted these reliefs. Proctor's job was to enhance the museum's primary entrance with symbolic cultural guardians.

Griffins had long been used as architectural embellishment. In Greek mythology they dwelled in Scythia, a land that according to legend was rich in gold and strewn with precious gems. These winged beasts with the bodies of lions and the heads of eagles protected those treasures from outsiders. In the 1980s, Proctor's *Griffins* were removed from the building to protect them from the elements, and replicas covered in gold leaf now stand in their place. Guarding the entrance to Saint Louis' art treasury, they sit at either side of the roof, peering down with menacing contempt. Their beaks are open and wings raised as if ready to spring into flight, a pose that stylistically resembles Renaissance models. The originals are made of hammered copper and were at one point gilded. Although many of the sculptural enhancements for the building had to be scrapped or made of staff rather than stone because of budget constraints, Proctor's copper *Griffins* were put in place on the original building.[4] Aside from their removal to repair damage incurred by winds in 1945 and to provide necessary periodic restoration and regilding, they remained on watch for most of the past century.

Exhibited: None known

Other known versions: None

Fig.85

Variant titles: None recorded
Modeled, c. 1903; cast initially, 1903
Bronze, 22 x 7 x 17 inches
Markings: "A. Phimister Proctor/The
Henry Bonnard Bronze Co. Founders-03"
Copyright: No record
Glenbow Museum, Calgary, Canada
(acquired 1966)

Plate 21 Caribou

In May 1903 the executive committee of the New York Zoological Society presented Professor Henry Fairfield Osborn with a bronze statuette by Proctor. An imperious, controlling, but visionary overseer of the society's operations and mission, Osborn had chaired the committee to select the society's first director, William Temple Hornaday. Supported by Hornaday's professionalism and the organizational skills of the society's first secretary, Madison Grant, he had guided the organization through its formative years.

Osborn graduated from Princeton in 1877, then traveled widely in the West and Europe. He had established himself in the forefront of American science by 1890. At the time of this presentation, he held the position of professor of zoology at Columbia University, and curator of vertebrate paleontology as well as vice president at the American Museum of Natural History in New York. Earlier Osborn had joined the U.S. Geological Survey as vertebrate paleontologist in 1900 and would hold that position until elevated to the rank of senior geologist in 1924.

The president of the society in 1903 was the banker and statesman Levi Parsons Morton, a past vice president of the United States and recent governor of New York. Proctor was acquainted with both Morton and Osborn. In 1890 he had sold a painting of two panthers to Morton's brother.[1] If perhaps not the impetus behind the Caribou commission, Morton was at least sufficiently familiar with Proctor's work and reputation to support the notion. A meeting of the society's executive board was held on May 28, 1903, at the residence of John S. Barnes. Although the gift is not mentioned in the minutes, Osborn probably received the bronze on that occasion.[2]

Proctor's Caribou stands out in the way it portrays the strength of the animal's focus, the effortlessness with which it supports its mighty rack of antlers, and its firmness of stance. Perhaps these were qualities that Proctor saw in the bronze's recipient. No other castings of this piece are known to exist; it was exhibited and offered commercially only once, and it was apparently not copyrighted by the artist. Most likely the Caribou was modeled with that single presentation in mind.

Exhibited: A. Phimister Proctor, Montross Gallery, New York, 1908

Other known versions: None

141

Variant titles: *Morgan Horse*
Modeled, 1904; cast initially, 1904
Bronze, 15½ x 4¾ x 15½ inches
Markings: None
Copyright: None recorded (a Gorham
Company photograph indicates that
Proctor copyrighted the bronze in 1913)

Fig.86
Croydon Prince with his trainer,
Billy Morrison, c. 1910

Photograph by William Ruger Jr.
Newport, N.H.

Fig.86

Plate 22 Morgan Stallion

History of the Louisiana Purchase Exposition, published in 1905, includes an illustration of a monumental sculpture of Louis Joliet by Proctor. The caption tells how this equestrian statue towered over the Plaza of Saint Louis and faced, across a wide esplanade, a similarly heroic plaster of Hernando De Soto. The Proctor statue was pronounced a "majestic and inspiring production" that did justice to Joliet, the seventeenth-century discoverer of the upper Mississippi River. The book acknowledged Proctor's diligence at conceiving a likeness of this historic figure:

> In the statue of Joliet the artist, A. Phimister Proctor, has followed tradition and contemporary descriptions for the portraiture of the figure, the attitude of which suggests a survey of the territory that lay before the explorer, who holds in his right hand a chart to which he seems to be referring for guidance through the wilderness.[1]

The extent of that wilderness emphasized the value of the horse under him.

Proctor's autobiography suggests that he received the commission for the Joliet monument early in 1903 and made his first sketch for the statue while staying with Michael and Mary Lawrence Tonetti at Sneden's Landing on the Hudson.[2] Evidently Proctor's initial sketch, which was illustrated in the art magazine *Brush and Pencil* in December 1903, proved unsatisfactory to either the jury committee or the artist. Among other things that may have disappointed Proctor was Joliet's mount. For such an explorer, a grand horse was required. Fortunately Proctor's friend Austin Corbin of Croydon, New Hampshire, who was, according to Proctor, "a

horse fancier and sportsman," raised Morgan horses.[3] One of his stallions, Corbin pronounced, would make a perfect model for the artist, and so Proctor and his family at Corbin's invitation moved north to New Hampshire for the summer of 1903.

Much of the artist's work that summer took place in the Corbin stables. There he sketched the recommended stallion, likely the famous Croydon Prince (fig. 86), then universally celebrated in American horse circles. The sketch would later serve as part of the maquette for the Joliet monument and as the model for his small bronze *Morgan Stallion*.

Corbin owned a vast game preserve that had been started by his father, also named Austin. Known as Corbin Park, the preserve spread over 25,000 acres and, at the time Proctor visited, contained the largest bison herd in the world. When not working on his Morgan portrait, Proctor enjoyed roaming the preserve sketching elk and bison.

Happy with his summer's work, Proctor quickly had the *Morgan Stallion* cast in bronze and exhibited it at the National Academy of Design's 1904 annual exhibition. He later added the Joliet figure and used the group as his maquette for the Saint Louis exposition commission, exhibiting the maquette at both the National Academy of Design and the Century Club in 1905.

Exhibited: Annual exhibition, National Academy of Design, New York, 1904 and 1905 (latter as horse in *Joliet* plaster); Century Club, New York, 1905 (as horse in *Joliet* plaster); *A. Phimister Proctor*, Montross Gallery, New York, 1908 (as *Morgan Stallion* and as horse in *Joliet*); *Exhibition of Bronzes and Plaster Models by A. Phimister Proctor*, The Gorham Company, New York, 1913; *Small Bronzes by A. Phimister Proctor*, Art Institute of Chicago, Chicago, 1917; *Works in*

Sculpture by A. Phimister Proctor, Corcoran Gallery of Art, Washington, D.C., 1918

Other known versions: A. Phimister Proctor Museum, Poulsbo, Wash. (a bronze cast and a plaster maquette)

Variant titles: *Sleeping Lions;*
McKinley Lions
Modeled, 1904–1906; dedicated, 1907
Marble, monumental sculpture
Markings: None
Copyright: None recorded
Niagara Square, Buffalo, N.Y.

Photograph by Wilbur H. Porterfield, the Wilbur H.
Porterfield Collection, Buffalo and Erie County
Historical Society, Buffalo, N.Y.

Plate 23 Lions (McKinley Monument)

In late 1903 the New York architectural firm of Carrère and Hastings commissioned Proctor to produce four massive male lions in marble for a memorial monument in Buffalo to William McKinley. An anarchist had assassinated the president on September 6, 1901. Within less than two weeks, the people of Buffalo, where the tragedy had occurred, were calling for a "fitting memorial" for the fallen leader, "the beloved chief of the nation, shot down by an alien hand within our gates."[1]

A McKinley Memorial Fund was established, and ideas began to come forward regarding what might be most appropriate. Elliott McDougall, president of the Bank of Buffalo, immediately endorsed the idea of a monument, defining the project in his mind as "a life size bronze statue, done by the best American sculptor, the pedestal to be inscribed with the president's last words and with selections from his address, which is already historic."[2]

The State of New York appropriated $100,000 within the next several months, and another of Buffalo's worthy citizens, Edward H. Butler of the *Evening News*, assumed the chairmanship of a citizens' committee to see the project through to completion. Following the suggestion of his banker friend McDougall, Butler's group wrote to Augustus Saint-Gaudens in the late summer of 1902. The sculptor, together with the Chicago and New York architects Daniel Burnham and Charles McKim, were invited to act as an advisory committee. Not only did Saint-Gaudens consent to the request, but he also made such a favorable impression that the committee beseeched him to accept the commission for the McKinley sculpture himself.[3] No less than the new president, Theodore Roosevelt, was brought in to persuade the illustrious Saint-Gaudens to set his hand to the task.

Saint-Gaudens instead recommended Proctor for the job.[4] In the end the New York architects Carrère and Hastings provided the overall plan for the monument while Proctor worked on his part. Together with the committee, they decided to abandon the idea of a portrait of the late president for a symbolic reference to his powerful leadership laid to rest. Thus Proctor chose a sleeping lion for the motif.

Proctor and his family moved to the Bronx in 1904 so that he might be close to the Bronx Zoological Gardens. There, he worked up sketches modeled on a particularly grand old "veteran lion" named Sultan. "No finer specimen of the jungle cat existed in captivity," wrote one newspaper account. "Week after week Mr. Proctor spent before Sultan's cage in the lion house … working on his first sketch, and afterward on the small model."[5] Proctor observed that the big cats "of all the wild animals … are the most interesting to artists. They not only have color and form, but their natures are so subtle and interesting that one never feels he knows them, yet is always fascinated in trying to learn something of them."[6]

Once Proctor completed his preliminary models, he and his family made another move, this time to a farm near Bedford, New York, called Indian Hill. There he built a barn studio and embarked on two four-foot enlargements in plaster that would be taken up to the final scale: two pieces four times life size. As with the Brooklyn *Pumas* (see plates 14 and 15) and the Q Street Bridge *Buffalo* (see plate 34), the lions assumed two poses, one for the left side of the monument and another for the right side.

As Proctor put the finishing touches on the huge plasters during the spring of 1906, the press proclaimed that these were "perhaps the largest of [their] kind to the credit of an American

sculptor."[7] Yet the most formidable task lay ahead of him still: working over a three-month period with stonecutters to transfer the lions from plaster to marble. He had worked with granite on the New York Zoological Society commissions, but never in marble for other than small statues.[8] Proctor moved to Buffalo for the summer of 1906 and took up residence at the University Club. He worked long hours trying to bring life into the Vermont stone. "I plied the hammer from early morn till six this evening," he wrote to Saint-Gaudens on June 5. "I am tired in the hands, as you may imagine. I enjoy it, very much."[9]

Saint-Gaudens had recently provided, at Proctor's request, a critique of a sketch for another commission that Proctor was considering. In his criticism, Saint-Gaudens had suggested that Proctor strive to capture more nobility and power in his lions and give them less of a feeling of zoo animals. Proctor responded with alacrity and at length, making special reference to the lions he was just then cutting in stone:

The lion I had for model was all mane, and I have had the worst job of my life trying to do it. Have not succeeded with a single look as yet. I hope the marble will hold out long enough for me to get something out of it—I would give a great deal for your criticisms on these lions, before it is too late—I shall hope to get some of the finer qualities in the next lions, that may be lacking in these."[10]

Construction of the McKinley monument was completed on July 1, 1906. The four lions, each weighing about twelve tons and measuring twelve feet in length, slumbered grandly beneath the obelisk that towered skyward to a height of ninety-three feet, including its marble base.[11] Proctor recounted in his autobiography how difficult it was to place the giant lions on their pedestals:

> *Heavy ropes were wound around the huge figures, in preparation for hoisting them into position with a derrick. The man in charge of the moving was afraid that the plinths — the bases of the pedestals — might crack if the figures were not settled perfectly evenly. Consequently, the pedestals were covered with finely crushed ice, and the lions were lowered onto it. As the ice melted, the figures slowly settled into place. To prevent the ice from melting more rapidly in one spot than in another, a man with a hose stood by to turn a stream of water on the ice.*[12]

Over the years the city of Buffalo gradually grew up around Niagara Plaza and the open sweep of the McKinley monument. City Hall, as well as several state and federal buildings, now look out over Proctor's guardian lions. Even as the great obelisk became the hub of the city, the monument started to represent something of an embarrassment: the reflecting pools began to leak, and the lions were discolored in Buffalo's polluted air. Conservation efforts attempted in the mid-1970s proved to be controversial, many observers considering them hasty and ill conceived.[13] More careful restoration efforts have been undertaken in the new millennium.

Proctor produced and sold small versions of the McKinley monument lions. As early as 1906, he displayed *Sleeping Lion: A Study* at the annual exhibition of the National Academy of Design in New York. Two years later, in his comprehensive exhibition of "sculptures, bronzes, watercolors and sketches" at the Montross Gallery in New York, he presented one marble "reduction" and a plaster "companion" of *Lions*. The *Sleeping Lion* appeared again in 1922 at a special showing of Proctor's work, where it and other animal pieces were regarded as "profoundly entertaining … by a man who has made a life study of them."[14] The McKinley *Lions,* in reduced and monumental form, continued through Proctor's life to be listed as one of his sterling accomplishments. Along with the Princeton *Tiger Couchant* (see plate 32) and the Q Street Bridge *Buffalo,* they are mentioned in nearly every biographical sketch of Proctor that appeared after 1907.

Exhibited (small versions): Annual exhibition, National Academy of Design, New York, 1906 (a study); *A. Phimister Proctor,* Montross Gallery, New York, 1908 (a marble reduction and a plaster second version); *A. Phimister Proctor,* Montross Gallery, New York, 1922

Other known versions: A. Phimister Proctor Museum, Poulsbo, Wash. (two plasters, a small study 7½ inches long and a large maquette 48 inches long)

Variant titles: *Panther and Kill;*
Panther with Deer
Modeled, 1907; cast initially, 1908
Bronze, 11½ x 5½ x 5½ inches
Markings: "A. Phimister Proctor,
SC/copyright 08"
Copyright: None recorded

A. Phimister Proctor Museum, Poulsbo, Wash.
Photograph by Howard Giske

Fig.87
Antoine-Louis Barye (1795–1875)
Jaguar Devouring a Hare, modeled 1850
Bronze, 23 inches in height

National Museum of Wildlife Art, Jackson, Wyo.

Fig.88
Henri Matisse (1869–1954)
Jaguar Devouring a Hare
(after Antoine-Louis Barye), 1899–1901
Bronze, 22 x 9⅛ x 9⅛ inches

Musée National d'Art Moderne, Centre Georges
Pompidou, Paris
CNAC/MNAM/Dist. Réunion des Musées
Nationaux/Art Resource, N.Y.
© 2003 Succession H. Matisse, Paris/Artists
Rights Society (ARS), New York
Photograph by Philippe Migeat

Plate 24 Panther with Kill

Proctor's talents as an animalier sculptor once attracted a gift from America's premier animal reserve, Yellowstone National Park. One of his old friends and hunting companions, Major John Pitcher, was acting superintendent of the park from 1901 to 1907. Pitcher was an extremely popular administrator who paid close attention to the needs of park visitors. While he was a zealous guardian of the park's resources, he also insisted that tourists should have the most positive experience possible. His vision of accessibility went beyond the park's boundaries, and Proctor and the world of art became its beneficiaries.[1]

Reports and stories had been circulating for several years about the impact that cougars were having on the park's mountain sheep, deer, and elk populations. Some, like Theodore Roosevelt, suggested that despite the serious attrition in elk herd numbers caused by hungry mountain lions, the elk in the park were actually "rather too numerous" and the cougars represented little long-term threat.[2] Others were not so sanguine. Frederic Remington, who had taken a winter tour of the park in 1900, referred to the cougars as "outlaws." In an article published in *Collier's* shortly after his visit, Remington pronounced the cougars a menace and called for them to be dealt with summarily.[3] Pitcher, in his desire for visitors to see as much wildlife as possible, leaned more toward Remington's attitude. He felt a reduction in lion population was necessary, arguing that they "seriously threaten[ed] the extinction of the deer and other game" in the park.[4] In the spring of 1907, he set out with a party of men and dogs to remedy the situation. One lion, a female who was affectionately, though inaccurately, nicknamed Yellowstone Pete, was treed and about to be dispatched, when Pitcher thought of his friend Proctor. The superintendent, according to an article in the *New York World,*

remembered that in the Bronx in New York was the most extraordinary art studio in the country—a big building, where a former westerner, now a sculptor, worked from live animal models in the moist clay and afterward fixed the forms into bronze and marble. The major had hunted across the Rocky mountains with A. Phimister Proctor, the sculptor, when Proctor lived with the cowboys and mountaineers and spent his life studying the denizens of the plains and the hill country. They had gone hungry together among the crags and slept under the same blanket and cut the same venison before the camp fires in the wilds. He determined to capture Pete alive and send him to Proctor.[5]

Proctor had just completed his huge marble lions for the McKinley monument in Buffalo, New York, each twelve feet long and weighing about twelve tons. Dealing with this scale and working in Vermont marble had challenged the artist. Thus he welcomed the chance to work once again on a small sculptural group. The product of Pitcher's generosity would eventually be cast in bronze with the title of *Panther with Kill.* After the cougar was donated to New York's Zoological Park, Proctor began visiting Yellowstone Pete there. He soon found, however, that Pitcher's trophy was a "wild and unwilling model" under those circumstances.[6] After many efforts to cajole the animal into posing, Proctor persuaded the zookeepers into letting him borrow Yellowstone Pete for the summer. Thus the cat was moved to the artist's farm at Indian Hill, north of the city near Bedford, New York. Placed in a smaller cage there in the country, it was "a captive to the interests of art."[7] The Proctor children long remembered the feline yowls that pierced the calm of their Westchester evenings.

Comparing it to the McKinley commission, Proctor spoke of the *Panther with Kill* in relaxed terms:

Models for the group presented no problem, for we had a caged panther at the farm, and I was permitted to make sketches of a deer that had died at the [New York City] menagerie. I had to prod the panther with a pole to get her into the position that I wanted. After a period of poking she seemed to grasp the situation and kept the pose pretty well.[8]

It took several months to complete the model, and once finished, the dramatic little group was sent to the foundry, presumably the Gorham Company. In its final form, the bronze paid a romantic tribute to Yellowstone National Park and the West, to the wild instinct for survival, and to the fundamental realities of predation in the balance of nature. It is not known if Proctor agreed with Roosevelt or Pitcher in the numbers debate, but he definitely privileged the cougar as a dominant, pervasive force in nature's scheme.

Proctor also paid special tribute in this work to his artistic hero Antoine-Louis Barye. In pose, theme, and dramatic essence, Proctor's *Panther with Kill* was patterned after Barye's famous, convulsively powerful bronze *Jaguar Devouring a Hare* (fig. 87), which was sculpted in France around 1850. In everything from the highly articulated musculature of the cat's massive shoulders and its taut, twitching tail to the formal base panel, Barye's influence is evident. Just as Barye was reacting in his "animal combat" sculptures against neoclassicism in favor of romanticism's ideal of truth in nature, so, too, was Proctor making a statement.[9] His McKinley lions, by virtue of their memorial function for a head of state, had possessed a regal, staid air with bows to classicism. In his *Panther*

Fig.87

Fig.88

with Kill, Proctor could step vicariously into the wilds and aesthetically into romanticism's more dramatic realm.

In 1901 Henri Matisse, the French modernist painter and sculptor, had used Barye's *Jaguar Devouring a Hare* in a similarly transitional way. Matisse's first serious sculptural piece, also titled *Jaguar Devouring a Hare* (fig. 88), was a freely formed mass of faceted planes crafted as a study after the Barye bronze. Matisse was reacting against Beaux-Arts productions of his time, which to him were uninspiring and crisply represen-

tational.[10] While Proctor was not willing to move beyond accepted French and American norms, he was interested in varying his output only within the Beaux-Arts perimeters.

Exhibited: Winter exhibition, National Academy of Design, New York, 1908; *Second Annual Exhibition*, Canadian Art Club, Toronto, 1909; *Small Bronzes by A. Phimister Proctor*, Art Institute of Chicago, Chicago, 1917; *An Exhibition of Small Bronzes by American Sculptors*, Buffalo Fine Arts Academy,

Albright Art Gallery, Buffalo, N.Y., 1918; *Works in Sculpture by A. Phimister Proctor*, Corcoran Gallery of Art, Washington, D.C., 1918; *Paintings and Sculpture by Four Artists of Taos*, Art Institute of Chicago, Chicago, 1919

Other known versions: A. Phimister Proctor Museum, Poulsbo, Wash. (plaster cast)

Variant titles: *Tarpon; Leaping Tarpon;*
Silver King Fish; Tarpon: Silver King
Modeled, 1907; cast initially, 1907
Silver-coated bronze sculpture,
10⅝ x 4 x 13½ inches
Markings: "COPY RT AP PROCTOR-07"
Copyright: By Alexander Phimister
Proctor under No. I28385 on
February 16, 1909

Brooklyn Museum of Art. 12.894.
Gift of George D. Pratt

Plate 25 Silver King

Proctor and Gifford Pinchot communicated frequently during the first two decades of the twentieth century. They spoke of business matters related to the Century Club and the Boone and Crockett Club, they bemoaned the personal and professional vicissitudes of their lives, and they talked of hunting and fishing. Of all the topics, sporting life received by far the most attention.

The many schemes for getting together in the backcountry included plans to visit Yellowstone National Park in 1906 in the more general pursuit of wild game. Both were interested in deep-sea fishing off the Florida or Texas coasts. In 1905 they began arranging a trip, but they found coordinating schedules to be impossible. Pinchot went anyway with their mutual friend from New York, James R. Garfield. Proctor was envious. The next fall, Pinchot wrote Proctor about further plans:

> *I have had two schemes, one to go to Montana, where*
> *there is a grizzly who has a habit of running sheep herders*
> *out of the country; the other to go to Aransas Pass [Texas]*
> *and catch a few tarpon on an 8-oz. rod. If I can get away at*
> *all I could leave on the 22nd or 23rd of this month. Could*
> *you leave, and have you any alternative scheme? If you*
> *and I could get into the woods together once it would be a*
> *gorgeous thing. If we went to Montana we should be right*
> *on the edge of the Nat. Park, and by the time we got out of*
> *the woods the game would have begun to come down.*
> *Both Major Pitcher [Yellowstone Park superintendent]*
> *and Mrs. Pitcher are exceedingly anxious to have you*
> *come out there. I saw them recently and they both spoke*
> *enthusiastically of you coming. How about it?*[1]

Although neither of those trips worked out either, Pinchot was persistent, and in the spring of 1907 he reissued the invitation, this time through Proctor's wife, Margaret. He told her that "nothing will do me so much good as his company."[2] That extra bit of cajoling paid off, and the trip, slated for late May, was a successful one. The tarpon that Proctor brought home, along with the memories of the catch, inspired his bronze *Silver King*, which was first cast in 1907 in multiples. As soon as the initial bronzes were complete, Proctor wrote to Pinchot, who had reserved a casting:

The Tarpons have been cast & we silvered one yesterday, & it is coming out finely — Tho Hastings, Carrère & Grant La Farge saw it yesterday before it was patinaed, they were exceeding[ly] pleased & enthusiastic over it. All said it had a heap of "get up in the air" feeling.[3]

The *Silver King* was exhibited at the Century Club in December 1907. According to Proctor, "all the artists and one or two art critics spoke very highly of it." Proctor credited Pinchot with helping to design it. "I ought really to pay you a royalty on it," he told his friend and fishing partner.[4] He insisted that Pinchot, who had paid for his trip to Aransas, not be assessed for more than the casting costs. The argument went back and forth, but Pinchot ultimately prevailed and paid the full tab, plus ordering another as a Christmas present for a friend. When Proctor asked him which title he preferred, *Tarpon* or *Silver King*, Pinchot felt the latter was "more attractive."[5] So in 1909, when Proctor copyrighted his vigorous tarpon, it was formally recorded as *Silver King*.

When Proctor exhibited the work at New York's Montross Gallery in 1908, he included both the patinated bronze and a silver-plated version. From the beginning, Proctor's fish story — the tale of his Texas trip with Pinchot in 1907 — was as much a part of the sculpture's exhibition scheme as its placement on the pedestal. Some critics appreciated the work as a technical tour de force, "a subject that is unique, of great difficulty, and worth the effort it demanded," and for the formal achievement of its ambitiously graceful curving rhythms.[6] Others simply enjoyed repeating Proctor's account of the catch:

I made the model of that fellow while on a fishing trip with Gifford Pinchot off the coast of Texas. I was lucky enough to haul in a big fellow over seven feet long. His grace, the beautiful lines of his body as he made the fight for his life appealed to me so strongly that after he had been landed I dropped my tackle and began a search for some clay. I found a bit that would do and made the model on the spot, later having it cast in the bronze.[7]

Silver King remained a popular and financially rewarding work for Proctor. Considering it a unique part of his oeuvre, he would feature the bronze in exhibitions over the next two decades. In these shows he often preferred to display the silvered bronze as it so effectively replicated the flash of the game fish and the sparkle of the curling wave that follows its combative leap.

Exhibited: Century Club, New York, 1907; *A. Phimister Proctor*, Montross Gallery, New York, 1908; *Second Annual Exhibition*, Canadian Art Club, Toronto, 1909; *Exhibition of Bronzes and Plaster Models by A. Phimister Proctor*, The Gorham Company, New York, 1913; *Contemporary American Sculpture*, Buffalo Fine Arts Academy, Albright Art Gallery, Buffalo, N.Y., 1916; *Twenty-ninth Annual Exhibition of American Oil Paintings and Sculpture*, Art Institute of Chicago, Chicago, 1916; *Small Bronzes by A. Phimister Proctor*, Art Institute of Chicago, Chicago, 1917; *Works in Sculpture by A. Phimister Proctor*, Corcoran Gallery of Art, Washington, D.C., 1918; *Painters and Sculptors of Animal Life*, Babcock Gallery, New York, 1920; *A. Phimister Proctor*, Stendahl Art Gallery, Los Angeles, 1923; *Sculpture by A. Phimister Proctor [and] Harold Swartz, Paintings by Conrad Buff [and] Shiyei Y. Kotoku*, Los Angeles Museum, 1924

Other known versions: None

Variant titles: *Bull Moose*
Modeled, c. 1907; cast, 1907
Bronze, 15 x 5½ x 19½ inches
Markings: "A.P. Proctor" and "COPY
RT.-07" on base
Copyright: By Nona Proctor Church
under No. H53320 on July 15, 1973
Buffalo Bill Historical Center, Cody, Wyo.; 53.61

Fig.89
Henry Merwin Shrady (1871–1922)
Bull Moose, 1900
Bronze, 20¾ inches in height
Gilcrease Museum, Tulsa, Okla.

Plate 26 Moose

Fig.89

Proctor cast this bronze statue of a bull moose in 1907.[1] According to William B. McCormick of the *New York Press*, it was originally modeled for the artist's old friend Gifford Pinchot.[2] The two men shared an affection for nature and an interest in the preservation of its wonders. Serving as chief of the federal Forestry Division, Pinchot had just that year coined the word "conservation." He and President Theodore Roosevelt were about to embark on a national program of managed natural resources that would revolutionize American use of public lands.

The predecessors to Proctor's *Moose* also had associations with conservation. Fourteen years earlier Proctor had sculpted four large plaster moose for the bridges at the 1893 World's Columbian Exposition in Chicago. Supposedly male and female pairs,[3] all four were in fact bulls, posed with their heads up looking straight ahead. One pair guarded "The Farmers' Bridge" at the northwest corner of the mammoth Agricultural Hall, festooned with sixty caryatids and containing vast displays of domesticated animals and crops — a harvest cornucopia of America's potential as a farming nation. The other pair of monumental plaster moose rested atop the initial posts of the balustrade for "The Moose Bridge," which spanned a stretch of water to the "Wooded Island" featuring the "Hunters' Cabin," built by Theodore Roosevelt to promote the nascent Boone and Crockett Club, America's first conservation organization, and accommodate its meetings.

While Proctor's *Moose* sculptures on the bridges in Chicago were statements of neither high art nor nature conservation, their proximity to the Agriculture Hall and the Hunters' Cabin associated them with the latter function. One of the souvenir albums that illustrated Proctor's Chicago

Moose claimed it was commonly believed in 1893 that the animals were on the verge of extinction. The declared mandate of the Boone and Crockett Club was to preserve huntable populations of America's game animals, a mission with which the artist was in full accord, and Proctor doubtless felt that his *Moose* symbolized both the glory of one of nature's most eccentric forms and the hope for its continuance as a viable species.

Proctor wrote that these plaster figures were "sullen" creatures, "with shaggy manes, disproportionately long legs, short thick necks and ugly noses."[4] Others were more charitable. One critic was quoted as finding them "very decorative and beautiful, with their immense antlers and long, graceful legs, seen as they are above the spectator and against the deep blue of the sky."[5]

After Pinchot had graduated from Yale University in 1889, he set sail for Europe to study professional forestry. Likewise, when Proctor completed his exposition commission, he also departed for Europe to advance his studies as a sculptor. By 1907 Proctor's skills were fully matured and he felt confident that reworking the old model for the exposition *Moose* would produce good results. He was right: the new bronze succeeded in formally revitalizing Proctor's earlier composition. Further motivation came from the fact that a fellow artist, Henry Shrady, was casting and selling tabletop reductions of his own *Bull Moose* (fig. 89), which had decorated the grounds of the 1901 Pan-American Exposition in Buffalo, New York. Proctor figured there was no reason why he should not share in the popularity of such work.

Proctor was able later to joke about some of his early Chicago works. The *Wichita Evening Eagle* in 1931 quoted Proctor as confessing humorously that while the exposition

work had "started him on his road to fame," he had to admit, "thank goodness," that plasters like *Moose* were "destructible. I thought [the work] was good then but I know now how rotten it was and am glad that it is gone...."[6] That had not stopped him from bringing fresh life and renewed vigor to what, even in its original form, was a remarkable tribute to one of America's most unique animals.

Exhibited: *A. Phimister Proctor*, Montross Gallery, New York, 1908; *Third Annual Exhibition*, Canadian Art Club, Toronto, 1910; *Canadian Art Club Exhibition*, Art Association of Montreal, Montreal, 1910; *Exhibition of Bronzes and Plaster Models by A. Phimister Proctor*, The Gorham Company, New York, 1913; *Small Bronzes by A. Phimister Proctor*, Art Institute of Chicago, Chicago, 1917

Other known versions: R. W. Norton Art Gallery, Shreveport, La. (gift of Richard W. Norton Jr., 1948); Rockwell Museum, Corning, N.Y. (gift of Robert Rockwell, acquired 1964); Brooklyn Museum of Art, Brooklyn, N.Y. (gift of George D. Pratt, 1913)

Variant titles: *Head of Alaska Brown Bear;*
Brown Bear Head; Alaskan Bear's Head;
Alaska Brown Bear Head; Bear Head
Modeled, 1908; cast initially, 1908
Bronze, 6 x 4½ x 6 inches
Markings: "BOONE AND CROCKETT
CLUB/A.P.PROCTOR/COPYRIGHT 1909"
Copyright: None recorded in Proctor's
lifetime, although some castings are
inscribed "COPYRIGHT 1908"; by Nona
Proctor Church as *Boone and Crockett*
Plaque under No. H53496 on
December 1, 1973

A. Phimister Proctor Museum, Poulsbo, Wash.
Photograph by Howard Giske

Fig.90
Bear head on the title page of
A. Pendarves Vivian,*Wanderings in the*
Western Land (1879)

Buffalo Bill Historical Center, Cody, Wyo.;
RB594.V58 1879

Plate 27 Head of Brown Bear

In the late fall of 1908, Proctor held a major solo exhibition
with his prime dealer, N. E. Montross. The show included watercolors, bronzes and plaster sketches, architectural details, and
photographs of monuments — 185 items in all. One of his most
recent creations, a sculptured frontal relief of an Alaskan
brown bear's head, was listed in the catalogue as having been
made for the Boone and Crockett Club of New York that year.[1]

Proctor had been a member of the Boone and Crockett
Club since 1892. As an animalier sculptor at the World's
Columbian Exposition in Chicago and a highly reputed
hunter-sportsman, he had been issued an invitation in
advance of the 1893 fair to a special luncheon at the club's
island, a log cabin retreat in the lagoon. There, as a guest of
Charles Deering, he was initiated into the early conservation
fraternity.[2] After that, whenever possible, Proctor attended
the club's annual banquets and befriended fellow members.
He remained active until the early 1940s.

The club's banquets were traditionally held in December,
so some members may well have made an effort to view
Proctor's 1908 exhibition at the Montross Gallery at 372 Fifth
Avenue. Many members bought bronze castings of the brown
bear over the years, and Dr. C. Hart Merriam of the
Smithsonian Institution recalled that members attending the
1908 banquet received plaster castings of the club's "mascot"
as a gift from the artist.[3]

One review of Proctor's Montross Gallery show suggests
why he was selected by the club for such a commission: "The
chief interest of the exhibition lies in the sculpture of the animals that Mr. Proctor has studied and hunted in their native
lairs...."[4] This was in tune with the club's philosophy, which
reflected Theodore Roosevelt's advocacy of the nationalistic

as well as personal ethos of hunting and nature study.
Roosevelt stressed self-reliance, adventure, manliness, woodcraft, and an appreciation of the wilderness, concluding that
they combined to form the very foundation of democracy.

The relationship between Proctor and the Boone and
Crockett Club remained close and mutually supportive. Other
artists were members of the club, including Albert Bierstadt,
the painter of grand Rocky Mountain landscapes, who was a
charter member, adding his name to the rolls in 1887 when
the organization was founded. The head of his New Brunswick
moose, killed in 1880, was famous in hunting literature of the
day, and he illustrated one of the most widely acclaimed
hunting books of the period, A. Pendarves Vivian's
Wanderings in the Western Land of 1879. The book described a
bear encounter in Colorado's North Park, Proctor's old stomp-
ing grounds, and its title page illustration showed a bear
head mounted on a plaque, a trophy of a western hunt (fig.
90).[5] That bear, unlike Proctor's model, grimaces with a ferocious, fang-baring, almost audible roar.

Proctor's bear faces the viewer straight on. It projects confidence without overt threat, seeming willing to share its world
with the viewer. The artist's tenure with the Boone and Crockett
Club would have taught him the value of that kind of tolerance.

Exhibited: *A. Phimister Proctor*, Montross Gallery, New York,
1908; *Second Annual Exhibition*, Canadian Art Club, Toronto,
1909; *Canadian Art Club Exhibition*, Art Association of
Montreal, Montreal, 1910; *Sculptures by Olin Warner and A.*
Phimister Proctor, Portland Art Association, Portland, Ore.,
1911; *Exhibition of Bronzes and Plaster Models by A. Phimister*
Proctor, The Gorham Company, New York, 1913; Panama-

Pacific Exposition, San Francisco, 1915; *Small Bronzes by A.*
Phimister Proctor, Art Institute of Chicago, Chicago, 1917;
Works in Sculpture By A. Phimister Proctor, Corcoran Gallery of
Art, Washington, D.C., 1918; *Paintings and Sculpture by Four*
Artists of Taos, Art Institute of Chicago, Chicago, 1919 (possi-
bly bronze titled *One Kediac* [sic] *Bear*, no. 31)

Other known versions: A. Phimister Proctor Museum, Poulsbo,
Wash. (Gorham bronze pattern); Grey Towers National Historic
Landmark, Milford, Pa. (gift from Proctor to Gifford Pinchot);
Lowell Baier, Bethesda, Md.; Henry O. Smith III, New York

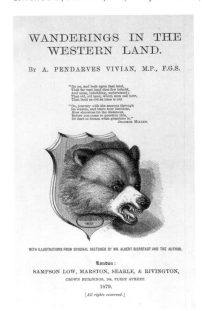

Fig.90

Variant titles: *Bear Cub with Frog; Bear Startled by a Frog*

Modeled, c. 1908; cast initially, c. 1908

Bronze, 6¾ x 6¾ x 12 inches

Markings: "A. P. Proctor/1922"

Copyright: None recorded in Proctor's lifetime (perhaps subsumed under *Cub Bear and Rabbit* of 1895); by Nona Proctor Church under No. H55769 on September 1, 1973

The R. W. Norton Art Gallery, Shreveport, La. (gift of Mrs. Richard W. Norton, 1944)

Plate 28 Bear Cub

Proctor described in his autobiography a hunting and fishing expedition that took place near Denver in 1874 when he was fourteen years old. Late in the day, after he had abandoned rabbit hunting in frustration and taken to the trout stream, he hooked a hefty and lively trout. At that moment the largest grizzly bear he had ever seen or imagined emerged from the woods. The bear made a mock charge at the boy, who fled the stream for his rifle onshore. By the time he grabbed his gun and got it cocked, however, the grizzly had disappeared in the opposite direction. For as long as he lived, that moment perplexed Proctor: Why would a huge bear turn tail and run from such a small boy?[1]

Proctor drew on that experience and other observations while making a series of animal sculptures related to bear cubs. In 1895 he copyrighted a small work that he titled *Cub Bear and Rabbit* (see plate 10) showing a young bear being startled by a tiny rabbit. As early as 1908 Proctor was exhibiting with that work a companion bronze simply titled *Bear Cub*.[2] It is conjectured that this earlier *Bear Cub* was a larger version (twelve inches rather than four and one-half inches high) of the original copyrighted work but without the rabbit: only the cub appeared posed erect on his back legs, with his head cocked over to the right and his forepaws held out to each side. By the early 1920s, the artist had inserted another element into the composition, and *Bear Cub* here shows the curious bear being surprised by a frog.

The immediate inspiration for adding a frog may have come from the popular story of a bear cub named Bruno told in William Lyman Underwood's 1921 book *Wild Brother: Strangest of True Stories from the North Woods*. Bruno was a captive black bear raised by the author. One of Bruno's adventures growing up involved a similar surprise (fig. 91):

Fig.92

Owing to his unusual bringing up, Bruno had never become acquainted with the ordinary animals of the woods and fields, and so I was curious to see what he would do when he met any of them. Down in the garden one day I found a large fat toad, and when Bruno was at lunch I placed the warty creature on the ground beside the saucer from which the cub was taking his food. Being quite hungry, at first he paid no attention to the intruder; but presently, as the saucer became empty, he caught sight of his curious visitor. With a jerk he raised his head, and for a moment, without moving a muscle, gazed in astonishment and with some misgiving at the strange monstrosity in front of him. His natural curiosity, however, soon overcame his doubtful frame of mind; he was a born investigator and this thing must be looked into. Very cautiously he reached forward his paw and ever so gently he touched the curious thing on the back.

The toad did as toads usually do when tickled from behind. It hopped, and with such force that it went quite over the saucer. Simultaneously the bear stood erect. He had a puzzled look of amazement and dismay on his hairy visage; he appeared to be utterly overcome with astonishment. It didn't seem reasonable that an insignificant misshapen creature like that could, with no apparent effort, cover so much ground in one leap. Bruno's paws hung inertly in front of him and his tongue lolled stupidly from his mouth. His breath came in short explosive gasps.[3]

Other anecdotal accounts of bears relating to the curiosities around them appeared in the literature and art of the day. The naturalist artist Ernest Thompson Seton described the lives of both black bears and grizzlies living in Yellowstone National Park in the 1913 book *Wild Animals at Home*.[4] Proctor's New York friend and fellow animal sculptor Edwin Willard Deming modeled a humorous statuette, *Mutual Surprise*, featuring a bear and had it cast in bronze of 1907 (see fig.72). Charles Russell also produced a series of bronzes of grizzly bear mothers and cubs: both *The Lunch Hour* of 1910 and *Oh! Mother, What Is It?* of 1914 (fig. 92) were exhibited at Folsom Galleries, New York, in 1916.[5] In the latter work, two cubs wisely seek the protective counsel of their mother about an approaching porcupine. Very much in the spirit of progressive writers on nature like Seton, Russell anthropomorphized the animals in ways that cultivated popular interest and potential markets. In contrast, Proctor, who had led the way with such interpretations in the mid-1890s, used images like the startled cub to reveal the more tender side of himself.

Exhibited: Presumed to be the *Bear Cub* listed as exhibited at *A. Phimister Proctor*, Montross Gallery, New York, 1908; *Second Annual Exhibition*, Canadian Art Club, Toronto, 1909; *Third Annual Exhibition*, Canadian Art Club, Toronto, 1910; *Small Bronzes by A. Phimister Proctor*, Art Institute of Chicago, Chicago, 1917; *Works in Sculpture by A. Phimister Proctor*, Corcoran Gallery of Art, Washington, D.C., 1918

Other known versions: A. Phimister Proctor Museum, Poulsbo, Wash. (the plaster)

Fig.91

Variant titles: None recorded
Modeled, c. 1908; cast initially,
date unknown
Bronze, 15¾ x 4¼ x 10⅞ inches
Markings: "A.P. Proctor Sc. /Gorham Co.
Founders QGON"
Copyright: None recorded

J. Frank Dobie Collection, Harry Ransom
Humanities Research Center, The University of
Texas at Austin

Fig. 93
Proctor's *Caged Wolf*

A. Phimister Proctor Museum, Poulsbo, Wash.
Photograph by Howard Giske

Plate 29 Wolf

Fig.93

Proctor first met the Texas historian and western folklorist J. Frank Dobie in 1938 when Dobie asked Proctor to sculpt the *Mustangs* (see plate 55) for the University of Texas at Austin. In very short order, that acquaintance evolved into a strong and close personal friendship, built on the high professional regard that they held for one another. In a letter to Dobie's wife, Bertha, written in the spring of 1944, Proctor proudly asserted that Dobie had "taken a place in my life held by only my oldest friends."[1]

Proctor and Dobie carried on a voluminous correspondence through the 1940s. Most of their letters concerned the *Mustangs* and the problematic status of the project over the years, but often they exchanged ideas about politics, society, and art. Dobie at one point acquired a casting of Proctor's bronze *Panther* (see plate 5). In late 1949, only months before the artist's death, Dobie also discovered another of Proctor's sculptures that especially struck his fancy, the *Wolf*. Dobie had just published what is considered one of his classics, *The Voice of the Coyote*, an ecological account of one of the most beleaguered predators of the West. Proctor's *Wolf* must have suggested many of the analogies between wolf and coyote that Dobie had pointed out in his book, including the early Anglo explorer's name for the coyote, "the prairie wolf."[2] Like the coyote, the wolf had suffered from official U.S. government policy to exterminate it. Efforts had been underway since 1915 to eliminate the predator from the entire West. Dobie saw this as a tragic overreaction, and he discussed the wolf's demise in vivid terms in his book on the coyote:

While federally controlled operations — since 1915 — accounted for nearly 2,000,000 coyotes, they accounted for over 30,000 gray wolves (including the lesser red wolves). By 1880, at which time most of the buffaloes had been slaughtered and range cattle were rapidly taking their place, professional wolfers were poisoning and otherwise killing gray wolves — along with coyotes — in enormous numbers. To see a gray wolf on his own range now, a citizen of the United States must go to Mexico or far into Canada, perhaps clear to Alaska. The size and habits of the gray wolf prevent its hiding itself; its power and predatory nature make it intolerable to owners of livestock. The lone lobo, noble in isolation, was as unadapted as the pack.[3]

Dobie had spent several weeks in Montana in 1940 collecting stories on northwestern wildlife. In 1952 he published some of his findings under the title "The Lonest Wolf" in *Outdoor Magazine*.[4] It was the tale of a white wolf, Snowdrift, who survived by cunning and stealth. Like Dobie himself, under pressure from the University of Texas, Snowdrift lived "year in and year out ... on the dodge."[5] When Dobie was fired in 1947 for refusing to conform to university policies, he made do with large research and writing grants, targeting such sizable prey as the Rockefeller Foundation. No doubt Proctor's *Wolf* felt like an autobiographical tribute to Dobie's legendary perseverance and solitude.

"I'm glad you like my wolf," Proctor wrote to Dobie in December 1949. Proctor offered to make arrangements to have a cast made for his friend or to send him the bronze pattern, which the artist had on hand.[6] But a month later the artist passed on some bad news about the *Wolf*. Proctor was willing to see the bronze go to Dobie at cost, but he had been flabbergasted by the casting fees of the postwar years. "I nearly fell over," he told Dobie, "they used to cost $25.00" and now the foundry demanded $173.00."[7]

To provide Dobie with an alternative, Proctor mentioned another version, a wolf in plaster that was stored in Wilton, Connecticut. This was probably the wolf (fig. 93) still owned by the artist's family, a substantially more spirited work. Dobie selected the original version, although there is no evidence as to when it was delivered or how much he ultimately had to pay for it (the second version showed the wolf in a posture of submission and fright, and Dobie no doubt preferred an interpretation portraying the wolf as dominant). At the end of Dobie's story about Snowdrift, the writer tells how a rancher finally shot the lone lobo, whose teeth and hearing had gone with the years. "No hunter," he concluded, "ever outwitted him. Old age and chance combined to end his life."[8] The same could be said for Dobie and his old friend.

It is not known when Dobie's version of the *Wolf* was first made. As part of Proctor's large solo show at the Montross Gallery in 1908, a *Sketch of Wolf* in wax was exhibited.[9] There is no copyright record for this sculpture and no information to show where and how Dobie first saw the *Wolf* of which he ultimately acquired a casting.

Exhibited: *A. Phimister Proctor*, Montross Gallery, New York, 1908 (as *Sketch of Wolf*: wax)

Other known versions: None

Variant titles: *Piney Branch Bridge
Panthers; Sixteenth Street Bridge Tigers*
Modeled, 1908–1909; cast, 1910
Bronze, monumental sculpture
Markings: Signed "Alexander Phimister
Proctor 1910" with foundry marking
"JNO Williams"
Copyright: None recorded
Piney Branch Bridge, also known as
Sixteenth Street Bridge, Washington, D.C.

Photograph courtesy Historical Society of
Washington, D.C.

Plate 30 Piney Branch Tigers

Adorning the first "parabolic arched bridge" in Washington, the *Piney Branch Tigers* was a critical commission for Proctor. It brought national recognition to his work and led to a second commission, the celebrated *Buffalo* for the Q Street Bridge in Washington, D.C. (see plate 34).[1] Originally the colossal bison sculptures that would ultimately embellish the Q Street Bridge were intended to decorate Piney Branch Bridge. As Proctor's friend Gifford Pinchot stated in a letter to Proctor on August 2, 1909, Henry F. B. MacFarland of the District Committee "would greatly prefer bison, and I think he may make a stab in that direction."[2] "The trouble with bison in this case," Proctor practically replied, "is the expense."[3]

As the Piney Branch Bridge sculpture project was also time-sensitive, a group of tigers proved a more efficient solution. Proctor had recently completed his *Tiger Couchant* (see plate 32) for Princeton University, and the models and compositional schemes were still fresh in his mind. This is noted in a letter to Pinchot of July 28, 1909: "I have been studying tigers, & he [W. J. Douglas, Consulting Engineer for the District] wants a position similar to the one I am now doing, so that I could use a lot of material I already have."[4] While being resourceful with time and materials, Proctor also devoted himself to improving the tigers beyond what was originally proposed by the committee. They had suggested that the tigers be made of concrete. The artist offered to do them as bronzes for "about [the] same price as cement," a modification that, according to Proctor, was "one hundred times better." Proctor hoped the embellished tigers would impress civic leaders as well as citizens, thereby making it "easier to get the next job in Washington."[5]

Proctor secured the Piney Branch commission in late 1909, which began under W. J. Douglas, Engineer of Bridges, and then continued under his successor, T. J. C. Bailey.[6] Once the large-scale models were completed, a Washington state

newspaper confirmed that the New York Bridge Commission had looked upon the *Tigers* "favorably" after viewing them in Proctor's studio, and had commented a bit covetously that soon those "who walk and ride about Washington … will have the opportunity … of seeing four bronze tigers of heroic size."[7]

Other newspapers underscored the artist's talent at achieving lifelike accuracy in the sculpting from a feline model that many people had allegedly already seen "behind bars in the animal tent of a great three-ring show that [came to] … Washington once every year." According to the *Evening Star*, Proctor "chose [the] circus tiger because it appeared to him to be the most perfect specimen obtainable." Fantastic tales of the connection between the "circus" beast and its admiring artist circulated from the city engineer's office:

> Proctor found this tiger … and then set about traveling with the [circus] show getting the tiger's poses firmly fixed in his mind and making sketches and models of it. For two months he virtually lived with the circus tiger, finding in it something that the gaping crowds that paid a half dollar to 'get in' never would see — until they coupled the fine beast with the crouching bronzes on the Piney Branch Bridge.[8]

The *New York Herald* reported the more probable story that Proctor had modeled the sculptures after tigers from the zoological park in the Bronx.[9]

Cast for the sum of three thousand dollars, and completed at the same time as his *Tiger Couchant* for Princeton, the plaster models for the *Piney Branch Tigers* had been sent to Jno. Williams & Co. Founders before the winter of 1910.[10] A story from the *Evening Star* — the same article that reported Proctor's rooming with the circus beasts — claimed that the foundry experimented with alloys used for the *Tigers*. "Gold

was tossed into the molten swirl to the value of about $20 to a tiger," apparently making the molten metal flow more readily and thus preventing the bronze from hardening too quickly.[11]

By early 1911 the gracefully posed *Tigers* were complete and ready for installation on the corner parapets of Piney Branch Bridge. Once the "1,550 pound beasts" were dedicated, Washington responded enthusiastically to the bridge's elegant new guardians:

> The four bronze tigers are very nearly alike, except that the artist has caught the waving motion of the tail and fastened it in bronze so that it points inward toward the roadway of the bridge… Most of the detail has been worked out so that it will show the most from the roadway, over which tens of thousands of people pass in a year's time … The District building contract which called for so many tigers at a certain time … fretted and fumed and shuffled papers, made red ink marks and piled up red tape, while the time limit expired. But that made no difference to the artist. He was bound to make those tigers the world's best, and time limit or not, auditors, controllers and musty contracts against him, he was going to finish those tigers so that they would eventually be The Tigers.[12]

Maintaining a prominent position on the world-famous avenue, the *Tigers*, as one critic professed, lent "an appreciable dignity and elegance to the highway."[13]

Exhibited: None known

Other known versions: None

(KCE)

Variant titles: None recorded
Modeled, 1909
Plaster, 9 x 3½ x 7½ inches
Markings: "EXHIBIT A-WHITE
HOU[S]E-FEBY 26-09/TO
PRESIDENT ROOSEVELT/
A.P. PROCTOR 1909"
Copyright: None recorded

Sagamore Hill National Historic Site, National
Park Service, Oyster Bay, N.Y. (gift to Theodore
Roosevelt from the artist, 1909)
Photograph by Marc Witz

Plate 31 Buffalo Head

During the Theodore Roosevelt administration, Senator James McMillan called for a sweeping redesign of what is now the National Mall area in Washington, D.C. His congressionally appointed group, the McMillan Commission, aspired to return the area to a unified architectural statement, with mighty neoclassical buildings and broad vistas replacing a jumble of stylistic intrusions and unplanned natural elements. The commission also dreamed of returning the "White House," as Roosevelt officially dubbed it, to the splendor of its original federal period elegance.

To accommodate the program, First Lady Edith Roosevelt secured the services of the architect Charles Follen McKim of the New York firm McKim, Meade and White. A member of the McMillan Commission, McKim was the leading American proponent of classicism in architecture. McKim's orders were to revamp and reshape the White House in the classical manner. The year was 1902 and he was given six months to complete the work.[1]

Among the many changes resulting from this return to the architectural idiom of antiquity was the fireplace in the State Dining Room. Redesigned in the style of a Georgian country house, the room featured polished wood-paneled walls relieved by boldly fluted, square pilasters topped with Corinthian capitals. The centerpiece of the room, a New England limestone mantel that measured seven feet high, focused attention on the fireplace, the symbolic essence of the home. Above the hearth rose two graceful serpentine stone pilasters, which were capped below the mantelpiece by animal heads in relief. High above the fireplace, flanking it on either side, were mounted specimens of the hunt: a huge stuffed moose and two bighorn sheep. They had been provided

Fig.94

not by Roosevelt, famous for his exploits with the rifle, but by an interior decorator friend of the family, William Hart.[2]

The mantel, as installed in 1902, originally incorporated lion heads in the upper right and left corners. President Roosevelt expressed displeasure with the lions because they were not indigenous to the United States. He preferred decorations that would reflect native wildlife and so requested that the lions be substituted with buffalo heads. Proctor, a friend of both McKim and Roosevelt, was selected to sculpt a suitable replacement. Once this was completed, which according to most accounts took place in 1902, the Beaux-Arts mantel with western motifs was given the name of the "Buffalo Mantel" (fig. 94).[3]

Proctor's autobiography dates this modification to the State Dining Room fireplace as 1909, rather than 1902. Noting that he was engaged by Roosevelt just before the president left the White House, he added that the president was pleased by the design Proctor conceived and that Proctor, with the small buffalo head model in hand (probably the one pictured here and dated "FEBY 26-09"), was then presented to the National Art Commission.[4] Two subsequent letters to Proctor dated February 1909 — one from William Loeb Jr., the president's secretary, and the other from Roosevelt himself — are less enthusiastic. Loeb wrote on February 1 that the president wanted to know when the heads would "be put into the mantels in the state dining room in the White House. He thinks the work should be hurried up." And at the end of the month, when the work had evidently not been completed as promised, the president's impatience found furious expression:

Am greatly chagrined and disappointed at your failure to have work ready. It is a distinct breach of promise on your

part. You should have it here without fail on Friday morning. Under no consideration must you have it later. I am very greatly disappointed that you should have failed to keep your agreement.   Theodore Roosevelt[5]

What caused the delay is not known. The president was scheduled to leave office in March 1909, which may explain his anger. In any event, the artist and Roosevelt later mended their fences.

The Buffalo Mantel was less fortunate. Between 1949 and 1952, when the White House again underwent major remodeling, the stone mantel was replaced by a "simply designed Verde-antique marble mantel" that the Renovation Commission felt more suitably reflected modern tastes.[6] According to the president at the time, Harry S. Truman, the commission acted cavalierly:

When the White House was renovated during my administration the Congressional Committee who handled the renovation of the Executive Mansion went ahead with plans as set out by Congress and did not inform me of the changes they planned to make.

During the renovation that mantel ... was thrown out on the junk pile by the Renovation Commission. I rescued it and kept it until my Library here in Independence was built and had it brought here and that is where I intend to keep it.[7]

The Buffalo Mantel resides today in the Harry S. Truman Library Museum, where it has been placed on permanent display. A replica eventually found its way back into the White House in 1962 when President and Mrs. John F. Kennedy restored the State Dining Room fireplace. Two craftsmen,

Guido Ratti and Alex Salvioli, copied the McKim mantel with the Proctor buffalo relief embellishments. Roosevelt's daughter, Mrs. Nicholas Longsworth, attended the rededication and said she had been there in 1902 when, as she recalled, the original mantel had been set in place. She remembered how important it had been to her father "that there should be an American animal on the mantel" in that room.[8]

The bison head shown here was conceptually modified by Proctor nearly twenty years later when he was working on the heroic-sized keystone reliefs for Washington's Arlington Memorial Bridge (plate 48). The bridge had also been part of the McMillan Commission's plan to return the nation's capital to the look of Pierre L'Enfant's eighteenth-century design.

Exhibited: *Exhibition of Bronzes and Plaster Models by A. Phimister Proctor*, The Gorham Company, New York, 1913 (plaster)

Other known versions: Limestone reliefs at the Harry S. Truman Library Museum, Independence, Mo. (gift of President Harry S. Truman, 1957)

Variant titles: *Princeton Tiger*
Modeled, 1908–1909; cast, 1912
Bronze, 9⅜ x 2⅝ x 4 inches
Markings: "A. P. PROCTOR 1912/C/
PRINCETON TIGER/79/GORHAM CO.
FOUNDERS/C454"
Copyright: By Alexander Phimister
Proctor under No. G42747 on
January 15, 1913

© The Cleveland Museum of Art, 2003
Gift of Mrs. Henry A. Everett for the Dorothy Burnham
Everett Memorial Collection, 1923.734

Plate 32 Tiger Couchant

In mid-April 1909, the *Denver Rocky Mountain News* published a lengthy article on Proctor, "an old Denver boy and now one of the leading sculptors in New York." In discussing the artist, the writer observed that "perhaps nothing he has done yet will give him more permanent and popular fame than his selection to design two tigers to guard the steps of Nassau Hall at Princeton University."[1] Proctor had contracted with a group of Princeton alumni on February 1 of that year to produce two monumental tigers in bronze. The dedication was slated for April 1910.[2]

As with all of Proctor's work, the first task for him was finding the appropriate model. After considerable searching through available zoos, the sculptor happened upon just the right tiger at Madison Square Garden. There among the caged and performing animals of the Ringling Brothers Circus was a prize Bengal tiger named Jerry. The engagement of artist with beast produced an immediate burst of publicity for both Proctor and the circus. The Ringling Brothers press agent, a Mr. Brady, made special arrangements for the sculptor to have lengthy sittings with Jerry. Crowds soon came to watch the artist at work, creating something of a sideshow for circus visitors.

Jerry proved to be the perfect model in most respects, but there were troubles as well:

Mr. Proctor couldn't say enough for the symmetry of Jerry. The only trouble with him was that he was a poor poser. Whenever Jerry struck a particularly appropriate posture, with both paws extended and head raised as if scenting the approach of a jungle foe, the plastaline would fly under Mr. Proctor's fingers until Jerry would tire of the proceedings and indulge in a yawn as he rolled over on his

back. Right there was the trouble Mr. Proctor explained. If he would only keep still the two-foot model could be finished in a hurry, but as it is the sculptor is afraid he will have to follow the circus for the next month or so.[3]

By November 1909 Proctor had progressed far enough with the two models to allow art critic Royal Cortissoz a look. "For a certain breadth and dignity, richly imbued with life, I think they are the best," Cortissoz wrote in *Scribner's* shortly after visiting Proctor's studio. With their linear clarity, their elegant yet powerful silhouette, their harmonious balance as an ensemble, and their bold treatment of structural massing of form, these dual portraits of Jerry reached a zenith in the artist's work to that date. "Though his tigers are recumbent and immobile with the placidity suiting their decorative purpose," wrote Cortissoz, "they are sentient bodies with a kind of grim vitality made manifest in their heavy yet lithe forms."[4]

According to Proctor's autobiography, the two *Tigers Couchant* were dedicated at Princeton on Commencement Day of 1909.[5] Perhaps the plasters were temporarily placed on the steps for the occasion, but not the big bronzes. The *New York Herald* on June 11, 1910, remarked that the pieces had not yet been cast in bronze, and a letter to Proctor from William A. Day of the Gorham Company dated June 17, 1910, stated that the casting of the tigers would be completed in "eight weeks from receipt of the last model."[6]

The *Tigers Couchant* were gifts to Princeton from the class of 1879. They replaced a pair of cast-iron lions that, in increasingly dilapidated condition, first guarded the front steps of the university's venerated Nassau Hall. The bronzes are slightly different, each with the opposite leg and paw extended. A few years after the two works were finally installed,

another art critic, Charles H. Caffin, commented again on the special "nobility" of Proctor's tigers, with their powerful "masses and contour lines." "Long after one has admired the lifelike quality" of these cats, he concluded, "one can continue to be absorbed by [their] artistic grandeur."[7]

Proctor later produced two smaller versions of the *Tiger Couchant, Pose #1*, one nearly two feet long and another slightly over nine inches in length. The first casting of the larger of the two reductions, made from the original models, was presented to President Woodrow Wilson in June 1914. A casting of the smaller reduction went to the first lady.[8] Princeton used the other castings, like the one shown here, for alumni promotion and fund-raising, and Proctor enjoyed continued acclaim and profits from their sales over the years.

Exhibited: *Third Annual Exhibition*, Canadian Art Club, Toronto, 1910 (plaster cast); *Canadian Art Club Exhibition*, Art Association of Montreal, Montreal, 1910 (working models for both poses); *Fourth Annual Exhibition*, Canadian Art Club, Toronto, 1911 (both models); *Sculptures by Olin Warner and A. Phimister Proctor*, Portland Art Association, Portland, Ore., 1911 (both models); *Exhibition of Bronzes and Plaster Models by A. Phimister Proctor*, The Gorham Company, New York, 1913 (reduction); Century Club, New York, 1913 (as *Tiger in Bronze*); *Seventh Annual Exhibition*, Canadian Art Club, Toronto, 1914; *Contemporary American Sculpture*, Buffalo Fine Arts Academy, Albright Art Gallery, Buffalo, N.Y., 1916; *Twenty-ninth Annual Exhibition of American Oil Paintings and Sculpture*, Art Institute of Chicago, Chicago, 1916 (reduction); *Small Bronzes by A. Phimister Proctor*, Art Institute of Chicago, Chicago, 1917 (both sizes of reduction); *Works in Sculpture by A. Phimister Proctor*, Corcoran Gallery of Art, Washington,

D.C., 1918 (both sizes of reduction); A. Phimister Proctor, Stendahl Art Gallery, Los Angeles, 1923; National Sculpture Society, New York, 1923 (plasters of both poses)

Other known versions: *Small version*: Gifford Proctor, Wilton, Conn.; R. W. Norton Art Gallery, Shreveport, La. (gift of Richard W. Norton Jr., 1942); Cleveland Museum of Art, Cleveland (Dorothy Burnham Everett Memorial Collection, acquired 1925); A. Phimister Proctor Museum, Poulsbo, Wash.; Lowell Baier, Bethesda, Md. *Large version*: Brooklyn Museum of Art, Brooklyn, N.Y. (gift of George D. Pratt, 1914); Nels Westman, Capitola, Calif. (through inheritance in 1970); A. Phimister Proctor Museum, Poulsbo, Wash. (a plaster cast, probably one of the original maquettes of *Tiger Couchant, Pose #2*)

Variant titles: *Lions of the Desert;*
Lions Panel
Modeled, 1911; cast initially, 1911
Bronze, 75 x 2¼ x 36½ inches
Markings: "Alexander Phimister
Proctor/MCMX1"
Copyright: None recorded

Portland Art Museum, Portland, Ore. (bequest
of Wilson B. Ayer)

Fig.95
Proctor with *Lions,* New York, 1912

A. Phimister Proctor Museum Archives,
Poulsbo, Wash.

Plate 33 Lions

Quite often Proctor regarded his travels as a combination of relaxation, artistic inspiration, recreation, family bonding, and patron development. In the fall of 1911, he toured the West. His stops included a sketching trip to the Stoney Agency of western Canada, where he was joined by his friend the Toronto painter Edmund Morris, a hunting trip in British Columbia, a roam through a bison preserve near Wainwright, Canada, a visit with family in Seattle, and a prospecting-for-patrons swing into Portland. When he returned to New York in early November, he wrote to his fellow explorer Morris that he "had a bully time," gathering both creative fuel and economic encouragement along the way. "I made enough in two weeks," he wrote in a postscript about his time in Seattle and Portland, "... to pay my expenses several times and brought order[s] for $4,500.00. Not so worse for a Canadian."[1]

The primary order Proctor referred to in the letter was for "a relief of lions, 6 ft. 3 in.," a casting of which he hoped to send to the 1912 Canadian Art Club exhibition in Toronto the next February. Wilson B. Ayer, a trustee of the Portland Art Association and chairman of the museum's collections committee, had commissioned it.[2] That order, combined with the Portland Art Association's earlier exhibition and subsequent purchase of a large *Indian Warrior* bronze (see plate 12), led Proctor to pronounce Oregon's largest city the veritable center for art activity in the Pacific Northwest. Portland "has the breadth and breeziness of the West with the taste and culture of the East," he told a reporter from the *Portland Oregonian*.[3] Proctor found its gracious and enlightened attitude toward art unprecedented among western cities.

In conceptualizing his large lion relief for Ayer, Proctor relied on the successful formula used in his *Moose Family* (see plate 19), sculpted earlier for Gifford Pinchot. *Lions* commands

authority with its series of strong, overlapping forms and contrasting textures. The powerful hindquarters and interlaced tails of the lion and two lionesses counterbalance the high head and mane of the lead figure. The focused stares of all three great cats project the kinetic force established by the patterned profusion of legs crowding the lower third of the composition.

Proctor had himself photographed before the finished plaster sometime in 1912 (fig. 95). His fixed gaze and firmly set mouth show the American hunter-artist as comparable to the king of the beasts, Africa's supreme artist of the hunt. The bond is at once immediate and compelling.

The plaster relief appeared in exhibitions of Proctor's work in the years following the bronze's installation over a mantel in the Ayer family home in Portland. When the plaster was shown in Proctor's large solo show at the Gorham Company galleries in New York in the fall of 1913, it was noted as possessing a different quality from other of his animal sculptures. "It is only occasionally here that one feels the sense of convention," wrote the critic William B. McCormick after touring the exhibit.[4] He found that convention in the bas-relief *Lions.* Another critic, Charles H. Caffin, made the same observation. Proctor's characteristic naturalism here achieved a happy balance with the artistic. As he wrote:

These creatures do not show either the restlessness or the drowsy stupidity, equally pitiable of the caged beasts. Magnificently self-composed, yet alert to every sound and scent, they are noble in the ease of their untrammeled freedom. But they exhibit an enhanced nobility, product of the sculptor's own possession of artistic control and liberty, which gives this relief a durable aesthetic value.[5]

Thus, for the city in Oregon that he considered the most aesthetically spirited of any in the West, Proctor had produced one of his most purely artistic works. Appropriately, Ayer willed the *Lions* to the Portland Art Museum in 1935. Unfortunately, within a generation its artistic merits had ceased to be appreciated. The museum's director, Francis J. Newton, felt that the bronze might be more suitable as adjunct decoration, or what was referred to as "shared attention with elephants," and saw to its removal from the gallery and its placement on an exterior wall of the "feline house" of the Portland zoo.[6] There it suffered considerable neglect. According to a conservation survey undertaken by the museum thirty-six years after the initial loan, the unprotected bronze had been spattered with mortar and paint, and had lost the chroma of its original patina through corrosion and oxidation. In 1998 the museum, under the guidance of its curator of American art, Prudence Roberts, retrieved the monumental bronze panel, ordered proper conservation treatment, and reinstalled the piece in an outdoor sculpture garden. Proctor's city of "taste and culture" had reclaimed one of its early art treasures.

Exhibited: *Sixth Annual Exhibition,* Canadian Art Club, Toronto, 1913; *Exhibition of Bronzes and Plaster Models by A. Phimister Proctor,* The Gorham Company, New York, 1913 (as a plaster); Panama-Pacific Exposition, San Francisco, 1915; National Sculpture Society, New York, 1923 (as a "colored plaster")

Other known versions: A. Phimister Proctor Museum, Poulsbo, Wash. (plaster model and at least one sketch)

Fig.95

Variant titles: *Q Street Bridge Buffalo,*
Buffalo I, Buffalo II
Modeled, c. 1911; cast, 1913
Bronze, monumental sculpture
Markings: "A PHIMISTER PROCTOR/1913"
Copyright: By Alexander Phimister Proctor,
registered in the name of Mrs. A. Phimister
Proctor, *Buffalo I* (Pose #1), on April 4, 1913,
under No. G43654, and *Buffalo II* (Pose #2),
under G43655. Buffalo in bronze for bridge
in Washington, D.C. In 1973, Nona Proctor
Church reproduced this work in smaller
scale and on a base, as well as figurine size,
under H53098.
Q Street Bridge, Washington, D.C.
(Georgetown)

Plate 34 Buffalo

By the end of the 1800s the United States government had declared the western frontier closed, as natural resources including the buffalo were rapidly depleting. Even so, America emphatically held on to the dream of the West, and, as a result, this dream was openly symbolized in the art of this time. Above all, the huge and wooly buffalo became the popular emblem of this nostalgic past as America entered the twentieth century. The spirit of the American West that the buffalo embodies is certainly evident in Proctor's massive and most celebrated work *Buffalo,* created for the Q Street Bridge located in the Georgetown neighborhood of Washington, D.C.

During the late 1890s the land surrounding Q Street was approved for survey in preparation for its extension over Rock Creek. This real estate transaction was "proposed to span [the water] with a magnificent iron bridge of the latest design and construction, thus bringing in direct communication the very desirable ... section of Washington with one of the choicest sections of Georgetown."[1] Consequently, while the practical matter was to connect the affluent neighborhood to downtown Washington, of equal importance to the community — specifically the women of the community — was the aesthetic quality of the bridge. As recorded in a hearing regarding the approval of the proposed bridge for Rock Creek, on January 25, 1905, a representative stated to the commissioners: "I am here to represent not the men of Georgetown, but the ladies...."[2] Indeed, it was the tenacious Georgetown ladies who for years wrote voluminous letters, some in poetic verse, to U.S. senators beseeching their help to acquire the bridge.[3] It was also these women who took the petition door-to-door, acquiring signatures from the predominantly male homeowners.[4]

Eventually, the city responded to the requests of Georgetown by approving the bridge project. To design and build the expanse, the commissioners chose Glen Brown and his son, Bedford, who together formed an architectural team known for their restoration efforts of the area's historic sites. This proposed undertaking proved challenging as the connecting streets were parallel but differed by "about 185 feet" in alignment, which meant the bridge itself would have to be curved. In an interview with *The American Architect*, Glen Brown later admitted: "As there are few curved bridges in the world, it was difficult to get the Engineer Department to agree to [the] plan."[5]

It was most likely the city's Fine Arts Commission that collectively chose Proctor to create the large-scale sculptures. He was certainly a plausible choice. Widely acclaimed for his sculptural works depicting American subjects, Proctor was already a hit in Washington with his bronze *Tigers* of the Piney Branch Bridge (see plate 30), which had been installed only a few years prior to the Q Street commission. The architectural team stood "determined to give the carving in other portions of the structure an American character" and included fifty-six Indian-head reliefs to decorate the span of the bridge.[6] The reliefs were designed by the concrete sculptor and innovator John Joseph Earley.[7] Like Proctor's *Buffalo*, the Indian heads, modeled after the famous Sioux Chief Kicking Bear, known for his tours with Buffalo Bill Cody's Wild West shows, symbolized the American West.

Once Proctor set to work on the sculptures, his first task was finding a model. In the fall of 1911, he visited Wainwright, a buffalo sanctuary in Alberta, with the dual purpose to "look over the herd of buffaloes on the 200,000 acre game preserve" and do a little duck hunting.[8] Here, Proctor would become

reacquainted with the bison, producing several sketches to take back to his New York studio. According to one newspaper account, the buffalo from Wainwright that Proctor used as his model was a "Western type, [that] ... differs much from Black Diamond or Toby, the famous Central Park buffalo," which decorated the buffalo nickel by James Earle Fraser.[9]

Something of a champion of the buffalo, Proctor demonstrated his affinity with the western animal in earlier versions of this subject, as with *Buffalo* of 1897, which he exhibited in Paris during the spring of 1898 at the National Sculpture Society's *Third Annual Exhibition*. Some years earlier, Proctor's Chicago experience and his association with Edward Kemeys — who had sculpted his monumental *Bison* that adorned the grounds of the World's Columbian Exposition — were obvious influences for the Q Street *Buffalo*. Like Kemeys' commanding bison, Proctor's Q Street *Buffalo* of 1913 conveys a naturalistic style reflective of the creature's strength and resilience. Yet Proctor's *Buffalo* delivers a dynamic punch generated by the curvilinear repetitions of mass and bulk, precisely textured and playfully topped off by a tail with an upward flip.

When Proctor first set to work on the models for *Buffalo I* and *Buffalo II*, he soon found their size to be problematic, not only in terms of acquiring funds to pay for such a casting, but with regard to housing them. He found it necessary "to build a studio for the buffaloes, as there was none available in [New York] large enough...."[10] Several letters between Mark Brooke, the Acting Engineer Commissioner for the city, and Proctor discuss the duplication of the full-size model made for the Q Street Bridge and Proctor's need for payment — insurance and studio space were important factors. Proctor insistently wrote in one letter, "I have built up these two full size figures at great expense to me, and naturally am much in need of money — I would be greatly obliged if you would forward check as soon as convenient."[11]

As anticipated, Proctor received support and soon completed the models. During a winter day in January 1914, he opened his studio and invited the public to see his completed models. When nearly three hundred people came to his reception, Proctor said he was "surprised that [the] old bull bison would bring out so many New Yorkers."[12] Ultimately, the full-size models were cast in one piece at the Henry-Bonnard Bronze Company in Mount Vernon, New York. The two *Buffalo* were often touted in newspapers as the "largest single casting of bronze ever made in the United States."[13] The equally hefty price tag to cast such large works was estimated by the Anton Kunst Art and Architectural Bronze Foundry at the cost of $4,500 each.[14]

Following the opening of the Q Street Bridge, historian R. W. Shufeldt wrote on the subject of zoological statuary in the capital city. He declared that Americans "should like to see immortalized our Native American fauna, in connection with which the pioneer history of the United States has developed." During Proctor's lifetime, few of Washington's public spaces were decorated with indigenous animal subjects other than eagles. A champion of Proctor's profoundly American *Buffalo*, Shufeldt concluded that:

Mr. Proctor does not let what is natural in form and pose be overruled by the principles of conventionalism in art ... [they] are sculptured or cast so close to nature that their grandeur and naturalness impress all beholders favorably.... And it is to be fervently hoped when Washington comes to repeat

such work ... that it will prove to be an exposition of all that constitutes a correct conception of zoological and anatomical facts....[15]

Nearly one hundred years later, Proctor's impressive *Buffalo* continue to tower over the capital city's commuters and pedestrians as they cross Q Street Bridge. Dually reinforcing the demise of the "real" West, yet assuring the preservation of the dreams invoked by such American symbols, Proctor's *Buffalo* represent more than American fauna — they represent the historic West, a vital ingredient in the formation of America's national heritage.

While there are no known versions of *Buffalo II*, several smaller castings of *Buffalo I*, which measure about thirteen inches in height, were made in 1912 by Gorham Company Founders. One of these was given to the artist's friend and patron, George D. Pratt of New York, who later contributed it to the Cleveland Museum of Art. Pratt also donated a similar cast to the Toledo Museum of Art. And, in 1964, the Gorham Corporation gifted a casting to the collections of the university gallery at the University of Delaware. In addition to the Gorham bronzes, the Roman Bronze Works foundry produced two known casts in 1913. Pratt, who seems to have favored this particular work regardless of foundry, purchased one of them to donate to the Brooklyn Museum of Art. The other is on loan to the Denver Art Museum from St. Hubert's Giralda, Madison, New Jersey. In 1973, the artist's daughter, Nona Proctor Church, reproduced the piece in a smaller scale with a base using the title of *Q Street Buffalo*, adapted from an early model, and in a figurine size as *Q Street Study Buffalo*.

Exhibited: All shows exhibited works cast from smaller versions of *Buffalo I* (facing left) except the winter exhibition, National Academy of Design, New York, 1912, where the full-size "Buffalo, Working Model for Q Street Bridge" was exhibited as no. 137; *Sixth Annual Exhibition,* Canadian Art Club, 1913; Frazier Book Store, Pendleton, Ore., 1914; Annual exhibition, National Academy of Design, 1914; *Twenty-ninth Annual Exhibition of American Oil Paintings and Sculpture*, Art Institute of Chicago, Chicago, 1916; *Small Bronzes by A. Phimister Proctor*, Art Institute of Chicago, Chicago, 1917; *Works in Sculpture by A. Phimister Proctor,* Corcoran Gallery of Art, Washington, D.C., 1918; Army Air Forces Convalescent Center and Station Hospital, Pawling, N.Y. 1944

Other known versions: St. Hubert's Giralda, Madison, N.J., on loan to the Denver Art Museum, Denver; Toledo Museum of Art, Toledo, Ohio (gift of George D. Pratt, 1927); A. Phimister Proctor Museum, Poulsbo, Wash. (plaster and bronze); Indianapolis Museum of Art, Indianapolis (acquired in 1921, General Fund); Collection of Arthur Phelan, Chevy Chase, Md.; Collection of the University Gallery, University of Delaware (gift of the Gorham Corporation, 1964); Art Institute of Chicago, Chicago (gift of George D. Pratt, 1927); Brooklyn Museum of Art, Brooklyn, N.Y. (gift of George D. Pratt); Gilcrease Museum, Tulsa, Okla. (Cole Collection); Cleveland Museum of Art, Cleveland (gift of George D. Pratt, 1927); Metropolitan Museum of Art, New York (bequest of Jacob Ruppert, 1939); Elvehjem Museum of Art, University of Wisconsin, Madison (provenance unknown); Cosmos Club, Washington, D.C.
(KCE)

Variant titles: None recorded
Modeled, 1914; cast initially, 1915
Bronze, 21½ x 9¼ x 28½ inches
Markings: "A.P. PROCTOR
C1915/ROMAN BRONZE WORKS N.Y."
Copyright: By Alexander Phimister
Proctor under No. G50117 on July 8, 1915
Denver Public Library, Denver

Plate 35 Buckaroo

On July 8, 1915, Proctor copyrighted his first bronze celebrating the American cowboy. He titled it *Buckaroo*, a term used in the common parlance of the Northwest to describe cowboys, especially those who rode and broke wild horses. In his autobiography Proctor acknowledged that this was his second attempt to produce an equestrian cowboy sculpture: "I had made one in plaster for the Columbian Exposition in Chicago twenty years before."[1] What he now had in mind, however, was dramatically different in pose and (at least to begin with) in scale. The result would be one of Proctor's most successful and popular works.

In pursuit of this second cowboy sculpture, Proctor decided in the fall of 1914 to visit Pendleton, Oregon, and take in the annual rodeo. He had spent the summer with his wife, Margaret, on the Cheyenne Indian reservation in Montana, followed by a trip to Portland where he filled commissions for several portraits. These included bas-relief bronzes of Colonel Charles Erskine Scott Wood, his daughter Lisa, and the young Martin Biddle.

The Pendleton Round-Up was in its fourth year and already enjoyed a national reputation. Fellow artist Herbert Dunton had written about it in *Scribner's* that spring, comparing it with the Cheyenne Frontier Days rodeo and the popular old Wild West shows that once toured America. As rodeos went, Pendleton was one of the "more pretentious affair[s]" in Dunton's mind.[2] The writer Charles Wellington Furlong was also in Pendleton that fall, planning to write a book on the Round-Up, an event that he called the "greatest of all human shows ... a magnificent three-day cowboy carnival ... in which the Old West stalks before one in the flesh."[3] The scene was rich with reminders of Proctor's early years in Colorado.

Proctor was especially impressed with the horses, supplied mostly by Bill Switzler, a local rancher from the Umatilla area. The wild horses at Pendleton were, in Furlong's estimation, a particularly unruly bunch. They milled and churned around the corral, "shy, fighting, biting, kicking, squealing, cautious and cunning as the coyotes with whom they had been reared" on the eastern Oregon range. Next in unruliness were the buckers, horses that in the Northwest were as well-known as Ty Cobb and Babe Ruth.[4] The most authoritative voice on the buckers was a tall, thin local wrangler and buckaroo named Bill ("Slim") Ridings. He helped Furlong distinguish individuals among the fierce assemblage of horseflesh: Long Tom was heavy, like a plowhorse, but defied even the best cowboys, while Angel was a devil horse in disguise. Ridings also pointed out a white-faced black horse, Hot Foot, that "chills 'em when he stalls skyward and then volplanes down."[5]

Proctor soon knew the scene well, making sketches of many of the horses. "I used Angel, Grandma, Long Tom and Hot Foot," he later mused to a Portland reporter, although the finished sculpture had "more of Long Tom in it than any of the other horses."[6] This was a preference he shared with Ridings, who described the "big, heavy-built, dark sorrel" as "[the] king of 'em all."[7]

In fact Proctor went on to select Ridings as the model for his rider (fig. 96). While Ridings did not win the riding title that year, an honor that went instead to a fellow named Red Parker, he proved to be perfect for Proctor's needs. What Proctor required of Ridings was repeated performances in front of the barn studio that had been assigned to him. As described to a reporter, Proctor's artistic process was "quite simple ... when you want to get a figure of a cowboy on a

Fig.96
Bill ("Slim") Ridings

A. Phimister Proctor Museum Archives,
Poulsbo, Wash.

Fig.97
A photograph acquired by Proctor at
the Pendleton Round-Up, Pendleton,
Oregon, c. 1914

A. Phimister Proctor Museum Archives,
Poulsbo, Wash.

bucking horse, you get a cowboy and put him on the horse and then let them buck past the door of your studio."[8]

Proctor also sketched voraciously, and sometimes precariously, in and around the arena. He took or acquired photographs of the events that suggested poses for the statue he had in mind (fig. 97).

The people of Pendleton treated Proctor like a celebrity. The local *East Oregonian* announced his mission with great fanfare; according to Proctor, "since sculptors were then quite a novelty in eastern Oregon, I was almost considered an exhibit myself."[9] The admiration was mutual. The event organizers and the artist both benefited from the resulting publicity. A similar association had formed between Charles Russell and the Calgary Stampede beginning in 1912. The renown won by Russell during a few years of collaboration with the Canadian show eventually opened the way to international patronage that included the Royal Family and a 1914 exhibition of his work in London.[10] Unlike Russell, though, Proctor found the dusty western rodeo town appealing for itself. Asked later how he felt about eastern Oregon, he would reply, "This is an artist's country. It is the natural haunt for creators."[11] So pleased was he with the Pendleton ambiance that he telegrammed Margaret in New York to pack up and come west. The family rented a house in Pendleton and spent the whole winter there.

Proctor began work on the *Buckaroo* in the late fall of 1914. On November 12, though, the Proctor home and studio suffered substantial damage by fire, destroying personal effects as well as many of the artist's tools. In addition, the *Pendleton East Oregonian* lamented, "the start which he made upon the figure of a bucking horse was completely

burned."[12] In all the loss totaled between $500 and $1,000, a shock that would have set back all but the most resilient characters.[13] Within a week of the fire, however, Proctor was exhibiting his latest work, some of it tinged with smoke, at the Frazier Book Store in Pendleton. He wanted the town to know what he had accomplished since his arrival.

Proctor started again on the *Buckaroo* in December. In July 1915 he presented what was probably a plaster casting in Seattle at the Washington State Art Association galleries. Lillian Tingle, a critic for Portland's *Morning Oregonian* would announce later in the month that Proctor and his new statuette had moved to Portland. The *Buckaroo*, she observed, was "full of verve and action, both horse and man typically American, typically Western." She continued, "Yet even when, as in 'The Buckaroo,' the sculptor is primarily concerned with the expression of action, he never loses the rare sense of decorative beauty which is characteristic of his more monumental works."[14] No matter how far west Proctor went, he never abandoned the essential lessons in the Beaux-Arts ideal learned from his Paris instructors and Augustus Saint-Gaudens.

Tingle's sense of the monumentality of the *Buckaroo* proved prophetic. When in late July 1915 Proctor returned to Pendleton and displayed a plaster model of the statuette at the Frazier Book Store, the local paper excited its readership by proclaiming that a heroic-sized bronze version had been proposed for the town.[15] But it was the city of Denver that eventually took an interest in the work, which would find its full expression as a monument in Colorado's capital (see *Broncho Buster*, plate 41). A few days after its showing at the bookstore, Proctor shipped the *Buckaroo* to New York for further casting. Because it had, according to the *Pendleton*

Fig.96

Tribune, "created a furor in art circles," the townsfolk looked forward to the following summer when it would return as a bronze.[16] Yet the *Buckaroo* returned to Oregon somewhat sooner and with greater impact when a bronze casting found its way to the Portland Art Museum in early November 1915 and another was sent to the Oregon Pavilion of the Panama-Pacific Exposition in San Francisco. In California the *Buckaroo* was unveiled with a flourish from beneath an American flag, while Proctor was claimed as an Oregon artist and his bucking horse bronze as a true testament to the state's cultural ascendancy.[17] "It reflects no little glory on Oregon in general," wrote an admiring writer from Pendleton.[18]

Proctor cast the *Buckaroo* both at the Gorham Company, where the casts were priced at $240 in 1917, and at Roman Bronze Works. One of the Gorham casts, possibly the one recorded as completed on September 15, 1915, graced the galleries of the Art Institute of Chicago in the solo exhibition of Proctor's works presented there in 1917.[19] The ledger books of Roman Bronze Works reveal that they produced seven bronzes between 1916 and 1917, so the *Buckaroo* appears to have sold well.[20] Proctor's account books record two later sales of this work, one in 1932 to George D. Pratt as a gift for Amherst College at a special price of $375 and the other in 1935 to Ernest Quantrell at another special price of $400. (Casting costs at Roman Bronze Works in 1935 were $210, and the normal retail prices ranged from $450 to $475.)[21]

Exhibited: Frazier Book Store, Pendleton, Ore., 1915 (plaster); Washington State Art Association, Seattle, 1915 (plaster); Panama-Pacific Exposition, San Francisco, 1915; *Small Bronzes by A. Phimister Proctor,* Art Institute of Chicago, Chicago, 1917; *Works in Sculpture by A. Phimister Proctor,* Corcoran Gallery of Art, Washington, D.C., 1918; *A. Phimister Proctor,* Stendahl Art Gallery, Los Angeles, 1923

Other known versions: George Gund Collection of Western Art, Princeton, N.J.; Oregon Historical Society, Portland, Ore. (bequest of Charles S. Jackson, 1958); Mead Museum of Art, Amherst College, Amherst, Mass. (gift of George D. Pratt, 1932); John L. Wehle Gallery of Sporting Art, Genesee Country Village and Museum, Mumford, N.Y. (acquired 1990); Michael Greenbaum, Paradise Valley, Ariz. (acquired 1998); Metropolitan Museum of Art, New York (bequest of George D. Pratt, 1935); R. W. Norton Art Gallery, Shreveport, La. (gift of Richard W. Norton, 1946); Britt Brown, Wichita, Kans.; Thomas A. Petrie, Denver; A. Phimister Proctor Museum, Poulsbo, Wash. (two plasters from Roman Bronze Works)

Fig.97

Variant titles: *Iron Tail; Iron Tails; Iron Tail: Head Chief of the Sioux Indians; Indian Bust — "Chief Irontail"; Indian Head: Iron Tail*
Modeled, 1914; cast initially, 1914
Bronze, 18 x 9½ x 25 inches
Markings: "A.P. Proctor/1914/Gorham Co. Founders"
Copyright: By Alexander Phimister Proctor under No. G47278 on July 25, 1914

Henry O. Smith III, New York
(acquired 2001)

Fig.98
Alexander Phimister Proctor
Iron Tail (sketch), c. 1914
Bronze, 5½ x 7⅛ inches
Gilcrease Museum, Tulsa, Okla.

Plate 36 Bust of Iron Tail

Fig.98

Iron Tail, or Sinte Maza as he was known among his Oglala Sioux family, played an important role in western history. He was born in 1850 in South Dakota and received his name from his mother who had watched a buffalo hunt around the time of his birth and been impressed by the ironlike erectness of the bisons' tails as they ran. Like his namesake, Iron Tail was upright and highly respected among his people. He gained the title of war chief and a reputation as a gallant warrior. He fought in the Battle of the Little Big Horn, at which time he carried the name Plenty Scalps, and he later succeeded Sitting Bull as chief.

Near the close of the Indian Wars, Iron Tail befriended William F. Cody. The scout and showman saw in Iron Tail an ideal native figure to represent his people in Buffalo Bill's version of the western saga. In fact, Iron Tail was the perfect foil for Cody himself in the popular Wild West shows. Like Cody, Iron Tail was both physically striking and known for his sagacity and bravery. He signed up to tour with Buffalo Bill's troupe as early as 1889, when the show toured England and the European continent. Iron Tail became an overnight sensation and stayed with Cody's extravaganza, off and on, throughout the remainder of his life. He died in 1916 on a train home to the West from Philadelphia, where he had been performing with his old and by then equally infirm friend Cody in the Sells-Floto Circus.[1]

Exactly when Proctor met Iron Tail is not known, though it would appear that the first contact was made in the spring of 1914. The story of their interaction was published the next year in Portland's *Evening Telegram*:

There was also the story of the modeling of Iron Tail, the Sioux chief. Proctor made a bust of the old man. When it was finished Iron Tail gazed long and fixedly at the stern portrait of himself. The sculptor couldn't tell whether he *was pleased or angry. Finally the old Indian drew a bundle from inside his shirt. Slowly he unwrapped the old newspaper. "Yours," said Iron Tail holding out the gift. It was the withered scalp of a Blackfoot the chief had killed in battle.*[2]

The *Gotham Weekly Gazette* also reported Iron Tail's gift to Proctor: "A. Phim Proctor, the animal modeler has received a valuable memento from an Indian friend of his, George W. Iron-Tail Esq., same being the scalp and top not of a Crow Chief."[3] Despite the confusion about the victim's tribe, the story was substantiated by the inclusion among the several dozen Indian artifacts that Proctor loaned to New York's American Museum of Natural History between 1925 and 1943 of a "Scalp presented to A. Phimister Proctor by Iron-Tail, head chief of the Sioux on completion of a bust which Mr. Proctor made." In the mid-1950s, the museum purchased many of these items from Proctor's son Gifford, but the scalp was not one of them.[4]

A casting of Proctor's initial sketch, a Roman Bronze Works bronze marked as "N 2," is in the collections of the Gilcrease Museum, Tulsa, Oklahoma (fig. 98). Assuming that Proctor made the sketch for the *Iron Tail* bronze in the spring of 1914, both the sketch and the finished portrait bronze mark a significant new direction for the artist. Not only did they underscore Proctor's renewed focus on the West and its people, but they also revealed an interest in moving away from animal subject matter and toward human themes and figures. Later that spring the Proctors would depart for Montana and the Cheyenne reservation. Iron Tail, though wizened and tinged with melancholy in this portrait, had launched a fresh path for Proctor's art, one he had not explored since 1896 and his time among the Blackfeet.

Exhibited: *Seventh Annual Exhibition*, Canadian Art Club, Toronto, 1914 (*Indian Head, No. 61*, may have been either the *Iron Tail* sketch or the finished bronze); Washington State Art Association, Seattle, 1915; *Small Bronzes by A. Phimister Proctor*, Art Institute of Chicago, Chicago, 1917; *Works in Sculpture by A. Phimister Proctor*, Corcoran Gallery of Art, Washington, D.C., 1918; *Paintings and Sculpture by Four Artists of Taos*, Art Institute of Chicago, Chicago, 1919

Other known versions: Gilcrease Museum, Tulsa, Okla. (bronze sketch); Walter D. Harris, Fresno, Calif.

Variant titles: *Little Wolf Bust; Bust of Indian; Little Wolf: Cheyenne Indian; Indian Head "Little Wolf"*
Modeled, 1914; cast initially, c. 1919
Bronze, 10¾ x 6½ x 11¼ inches
Markings: "A PHIMISTER PROCTOR/ Little Wolf 1914/Gorham Co. Founders"
Copyright: By Alexander Phimister Proctor under No. G50116 on July 8, 1915; by Nona Proctor Church as *Little Wolf Bust* under No. H55361 on March 1, 1993

Fig.99
Olin Levi Warner (1844–1896)
Joseph, Chief of the Nez Perce Indians, 1889
Bronze, 17½ inches in diameter

Plate 37 Little Wolf

During Proctor's stay with the Northern Cheyenne near Lame Deer, Montana, over the summer of 1914, he sculpted two works with Robert, the son of Laban and Laura Little Wolf, as a model. *Pursued* (see plate 38), a dramatic equestrian sculpture, transformed the young ranch hand who normally spent his time mending fences, tending cattle, and working the hayfield into a mythic warrior fleeing some unseen peril. The second sculpture concerned less the romantic past than the pursuit of immediate beauty, portraying the young man with such skill and sympathy that Robert firmly inhabited the present.

In choosing Robert Little Wolf as his model for a bust portrait, Proctor forged a new path in the sculptural treatment of native peoples. Although Robert was by birth part of Laban Little Wolf's legacy, and the artist portrayed him as a warrior, bare-shouldered and with hair tied tightly in braids, Proctor nonetheless focused on Robert's youth and individuality rather than his heritage. Proctor was familiar with Olin Warner's portrait medallions of Indians, which had been shown side by side with Proctor's own work at the Portland Art Association in 1911. Warner lavished his attention and skill primarily on celebrated tribal headmen like Chief Joseph of the Nez Perce (fig. 99). Likewise, Proctor's contemporary Charles Schreyvogel selected for his only Indian portrait the revered Ponca chief White Eagle. In both cases the bronzes served as memorials to men who were concluding vital and venerated political and military careers within their cultures. White Eagle was known as the last of the great Ponca chiefs of Oklahoma, while Chief Joseph had been forced by fate to surrender his people to the wily and persistent Colonel Nelson A. Miles in 1877. Both figures were thus symbols of loss, romanticized to conform to the American appetite for images of Indians as a defeated, once noble people.

Proctor's *Little Wolf,* on the contrary, evinces hope. The model's youth promises a future that, rather than lost in time, is restorative and alive. Under the reservation agent J. R. Eddy and others from 1903 to the early 1920s, the Cheyenne enjoyed what they referred to as "good times." They prospered in the business of cattle-ranching, which allowed them to reestablish cultural and economic self-sufficiency, feeling what tribal historian Tom Weist called "a growing sense of accomplishment among the people."[1] This was the Cheyenne world to which the Proctors were introduced in 1914. Through his portrait of Little Wolf, Proctor presented not stoic resignation but youthful vitality. The man shown is wary, not weary; determined, not despondent.

This work revitalized Proctor, reconnecting him to the West and to his vision of himself as a sculptor of people as well as animals. He was soon showing the bronze from coast to coast. The Washington State Art Association in Seattle exhibited the statue in 1915. By 1918 it had appeared in Denver, Chicago, and Washington, D.C. In May 1917 the *Denver Post* illustrated a casting of *Little Wolf* to accompany a story about Proctor's discussions with the Buffalo Bill Memorial Association on a heroic monument to William F. Cody.[2] *Little Wolf* was testimony to Proctor's ability to depict a man of action, confident of the future.

Exhibited: Frazier Book Store, Pendleton, Ore., 1914 (a plaster); Washington State Art Association, Seattle, 1915 (plaster); *Small Bronzes by A. Phimister Proctor*, Art Institute of Chicago, Chicago, 1917; *Works in Sculpture by A. Phimister Proctor*, Corcoran Gallery of Art, Washington, D.C., 1918; *A. Phimister Proctor*, Stendahl Art Gallery, Los Angeles, 1923

Other known versions: A. Phimister Proctor Museum, Poulsbo, Wash. (painted plaster model)

Fig.99

Variant titles: *Pursued: Cheyenne Indian;*
Indian Pursued
Modeled, 1914; cast initially, 1914
Bronze, 24 x 8 x 17¼ inches
Markings: "A. PHIMISTER PROCTOR
1914/ROMAN BRONZE WORKS, N.Y."
Copyright: By Alexander Phimister Proctor
under No. G50025 on June 24, 1915;
by Nona Proctor Church under No. H53099
on December 1, 1973

Gilcrease Museum, Tulsa, Okla.

Plate 38 Pursued

In Proctor's major exhibition at the Gorham Company's New York galleries in 1913, only three sculptures out of forty-three incorporated human figures. All three were products of his late nineteenth-century travels among the Blackfeet of Montana; the *Indian Warrior* (plate 12) was the only formally finished work. Proctor had attempted on several occasions to have himself recognized as a sculptor who could treat human subjects as well as animals, but potential patrons were unconvinced without a record of accomplishment in that regard. So, to change that perception, he dedicated a healthy portion of the summer of 1914 to remedy the situation. He and his wife, Margaret, headed for Montana, the site of his earlier inspiration, but this time he chose the Northern Cheyenne rather than the Blackfeet for his models.

There may have been other motivations, too. The bronze model for Proctor's *Buffalo* for the Q Street Bridge (plate 34) shared gallery space that spring with two spirited cowboy sculptures by Joseph Mora at the National Academy of Design. Mora's bronzes signaled a fresh western talent on the scene who, like Frederic Remington eighteen years before, dared to present parochial themes such as rodeo riders before a New York audience. Proctor clipped the review from *Scribner's,* which showed his and Mora's bronzes together on the same page.[1] In the previous issue of that magazine, Proctor probably also read a story by William Herbert Dunton, a young illustrator from New York who had recently moved to Taos and was enthusiastically immersing himself in western life. Dunton's article, "The Fair in the Cow Country," recounted his experiences at the Cheyenne Frontier Days rodeo in Wyoming.[2] These small town "events," as Dunton described them, possessed a vitality and charm unequaled by the big

tent Wild West shows that toured the eastern cities. Cheyenne's rodeo, in Dunton's opinion, was not just the best but the "largest Wild West show in the world."[3] One painting was inspired by the author's text: "In the Indian race it is not the speed of the horses that counts; it is the spectacle of these little, scrawny, off-colored ponies and their bronzed, picturesque riders, sweeping, all bunched, into the stretch" (fig. 100).[4] Both the Dunton story and Mora's little bronzes must have reminded Proctor of his western roots, his Indian ties, his love of horses and men in action, and his fundamental desire to portray western themes.

Also at this time, Proctor's friend and fellow Boone and Crockett Club member George Bird Grinnell was putting the finishing touches on the first of his three books on the Cheyenne Indians, *The Fighting Cheyennes.*[5] Among New York writers, artists, and scholars, the Cheyenne Indians commanded growing attention. Proctor went west to see for himself.

After settling in a camp on the Cheyenne reservation six miles out of Lame Deer, Montana, the Proctors befriended the agent J. R. Eddy. The artist and Eddy went in search of "picturesque riders," eventually connecting with the famous Little Wolf family. The senior Little Wolf, Laban, was a tribal chief. His son Robert Little Wolf, handsome, athletic, and enthusiastic, was willing, in an indefatigable way that surprised even Proctor, to model for an ambitious sculpture celebrating the distinguished heritage of a Great Plains horse culture:[6]

My idea was to depict the Indian riding downhill and at
the same time making a wheeling motion. To capture the
motion and the realism, I had Wolf ride uphill on the walk,
turn, and then gallop down, sometimes on one side of me,

Fig.100
William Herbert Dunton (1878–1936)
Fair in the Cow Country, 1914
Oil on canvas, 26 x 39 inches

Eiteljorg Museum of American Indians and
Western Art, Indianapolis

Fig.100

sometimes on the other. *This arduous work — for both model and sculptor — went on for several days while the eighteen-inch statuette,* Indian Pursued, *took shape.*[7]

The first critics of the work were the Little Wolf family. They were so pleased with the results that they paid Proctor the supreme compliment of giving him their name. "I'm Little Wolf, too, now," he boasted to friends in Portland the next year. "That is the highest honor an Indian can pay you."[8]

Pursued represented Proctor's dynamic return to western themes. Following the energetic examples provided by Mora and Dunton, he successfully formulated an alternative to the static, formally posed *Indian Warrior.* Even though the rider is in flight, his expression of resistance and turn of defiance speak to his survival. This was in distinct contrast to other artists, like James Earle Fraser, another Saint-Gaudens protégé, whose *The End of the Trail* conveys despair and defeat, a resignation in the face of impossible odds.

In 1928, while Proctor was living in Brussels, he reworked *Pursued,* one of his favorite and most energetic statuettes. Hoping to improve on his original concept, he replaced the spear in the warrior's hand with a war club, added a quiver over the man's shoulder, rearticulated the grass supporting the horse's single foot touching the ground, and lowered the flapping breechcloth — in all tightening the composition and making the horse and rider flow more gracefully past the viewer's gaze. Later versions are generally marked with two dates, 1915 and 1928.

Exhibited: Frazier Book Store, Pendleton, Ore., 1914 (probably a plaster); Washington State Art Association, Seattle, 1915 (plaster); *Small Bronzes by A. Phimister Proctor*, Art Institute of Chicago, Chicago, 1917; *Works in Sculpture by A. Phimister Proctor,* Corcoran Gallery of Art, Washington, D.C., 1918; *A. Phimister Proctor*, Stendahl Art Gallery, Los Angeles, 1923; *Exhibition of Paintings and Sculpture*, Fort Worth Frontier Centennial Exposition, Fort Worth, Tex., 1936

Other known versions: R. W. Norton Art Gallery, Shreveport, La. (1914 version, gift of Mrs. Richard W. Norton, 1946); Anson M. Beard Jr., Greenwich, Conn. (1914 version); Smithsonian American Art Museum, Washington, D.C. (1928 version, acquired 1992); Mead Museum of Art, Amherst College, Amherst, Mass. (gift of George D. Pratt, 1933); Buffalo Bill Historical Center, Cody, Wyo. (1928 version, William E. Weiss Purchase Fund acquisition, 1975); Brookgreen Gardens, Pawleys Island, S.C.

Variant titles: *Cowboy; Slim-Cowboy*
Modeled, 1914; cast initially, 1915
Bronze, 10 x 6½ x 12 inches
Markings: "A.P. Proctor c./Gorham Co.
Founders QACU"
Copyright: By Alexander Phimister
Proctor under No. G50115 on July 8, 1915

Oregon Historical Society, Portland (bequest of
Mrs. Hamilton [Charlotte] Corbett, 1982)

Plate 39 Slim

During Proctor's first season at the Pendleton Round-Up, he found a number of potential subjects. By the time the rodeo had concluded, the artist boasted dozens of sketches, any one of which could have been made into finished sculptures. He later said it was difficult selecting from the variety of "cowboys and Indians, buffaloes owned by the Round-Up Association, frontiersmen, and a western atmosphere" that he said reminded him of what he "had known in Colorado" years before.[1] Despite the myriad choices, Proctor focused on the theme he had come to develop, the bucking horse and rider that became his famous *Buckaroo* (see plate 35).

As Proctor worked on the *Buckaroo*, he also made a separate bust portrait of the cowboy model he was using, Bill ("Slim") Ridings. The dual process was one Proctor had adopted when he sculpted both *Pursued* (see plate 38) and the attendant portrait *Little Wolf* (see plate 37). The artist kept fresh by working on more than one piece at a time, and combining a complicated equestrian sculpture with a sensitive portrait rendering helped relieve tensions and monotony.

As one newspaper account reported, Proctor bought two horses, one to ride and one to model from, and then "retained Slim Ridings as a model," working with his horse and cowboy all winter and spring. In fact, the paper continued, "it was July 1 [1915] before Mr. Proctor felt he could sell his bronzes and let Slim go back into the sage."[2] In the course of that nine-month gestation period, the artist finished both the *Buckaroo* and his portrait bust *Slim*.

Slim Ridings placed high among the cowboy ranks at the Round-Up. One newspaper referred to him as the "Round-Up hero," and artists other than Proctor had turned to him for inspiration. The writer Charles Wellington Furlong relied on

Ridings to describe the bucking horse stock that was used by the Round-Up Association. Unlike most of his laconic colleagues, Ridings impressed audiences with his garrulous banter. Furlong described him as tall and slim, looking like any one of the wranglers. Sitting on a fence assessing the assembled buckers, Ridings was quoted as follows:

> That sorrel mare is Whistling Annie. You can sure hear the wind go by when yer on her. The white horse with the half moon circle brand on his left flank is a good un — that means a bad un, get me? He's Snake, a sun-fishing devil and one of the hardest to wrangle; so's Sledgehammer, that big dapple gray. Last year at the Round-Up in the Friday mornin', old Sledge wanted to ride himself, so he just chased the boy right off the saddle of the snubbing horse and got right up in the saddle himself, but the judges wouldn't allow it.[3]

Proctor portrayed Bill Ridings as alert and open. Wearing a broad-brimmed Stetson, denim shirt, and knotted bandana, Slim looks observantly over his left shoulder as if reciting some horseflesh homily for an onlooker. His mouth and eyes, shaded by the hat's brim, express honesty and forthrightness, characteristics that Proctor saw as typical of western character. When he first brought his new work back to New York and its eastern audiences, the *New York Herald* showed Proctor next to his statue of *Slim* as a rough western type himself (fig. 101). Though his headquarters were the posh Fifth Avenue offices of the Montross Gallery, Proctor was said to be seen there garbed in "his outfit — a buckskin shirt made from a buck he himself had killed and his buckaroo hat flung on a desk chair."[4]

Fig.101

Proctor often showed the *Buckaroo* and *Slim* together.
Shortly after he completed the two models, he visited friends
in Portland. His hosts Mr. and Mrs. Jack G. Edwards opened
their house on July 22, 1915, as a gallery to feature Proctor's
latest works in plaster. In appreciation of the hospitality, Proctor
gave the Edwardses a copy of *Slim*, which soon decorated the
mantel of the family library. The next day, the *Portland
Morning Oregonian*'s art critic, Lillian Tingle, highlighted the
work's depiction of a true western type:

> *"Slim," a small "character" bust is a portrait of a real man.
> But it is also more than a portrait; it records for future gen-
> erations the typical cowboy of story and tradition. There is
> an indefinable something in the carriage and poise of the
> head and neck, the "long distance look" in the eyes, the
> firmly modeled chin and the lean lines of the cheek that
> would be recognizable as "cowboy" even without the
> "costume touch" of hat and knotted handkerchief.*[5]

A writer for another Portland paper offered a subsequent
observation about Proctor that proved prophetic: "He has
this difference from his brother sculptors; instead of modeling young Grecian goddesses with more curves than mod-
esty, he prefers Indians, mountain lions and bad men."[6] Only
four days later, the *Pendleton East Oregonian* ran a headline
suggesting that Bill Ridings was not the virtuous cowboy
Proctor had depicted in his "character" portrait: "'The
Buckaroo' Is Now in Jail." Evidently Slim had sold a horse to
James Roach, a local stockman, that proved to belong to
someone other than Slim. He was accused of larceny.[7] The
Pendleton Tribune captured the irony of the situation:

Slim" Bill Ridings, idol of thousands of Roundup [sic] *spectators and the model for, if not the inspiration of "The Buckaroo," the latest of A. Phimister Proctor's sculptured works which has created a sensation in Portland and Seattle as the most typical of all artist's depictions of the Western spirit, is in the Umatilla County jail this afternoon facing a charge of horse stealing.*[8]

Ridings claimed that he had been selling Roach the horse for a second party, but the facts in the case proved Slim wrong, and he was sentenced to the state prison for one to ten years.[9]

Stories circulated that Proctor's friend, the Oregon rancher and businessman Bill Hanley, had bailed Ridings out of jail earlier in the summer. Or that authorities had known Ridings was a culprit before Proctor was finished with his work and obligingly released the felon into Proctor's custody so the modeling could be completed. The latter is unlikely: there are no formal accounts of such an arrangement and the sheriff had to travel all the way to Boise to arrest Ridings. There is a letter from Ridings' wife to Proctor asking that the artist consider putting up bail, but that arrived after the culprit was in jail.

In later years Proctor made light of this problem. However, when he wrote his autobiography in the 1940s, he left out all mention of Ridings, claiming that his model for the *Buckaroo* was named "Red." Perhaps he confused Slim with Red Parker, or perhaps Red was another nickname for Slim. Either way he probably hoped to rewrite the part of his history that celebrated a man whose honor was found sorely wanting.

Exhibited: Frazier Book Store, Pendleton, Ore., 1915; *Small Bronzes by A. Phimister Proctor*, Art Institute of Chicago, Chicago, 1917; *Exhibition of Paintings and Sculpture*, Fort Worth Frontier Centennial Exhibition, Fort Worth, Tex., 1936

Other known versions: Gilcrease Museum, Tulsa, Okla.; A. Phimister Proctor Museum, Poulsbo, Wash. (plaster model)

Plate 40 Buffalo Hunt

In the spring of 1916, Proctor left Pendleton, Oregon, for New York. Newly full of enthusiasm for life in the West, he regaled friends and potential patrons whenever possible with stories of the Pendleton Round-Up and the characters that gave it such novel flair and excitement. At this time Pendleton was claiming Proctor as her own and profoundly appreciated the promotion he offered in the East. H. Blanchard Dimick, a silver manufacturer and the president of several New York banks, hosted a dinner for Proctor at which the artist entertained the guests with hair-raising tales of the rodeo. "His enthusiasm on that subject lent eloquence to his modest tongue," noted a Pendleton newspaper account, and he depicted events so vividly "that everyone present expressed an almost irresistible desire to come west to Pendleton this fall."[1] In fact Dimick and several other New York worthies did show up there in September.[2]

Of more importance to the artist's own promotion was a full-page article in the Sunday *New York Herald*. Titled "Sculptures of the Western Frontier," it featured Proctor in his western regalia along with images of his latest sculptures, the *Buckaroo* and *Slim*. Also pictured was a work in progress, a plaster running buffalo that Proctor had sculpted at the Round-Up using bison owned by the Rodeo Association. Although he had already produced multiple versions of the buffalo in bronze and plaster, beginning with his small 1897 *Buffalo* (see plate 16) and culminating a short time before with the mammoth Q Street Bridge *Buffalo*, this was something quite new for him. Proctor intended this work to move beyond the staid and formal eloquence of animal grandeur to a more dynamic rendition. Here he would show the West as living on, whether as a place for artistic revitalization or as a home for working cowboys, Indians, and frontier characters. And he would be working from experience: the *New York Herald* article described a wild buffalo bull that might have brought disaster to an inattentive group of cowboys at the Round-Up, had Proctor not distracted the bison's charge.[3] That encounter possibly inspired Proctor's vision of his charging buffalo; by introducing an Indian hunter into the mix, he would also invest the work with historical association.

Other artists had dynamically recreated history before Proctor. Frederic Remington had explored the subject in his bronzes and paintings. More recently, Charles M. Russell had garnered public and critical acclaim with the bronze *Buffalo Hunt* (fig. 102). Proctor would have seen Russell's spirited piece at Tiffany's and the Roman Bronze Works foundry, as well as read about it in art magazines and New York newspapers as early as 1911.[4]

Proctor wanted to do what Russell had done, except in a somewhat more formal, precise interpretation that would also be more monumental in scale and treatment. Like Russell, Proctor imagined his buffalo sculpture as a hunting scene, pitting the speed and mass of the bison against the equestrian skill and valor of the native huntsman. His version would capture the moment of the kill, as Russell's had, in a way that defied the soft sentimentalism of Hermon Atkins MacNeil's *Physical Liberty*, one of the staff monuments at the Louisiana Purchase Exposition in 1904 (MacNeil, according to Lorado Taft, had not yet been able "to essay the horse").[5] Proctor's (or Russell's) Indian did not run *with* the buffalo but *after* it. This was a visceral rather than philosophical encounter in which the horse and rider worked in unison to guarantee their mutual survival. For this Proctor needed the ideal Indian model, a

Fig. 102
Charles M. Russell (1864–1926)
Buffalo Hunt
Bronze, 18¾ x 13 x 10 inches
Modeled 1903, cast 1905

Amon Carter Museum, Fort Worth, Tex.

Fig.103
Newspaper photograph of Proctor
(right), Jackson Sundown (center),
and Charles Wellington Furlong (left)
at the Pendleton Round-Up, 1916

A. Phimister Proctor Museum Archives,
Poulsbo, Wash.

Fig.102

man whose acquaintance with horses was as natural as the
"natural man" he wished to commemorate.

He knew just the person: a Nez Perce who was the
nephew of Chief Joseph. Though he went by the name of
Jackson Sundown, he had been born in 1863 with the name
Earth Left by the Setting Sun. Sundown was a formidable
horseman. While fighting as a youth in the Nez Perce war, he
had been wounded and survived by clinging to the side of his
horse. Unlike many of his band, he was able to escape to
Canada, where he lived for about two years with Sitting Bull's
band of Sioux. He was eventually granted land on the
Flathead Indian reservation. By the time Proctor met
Sundown, he was married and had settled on a ranch in Idaho.

As early as 1910, Sundown had begun to participate in
rodeos. His formidable skill, height (six feet tall), and colorful
attire soon won him wide favor among rodeo crowds. By the
time Proctor first saw him in Pendleton in 1914, Sundown was
something of a sensation. The artist, according to his daughter Hester, immediately prevailed upon Sundown to serve as
his model, coming early to the Round-Up in 1915 so "he could
make sketches and measurements and watch him ride."[6]
Later, during the summer of 1916, the artist and his family
spent approximately six weeks living on Sundown's ranch in a
special tipi pitched under majestic cottonwood trees.

"Serious work began as soon as we were settled," Proctor
later recalled. "Every day Sundown rode back and forth in
front of me or posed quietly while I modeled details."[7] Hester
remembered that when Sundown posed for her father, "he
wore only a breach [*sic*] cloth and moccasins. He rode bare-
back with an Indian-style halter. He would come at full gallop
directly at Dad, and I would hold my breath wondering if he
would stop in time or turn."[8]

Fig.103

On the 170-mile trip to Sundown's Idaho ranch, Proctor's model of the horse and buffalo suffered considerable damage—enough so that the artist felt his progress had been set back two months. But after making necessary repairs, he added the Indian figure, and by September 19, 1916, the *Pendleton Evening Tribune* was announcing that the work was nearing completion.[9] The Proctors then left their shaded outdoor studio and returned to Pendleton for the Round-Up. There the *Portland Journal* would describe Proctor and Sundown's collaboration:

> *Though past the half-century mark, Sundown is one of the most handsome Indians of the west. So typical and ideal is he that A. Phimister Proctor, New York sculptor, had been using him all summer as a model for a piece of Indian bronze sculpture. He is tall, slender, dignified and wonderfully picturesque. He owns land on the Nez Perce reservation near Culdesac, Idaho.[10]*

Although Sundown had ridden bucking horses in five previous Round-Ups and qualified for the finals in three, he had vowed not to enter the 1916 contest: the general sentiment was that in earlier contests he had not been given a fair score. But Proctor convinced him to make a final try. Arriving in Pendleton early, the artist secured a special box in the grandstands to watch, then registered Sundown for the bucking horse events, paying the entry fees. Competing before a crowd of 30,000, Sundown won the major event and the year's title, turning the 1916 Round-Up into "the most popular championship ever made."[11] Sundown, a certified champion, an honorable and gracious host, and an epic figure in Indian history, fully vindicated Proctor's interest through his

own remarkable efforts. And in almost every story about Sundown's victory in the arena, Proctor and his *Buffalo Hunt* sculpture found ample play. Sundown left Pendleton with $500 in his pocket and a fancy commemorative saddle on his horse's back. Proctor left with a sculptural sensation almost ready for the foundry and for enthusiastic audiences east and west. Sundown posed with Proctor and the writer Charles Wellington Furlong after the ride (fig. 103), which forty-five Nez Perce had watched, joining in as the "crowd cheered with a frenzy."[12]

Later the next year, when the *Buffalo Hunt* had been cast in bronze and was being exhibited and sold nationally, the New York press proclaimed its importance. Though merely a tabletop statue, it was "possessed of such monumental quality as to make it well worthy of being cast in heroic size for erection in some park. We would like to see it in New York City, where," in the critic's mind at least, "no truly great Indian sculpture has been erected." The group compared in "vigor of ... creation" with the finest examples of Remington's sculptures, yet it exceeded those in its "fine feeling of artistic values." And the three figures in the group played brilliantly next to one another:

> *There is rapid forward motion in the pose of the mustang obedient to his savage rider's will; there is an unusual exhibition of energy, activity and alertness in the Indian himself. The huge bulk of the bison is contrasted admirably with the slender grace of the horse as he strains forward in the effort to overtake the terrified beast.[13]*

Proctor, with his penchant for combining monumental expression and aesthetic finesse, had accomplished a special balance between art and reality, just as Sundown had in his famous ride.

Exhibited: *Small Bronzes by A. Phimister Proctor,* Art Institute of Chicago, Chicago, 1917; Annual exhibition, National Academy of Design, New York, 1918; *Works in Sculpture by A. Phimister Proctor,* Corcoran Gallery of Art, Washington, D.C., 1918; *A. Phimister Proctor,* Stendahl Art Gallery, Los Angeles, 1923

Other known versions: Corcoran Gallery of Art, Washington, D.C. (acquired 1919)

Variant titles: *The Bucking Bronco; Bronco Buster; Buckaroo; The Bucking Broncho*
Modeled, 1915; completed in plaster to heroic size, 1918; cast, 1919; dedicated, 1920
Bronze, monumental sculpture
Markings: "A.PHIMISTER PROCTOR/GORHAM CO. FOUNDERS"
Copyright: Presumably under *Buckaroo* of 1915
Civic Center, Denver

Plate 41 Broncho Buster

In the spring of 1903, Proctor received a long and cordial letter from an old Denver crony, Curtis Chamberlain. Together with painter Charles Partridge Adams, Chamberlain and Proctor had been boyhood friends who grew up sharing an interest in art. All three went on to make a livelihood as artists.

Proctor was pleased to hear from Chamberlain that his big *Cowboy* and *Indian* (see figs. 13 and 14, p. 37) were still standing in Denver's City Park after a decade of exposure to the elements. They had been made of plaster staff for the 1893 World's Columbian Exposition, and he wrote in amazement, "When I modeled those two groups I had no idea they would be in existence ten years from that date."[1] In his letter Chamberlain had also suggested that many citizens of Denver would enjoy having Proctor's two sculptures made a permanent part of the city's landscape. Proctor responded with unreserved pleasure:

What you say about having those two groups remodeled and put in bronze is very interesting to me. This has been my cherished hope for years — to remodel those two equestrian statues, which were my first important work, and have them in Denver, of all places, appeals to me more than anything I know of. To have them where I as a youngster used to hunt jack rabbits nearly every holiday in the season — for the town where I was raised and grew to man's estate — well, it would give me a lot of pleasure to do them. I am afraid Denver would think the price too high. It seems to me she is of sufficient importance now to begin to think of the artistic things. What better beginning could she make than perpetuate the Indian and cowboy, two types inseparably connected with Denver's early history.[2]

Nothing came of this idea, but a seed had been planted that would some day sprout. A dozen years later, after a summer at the Pendleton Round-Up in Oregon, Proctor produced a model for what would ultimately become his first permanent monumental sculpture in Denver. *Buckaroo* (see plate 35) was completed as a plaster in early July 1915.[3] Shortly thereafter the artist exhibited the group in Seattle and Portland, receiving rave reviews in both venues. Rex Lampman, a critic for Portland's *Oregon Journal,* emphasized the preservation aspect of Proctor's effort: "The Pendleton Round-Up, action epic of the old west, is to endure in bronze. The spirit of a day that is passing, of a life that is fast slipping into the realm of legend, has been caught and crystallized by the sculptor."[4]

Those who saw the thirty-inch plaster immediately sensed that it was bigger than life. A fellow sculptor from New York, Victor Salvatore, was visiting Portland when Proctor and his plaster hit town. Salvatore had been a friend of the Proctors for some time, and he told the press that this cowboy sculpture deserved to be made into a heroic-sized bronze for some worthy western park. The consensus was that Pendleton would be the most appropriate site, "perhaps in the depot park, so that travelers may know when they have arrived in the very heart of the old-time cow country, and a place where bronchos and buckaroos are honored for their part in the winning of the west as they are nowhere else."[5] Portland, urged on by boosters of the Pendleton Round-Up, started a fund to accomplish the task; according to one newspaper account, even the railroad, the O.W.R.& N., was prepared to assist.[6] But then something happened to derail the project. As the local papers began running headlines like "Bill Ridings in Jail as a Horse Thief,"[7] it became evident that

191

Proctor's colorful model, while skilled as a cowboy, was also an accused felon — probably not someone that city leaders would want decorating a municipal park. By late January 1916, Ridings had been found guilty and sent to the state penitentiary. Proctor would have to look further afield to find an accepting, as well as acceptable, location for his cowboy monument.

To soften the negative associations, Proctor began to add to his stories about sculpting the original *Buckaroo* model. The local sheriff evidently knew of Ridings' criminal activities long before the arrest in June, but had allowed Proctor to finish his model before cuffing the culprit and putting him behind bars. "He said yesterday," wrote the *San Francisco Examiner,* "that the Pendleton officers kindly allowed his cowboy model to remain out of the penitentiary while his statue was made," citing this as evidence of Oregon's "responsiveness to the appeal of art."[8]

Proctor's desire to "eventually … have [the *Buckaroo*] cast lifesize"[9] or larger materialized a couple of years later in Denver, and the site was one of the most prominent possible: the new Civic Center. This development came about when Proctor and his wife, Margaret, arrived in Denver in late May 1917. They were there to attend Buffalo Bill's funeral and to discuss with Denver's Buffalo Bill Memorial Association ideas for a heroic-sized monument to the celebrated scout and showman.[10] To demonstrate his abilities with the human as well as the equine figure, Proctor brought with him a casting of the *Buckaroo*. When not meeting with the committee, he showed the work off to other interested parties. His old friend and fellow Denver artist Helen Henderson Chain later took credit for introducing the Proctors to the city's dynamic

mayor, Robert Walter Speer. Chain would recall that Margaret made the first approach to Speer (Proctor was recovering from an ulcer). Speer remembered the plaster groups in City Park and was "very enthusiastic," telling her, "I am proud to show this work of a former Denver boy to some of our wealthy citizens. I have no doubt Mr. [John K.] Mullen … may wish a life size figure of this subject for our Civic Center."[11]

Speer's vision for monumental art in Denver, while including Proctor's work, went well beyond that in scope. He had been impressed with the buildings and grounds at the World's Columbian Exposition in Chicago. Inspired like other city builders of the era with the ensuing City Beautiful movement, Speer returned to Denver with a dream for the Queen City. Once he was elected mayor in 1904, he had the political clout to turn Denver into one of America's flagship City Beautiful models.[12] In pursuing his dream of a monumental civic design, Speer sought out architects and urban designers such as Daniel Burnham, Charles Mulford Robinson, and Frederick Law Olmstead. Eventually a plan for downtown Denver's Civic Center was pieced together, primarily from ideas drafted by Proctor's friend and fellow sculptor Frederick MacMonnies, with refinements by Chicago architect Edward H. Bennett. Speer had strong ideas on the subject, many of them sparked by his recent visits to some of Europe's capitals. The design therefore included monumental companion buildings (fashioned after Renaissance models) that were to contain an art museum and a public library, government office structures, vast open courtyards for large public gatherings, and a lagoon. At every outlook were to be heroic-sized bronze sculptures. MacMonnies already had one sculpture group in place, his *Pioneer Monument,* a spire capped by an equestrian

portrait of Kit Carson and surrounded by other characters from Colorado's colorful frontier history. Further up the hill, near the state capitol, was Preston Powers' bronze monument *The Closing Era*, an 1893 tribute to Colorado's native people that had been imported from the fair in Chicago. Speer originally wanted to center Proctor's *Broncho Buster* in the middle of the grand plaza. But Bennett objected, contending that even in a heroic size the work was not of sufficient scale to hold the space. According to modern architectural historian William H. Wilson, Bennett deemed it conceptually "incongruous" as well.[13] Yet Proctor's *Cowboy* and *Indian* were clearly compatible with the monuments by MacMonnies and Powers that were already in place. When Proctor returned to Denver in September to meet with Speer, the newspapers at least felt the Civic Center was ripe for similar additions. "Sculptural designs that would typify the peoples of the early days of the West, and accurately preserve in stone and bronze wild life of mountain and plain as it existed, may yet find a place in the civic center," wrote the *Rocky Mountain News.*[14] By the following summer, Speer had persuaded Mullen, a Denver miller, to give the *Broncho Buster* monument to the city and convinced another benefactor, Stephen Knight, to donate its companion piece, *On the War Trail* (see plate 43). The press called the Proctor monuments "important additions to the group of bronze works of the greatest sculptors in the country which the city is steadily acquiring."[15]

Because MacMonnies was renting Proctor's New York studio at the time, Proctor decided to move to California to work on the latest commissions. Los Altos became the Proctors' new home, with a big red barn for the sculptor's studio. A friend from Proctor's Saint-Gaudens days, Robert

Payne, was also living in the area and he helped to point up the *Buckaroo* plaster into its heroic dimension (see fig. 48, p. 77). By late July 1918, they had the monument in plaster and soon shipped it to Providence, Rhode Island, to be cast by the Gorham Company.[16] By then the press was circulating a different story about Proctor's model, claiming that another Oregon cowboy, Del Blancett, had posed for the rider. Ridings could not object as he was locked away in prison, nor could Blancett confirm or deny the claim as he had died fighting in France with a regiment of Canadians.[17]

Proctor was awarded $15,000 for the *Broncho Buster*. With the pedestal and other fees, it cost Denver $18,500 and was dedicated on December 1, 1920. The bronze was placed on the south side of the plaza, in front of what was hoped would be the city's art museum. Alongside the statue rose the elegant Corinthian-styled Colonnade of Civic Benefactors that honored Mullen and his fellow contributors to Speer's City Beautiful project. The Colonnade, also known as the Greek Theater, featured murals by Allen True that depicted pioneer scenes of trappers and prospectors.[18] Speer's ambitious city center design, thanks to Proctor and other artists, had flourished.

Other communities would look to Denver as a model, including Seattle, which earlier had made futile efforts to introduce the City Beautiful concept into its plans for growth and development. And Proctor wasted little time before trying to parlay his Rocky Mountain success into Pacific Coast sales. Using Speer's pitch of European achievements, Proctor told the Seattle press in 1919, "What would France and Italy be without its art? People swarm to those countries because of the famous pieces of art to be seen there. There is no reason why the United States should not be famous for its art. Cities should be more beautiful.... How much more beautiful Seattle would be with several statues typical of the real West."[19]

In Denver, when he arrived on Christmas 1919 to welcome his giant bronze *Broncho Buster* to the railyards, Proctor told the press how advanced Colorado's capital was by contrast. "Denver is rapidly coming to the front as an art center," he assured *Denver Post* reporter Arthur Frenzel. "The city has improved much within the last few years and the statues it has are of a high and excellent type."[20] Over the next several decades, Proctor and his *Broncho Buster* continued to bolster Denver's civic pride. *Municipal Facts*, a Denver promotional magazine, boasted in 1926 that the "Civic Center is conceded by artists to be the spoke of the most effective city plan in America," and below a photograph of Proctor's bronze silhouetted before silver-lined clouds, the magazine concluded grandly that "in a few years more ... Denver will be generally acknowledged as 'The Paris of America.'"[21] Proctor had helped issue that passport to international acclaim even if it represented a leap nearly as large as that of the monument's bucking horse.

Exhibited: None known

Other known versions: None

Variant titles: *Chief Sundown: Nez Perce's Indian; Indian Head — "Sundown"; Indian Head — Sundown; Chief Sundown*
Modeled, 1916; cast initially, 1917
Bronze, 11 x 13½ x 11½ inches
Markings: "A. PHIMISTER PROCTOR 1917/(copyright mark) 1917/ CASTING PATTERN"
Copyright: By Alexander Phimister Proctor under No. G54629 on July 20, 1917; by Nona Proctor Church as *Jackson Sundown Bust* under No. H53330 on October 1, 1973

A. Phimister Proctor Museum, Poulsbo, Wash.
Photograph by Howard Giske

Plate 42 "Sundown" Nez Perce's Chief

By the time Proctor settled on Jackson Sundown's ranch for the summer of 1916, he had perfected a process of working that enabled him to remain creatively energized and productive: he developed two or more sculptures at once. In this case, he divided his time between his dynamic group the *Buffalo Hunt* (see plate 40) and a staid but dramatic bust portrait of his model, Sundown. One newspaper in early October suggested, without foundation, that multiple portraits would result. "A. P. Proctor, a New York sculptor, has been using [Sundown] all summer as a model for bronze Indian busts," it wrote. But only one rendition ever emerged.[1] *"Sundown" Nez Perce's Chief* was copyrighted as a bronze the following July.

In the interim Proctor showed the plaster bust from coast to coast. In February 1917 the portrait received rave reviews in Portland, where it was shown privately at the home of Mrs. Helen Ladd Corbett. Proctor's loyalty to his Beaux-Arts mentors was alluded to when a reviewer for the *Portland Oregon Sunday Journal* reminisced that "just as the ancient Greeks put the physical perfection of their athletes into marble for all time, so A. Phimister Proctor ... is to make immortal Jackson Sundown." The writer went on to ascribe to Proctor the same search for ideal qualities of beauty and character that had consumed artists in antiquity. "Sundown afforded an ideal type," concluded the writer. "He is the Indian as one conceives him at the height of his glory — proud, noble of bearing, free, active, resourceful, verily a chieftain."[2]

Of course Sundown was many things. He had earned the title of world champion bronc rider a few months earlier; history testified to his brave performance as a warrior; he was a gracious host for the artist and his family; and he proved to be an indefatigable and inspiring model. He was also known locally in Idaho as a successful rancher. But Sundown could not and never did claim the status of tribal leader or chief. Proctor and his world fashioned that title for him.

By placing the elegant feathered bonnet atop Sundown's dignified head and adorning his left shoulder with a decorated shield, Proctor created a new history for Sundown. He was responding to the need to embellish real people with conventional conceptions of historical grandeur that conformed to popular stereotypes of the period. Proctor was not interested in celebrating Sundown's triumphant victory as a bronc buster or his place in the pantheon of America's cowboys. He did not emphasize Sundown's "modest and dignified" demeanor or his ebullient joy, "the expression of happiness which wreathed his face in smiles" at winning the championship.[3] Instead he showed Sundown as grim and defiant.

In the mid-teens, when Proctor knew him, Sundown lived in two worlds. One involved reservation life and day-to-day survival as the head of a ranching family in Idaho. The other was the rough-and-tumble world of the rodeo and the difficulty an Indian athlete faced in a sport that was dominated by white cowboys. Proctor was familiar with both of these aspects of Sundown's life, yet whether by personal artistic preference or in concession to the market, Proctor chose historical ideal over contemporary celebrity. The effect, if not paradoxical, was certainly confusing. A writer for the *Los Angeles Times* some years later invented the notion that Sundown had "won the feathers that he is wearing at a bucking contest."[4] But a Nez Perce man would not have won eagle feathers for riding a bucking horse. Prize money, a nice saddle, and even a silver buckle, along with the adulation of the

huge crowd, but not a bonnet. That was loaned to him by a friend or perhaps from the artist's own collection.

Proctor's two sculptures of Sundown, the *Buffalo Hunt* and the bust portrait, were given their first museum exhibition by the Art Institute of Chicago in 1917. Both were presented as plasters. So accustomed was the public to Proctor as an animalier sculptor, the critic for the *Chicago Tribune* neglected to mention any of Proctor's western work.[5] The *Christian Science Monitor* described the western work as convincing because of Proctor's direct experience with the subject, particularly his close personal friendships with his sitters.[6]

Once Proctor had the two works cast in bronze and displayed in the showrooms at the Gorham Company gallery in New York, the two Sundown-inspired works received more focused attention and wider recognition. The critic Frank Owen Payne, writing about the bust portrait, compared it with similar work by other noted American sculptors:

It possesses the ethnological accuracy of Olin Warner's chieftains, the faithful likeness seen in the best Indian sculptures of MacNeil and Weinman, and the fine spiritual aspects of Indian nature so characteristic of the works of Dallin.... There is delicacy of touch and masterly workmanship of modelling — an exquisite finish withal — in this admirable piece of sculpture. Every detail of the intricate feather-work head-dress has been modelled with infinite pains and loving care. Surely, if future ages are to judge the aboriginal American from sculptured representations of him, such works as this cannot fail to place that abused race in a position worthy of high respect.[7]

Sundown died of pneumonia in December 1923. He was sixty-one years old. Grangeville's *Idaho County Free Press* ran an obituary lamenting the loss of "a picturesque Nez Perce Indian" and recalling that in the years before his death Sundown had frequented local rodeos dressed in full native regalia.[8] But on his tombstone, etched into one corner of the large marble slab, Sundown is shown in the costume of his grandest achievement — as a cowboy with lavish, wooly chaps, his wide-brimmed hat pushed back on his head, his trophy buckle in full view, hands on his hips, and a smile on his face.

Exhibited: *Small Bronzes by A. Phimister Proctor*, Art Institute of Chicago, Chicago, 1917 (plaster); *Works in Sculpture by A. Phimister Proctor*, Corcoran Gallery of Art, Washington, D.C., 1918; Annual exhibition, National Academy of Design, New York, 1918; *Paintings and Sculpture by Four Artists of Taos*, Art Institute of Chicago, Chicago, 1919; Winter exhibition, National Academy of Design, New York, 1919; *A. Phimister Proctor*, Stendahl Art Gallery, Los Angeles, 1923

Other known versions: None

Variant titles: None recorded
Modeled, 1918–1920; cast, 1921;
dedicated, 1922
Bronze, monumental sculpture
Markings: "A. PHIMISTER PROCTOR
C/ROMAN BRONZE WORKS N-Y"
Copyright: By A. Phimister Proctor,
registered in the name of the National
Sculpture Society, under No. J262794 on
May 9, 1923
Civic Center, Denver

Plate 43 On the War Trail

Denver's Civic Center park was completed in 1922. It began
with Mayor Robert Speer's dream of a City Beautiful in 1893
and was formally put in motion in 1904, absorbing the attentions and energies of countless talented planners and politicians for over a generation. Speer died in 1918 while in office,
still pushing through some of his most ambitious plans. But
even without him at the helm, the city pressed forward to
complete the work. One of the crowning achievements of the
visionary project was the installation and dedication of
Proctor's monumental tribute to the native people of
Colorado, *On the War Trail*, in May 1922.

In 1916 Speer had called on Denver's wealthier citizens
to contribute to the cause of decorating the Civic Center with
statuary, buildings, and fountains. He promised, in a speech
titled "Give While You Live," to build an elegant colonnade in
the Greek style that would acknowledge the donors and properly preserve the spirit of their generosity. Among those who
accepted the challenge was Stephen A. Knight, a boyhood
friend of Proctor's. Owner of the Eagle Milling Co. and a distinguished member of Denver's Board of Education, he offered a
gift of $16,500 to bring Proctor's monumental bronze, *On the
War Trail*, into the downtown park where it would stand side
by side with the *Broncho Buster* (see plate 41).[1] The *Denver
Post* cartoonist and Proctor's old friend A. Wilbur Steele wrote
the artist on May 23, 1922, enclosing some snapshots of the
monument, which he said were proof that the bronze "is in
place on his pedestal in the Denver Civic Center looking fine
and 'proud and haughty'! With the 'Buster' he makes the
picture complete.... The Indian," he assured Proctor, who had
not yet seen the work installed, "shows up fine from all along
Broadway."[2]

Fig.104
Frederic Remington (1861–1909)
Cowboy, 1908
Fairmount Park, Philadelphia

Photograph, Frederic Remington Art Museum,
Ogdensburg, N.Y.

Fig.105
Newspaper photograph of Proctor and
Red Belt with the maquette for *On the
War Trail*, 1919

A. Phimister Proctor Museum Archives, Poulsbo, Wash.
Reproduction photograph by Howard Giske

Fig.104

Proctor began work on the monument in the summer of 1918, shortly after he finished the *Broncho Buster* plaster and sent it east for casting. He and his family were living in Los Altos, California, at the time, and Proctor borrowed a pinto horse from Louis O'Neil, a San Jose lawyer, to begin the process. He fashioned the horse's pose somewhat after Frederic Remington's *Cowboy* monument in Philadelphia (fig. 104), except that in his monument, the horse has thrown both front feet into the ground as the rider has pulled him up to an abrupt stop.

Once the horse model was complete, Proctor loaded it into his car and drove to Idaho in search of an Indian to pose for his warrior. The *Pendleton East Oregonian* on June 4, 1918, reported that the artist was in town on his way to Lewiston, "where he hopes to secure the services of Jackson Sundown as a model for further Indian studies."[3] Proctor found Sundown, who, contrary to his expectations, was willing to work with him on this latest commission. Sundown, his wife, Cecilia, and his son Willie returned to California with Proctor and settled into a cottage that had been arranged for them in Los Altos. There Sundown and Proctor worked together on several poses over the next several months. Proctor saw something extraordinary in Sundown, and those who observed them working together recognized a special sense of harmony. As one writer observed after visiting Proctor's studio that summer and watching Sundown pose:

With such a man as this for a model — a being whose bud of personality, despite years of rigorous hardship and oppression, has not been crushed out; whose warm[th] of sense has not been destroyed past resurrection — what wondrous works might not a sculptor give to art?[4]

The *Denver Post* claimed that "The Indian," as it referred to Proctor's monument in progress, was a replacement for one of "the two figures in staff which for many years stood in City Park." But, the paper pointed out, this was "in no sense a copy" of the former work, "but rather a new and free treatment along the same lines."[5] In particular, the rider's pose in the initial model for *On the War Trail,* that of a scout shading his eyes with his hand and looking intently into the distance, was strongly reminiscent of the earlier design (see fig. 14, p. 37).

By March 1919 Proctor had completed the heroic-sized model of the horse. The figure of the Indian turned out to be more problematic. The *San Jose Mercury Herald* that month reported that Sundown and his family had returned to Idaho. Proctor blamed the departure on loneliness and a longing to return to life on the ranch. But Sundown had apparently also been bucked off too many times in the California rodeos he entered, and he had furthermore taken up with a shady fellow named "Foghorn" Murphy, with whom he roamed the bars and back streets of San Francisco.[6]

During the summer of 1919, Proctor visited Montana, working at various locations like Glacier National Park and Browning with at least two Blackfeet Indian models. His last model was variously known as Red Belt and Big Beaver.[7] In comparison with Sundown, Red Belt was urbane and engaging. He spoke English well, read and wrote poetry, and enjoyed social life among the Proctors and their peers. Like Sundown, he was also handsome and a fine horseman.[8] Red Belt returned briefly with Proctor to California, then, following the welcome news that Proctor's studio had been vacated by Frederick MacMonnies, they both headed east for New York where Proctor would complete the Denver monument. It was

like a "stray scene from one of the ubiquitous 'movie' rehearsals," wrote a San Francisco reporter who watched "the cultured gentleman and the handsome Indian in his unconventional cowboy costume" board the train.[9]

A photograph in the *San Francisco Chronicle* showed that the four-foot maquette was then complete (fig. 105). The warrior had a new pose, now sitting upright on his halting mount, his left shoulder turned forward, and holding a lance in his right hand. A hunting knife hung from the Indian's belt and a quiver of arrows from his shoulder. Instead of reconnoitering, the rider now projected defiance. Because the figure in the monument would face north toward Denver's city center, Proctor wanted his posture to reflect not accommodation with, or wonderment at the civilization that towered before him, but bold contempt. The spear, angled to conform to the pony's bowed neck and dropped hindquarters, presented a dynamic challenge to the city. It was not quite so bellicose a presentation as Cyrus Dallin's 1904 bronze *Protest*, but certainly expressive of a similar emotion.

Scribner's would refer to the new pose as "alert and spirited without being melodramatic or overdrawn." And the "shaggy Western pony" evinced "that thorough knowledge of anatomy, that fine feeling of form, that remarkably convincing air of reality that characterizes all of Mr. Proctor's work."[10] The monument was cast by Roman Bronze Works of New York and, according to the *Rocky Mountain News*, was ready to ship west by January 1922, when Proctor visited Denver to inspect the site and select granite for the pedestal.[11] By May 10 it had been placed in the Civic Center.[12]

Once the monument was finished, Proctor began a vigorous campaign promoting the smaller models. The National

Academy of Design exhibited a bronze of *On the War Trail* in 1922, and a colored plaster was displayed at the National Sculpture Society the next year. Also in 1923 the bronze was exhibited at Proctor's solo show at the Stendahl Art Gallery in Los Angeles, where it commanded the entryway, a powerful if somewhat delimiting introduction to the artist's oeuvre. Proctor copyrighted the piece through the National Sculpture Society that year and began to market both a twenty-inch bronze and a forty-eight-inch bronze through the Gorham Company. Proctor's records show the prices of the smaller castings in the early 1930s as ranging from $300 to $450. A superior casting of the forty-eight-inch version in bronze was sold to Geraldine Rockefeller Dodge. An inscription on a small casting now in the Gilcrease Museum collection in Tulsa indicates that Proctor reworked the plaster in 1928 while living in Brussels.

Exhibited: Annual exhibition, National Academy of Design, New York, 1922; Bohemian Club, San Francisco, 1922; National Sculpture Society, New York, 1923 (plaster); *A. Phimister Proctor*, Stendahl Art Gallery, Los Angeles, 1923; Winter exhibition, National Academy of Design, New York, 1930

Other known versions: Gilcrease Museum, Tulsa, Okla. (twenty-inch casting); Art Institute of Chicago, Chicago (forty-eight-inch casting); A. Phimister Proctor Museum, Poulsbo, Wash. (plasters of Indian torso and head, the head alone, and mask of Indian's face)

Fig.105

Variant titles: *Rough Rider*
Modeled, 1920–1922; cast, 1922;
dedicated, 1922
Bronze, monumental sculpture
Markings: "Alexander Phimister
Proctor Sc./© 1922"; "A Gift to the City of
Portland From Dr. Henry Waldo Coe."
Copyright: By Alexander Phimister Proctor
under No. G65849 on May 19, 1922
City of Portland, Oregon

Photograph by Will Gillham

Plate 44 Theodore Roosevelt

In May 1920 a Portland doctor, Henry Waldo Coe, dropped by Proctor's New York studio. He had been making the rounds of the city's sculptors, searching for the right talent to produce a monumental equestrian portrait of Theodore Roosevelt, who had recently died. While visiting Proctor, Coe saw a bronze relief portrait of fellow Oregonian William Hanley. He was so impressed with the likeness and the expression of character in the Hanley portrait that he decided to look no further: Proctor was his man.

Proctor promptly wrote his friends in Portland with the news. Coe wanted a casting of the monument for a Portland park, he told them, and was prepared to donate the statue to the city. "As far as I know," wrote Proctor, "I am the first one commissioned to do an equestrian of Roosevelt." Proctor felt extremely fortunate to be given the commission, yet somehow it also seemed natural. Roosevelt, he reminded them, had "strongly recommended me as the man to do one of Colonel William Cody (Buffalo Bill) which was proposed for Denver but which the war postponed."[1]

Because Proctor had been a friend of Roosevelt's since the early 1890s, many observers endorsed Coe's choice for that reason as much as for his stature as an artist. Other artists had lavished honors on Roosevelt by this date, especially Frederic Remington with his celebrated canvas *Charge of the Rough Riders at San Juan Hill* (1898, Frederic Remington Art Museum). The New York painter William R. Leigh had also depicted Roosevelt in action in his 1920 painting *Theodore Roosevelt and the Rough Riders* (fig. 106), a work prominently featured in the *Christian Science Monitor*.[2] Now it was Proctor's turn.

As Proctor began to sketch an initial composition for the work, he said that the first image to quickly take shape in his mind was of "the man on horseback in the uniform of Colonel of Rough Riders ... and my first thought was to make him in action."[3] An early sketch shows the colonel on a boldly striding horse (fig. 107). To assist with the details of proper attire, the sculptor called on his associate Carl E. Akeley at the American Museum of Natural History in New York. He needed the right uniforms and asked Akeley to pursue the matter with the family through Roosevelt's son Kermit. But Proctor's directions were less than clear, for Akeley responded with the following inquiry:

I suppose I am stupid, but when I had a talk with Kermit this morning about the clothing and accouterments. I could not answer his question as to just what you wanted — whether you are doing him in rough-rider or some other out-of-door costume. If you will answer this question I think we can get action. In other words just let me know the things you want.[4]

It was not until late spring that Proctor had what he wanted. Kermit and his mother, Edith, rummaged through trunks and closets in Oyster Bay and produced a couple of Rough Rider uniforms for the artist to use. "Mrs. Roosevelt sent me two of T.R.'s rough rider suits," Proctor reported to the *Portland Oregon Journal* in June 1921. Also included in the loan were appropriate "side arms, bridle and his actual rough rider hat, all of which fitted well the soldier boy who was my model. I felt very grateful for this consideration."[5]

By the time Proctor added the proper costumes, he had also chosen a more static pose for the group. He recalled later that he had "gradually decided if possible to show the rider and horse in partial repose. The rider is in control and the horse's feet are well under him, ready for instant action."[6] General Leonard Wood, who fought with Roosevelt in the Spanish-American War, helped Proctor identify the right horse: a northern range horse with a strain of thoroughbred.[7]

Coe approved the model at every stage, and once the final plaster maquette reached New York, the Roosevelt family was called in for their comments over the next several months.[8] Of special note were the president's sister's remarks after she visited Proctor's studio in the early summer of 1922. In an exuberant letter to Coe, she expressed her enthusiasm for the artist's efforts:

Yesterday I was able to go to see Mr. Proctor's wonderful equestrian statue of my brother, Colonel Roosevelt. I cannot tell you how greatly it has surprised me. The figure of my brother — and the face also — are both unusually like the original, and there is a mixture of energy and repose about the whole composition that is remarkably characteristic of Theodore Roosevelt.[9]

Out in Portland considerable debate went on about the site of the monument and its base. Proctor played little role in the first debate, saying only that he preferred that the monument not be stuck back in some shady recess in a park. Coe viewed the monument as especially educational for Portland's children, and so the final placement selection, on the boulevard median in what was known as "the Parks blocks" directly across from Ladd School, suited both artist and patron. The pedestal presented other problems. Proctor wanted to involve the New York architectural firm of McKim, Meade and White. S. C. Pier, Portland's city commissioner, preferred to keep that part of the project in local hands. In the end the New York firm offered conceptual plans and the work was carried out by local craftsmen.[10] Vice President Calvin Coolidge attended the groundbreaking ceremonies in August 1922, and throngs of Portlanders turned out on Armistice Day for the dedication. A message from President Warren G. Harding

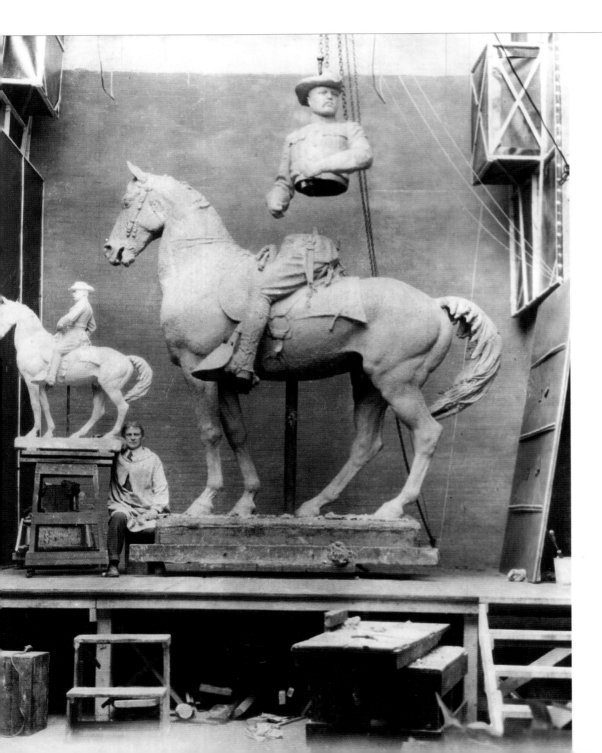

was read, formally commending the statue not just to
Portland's youth but to the children of America. In addition to
hundreds of students from Ladd School, over four hundred
Spanish-American War veterans turned out for the unveiling.

Proctor recalled on the occasion his long association
with Roosevelt: how they had met in 1893 at the World's
Columbian Exposition in Chicago, how Roosevelt facilitated
his Boone and Crockett Club membership, how the president
commissioned him to carve the buffalo heads for the White
House State Dining Room fireplace (see plate 31), and how
his *Panther* (see plate 5) had become an emblem for the
Roosevelt administration. He was much quoted at the time,
articulating his vision of the memorial:

> I wanted to give the world ... the impression of Roosevelt as
> I knew him — as, indeed, I always think of him. I most
> admired his fearlessness, his courage, and the energy
> always waiting to spring into action. I never thought of him
> as a man of hasty, ill-considered action. All his exuberance,
> all his restlessness, was only the surface that covered a
> quiet dignity and reserve. The popular idea of him is that he
> never was in repose. I wanted to show him as he appeared
> to me, with all his magnificent energy held in check.[11]

One of New York's most esteemed art critics, Royal Cortissoz,
had viewed the finished plaster in Proctor's studio in April. His
comments were in sympathy with the artist's mission:

> With admirable insight Mr. Proctor has reflected the dra-
> matic gesture into which this narrative might have
> tempted him and puts before us, instead, the character
> lying behind it. The Western type of horse upon which he

Fig.106   Fig.107

*has placed the Colonel is unmistakably a spirited animal,
but it is at the moment as serene and strong as its rider.
Technically this horse is perhaps the sculptor's finest
achievement as an interpreter of animals. It is modeled
with breadth and simplicity. Horse and rider together make
a very sound composition, effective from any point of view.
Its greatest virtue is its freedom from breezy picturesqueness. The keynote to the monument is one of restrained animation. The design has a dignified unity. It would be good if
a replica could be created here in the East.*[12]

Long before the Portland dedication, Coe had been working
to establish other sites for *Theodore Roosevelt.* By early spring
of 1922, he had negotiated a site for a second monument,
this one in Minot, North Dakota, near the ranch he had
owned as a young man. It was in North Dakota that Coe had
first befriended Roosevelt, back in the early 1880s. By the
time Coe finished distributing Theodore Roosevelt statues
across the country, the scope of his generosity had indeed
reached national proportions. Two smaller versions, each
over fifty inches high, were cast. One was placed in Depot
Park in front of what was then the Northern Pacific railroad
station in Mandan, North Dakota. The second was donated to
the Roosevelt Memorial Museum (now operated by the
National Park Service as the Theodore Roosevelt Birthplace)
in New York. Coe also gave a full-sized plaster cast to the
North Dakota Historical Society in Bismarck. He had denied
earlier requests from Philadelphia's Fairmont Park and from
Corinne Roosevelt Robinson, who wished to have a casting
displayed permanently in New York's Central Park.[13]

Proctor received national approbation for the monument. Crowds cheered him vigorously in Portland and again

in North Dakota, where he attended at least one of the other
dedications. But one politician, wishing to get his name in
the papers and professing to have the credentials of an art
critic, lambasted Proctor for supposedly misshaping
Roosevelt's mount. Oswald West, an Oregon ex-governor, was
quoted as saying that the horse Proctor modeled had "the
front legs of a giraffe, the neck of a stallion and the tail of a
fern."[14] Dozens came to Proctor's defense in the ensuing
debate. One champion of Proctor's assured readers that the
ex-governor was perpetrating nothing more than a "right
merry jest." Others were less forgiving. Proctor was a westerner and an artist with the "wonderful skill and cunning of the
great sculptor," said one of his allies, while West could claim
no aesthetic foundation and no higher ground than base political opportunism.[15] As with the controversy over Sherman's
horse, the matter filled newspaper columns for many months.
Everyone from old cowboys to fellow artists was invited to
offer testimonials. The general consensus was that readers
should not take West seriously and that the horse was just
fine—it was in fact "splendidly proportioned for range or cavalry purposes." Among the other equestrian monuments to be
found in America's public spaces—Edward Potters' *Custer,*
Frederick MacMonnies' *Kit Carson,* and Jean Antonin Mercie's
Robert E. Lee— Proctor's stood out as superior. The art critic of
the *Portland Oregonian* felt Proctor's *Theodore Roosevelt* was
by far the most faithful representation of horse flesh.[16]

Nevertheless, elements of the monument would be
debated for the next twenty years. In October 1948 Proctor had
to write a letter defending the double reins and the combined
snaffle and curb bits used in the work. His ultimate defense
rested on the fact that "the whole Roosevelt family saw and
approved the statue when it was finished in my New York

studio."[17] "I am quite sure that your horse is proof against mal-
ice," Roosevelt's widow, Edith, had written to Coe at the time
the original debate began back in 1926. Coe in turn defended
the work with a brief history of the monument's evolution:

*When the statue was made it was submitted to more than
20 sculptors, artists, painters, and they all commended it.
The Roosevelt family was called in, the sons, daughters,
every member except the widow. The Roosevelt family is a
family of horsemen and horsewomen. They know horses.
One of the boys said: "Where did you get father's sorrel
horse?"*[18]

Coe concluded that he had "wanted to get the best sculptor
in the world" and he felt he had found such a man in Proctor
who, he claimed, had "made more bronze horses than any
other man in history."[19] Oswald West failed in his reelection
bid, and Proctor moved seamlessly on to his next commission.

Exhibited: *A. Phimister Proctor*, Stendahl Art Gallery, Los
Angeles, 1923 (plaster maquette)

Other known versions: Minot, N. Dak. (heroic-sized bronze);
Mandan, N. Dak. (fifty-five-inch bronze); Theodore Roosevelt
Birthplace, New York (fifty-five-inch bronze); A. Phimister
Proctor Museum, Poulsbo, Wash. (plaster for small castings);
North Dakota Historical Society, Bismarck, N. Dak. (full plaster
of heroic-sized bronze)

Variant titles: None recorded
Modeled, 1921–1923; cast, 1923;
dedicated, 1924
Bronze, monumental sculpture
Markings: "A PHIMISTER PROCTOR
SCULPTOR/CAST BY ROMAN
BRONZE WORKS"
Copyright: By Alexander Phimister
Proctor under No. G68875 on June 18, 1923
State Capitol Building, Salem, Oregon

Plate 45 Circuit Rider

On January 8, 1922, the *Portland Telegram* announced that a former senator from Eugene, Robert A. Booth, had recently proposed to give the State of Oregon a statue honoring the early pioneer circuit ministers. The idea had come from discussions with Proctor the preceding summer, after which Booth had offered the artist a commission for a working model that, once approved, would be enlarged into a twelve-foot high bronze equestrian monument. The article included Proctor's initial concept sketch, which was reportedly being exhibited before several Portland artists as well as the patron.[1] As described by the newspaper, Proctor's sketch model (fig. 108) represented

> *the circuit rider jogging along reading his sermon to be preached at his next stop. The long cloak, which was found to be good protection against wind and rain, is featured by the sculptor and the saddlebags in which he carried most of his worldly possessions. The horse is convincingly done and the whole figure is natural and realistic and depicts the rugged force of the riders who stopped for no obstacle in their dissemination of their beliefs.*[2]

Booth had asked Oregon's governor, Benjamin W. Olcott, to appoint a site selection committee. Given the historic nature of the proposed work, many felt a location on the grounds of the state capitol in Salem would be appropriate.

Although focused on commemorating the state's early evangelists, Booth also saw the commission as a family tribute: Booth's father, Robert, had been a Methodist circuit rider, and contemplating the senior Booth's career had led the son to choose to memorialize the western preachers on horseback. Robert Booth, his wife, Mary Minor, and four chil-

dren had come west on the Oregon Trail in 1852. On the trip one of their sons nearly died of cholera, Robert became gravely ill as well, and Mary made him promise to preach in Oregon if God delivered him from death.[3] Robert survived, the family settled in Yamhill County, and Booth joined the conference of the Methodist Episcopal church in 1855. His first assignment as an itinerant parson was in the Willamette Valley, after which he branched out widely, covering a seven-county area. According to his son, Robert "continued in the ministry for many years, being retired a short time before his death … in 1917 in his ninety-seventh year."[4]

An Oregon judge, Charles H. Carey, wrote about Robert A. Booth's larger influence, suggesting that the dedicated circuit preachers were responsible not just for providing spiritual guidance in the wilderness, especially in their proselytizing among native peoples, but in enabling through their work a political organization to take hold in the region. These "selfless" crusaders harboring "heroic soul[s]" and the highest of "ideals" inculcated the lessons of civilization among the pioneers. It is true, wrote Judge Carey,

> *that after their arrival many of these enthusiasts learned the practical fact that to convert the Indians was not the whole duty of the Circuit Rider. The westward movement of the white population began, and among these settlers there was a work to be done, and a work not less important than among the aborigines themselves.*[5]

The preachers turned to the establishing of schools of learning and to the laying of the foundations of the future commonwealth. The academies, and colleges, and universities that

PRESENTED TO THE STATE OF OREGON
IN REVERENT AND GRATEFUL REMEMBRANCE OF ROBERT BOOTH
PIONEER MINISTER OF THE OREGON COUNTRY·BY HIS SON, ROBERT A. BOOTH

Fig.108

have had such profound influence upon the Oregon people were in many instances founded and nursed by the circuit riding preachers. The provisional government of the infant territory of Oregon grew under their hands. And the spiritual and moral influence of these worthy men penetrated and infiltrated the civilization that owes its peculiar character in no small degree to these same teachers and preachers of the West. After viewing the model, Judge Carey felt that Proctor had "grasped the big idea."[6]

Proctor, after presenting his model to Booth as well as the people of Oregon, returned to his Stanford University studio in Palo Alto, California, to perfect the design and work up a larger model of the final conception. By late January 1921, the Palo Alto newspapers were commenting on Proctor's efforts, and in February his new model began to assume a slightly different pose. Now, instead of trotting, the horse plodded forward; the new pace suggested deliberation and persistence rather than vigor and expedience. The hat that had covered the preacher's unshorn head would be removed by September and attached to the saddle, giving the figure, as many observers remarked, "a more spiritual look."[7]

Although the rider's mission had far-sighted goals, the horse and the pioneer apostle in the model seem humbled. The horse's ambling gait and blank expression suggest a weary pace propelled by resolve rather than energy. The minister looks no further ahead than the pages of his Bible. There is a sense of the two storing up energy for the conversions ahead, as if having crossed the continent to the Pacific shore, the preacher and his message are as much exhausted as exalted. Studious and burdened, he marches from county to county through the soggy Oregon forests and fields.

Fig.109

Proctor did not attempt a portrait of the Booth patriarch. Rather his purpose was "to build up a composite type which will reflect the strength of character possessed by the early day ministers."[8] For some reason the sculptor made the rider older with successive modelings. Increased age may, in the artist's mind, have imbued the figure with even more solemnity.

By November 1921 the working model was complete (fig. 109) and ready to enlarge to heroic scale.[9] A site had been selected in front of the state capitol building in Salem, and the artist and his patron anticipated a spring 1923 dedication. The original contract had called for all the work to take one year, but simply enlarging the working model to over twelve feet took that long. In late 1922, shortly before he shipped the monumental plaster to New York where Roman Bronze Works would cast it in bronze, Proctor hosted a public reception for his California neighbors. A reporter who saw the model there made the following observations:

The figure, of heroic size, depicts a 'circuit-rider' or travel-ing minister of the old West, mounted on the gaunt steed that bore him through his extensive parish. The earnest, almost ascetic face of the rider is bent over a book; his head is bare, and his long hair is tousled by the wind. The work is one of unusual interest, and vigor. In it the sculptor has caught the earnestness of spirit, the disregard for self, which typified the heroic preachers of the early days.[10]

The serene dignity with which Proctor had infused this work, and its combination of expressive, emotive power with under-stated simplicity, caused more than one California art critic to claim Proctor as "one of America's foremost sculptors" and

"one of the foremost exponents of western spirit and art."[11] For some Oregon critics, Proctor approached canonization. He had produced a work, according to Gertrude Robinson Ross, not simply shaped with "beauty and spirituality," but one that left "a sense of having looked on something sacred."[12]

After some of its members saw the work on its way to the foundry in early 1923, the National Sculpture Society in New York requested that Proctor allow them to exhibit the monu-mental plaster. Yet it was not included in the society's immense *Exhibition of American Sculptures* held at the Hispanic Society of America in New York that spring and sum-mer (Proctor did show five other works).[13] The reason was that Roman Bronze Works had been too busy to cast the group, and it was not until April 19, 1924, that the *Circuit Rider* mon-ument was finally dedicated in Salem.

In the primary address at the unveiling ceremony deliv-ered by Proctor's early Portland patron, the engineer Joseph N. Teal extolled the sculptor's artistic prowess and western ardor:

Mr. Proctor breathes the spirit of the West. He is true to its life and to its traditions. A western man himself, fond of all that makes it glorious, of its traditions, of its history, he has put into this group the very best that is in him. Fettered by no instructions, limited by no set designs, con-trolled by no preconceived notions, there was committed to him the task of expressing in bronze the high ideals the donor desired to commemorate and perpetuate.[14]

Proctor had told a Seattle reporter a few months earlier that he strove to "get as many of our great pioneers in bronze as possible.... I want to do my share in recording the historic

struggles of our great frontiersmen." At the time of the dedi-cation, the writer Charles J. Lisle affirmed Proctor's ambition. Not only had the pioneer preacher been properly document-ed and venerated, but an "ideal" had also been preserved, one that had "made Oregon a splendid Christian state out of a once howling wilderness."[15]

Proctor's monument weighed about three-and-a-half tons and sat on a thousand cubic feet of granite pedestal. Even so, in 1962 it was toppled off its base by strong winds. The rider's head was damaged, and the bronze underwent serious and much needed conservation treatment by Vancouver sculptor James Lee Hansen. In the process, a new head for the rider had to be cast and the full group repatinat-ed.[16] Thus the *Circuit Rider* continued its journey through his-tory once again.

Exhibited: *A. Phimister Proctor*, Stendahl Art Gallery, Los Angeles, 1923 (plaster)

Other known versions: None

Variant title: *Indian Maiden and Fawn;*
Indian Girl and Doe
Modeled, 1921–1926, cast initially, 1926
Leaded yellow brass, 48 x 23 x 70 inches
Markings: None
Copyright: By Alexander Phimister Proctor
under Nos. G78378 and G78379 on June 22,
1926; by Robert E. Maytag under No.
G53015 on January 14, 1974; by Nona
Proctor Church under No. H53322 on
December 1, 1973

Jasper County Historical Society, Newton, Iowa
(gift of Robert E. and Mona Maytag, 1993)

Fig.110
Photograph of Eliza Cowapoo, winner of
the Indian Beauty Contest, 1923

Howdyshell Photos/Matt Johnson

Plate 46 Indian Girl

Fig.110

In Proctor's autobiography he mentions starting on this work in his Stanford University studio in Palo Alto, California, during the year 1921.[1] It may have been inspired by Indian women he had seen at the Pendleton Round-Up, since the beaded headband was standard attire for young native women at the Oregon rodeo. In the early 1920s, the Round-Up began to award prizes for the loveliest of the women in an "Indian Beauty Contest."[2] Eliza Cowapoo (fig. 110), crowned princess in 1923, closely resembled Proctor's dryad. Proctor also knew many Indian women who were bucking horse contestants. One star rider, known as Princess Redbird, was known to wave a small American flag while she spurred her bronco before the crowd.[3] While there is no evidence to suggest that Proctor disapproved of female athletics, his interpretation of femininity did not allow for such themes in his art. He preferred instead to render women in the form of Indian nymphs, a paradigm of Mother Nature.

Proctor took the plaster model of *Indian Girl* with him in 1925 when he moved to Rome, where it attracted much attention. The King and Queen of Italy visited his studio in 1926 and were said to have especially admired the work; according to Proctor, the royal couple thought the "Indian girl group was very beautiful."[4] On the back of a photograph taken in Brussels in 1927, Proctor wrote the sculpture's title as *Indian Girl and Doe.* He indicated that the work was available in two sizes: one "about 16 inches high" and the "second & larger size 6 feet 3 inches high." The smaller castings cost $200, and the larger ones, $2,500 — in New York. For those who wished to take delivery of the larger casting in Brussels, the price went down to $1,500.

Three of the large bronzes and one smaller version sold while the Proctors were in Rome. One of the large castings,

when complete, was to go to Campbell Church of Eugene, Oregon. Ora Maytag of Newton, Iowa, had ordered another, and the third was destined for the Brooklyn Botanic Garden, a promised gift of George D. Pratt. California Senator James D. Phelan had requested a casting "somewhat smaller than the life" for the lawn of his estate, Villa Montalvo, in Saratoga, California.[5] Surviving correspondence between Proctor and Phelan indicates that the senator paid $2,500 for it in October 1926.[6] Proctor also sold the doe separately. It appeared in Loring Dodd's *The Golden Age of American Sculpture* (1936), and an example cast in Brussels shows the graceful deer nosing the air.[7]

The theme of Proctor's *Indian Girl*, while somewhat atypical for him, was not out of character for his work of this period. Conceived at the time he was completing his *Indian Drinking* (see fig. 50) in the early 1920s, the work relates to the bounty of nature, its connectivity with humankind, and the rewards of establishing and maintaining a spiritual union between the two. The Indian woman, as nature's symbolic innocent, nourishes the wild animal with maize. The roughly rectangular space defined by her arms and the deer's head suggest not only a bond among nature's creatures but a promise of continuity. These are messages similar to those in the *Indian Drinking* — a quiet, gentle, feminized view that is the opposite of the sense of rugged survival by wits and strength that pervades works like the stealthy *Panther* (see plate 5) or the defiant *Elk* (see plate 17). Absent also are any references to the hunter, man or animal. The Indian girl has harvested the corn from an unseen garden and shares the nourishment with her kindred spirit, the doe. Hers is an expression of charity and generosity.

A younger sculptor, Carl Paul Jennewein, was exploring similar themes at that time. In the 1922 *Nymph and Fawn*, however, Jennewein focused on the woman's instructing the innocent creature rather than apportioning nature's bounty. Yet both artists were addressing ideal beauty as found equally in wildlife and in the female form. Although Jennewein would soon turn to modernism and away from naturalistic depictions of the human figure, both he and Proctor would have supported Daniel Chester French's conviction, expressed shortly before the old master's death, "that the beauty of woman is beauty at its best."[8] While Jennewein chose a figure from antiquity, as did French in his final finished work, *Andromeda* (1929–1931, Chesterwood, Stockbridge, Mass.), Proctor elected to revere the woman he viewed as most ideal, the Indian woman of the American West. In its presentation, Proctor's *Indian Girl* was an aesthetic step back in time to the neoclassical expressions of Hiram Powers and William Henry Rinehart.[9]

Exhibited: None known

Other known versions: University of Oregon Museum of Art, Eugene (gift of Carl and Narcissa Washburne, 1962); Brooklyn Botanic Garden, Brooklyn, N.Y. (gift of George D. Pratt, 1927) *Small version*: A. Phimister Proctor Museum, Poulsbo, Wash.; Carol Church, Seattle, Wash.

Variant titles: None recorded
Modeled, 1925; cast, 1927; dedicated, 1927
Bronze, monumental sculpture
Markings: "A. PHIMISTER SCULPTOR 1927"
Copyright: By Alexander Phimister Proctor
under No. G 73646 on February 2, 1925
Penn Valley Park, Kansas City, Missouri

Plate 47 Pioneer Mother (Equestrian)

In his autobiography Proctor devoted a full chapter to the *Pioneer Mother*, perhaps his most complex and certainly one of his most accomplished and famous monuments. He wrote that he first conceptualized the work in 1922 after many years of wishing to produce a sculptural tribute to pioneer women but not knowing exactly what form it might take. The historian and novelist Emerson Hough had popularized the theme in 1922, when his book *The Covered Wagon* was serialized in the *Saturday Evening Post*. The cover of the magazine's April 1, 1922, issue featured William H. D. Koerner's illustration *Madonna of the Prairie* (fig. 111). It portrayed Molly Wingate, the novel's heroine, dressed in calico, framed by the halo of a Conestoga wagon, limply holding the horse's reins. Her gaze is distanced and her attitude is passive, her shoulders sloping gracefully though weakly from her beautiful face. It appears as if she is being led, rather helplessly, into America's promising future. Hough considered the image the absolute apex of the illustrator's art. "Here we have imagination and fidelity both," he wrote to the *Post*'s editor, George Horace Lorimer. "I don't know when an illustration has hit me in the face the way that one has."[1]

Proctor no doubt saw this exceedingly popular image. He hoped, however, to achieve the opposite impression with his interpretation. "I didn't want to show her doing ordinary tasks, plodding westward in a calico dress or driving cattle before her," he wrote. "I wanted to be true to life, but I also wanted to show another, no less heroic side." A peer of the men who went west, she would be portrayed as an active, self-determined partner in the pioneering experience:

It seemed to me that most people, in thinking of pioneers, thought solely of the men. I considered the heroism of the women equal to, and perhaps greater than, the men's. As Mark Twain said, "The women had to endure everything the pioneers did, and then they also had to endure the pioneers!"[2]

Proctor carried this concept in his mind for a year or more. Then in April 1923 Proctor met Howard Vanderslice, a wealthy grain broker from Kansas City, Missouri, at the Stendahl Art Gallery exhibition of his work in Los Angeles. Vanderslice had purchased a casting of Proctor's *Panther* (see plate 5), and in the course of talking together, the artist and the broker discovered a mutual aspiration: they both wished to see a monument erected some day to the pioneer mothers who had crossed the country on the western trails. Once Proctor described his ideas, Vanderslice encouraged him to develop a sketch. This Proctor did, and when Vanderslice saw the artist's concept in clay, he is reported to have trembled with excitement. His mother and his wife's mother had both been pioneers, and he could recall tales from his family history of his mother riding on horseback among the immigrants to Kansas.[3]

Because this was to be an extremely complicated group — two horses, a baby, and three adult human figures — and because Proctor thought that models would be more readily available in southern California, the family moved to Hollywood once the commission was assured. There Proctor fitted out a new studio while his wife, Margaret, made a dress for the central figure; he then hired models and bought a weary-looking horse. (One of his male models had been a stand-in for Ernest Torrence in the movie version of *The Covered Wagon* that had premiered in March 1923.) In his effort to make it "true to life," Proctor even acquired a sidesaddle from Eugene, Oregon, that had carried a woman across the Oregon Trail in 1852.[4]

According to the contract signed by Vanderslice and Proctor in February 1925, the artist was to be paid $40,000 for all work associated with the bronze monument including its casting, delivery, and placement on the pedestal in Kansas City.[5] By March the model was sufficiently developed that Proctor began to search for a foundry to cast the monument.[6] His original plan was to move to New York where he could supervise the enlargement as well as the casting, but during a trip there that spring, he discovered that the city would be too expensive. In addition, the foundries he approached — Gorham, Anton Kunst, and Roman Bronze Works — wanted far too much for their work to give Proctor the profit he felt he deserved.[7] Although he told the *Kansas City Star* in early April that he would have the monument cast in New York, he was considering other, more frugal options.[8] When Margaret suggested that he should pack it off to Rome, Proctor immediately agreed. Following discussions with several artists who had worked abroad and with William Mitchell Kendall, chairman of the American Academy in Rome, Proctor, his wife, and five of their eight children left for Italy later that fall.

They had shipped ahead the plaster maquette which measured nearly five feet in height. Kendall had arranged for a studio at the American Academy, and Proctor set to work using Italian artisans to enlarge the figures to monumental size. He discovered, however, that the Italian assistants were poor copyists: they wanted to "improve" on Proctor's design rather than stick to the enlargement function. He also found that the process would take rather longer than anticipated. What he had hoped would be a year's stay in Rome turned

Fig.111

into two. The *Pioneer Mother* was cast in Italy and did not find its way to its final resting place, Penn Valley Park in Kansas City, until November 11, 1927.

While in Italy, Proctor befriended a number of new artists like Frank P. Fairbanks, who encouraged and even documented Proctor's work. Fairbanks was a painter who served as director of the American Academy from 1922 to 1932. In 1928 he painted an eleven-foot tribute in oil to Proctor, his family, and the monumental sculpture that was taking shape within the academy's walls (see plate 2, p. 90). Pictured on a ladder below the plaster monument, but perched above his gathered family, is Proctor. Much as he stands at the apex of the family triangle in Fairbanks' composition, the pioneer woman with babe in arms crowns the sculptural tableau above. The untitled painting, according to Fairbanks, captured no specific scene but was "simply a romantic idea of a family in the open," even though the figures represented individual portraits.[9]

Many Americans also visited Proctor's studio. Kansas' ex-governor, Henry J. Allen, called on the artist in April 1927 and was emotionally moved by what he saw. "He has caught the fearlessness and energy of those rare pioneers," Allen wrote to the *Kansas City Star,* "and given them a deathless repose." Here stood the perfect "tribute to the eternal hope which characterized the pioneer women."[10] What particularly impressed Allen was the intensity of the mother's forward-leaning posture and gaze, as well as the courage and resolution in the lift of her chin. These were not qualities frequently seen in presentations of western women.

Other visitors brought international attention to the work. Proctor's old Académie Julian teacher, Denys Puech, who at the time was directing the French Academy in Rome,

Fig.112

came to admire his former student's work. And the King and Queen of Italy paid a visit to Proctor's studio in the summer of 1926. Standing next to the monument, dwarfed by the huge pioneers, they posed for pictures. The Italian and American press regarded the royal stop as a triumph for Proctor.[11]

"The theme, the Pioneer Mother, has an appeal to sentiment that is obvious," Proctor was quoted as saying at this time. "Yet the sculptor must carry beyond that, if the critical are to find his work worthy. The test," he concluded, "must be in composition, in bringing unity into an assemblage" of this magnitude.[12] Three adult figures, a baby, and two horses, while not an imposing challenge for a painter, represented a formidable one to the sculptor. The thirty thousand people said to have viewed the monument on its first day in Kansas City probably concurred that Proctor had met that challenge. Vanderslice declined to express an opinion. "As a business man, I do not presume to discuss the abstract qualities of art," he said when asked his thoughts at the unveiling.[13] But others voiced their approval, seeing in the *Pioneer Mother* "the great story of their own ancestry and heritage, incarnate in bronze."[14] The powerful unity of the group, its forward motion, and the symbolic force of the central maternal figure engaged, indeed overwhelmed, the crowds.

Although the Kansas City monument was dedicated to pioneers of the Southwest, especially travelers along the old Santa Fe Trail for which Kansas City had been a point of embarkation, it also served an autobiographical function for Proctor. His family had moved during his childhood first from Canada to Michigan, then to Iowa, and eventually on to Colorado. He knew that search for new opportunity, both the fatigue and the resolute determination that overcame it. As

the image of the pioneer family, especially pioneer mothers, became increasingly popular between 1920 and 1940, Proctor's interpretation stood out. Not only was it original in concept, formidable in scale and complexity, and one of the first, if not the first, of its genre, but it also expressed genuinely personal empathy with force and grace.[15]

The work recalls the gentle union of mother and child that Margaret had exemplified when she posed for Bessie Potter back in 1896. In *A Young Mother* (fig. 112) Margaret is portrayed affectionately cradling a baby in her arms. Potter had been Margaret's closest friend and a fellow artist who shared her reverence for motherhood. Significantly, in the contract between Vanderslice and Proctor, Margaret was named to complete the work in the event of the "death or disability of Proctor."[16]

Proctor had written into that same contract a provision that allowed him to cast and sell bronzes of the original four-foot, nine-inch maquette.[17] So far as is known, only one such bronze was produced: Proctor mentioned selling a bronze cast of the *Pioneer Mother* working model to a friend of Theodore Roosevelt's son Kermit in 1925. This was the one owned by the Douglas Clegg family of Calistoga, California, that was donated to the Santa Barbara Art Museum in 1991.[18]

In 1929 the sculptor Gutzon Borglum, a loquacious man of superior insight and vast ambition, stood before Proctor's monument in Kansas City. He concluded after some reflection that "it is the finest pioneer group in America today. It is the finest thought out, most carefully executed." Perched on a hill in the park astride a plain but dignified pink Minnesota granite base designed by Kansas City architects Wight & Wight, it also impressed Borglum as the most "admirably placed." And

giving Proctor the praise he would have relished most, Borglum claimed, "[H]ere you have something real."[19]

Exhibited: None known

Other known versions: Santa Barbara Museum of Art, Santa Barbara, Calif. (bronze of maquette, gift of Mrs. Douglas Clegg, 1991); A. Phimister Proctor Museum, Poulsbo, Wash. (plaster maquettes of the three adults and baby as well as the heads of the two horses)

one of four bison heads for arlington memorial
Bridge. Washington DC.

A. Phimister Proctor
sculptor.
Rome Italy.
1925.

Variant titles: *Arlington Memorial Bridge Buffalo Head; Buffalo Head*
Modeled, 1926; completed in plaster, 1927; installed with modification, 1932
Bronze, monumental sculpture
Markings: None
Copyright: By Alexander Phimister Proctor under No. 80895 on July 9, 1927
Arlington Memorial Bridge, Washington, D.C.

Vintage photograph A. Phimister Proctor Museum Archives, Poulsbo, Wash.
Reproduction photograph by Howard Giske

Fig.113
Proctor with his *High Relief of Bison Head* for the Arlington Memorial Bridge, Rome, c. 1927

Buffalo Bill Historical Center, Cody, Wyo.; P.69.677

Plate 48 High Relief of Bison Head

In the mid-1920s, Proctor benefited again from the commission established by Senator James McMillan to enhance the nation's capital architecturally. Proctor's friend, the architect Charles Follen McKim, was asked to design a bridge across the Potomac River connecting the Lincoln Memorial on one side with the Custis-Lee Mansion on the other. As a practical matter, the new stone bridge would replace a narrow wooden one that could not handle the increasing traffic pressures. As a symbolic gesture, the bridge provided a link between North and South, a psychological as well as physical union of two once bitterly divided segments of American society.[1]

Plans to build the bridge began in 1921. McKim asked Proctor to provide designs for the large bison heads that were to decorate the keystones over each of the bridge's nine spans. He had evidently remembered with favor the two marble relief buffalo heads that Proctor had sculpted for the Theodore Roosevelt White House State Dining Room fireplace mantel back in 1909 (see plate 31). In fact the bison heads for what was to be known as the Arlington Memorial Bridge, though somewhat lower in relief and slightly more decorative in style, were highly reminiscent of the Roosevelt White House heads.

The bridge was built between 1926 and 1932, and Proctor worked on his part of the job during his stay in Rome (fig. 113). Each head was to measure approximately six feet in height. According to documents in the artist's papers, he produced three "different sized heads—all large."[2] He worked on them in 1926 and completed them the next year, sending plaster casts back to Washington to be cut into stone and placed on the bridge façades.[3]

At some point in the process, however, Proctor's design was changed. A second sculptor, Carl Paul Jennewein, who

had been assigned the job of decorating the pylons for the bridge, was asked by the committee to rework Proctor's heads. Jennewein's reputation at the time centered on his ability to synthesize the ancient art of the Greco-Roman world with a decorative Art Nouveau stylization. Like Proctor, he was working in Rome in 1926. By the standards of the day, his modernized revival of antique forms was considered "conservative." Yet when set beside Proctor's production, the style's curvilinear patterns replaced naturalism with decorative contrivance.[4] Or, at least that was how Proctor reacted when he saw the changes that had been wrought on his large bison.

A photograph of Jennewein's modifications to Proctor's designs in the artist's papers is inscribed with comments by Proctor that reveal not just dissatisfaction and concern about the alterations but contempt for the direction art was moving in during the 1920s:

Bison Heads—modeled for Arlington Bridge Washington Bridge—Washington, D.C.—Tho this decoration was to go so high that nobody but the gods and angels could see it—The Art Commission, while I was in Rome thought the heads were not decorative enough—Had a spit-curls sculptor turn the hair on top of the head into rabbits entrails (or guts) and decorated the rest of the head with decorated rivet heads—This is the high art of today—A. Phimister Proctor—There were 3 different-sized heads—all large all modeled in Rome, 1926—Why a buffalo head 5'6" high, to be placed a hundred feet & more above the eye would be improved by putting several hundred little rivet heads, decorated with little circles... I don't see.[5]

The depth of Proctor's disdain for the commission's decision and for Jennewein's alterations was such that the sculptor refrained from mentioning the work in his autobiography. No doubt he did not identify with the heads after the severe modifications were effected. Fortunately he had other bridges in Washington in which he could take lasting pride.

Exhibited: None known

Other known versions: None

Fig.113

Variant titles: *Goodrich Riding Trophy;*
Draper Trophy
Modeled, 1926; cast initially, c. 1926
Bronze, 27 x 7 x 18 inches
Markings: "A. PHIMISTER PROCTOR"
Copyright: By Alexander Phimister
Proctor under No. G84150 on July 24, 1928
Third Cavalry Museum, Fort Carson, Colo.

Plate 49 U.S. Cavalryman

In early 1926 General Malin Craig, chief of the U.S. Cavalry, entertained a proposal from Major L. E. Goodrich, a member of the Cavalry Reserve from Miami, Florida. Goodrich had the idea that cavalry exercises might be more productive if the soldiers had a greater interest in the training process. Why not, he suggested, make training a competitive affair — offer an award for the unit that performed most effectively in training. As one writer observed in 1927, after the first award was conferred on Troop G of the Second Cavalry from Fort Riley, Kansas, recognition would be given "annually to that troop which excels all others in general cavalry proficiency — mobility, fire power, and shock action."[1] Goodrich not only proposed the idea but also provided the money to underwrite the program, contributing $50,000 to sponsor what was called a "Mounted Service Ride" and to pay for an appropriate trophy to honor the winners. With Craig's backing, the trophy was called the Goodrich Riding Trophy and the program was scheduled to begin the next year.

Proctor, who had been living and working at the American Academy in Rome since early 1926, received a letter from Craig's successor, Major General H. B. Crosby, inquiring if Proctor might be interested in sculpting the trophy. The artist's response was an enthusiastic yes. Even though the army offered him only $2,000 for the commission, "much below" the price he would charge for "such a piece for individual civilians," the thought of an artwork as a trophy appealed to him. In his response to Crosby, he noted that "small mounted or equestrian subjects are almost my specialty," and "it would be much better to have a distinctive work of art for trophies than a common place cup."[2] He went on to say that he was a "stickler for exact form in equipment," as evidenced in the

details to be found on his *Theodore Roosevelt* monument (see plate 44). He concluded with one condition:

I would be glad to do this model for you and the Army and to encourage the art idea for price mentioned & under the difficult conditions [presumably time constraints] if the commission were given to me outright. I would not care to go into any sort of competition with any other sculptors, however. I have done at least as many equestrian statues small and large as any other sculptor in America & probably more.[3]

The general accepted Proctor's conditions, Proctor met the tight time schedule, and the first *U.S. Cavalryman* trophy was awarded following the 1927 competition. In conceptualizing the trophy, Proctor had focused on the third day of the competition, described as a "most grueling" series of exercises testing physical endurance and marksmanship skills.[4] On that day the men demonstrated their prowess with pistols and sabers while charging in mounted combat. Crosby must have sent the artist photographs of similar exercises since Proctor was not known to have attended any military training maneuvers, though records of the Third Cavalry Museum indicate that he used a Sergeant Wotiski and his horse "Peggy" as his models.[5]

Although not created specifically for that purpose, two of Proctor's sculptures had been used previously as shooting trophies. Colonel Charles L. Potter, president of the Mississippi River Engineering Board, once gave a casting of Proctor's bronze "*Sundown*" *Nez Perce's Chief* (see plate 42) as a trophy for the Army Engineers annual competition. And, according to Proctor, his friend Gifford Pinchot, then governor of Pennsylvania, "is giving one of my bronzes as a trophy for the

Pennsylvania constabulary to shoot for in revolver practice." Proctor, who was a competitive marksman himself, found such use of his art "all gratifying to an old shooter like me."[6] Hester Proctor once wrote of her father that he personally "was much more proud of the medals he received from shooting than the ones he received from his sculpture.... He had trophies of every kind for shooting."[7]

The *U.S. Cavalryman* trophy was intended to go to the competition winners each year. It would be retired and become the permanent property of whichever unit won it three times. That victory eventually went to the Third Cavalry: its Troop F claimed the trophy in 1926, its Troop E in 1929, and its Troop B in 1934. At that point, the Third Cavalry became permanent custodian of the award. Forty years later the trophy was revived. Forty-six recasts were made of the trophy for use in another military training competition, an annual Armor Leadership Award.[8]

Exhibited: None known

Other known versions: None

Variant titles: *The Western Sheriff*
Modeled, 1927–1928; cast, 1928;
dedicated, 1929
Bronze, monumental sculpture
Markings: None
Copyright: None recorded
City of Pendleton, Oregon

Plate 50 Til Taylor

Tillman D. Taylor was the kind of sheriff every western town dreamed of having. Pendleton, Oregon, where he served as sheriff from 1900 to 1920, knew him as diligent, honest, courageous, and savvy. His instinct for crime detection and prevention became legendary within his lifetime. Even many of the criminals that he brought to justice, and there were many — by one report 2,500 — voiced appreciation for his skills as a lawman and his humanity as a custodian of justice. According to popular consensus, he was "the best sheriff the northwest ever knew," a man "who risked his life for 20 years in the cause of peace and order in this territory."[1]

Proctor came to know Sheriff Taylor in the mid-teens while the artist was in Pendleton studying cowboys and Indians in and around the Pendleton Round-Up. Taylor served as president of the Round-Up between 1911 and 1920, and in that capacity he helped Proctor secure a studio on the rodeo grounds, provided a permit for him to roam freely with his camera and sketchbook, and made other concessions to accommodate the special needs of the artist. It was also Taylor, according to Proctor, who allowed his model for the *Buckaroo* (see plate 35), Slim Ridings, to continue to pose despite a summons for his arrest.[2] The artist and the lawman shared a close bond.

Thus it must have come as quite a shock to Proctor to learn in late July 1920 that his friend Taylor had been fatally wounded in his office at the county court-house during a jail-break. An immediate call went up to erect a memorial to the fallen sheriff. By the end of August, Proctor was discussing a commissioned monument with a committee formed for the purpose. Oregon's governor, Benjamin W. Olcott, wrote Proctor at that time to encourage his involvement. "I under-stand through the press," he told the artist, "that you have tendered the commission of the Til Taylor memorial. You are the one man for this work and I trust you can take care of it."[3] In fact, knowing that funds for a full-scale heroic monument might be difficult to raise in Pendleton, Proctor had offered a variety of options that the community might consider. One, which was apparently accompanied by sketches, was for a bas-relief of the sheriff that could be mounted in a park or near the Round-Up grounds. An over life-sized bronze, Proctor told the committee, could cost as much as $30,000.[4]

Pendleton had attempted five years earlier to raise money for the heroic-sized *Buckaroo* for the Round-Up grounds. That had never reached fruition, in part at least because of the criminal conviction of Slim Ridings, who was the sculpture's model. But now the town had a real hero to celebrate, and its citizens systematically and energetically began searching for the right artist (Proctor was always at or near the top of their list) and collecting funds. As they made a "careful canvas for just the right sculptor," several of Proctor's previous patrons and fellow artists came forward with endorsements, including patrons Dr. Henry Waldo Coe and Joseph N. Teal, and artists Avard Fairbanks and Charles M. Russell.[5] Taylor "is worth an epic poem," wrote a reporter for the *Portland Journal* in 1921:

> He should be perpetuated in bronze, so that when future generations come to the Round-Up he shall not be a dim and dying memory, but shall stand forth, in bronze, in heroic size as his friends knew him in life. He will typify to coming generations the modesty, the courage and the resourcefulness of the men of the Old West.[6]

Fig.114

Fig.115

By the fall of 1921, Pendleton had $14,000 in the bank with the remaining funds on the horizon.[7] But it turned out to be a more distant horizon than anticipated. It was not until early 1927 that Proctor received the go-ahead to proceed with the Taylor monument. By that time the sculptor was living in Rome, so the conception for the piece had to rely on Proctor's memory, a group of photographs (fig. 114), and a selection of Taylor's clothes, including his hat and gloves, provided by the late sheriff's family. Proctor was also able to use Taylor's show saddle. Observers who watched the sculpture take shape in Rome sensed its uniqueness. "It will be the first American statue of its kind," wrote a correspondent for the Paris edition of the *New York Herald* in 1926.[8]

Proctor's initial sketch for the monument was a clay model portraying Taylor pulling back on the reins and with the horse's head erect (fig. 115). It appears to have been patterned after one of the photographs of Taylor taken in his later years at the Round-Up. But the composition crowded the figures together, so the sculptor altered the horse's pose to one with an arched neck and the head down. In that way the sheriff's stature remained uncompromised.

When the King and Queen of Italy visited Proctor's Rome studio in 1926, one of the entourage proclaimed that the Taylor monument "should be the statue of a king."[9] When Proctor moved the monumental plaster to Brussels for casting in 1928, the newspaper *L'Etoile Belge* went further: not only was this a remarkable American work, but its alluring simplicity gave it a charm lacking in most European monuments.[10] "They went wild over him in Belgium," noted the *Seattle Daily Times*, "made movies of him working on his heroic statue of Sheriff Til Taylor. His studio became the mecca for Europe's foremost art critics."[11]

The *Til Taylor* monument was cast in Brussels, and then shipped to Portland via Paris. It was too tall to transport overland by train, so arrangements were made for a special truck to carry it the 230 miles east to Pendleton. Sufficient funds had not been raised to pay for a granite base, so a painted wooden one sufficed for the dedication that took place on September 18, 1929. Appropriately, that was the first day of the Pendleton Round-Up and its twentieth anniversary as an event. With Proctor in attendance, the crowds applauded Taylor and his legacy, as well as the artist's accomplishment. One of the local papers reflected appreciatively that Proctor had "given us Til Taylor idealized somewhat, it is true and cast in heroic mould, yet the likeness is there."[12] Touches of gold leaf highlighted some of the details of costume and saddle. Proctor was quoted as saying that he regarded his big, stolid bronze figure as not simply "unique in conception and execution" but "his best work" ever.[13]

Over the years, as the bronze aged, Proctor liked it even more. In 1932 he returned to Pendleton and came away especially impressed by the work's patina. "I've never seen a bronze with so beautiful a color," he told a local reporter.[14] In 1939 the monument to the martyred sheriff received its long-awaited granite base.

Exhibited: None known

Other known versions: None

Variant titles: *Indian and Pioneer; The Spring; Indian and Trapper*
Modeled, 1929; cast, 1931; dedicated, 1931
Bronze, monumental sculpture
Markings: None
Copyright: None recorded
Wichita High School East, Wichita, Kansas

Photograph by Kirk Eck

Fig.116
Proctor with an early model for the
McKnight Memorial Fountain in his
studio, Wilton, Connecticut, 1929

A. Phimister Proctor Museum Archives,
Poulsbo, Wash.

Fig.116

Plate 51 McKnight Memorial Fountain

By the late 1920s, Proctor's reputation as a figurative sculptor, one who produced monuments that the public considered both art and faithful representations of life, had spread across the country. Proctor entered numerous competitions in those years; few went in his favor. However, none was more rewarding than his work for the McKnight family of Wichita.

In mid-June 1929, the *Wichita Eagle* announced that of several nationally acclaimed candidates, Proctor had just been awarded the commission for a monument on a western theme to decorate the grounds of the Wichita High School East. Proctor had been chosen (even over the hometown favorite Bruce Moore), because of his naturalistic style, his previous successes, his suggestion of combining an Anglo trapper and an Indian in the work, and his attractive price. His submission, noted the paper, fell "more in line with the amount of money they are allowed to spend."[1] To bring credibility to both the selection committee and Proctor, the paper also reported that either a National Sculpture Society commission or a selected group from the New York Art Commission would approve the final concept.[2]

Proctor developed several models before striking the right chord with his patrons and his own inclinations. The first, rather highly finished models—one with the Indian looking down at a spring below (fig. 116) and one with him looking up, as if for guidance, at the trapper—both showed the Indian with a roach hairpiece in the fashion of eastern woodland Indians. It must have soon been made clear to Proctor that the citizens strongly preferred an Indian more indigenous to their region. The progress on the statue would, according to one Wichita reporter, "be watched with more than ordinary popular vigilance" so that the New York artist

did not supply an Indian the likes of which "Fenimore Cooper may have dreamed about."[3] Since this was exactly what Proctor had initially conceived, it was fortunate that he had time to pay heed to local expectations. In the final model, the Indian appeared distinctly western. Once again Proctor could claim, as he did a few years later at the dedication, that he was at his best when "putting into bronze something which will commemorate the early days of the West."[4]

Proctor had offered to supply the bronze monument for $25,000. He kept his side of the bargain and had the two-figure bronze ready to ship west by August 1931. It was in place by September 18, the date school was to begin that year, resting on a massive rocky outcrop from which a spring flowed into a large reflecting pond below. Just as the work suggested a bonding of native and white people, the flowing water below was evidence of harmony between artist and architect. The natural rock garden that served as the monument's plinth had been set in place by Wichita Commissioner of Parks L. W. Clapp. The commissioner spent nearly two years, from the time ground was broken in 1929 until the dedication in 1931, searching for the perfect rock grouping to support the two bronze figures. When Proctor viewed the final installation on September 17, 1929, he commented that he had never "seen anything more beautiful in the way of setting in the United States." It was "perfection itself."[5] In such a setting, Proctor's work achieved its ultimate expressive force.

A crowd of nearly five thousand people assembled on September 18 to witness the unveiling and applaud the joint creative efforts of Proctor and Clapp. The program recognized the generosity of the late Eva McKnight who, in memory of her husband, J. Hudson McKnight, had left $25,000 to the city

for a proper monument. The McKnights had been early settlers in Wichita, moving there in 1891. Hudson McKnight amassed a fortune in the hardware and real estate businesses, later purchasing 140 acres east of the town where he settled into a substantial stone mansion. In the early 1920s, Wichita saw the need for a new high school and so appropriated the eastern portion of the McKnight land for that purpose. Hudson McKnight was embittered by the expropriation, but after he died in 1925, his widow relaxed the tensions by writing into her will a bequest to beautify the new school. Eva McKnight had long been interested in enhancing the cultural life of Wichita, particularly the city's art and music.[6]

Clapp situated the original *McKnight Memorial Fountain* between two buildings: Wichita High School East and its neighbor, Roosevelt Junior High School. As the landscaping matured around the monument (pleasing Proctor, who felt the "sharp outlines of modern school buildings"[7] detracted from the sculpture), it became increasingly difficult to see the monument from the main thoroughfare that it faced. In the mid-1970s, the school, in planning for a new cafeteria, moved the whole monument closer to the street. There it resides today, with its pool a bit stagnant and its presence exuding a sense of lonely endurance. But the trapper and his crouching cohort are still bonded against time and the elements.

Exhibited: None known

Other known versions: None

THE
PIONEER MOTHER

PAX

Variant titles: *The Pioneer Mother*
Modeled, 1929; cast, 1932; dedicated, 1932
Bronze, monumental sculpture
Markings: "ALEXANDER PHIMISTER
PROCTOR/SCULPTOR 1919"
Copyright: By Alexander Phimister Proctor
under No. G8610 on May 4, 1932
University of Oregon, Eugene

Photograph by Jack Liu

The Proctors were living in Brussels in November 1927 when the artist received an intriguing letter from a New York lawyer, Burt Brown Barker. Barker had seen Proctor's *Pioneer Mother* memorial (see plate 47) in Kansas City and was familiar with the highly publicized "Pioneer Woman" competition promoted and underwritten by Oklahoma oil tycoon Ernest W. Marland. Although he greatly admired both efforts, Barker's conception of female pioneers differed greatly from those formulated by Proctor and any of the twelve sculptors Marland had engaged. When recalling his own mother, Elvira Brown Barker, and his grandmothers, Lucinda Cox Brown and Christina Henckel Barker, the New York attorney told Proctor he would prefer to remember them in their "sunset" years. He wanted to downplay the hardships of travel that Proctor had previously documented in such an effective way, as well as the "battles and sorrows of pioneering" presented by Marland's artists. Rather, he wrote, he wished to commemorate the pioneer women as "they sat in the evening glow resting from their labors." Barker refined his idea further:

> *Others have perpetuated her struggles; I want to perpetuate the peace which followed her struggles. Others have perpetuated her adventure; I want to perpetuate the spirit which made the adventure possible, and the joy which crowned her declining years as she looked upon the fruits of her labor and caught but a faint glimpse of what it will mean for posterity.*[1]

Proctor later visited Barker at his Montclair, New Jersey, residence. There the two discussed Barker's proposal. At first Proctor confessed that he had done about all he could with the pioneer mother idea. But after Barker reread him the letter and described again his desire for a contemplative work, one in which reverie and contentment provided the essential elements, Proctor began to come around.[2] Barker, who had been educated in law at Harvard University and in art matters by his wife, Ella Star Merrill, had become in recent years a serious student of American art. He described his envisioned alternative as combining the serenity and peace of James Abbott McNeill Whistler's *Portrait of the Artist's Mother* (1871, Musée d'Orsay, Paris) and George Inness' rapturous, evanescent late landscapes. The result would present "the pioneer woman in the sunset of her life drinking in the beauty and peace of the afterglow of her twilight days."[3]

Proctor promised Barker that he would fit the project into his schedule as soon as time permitted. It was not an easy task, but over the next two years Proctor developed a composition conforming to Barker's vision. "His conception," as Proctor remembered in later years, "was an elderly woman sitting in repose with her hands in her lap. In her hands would be a half-closed book, her fingers marking a place. Her head would be tilted slightly forward in contemplation."[4] In October 1929 Barker arrived in New York to view the initial model (fig. 117). They agreed that she was a bit too youthful for Barker's purposes, but all else appeared to be in order. Barker consulted with several other New York sculptors at the time, asking them their impression of the work in progress. While James Earle Fraser's opinion was especially valued, all commented that they approved "without reservation," agreeing "that it was a monumental thing and they recommended it unqualifiedly as a great creation ..., [one that] would stand the test of time."[5] Proctor and Barker may have experimented

Fig.117
Proctor's plaster maquette for *Oregon Pioneer Mother*, photograph, 1930

A. Phimister Proctor Museum Archives, Poulsbo, Wash.

Fig. 118
One of the bas-reliefs around the base of the *Oregon Pioneer Mother*, 1932

Fig.117

with patina coloration as well at this time: the Roman Bronze Works foundry produced a small bronze in mid-October 1929 with a recorded color of "light green-brown."[6]

From this point on, Barker left Proctor to his work. On Mother's Day, May 7, 1932, the six-foot monument was dedicated at the University of Oregon, where it was appropriately placed in the center of the Women's Quad. It would garner special commendation for Proctor among the critical community. E. C. Sherburne in the *Christian Science Monitor* had voiced the feelings of many two years earlier when he wrote:

> *As an artist, Mr. Proctor has maintained a balance between the pressure of sentiment in his subject and the demands of aesthetic soundness. While keeping design at the service of sentiment he has avoided sentimentality. He has made his composition effective in an abstract sense. This is perhaps most noticeable in the side view, which is sweeping in continuity of line, a clear-cut, bold silhouette subtly accented by variations within repetitions. The draperies are beautiful in themselves, with their variety of direction of the folds with the large direction of the mass. The sturdy chair lends solidity to the composition and contrast to the soft, yielding lines of the figure.*[7]

Finding that balance between sentiment and art, and satisfying Barker's dream of pioneer reverie would have provided Proctor with a grand sense of accomplishment.

The dedication ceremonies were opened by Dr. Arnold Bennett Hall, the university president and a close colleague of Barker's. Barker had grown up in Oregon (his mother had been four years old when she came west on the Oregon Trail

Fig.118

in 1852). He had gone east to law school and enjoyed successful practices in both Chicago and New York before moving back to Oregon in 1928, where he settled in Portland. Barker was also appointed vice president of the University of Oregon on the understanding that he would not have to live in Eugene, but with the proviso that he not be paid. Hall insisted on some remuneration, and the two parties ultimately reached an accommodation whereby Barker's salary helped pay for the *Oregon Pioneer Mother*.

At the dedication a crowd of old Oregon pioneers, university supporters, and students, along with many of their mothers as specially invited guests, listened to Hall acknowledge Barker's vision and credit Proctor with what, on that day at least, was his masterpiece. He read a letter from the President of the United States, Herbert Hoover, who pontificated on the virtues of motherhood, as might be expected of a politician on such an occasion. But Hoover also proffered some compelling remarks on the freshness of the concept represented by Proctor's bronze monument. It "introduces a new thought," he observed. "It goes to the end of the trail and memorializes the spirit which made possible the journey, the peace which followed her struggles and the joy which consummated her victory."[8]

Hoover's remarks were simply another way of saying what Barker had written back in 1927, but they resonated with both the artist and the patron. The distinguished lady of the pioneer past, now cast in bronze and poised to reflect on the bygone era for near eternity, symbolized Proctor's and Barker's careers that were nearing an end. Barker would settle in as the grand historian of Oregon's past, serving for many years of his remaining long life on the board of directors

of the Oregon Historical Society. Proctor, though dedicated to preserving the pioneer types, would find that the *Oregon Pioneer Mother* was his last monument to the people of the West. Afterward Proctor metaphorically put his own hands to rest when it came to sculpting the human heroes of the region he called home.

Despite the quiescent, cerebral mood of Proctor's final pioneer tribute, one tangential element demonstrates the artist's persistent dedication to narrative. On the two sides of the pedestal are bronze bas-reliefs picturing the sorrow and hardship of life on the overland trek — exactly what Barker had wanted to avoid. One shows a prairie burial with a family and a minister standing solemnly before a grave. The other witnesses the uphill pull of an ox-drawn wagon. A man lashes at the laboring beasts and a woman's head can be seen awkwardly tilted beneath the canopy of the wagon's canvas cover (fig. 118). Both scenes could have been lifted from popular nineteenth-century artistic models, but Proctor derived his inspiration from old photographs he had in his studio. The covered wagon motif would later be developed into an etching. Apparently Barker had approved these historical tableaux two years before the statue's dedication.[9] As part of the base, they serve as thematic support for the work, although they also ultimately detract from its elegant simplicity.

In 1946 Barker contacted Proctor about the three-foot model for the *Oregon Pioneer Mother*. He had requested a bronze of the small version, and Proctor thought he had sent one to him many years before. It was evidently never received, so Proctor, then residing at the Bohemian Club in San Francisco, wrote to his artist son Gifford, who was living in his father's studio in Wilton, Connecticut. He told Gifford

that Barker seemed "sore" about the apparent oversight and asked his son to look around for either the small bronze from which he had pointed up or one of the plasters. What concerned him most was the fact that the small versions had a "younger face."[10] How this turned out is not known, but one hopes the two old men were eventually reconciled.

Exhibited: None known

Other known versions: A. Phimister Proctor Museum, Poulsbo, Wash. (three plasters of the *Oregon Pioneer Mother* and two plasters of the bas-relief plaques)

Variant titles: *Pony Express Plaque*
Modeled, c. 1930; cast initially, 1931
Bronze, 16 inches in diameter
Markings: "PONY EXPRESS/A.
PHIMISTER PROCTOR/C."
Copyright: By Alexander Phimister
Proctor under No. G5833 on
March 30, 1931; by Nona Proctor
Church as *Pony Express Plaque* under
No. H53325 on September 1, 1973

A. Phimister Proctor Museum, Poulsbo, Wash.
Photograph by Howard Giske

Plate 53 Pony Express

The Proctor family moved back to the United States from Europe in 1930. They took up residence in Wilton, Connecticut, and adopted a lifestyle that would accommodate the hardships of the Great Depression. Fortunately for them, Proctor kept busy with commissions. Thanks to his friend and patron George D. Pratt, and due to his own pioneering experiences in Colorado, he received a job that would catapult him back into the national limelight.

In 1926, inspired by Ezra Meeker, a veteran pioneer and tenacious booster of the West's place in public history, an organization known as the Oregon Trail Memorial Association was formed. Its purpose was "to honor the pioneers" by bringing to light through a vigorous marketing scheme and an elaborate series of memorial activities the "glories" of past epochs in the West. By "marking and monumenting" the "faded old pathway of the pioneers," the association hoped both to preserve and reinvigorate popular history. When Meeker died in 1929, he was succeeded by Dr. Howard R. Driggs, an associate professor of English at New York University and a champion of experiential education. As part of an umbrella program, the Covered-Wagon Centennial, he embarked on a project to commemorate the famous Pony Express. His plan was to mark sixty of the 190 original Pony Express stations that had been built along the route between Saint Joseph, Missouri, and Sacramento, California. Each monument would be decorated with a commemorative bronze plaque mounted into a building, a rock plinth, or some other suitable base.[1]

Driggs appointed the octogenarian Colorado artist, painter, and photographer William Henry Jackson to serve as research secretary for the association.[2] Jackson had ridden along the Oregon Trail in 1866 and 1867. Driggs asked him, as part of the research job, to produce a series of paintings related

Fig.119

Fig.119
William Henry Jackson (1843–1942)
Pony Express, 1930
Watercolor

Scotts Bluff National Monument, National Park Service, Gering, Nebr.

to the trail's history. Jackson's *Pony Express* (fig. 119), showing a rider pursued by three groups of Indians, was a testament to his fertile imagination, his somewhat primitive style, and his dedication to images of a romanticized West. Jackson completed the watercolor in 1930, one year before the association embarked on a nationally promoted celebration of the seventy-first anniversary of the first successful mail rides west.

The chairman of the association's board of trustees was George D. Pratt, Proctor's old friend and generous patron. The project had not proceeded far before Pratt commissioned Proctor to sculpt the plaques. The association announced that "one of America's eminent sculptors, whose intimate touch with the Old West had already found expression in many works of art," would design a plaque "expressive of the Pony Express."[3] Proctor chose as his theme for the plaque a composition similar to Jackson's, except that his rider faces forward, and seems a bit small, as if physically reduced to fit within the confines of the circular plaque. However, many of the Pony Express riders were boys and young men hired for their equestrian skill and endurance rather than their physical size. The most celebrated of them, William F. Cody, was in his mid-teens when he took the job with the Central Overland California and Pikes Peak Express Company in 1860.

To capture the essence of a Pony Express rider at work, Proctor made a series of photographs using one of his sons. He recorded the boy dismounting on the run, swinging back into the saddle, spurring forward, and galloping past. The last pose suited the sculptural concept best.

On April 3, 1931, Proctor was part of a group that presented the first plaque to President Herbert Hoover. In a ceremony on the lawn of the White House, Hoover expressed genuine pleasure at seeing the project underway. It reminded him of "some treasured memories of my boyhood when I was with the pioneers in the West."[4] What he liked most, however, was the boost such a program would give his "See America First" efforts. Ray Lyman Wilbur, Secretary of the Interior, and Horace Albright, recently appointed director of the National Park Service, were also on hand. They hoped to expand on a program attracting tourists to the nation's natural and historical sites.

Pratt saw to it that the first Pony Express plaque was dedicated in Salt Lake City. The procedure adopted in Utah would be followed by the other fifty-nine recipients. Pratt would provide the plaque (actually two in the case of Salt Lake City), and a local citizens' group would arrange for a proper monument to house it. In Salt Lake City, the Utah Pioneer Trails and Landmarks Association took on that task. In Gothenburg, Nebraska, the funding came from one generous person, Mrs. C. A. Williams; the plaque was fixed to an original Pony Express station that had been moved to a local park.

Not much was said in the press about the plaque as a work of art. Yet the *Newark Evening News* did take space to note certain details that they found wanting in accuracy. Claiming that Proctor was a long way from being a "plainsman," the critic complained:

> ... [T]he designer obviously has never studied the way a plains rider holds the lines in his left hand to guide his steed by "neck reining." As for the rider on the medal, he has his foot jammed in the stirrup as though it was frozen there, with the iron under the arch instead of under the ball. To old timers of the great open spaces, the medal is a libel on the greatest riders ever to handle leather.[5]

Proctor did not mention the plaques or the commission in his autobiography. Perhaps the sour note from New Jersey reduced his pleasure in this work.

Exhibited: None known

Other known versions: None

Variant titles: *Robert E. Lee and*
the Young Soldier
Modeled, 1935; cast, 1935–1936;
dedicated, 1936
Bronze, monumental sculpture
Markings: "A.P.PROCTOR - 1936,"
"ROMAN BRONZE WORKS N.Y"; and "©"
Copyright: By Alexander Phimister
Proctor under No. G18597 on January 8, 1935
Lee Park, Dallas

Photograph by Steven Watson

Plate 54 General Robert E. Lee

In 1963, when the *Dallas Herald* ran a feature article on her, Elizabeth Rogers, who was in her late eighties, was one of the reigning doyennes among the city's many club women. As second president of the Dallas Southern Memorial Association, a women's organization that had its beginnings as the Confederate Southern Memorial Association in 1922, she had spearheaded in the mid-1930s one of the city's most ambitious beautification projects. This involved a three-part plan to change the name of Dallas' serene Oak Lawn Park to Lee Park in memory of the Confederate hero General Robert E. Lee, to construct on the park grounds a replica of his Arlington mansion, and to commission a sculptor of national reputation to create a bronze monument to Lee to stand in the park. By the time she stepped down as chairman of the association's Lee Memorial Committee in 1936, she had raised sufficient additional funds to endow a substantial scholarship at Southern Methodist University to benefit descendants of Confederate soldiers, a distinction she shared with many other Texas families.[1]

Rogers approached Proctor by letter in 1931 inquiring if he might be interested in the commission. She spelled out the association's plans for a bronze memorial to Lee, explaining that it should be an equestrian monument and should include a young soldier to symbolize the youth of the South as well as a dramatic portrait of the great Confederate leader.[2]

Proctor, who had always considered himself a "damn Yankee," was surprised by the invitation, but accepted. He promptly set about to produce an initial model for Rogers to review. It showed Lee and an aide riding headlong into a gale. The horses trudge into the wind while the young soldier's cape billows behind him and General Lee pulls his own across

his chest with determined resistance (fig. 120). When Rogers and her sister visited Proctor's Wilton, Connecticut, studio, they were delighted with the sketch's drama but objected to its spirit. They wanted a general not beset by fate but showing stoic and noble resolve. After surveying Proctor's studio and portfolio, they felt assured that he could capture the likeness and stature of their hero but asked him to alter his interpretation of the general.[3] In April 1932 Proctor traveled to Dallas to present a second version and to lecture on "The Making of a Statue," an account of his work on the Theodore Roosevelt commission.[4] The lecture was well received, but once again Rogers and her associates rejected the model. At this point Rogers and Proctor dropped the project, according to the artist, because "the terms of the contract were unacceptable."[5] But the idea of a sizable commission lingered with the sculptor. Though he was in his early seventies, he still longed for a major project to work on, so about a year later, in the spring of 1933 while returning east from Los Angeles, he and his wife, Margaret, stopped once again in Dallas with the hope of reviving the negotiations. Rogers welcomed Proctor's rapprochement and later helped the artist get established in an apartment where he could work under her guidance until a satisfactory design solution was found. The *Dallas Times Herald* eventually ran an illustration of a plaster sketch next to the headline "Model Approved for Statue of R. E. Lee." The article said that Proctor had just left for New York where he would produce a four-foot working model, flesh out the secondary figure, and have it all ready within a year and a half.[6] Not only had he worked for several weeks on the approved sketch, but he had also collected "voluminous data" on Lee during recent visits to Richmond, Virginia, and promised to

use an exact replica of Lee's uniform as well as find an appropriately sized model for Lee himself and a faithful stand-in for the general's famous horse, Traveler.

By January 1934 Rogers could press forward with fundraising. She published a brochure with a collection of testimonials from New York artists and art aficionados. The association had promised Proctor $40,000 for his efforts, and in response Proctor's cohorts bolstered the association's funding efforts. The sculptors Hermon Atkins MacNeil and Charles Keck, then president of the National Sculpture Society, stepped forward with expressions of support. Proctor's old friend George D. Pratt, then treasurer of the Metropolitan Museum of Art, and the painter Charles Curran, representing the National Academy of Design, also lent their endorsement by sending letters to Rogers. Curran praised the good taste of the association and the effectiveness of the group, but MacNeil offered the most compelling remarks:

It gives me great pleasure to express my very high opinion of a group I have seen of Mr. Proctor's composition of two equestrians.... It is quite a unique thing to make any group of two equestrians, as well as a difficult thing, and in this study for a group Mr. Proctor has already solved, because of his many years of study of just this kind of monumental work, many of the problems that a sculptor less familiar would take years to attain.... I am convinced that he will make a most excellent group.[7]

At the same time that she embarked on her appeal for funds, Mrs. Rogers also took on the Dallas Park Board over the siting of the monument. At stake were decisions regarding its place-

Fig.120
Proctor's early, rejected sketch for *General
Robert E. Lee*, 1931

A. Phimister Proctor Museum, Poulsbo, Wash.
Photograph by Howard Giske

Fig.121
Proctor's monumental plaster for
General Robert E. Lee, 1934

A. Phimister Proctor Museum Archives, Poulsbo,
Wash.

Fig.120

ment in Oak Lawn Park and the possibility of renaming the park the Lee Memorial Park. If she did not get her way in those matters, she threatened, she would take the monument to Fort Worth.[8] Rogers prevailed. The site was approved and the park renamed Lee Park. The city obtained funds from the Works Progress Administration (or WPA) to pay for the monument's granite base, and a Dallas architect, Mark Lemmon, contributed his design for the plinth.

In the meantime Proctor proceeded with his work. When interviewed in Connecticut in August 1934 by the *Ridgefield Press,* he reported having found the perfect model for Traveler, a horse named "Uncle Sam" who was owned by a neighbor, the wife of Columbia University professor and writer John Erskine. Proctor also talked about the powerful influence that John Rogers, another Connecticut sculptor, had had on him.[9] In fact when Proctor rolled out the finished plaster model of the heroic work from his shingle-sided studio the next spring (fig. 121), it bore a striking resemblance to some of the Civil War plaster groups that Rogers had produced in the 1860s. Although the general was a figure of proud determination, heroic in scale and countenance, the young soldier peering up in adoration suggested an attendant genre element. Proctor had achieved a masterly tension between the grand gesture and the commonplace, between nobility and sentimentality.

Proctor delivered the large plaster to Roman Bronze Works on Long Island in December 1935. The Grand Central Galleries in New York had invited him to exhibit the plaster maquette in April, and a month later he placed it on long-term loan at the Corcoran Gallery of Art in Washington, D.C.[10] After viewing the stunning white tribute to "a great heritage," Leila Mechlin, who wrote art criticism for the

Washington Star, waxed eloquent. "When anything is as good as this there is no need for superlatives," she wrote. "It possesses that amazing quiet to which only great works attain." Few artists, Mechlin concluded, "have so correctly and vigorously set forth typical American subjects and given them artistic expression and beauty as has Mr. Proctor."[11]

When an image of the bronze monument appeared in the pages of the *New York Times* in early 1936, it prompted Proctor's New York friend Sherwood Trask to write him an extraordinarily perceptive letter. He pointed out that Proctor had achieved what Augustus Saint-Gaudens had called for early in the century: the union of true simplicity and nobility. He described the interlocking lines of movement as masterful in their relationship, one to the other. Lee himself was "sturdy, one could almost say stodgy," Trask went on, yet his soul transcended his formal bearing and was modulated by his lovingly carved features. Then he finished his letter with a summary statement on the irony that imbues the work:

> *Congratulations on having gotten the essence of the Lost Cause into these two figures, the Leader and the Led. And into their horses that were doomed, too, because life progresses on ahead even through the instrumentality of railroads, factories etc. which caused the downfall of Lee and his system (which he didn't believe in, in large part, and which therefore caused that exalted uplift of the head with which you top your work of art).*[12]

Rogers and others had decided that they would dedicate their new monument in their rechristened park in June 1936. The unveiling was scheduled to coincide with the Texas Centennial

Celebration, and President Franklin D. Roosevelt had been summoned into service for the ribbon cutting. When he appeared on June 13 in his long, black convertible for the ceremony, the *Dallas Morning News* wrote that the president and Mrs. Roosevelt were "not only the most distinguished, but undoubtedly the most friendly and charming visitors who ever responded to the oft repeated invitation, 'Light and hitch, stranger." He of course never left his car, so there was neither lighting nor hitching, but he did pull the cord that unveiled Proctor's masterpiece at which time, according to the sculptor, he exclaimed, "Magnificent!"[13] That simple but genuine response gratified Proctor immensely. He told the press that Roosevelt had been "the first president to recognize painting and sculpture on a large and comprehensive scale," and it was thus a "great compliment" to have his bronze "so graciously unveiled."[14]

On the podium that day, Rogers was given the task of formally acknowledging Proctor's work. She recognized his "great genius as an artist" and his "character as a gentleman," and she applauded his "patient endurance" as well. But one thing she added must have struck a particularly telling chord with Proctor. Rogers said she felt that he had "embodied in this memorial something of his own idealism of life," and that the monumental figures were a fine tribute not just to General Lee but "to a distinguished sculptor's conception of life."[15] Proctor had seen Lee not as a man in defeat but as ambition incarnate, not as a person but as an ideal force. For Proctor, his own art had risen to that level also.

Sometime in the late 1940s, Proctor wrote to Dallas journalist John William Rogers, reminiscing about the Lee monument. Rogers published the artist's letter, which included the following postscript:

Fig.121

You know, you can blame Mrs. Russell Rogers for selecting this sculptor to do the Lee statue. She stuck to me through thick and thin, and I am grateful to her for having the chance to do a statue to the great man as well as soldier. I put everything I had into it.[16]

The bond between Proctor and Rogers would endure through their long lives.

Exhibited: Dallas Public Art Gallery, Dallas, 1932 (plaster sketch); Grand Central Art Galleries, New York, 1935 (plaster maquette); Corcoran Gallery of Art, Washington, D.C., 1935 (plaster maquette)

Other known versions: Collections of the Lee Chapel and Museum, Washington and Lee University, Lexington, Va. (plaster maquette, gift of the artist, 1937); A. Phimister Proctor Museum, Poulsbo, Wash. (other maquettes and plaster sketches)

Variant titles: *The Manada; Manada Mustangs;*
Texas Mustangs; The Seven Mustangs
Modeled, 1939–1941; cast, 1948;
dedicated, 1948
Bronze, monumental sculpture
Markings: "A.PHIMISTER PROCTOR. 1941"
AND "GORHAM CO. FOUNDERS MUS-
TANGS/THEY CARRIED THE MEN/WHO
MADE TEXAS/PRESENTED TO/THE PEOPLE
OF TEXAS/BY RALPH ROGERS
OGDEN/AND/ETHEL OGDEN/ALEC [*sic*]
PHIMISTER PROCTOR,
SCULPTOR/MCMXLVII
Copyright: By Alexander Phimister Proctor
under No. G232819 in June 14, 1939

The University of Texas at Austin
(gift of Ralph and Ethel Ogden, 1948)

Plate 55 Mustangs

For many westerners, the mustang represented not only the West but also the stubborn if ephemeral way of life that evolved there. The name "mustang" came from the Spanish word *mesteñas*, a term for unbranded horses that had escaped onto the southwestern and Mexican prairies since the sixteenth century. These Spanish horses proliferated on the Texas plains, and when corralled and tamed in later years, they were used to drive longhorns north to the railheads of Kansas. The Texas historian J. Frank Dobie considered them special enough to write a book on the breed. He also helped orchestrate a remarkable monument to them in his home state at the University of Texas at Austin.[1] Because he saw mustangs as on the verge of extinction, threatened by wide-spread cross-breeding, it was with a sense of mission and urgency that Dobie sought a way to immortalize them.

In 1938 Dobie, who taught at the University of Texas, contacted an oilman from Austin, Ralph Ogden. In a lengthy account of Ogden's life written some years later, Dobie characterized Ogden as a resourceful, undaunted boom-and-bust entrepreneur who, after countless misadventures in business, had settled into a successful career as an oilman.[2] But Ogden had started out on a ranch, where an uncle gave him a mustang pony as a boy. By age ten, young Ogden had his own string of mustangs, one of which he rode to Kansas in 1886 with a herd of longhorn steers. The experience remained fresh in his memory, and in subsequent years he, too, became interested in finding ways to write the mustang into history.

Ogden's first efforts took shape in San Antonio in the 1920s when he attempted to persuade a group of Texas cattlemen to erect a monument to the range horse. Nothing came of the idea, primarily because, according to Dobie, the cattle market plummeted. But it is also true that the central source of patronage in San Antonio at the time, the Trail Drivers Association, had already engaged Gutzon Borglum to sculpt a monument to trail drivers and could not share their resources with Ogden's mustang memorial.[3]

By the time Ogden approached Dobie about a mustang memorial for the university, over a decade had passed. He proposed to donate the money if Dobie, who was referred to as Ogden's "art confessor," would find an acceptable sculptor.[4] Dobie surveyed the field and, after receiving what one source called "scores of models," selected Proctor for the job.[5] Dobie had seen Proctor's monument *General Robert E. Lee* (see plate 54) in Dallas when it was dedicated as part of the Texas Centennial celebration in 1936. He had also been vocal in his objections to the work of another Texas Centennial artist, the Italian-American sculptor Pompeo Luigi Coppini, whose group of Texas heroes cavorted with bugles in such an inert and mannered way that Dobie felt them an insult to Texas history and its people.[6] In contrast, Proctor's style fit nicely within Dobie's aesthetic parameters, and he was duly invited to contribute a model. The Proctors were living in Seattle when Dobie's letter arrived. The sculptor responded immediately by sculpting a plasticene model of five mares and a stallion cresting a hill at full gallop. He built a carrying box for the eight-and-a-half-inch sketch (fig. 122), then rounded up Margaret and his youngest daughter, Joanne, and drove south. Proctor and Dobie had never met, but they and their families became instant friends. Dobie and Ogden filled with enthusiasm at the first sight of Proctor's handiwork. They suggested that he should add a colt to the group, the sculptor assented, and a contract was drafted on the spot.

By April 1939 newspapers across the country carried the story that Proctor had holed up on a Texas ranch and was making models of the "rapidly disappearing mustangs," five mares, one stallion, and a colt, for a $60,000 bronze tribute to their enduring spirit. "These are the prairie horses on which Texans scouted, fought, and drove cattle in pioneer days," the article concluded.[7] To capture the true essence of the mustangs, Proctor had requested as part of his contract a period of study among an established herd, and Dobie arranged for him to stay at the King Ranch in South Texas. There, near Hebbronville, as a guest of the ranch owner's son-in-law Tom East, Proctor spent the next several months perfecting a larger-sized model. He photographed the horses (fig. 123), measured them, communed with them, and watched out for their unpredictable antics. They were wild horses, "as wild as the outdoors in which they lived."[8] He selected fifteen dun mares out of the seventy that East considered to be a pure strain. They, along with the stallion and colt, proved to be the most unruly models he had ever tried to manage. Over the weeks that ensued, he slowly developed a dramatic plunge of horses in motion — a *manada*, or herd, of wild Texas ponies on the run.

Each of the three main participants in the project had similar desires for the evolving monument. Proctor spoke out as early as May 1939: "I want to show the children of this country what the horse was like that carried the men who redeemed Texas from the wilderness."[9] Ogden, too, wanted a "monument to the horses that drove up trails as far as the grass grows and carried men who established ranches from the Gulf of Mexico to the Pacific and all the way to the Canadian line."[10] And Dobie said: "These mustangs will go towards making it unnecessary to put up signs on the campus

Fig.122
Alexander Phimister Proctor
Study for Mustangs, 1938
Plasticene, 7 x 8½ x 8½ inches

A. Phimister Proctor Museum, Poulsbo, Wash.

Fig.123
Photograph by Proctor of mustangs at
the King Ranch in Texas, 1939

A. Phimister Proctor Museum Archives,
Poulsbo, Wash.

Fig.124
Proctor with clay relief model intended
for base of *Mustangs*

A. Phimister Proctor Museum Archives,
Poulsbo, Wash.

Fig.122

of the University of Texas informing strangers that they are in Texas." He went on, "They will do something towards making the university grounds seem to belong to Texas as well as being in Texas."[11]

From the beginning of the project, well before Proctor was brought in, Dobie had spoken with Dr. E. H. Sellards, the director of a developing natural history facility for the university, the Texas Memorial Museum, about including a representation of the American horse to complement the galleries' scientific displays. Sellards hoped to design an exhibit on the history of the horse going back to Pleistocene times and earlier, and agreed to add the *Mustangs* in front of his building.[12] Once that arrangement was in place, Proctor's reputation as an animalier sculptor positioned him favorably to receive the commission. In Dobie's mind Proctor was perfect for the job because "he has been preparing for it all his life." Dobie assured the Texas press, "Mr. Proctor will deliver one of the supremely outstanding sculptural achievements of America."[13]

Even the King Ranch cowboys praised Proctor's efforts as the final model took shape in the fall of 1939. East, who was impressed with the amount of time Proctor had expended on his finished study ("I thought he would be through in a day or two, but he stayed around for nine months"), said that his cowhands thought the statue "was so perfect,... they could recognize every one of the horses."[14]

Proctor announced the completion of the first working model in late October 1939.[15] It was not until May 1940, however, that the final maquette reached its finished form.[16] That plaster was then sent to the Wilton, Connecticut, studio to be pointed up by Proctor's son Gifford and the sculptor's long-time assistant, Gozo Kawamura. Proctor remained in Texas a bit longer to sculpt two relief panels that he hoped would be

used on the base (fig. 124). The enlargement of the complicated horse group took the Wilton team over a year to finish. It was not until July 1941 that Proctor had it ready to ship to the Gorham foundry in Providence.[17]

The slow pace of the project at this stage was only partly due to Proctor's perfectionism. Evidently Ogden had not kept up with his payments to Proctor, which caused delays as well. And though Proctor had purchased enough bronze for the job, with American involvement in the European war looming, the government was threatening to sequester valuable metals like copper for possible future needs; a letter from the Gorham Company to Proctor in June had warned him that the foundry's energies were being pulled almost entirely into filling commitments to the "Defense Program."[18] By the end of the year, metals for non-war use had been frozen, and the *Mustangs* went on indefinite hold. Proctor found himself helplessly caught in the middle between an unresponsive patron and a distracted government with a wartime agenda. "I am wondering what I'll have to do to have [Ogden] pay up what's due me," he wrote Dobie that fall. "If he had come across, we would not now be messed up with [the] Government."[19] By February of the next year, Proctor was resigned but bitter. "It's hell that we can't go on with the *Mustangs*," he bemoaned, "and to think, I bought the copper a year and a half before the trouble broke — I wonder if boss Ogden realizes that his holding back my money got us into that trouble."[20]

Gorham stored the huge plaster during the war (Dobie eventually convinced Ogden to pay for that and for insuring the fragile group) while Proctor waited for the day when it would be completed. At one point he even suggested that Ogden and the university consider completing the *Mustangs* in marble

rather than bronze.[21] But that proposition did not fly, nor did his idea of setting the pedestal in place before the war ended.

Readying the final plaster for casting back in 1941 had put a tremendous physical strain on Proctor. He told Dobie that it took him a year to recover from the effort. Emotionally, too, he was stretched thin, especially as the health of his wife, Margaret, began to fail in the early 1940s. At age eighty-three, Proctor wasn't sure he would live to see the project completed. His son Gifford was listed in the contract as the one who would finish things up if his father died before completing the group. Proctor reassured Dobie that Gifford would be the perfect one "to oversee the casting ... and take care of any small breaks" in the event that "I croak" before the project was done.[22] But Proctor had not counted on the demise of the patron. Ogden died in April 1944, throwing things once again into uncertainty. At the time Dobie was teaching at Cambridge in England, which left no one in Texas to press the artist's cause. Proctor finally wrote Sellards, his only link to the university:

June 2nd, 44
Dear Mr. Sellards:
I learned a month after it happened of the death of Mr. Ogden.

Now I am wondering what will happen to me and my group of "Mustangs" — Frank Dobie told me that if I wanted to know anything about the situation, to write to you in his absence.

My lawyer friend tells me that I may have to file a claim against the estate, for bal. of money due — He didn't think that Mr. Ogden's death would have anything to do with the continuation of the case. At the same time he thought I might have to make the claim, according to the

Fig.123   Fig.124

law of Texas — He said that it could be carried out in a friendly way. I naturally don't want to inconvenience Mrs. Ogden in any way as she has been most friendly to Mrs. Proctor & me.

You know of course that the Gov't stopped the casting of the group — If Mr. Ogden had kept up his payments as the work progressed, the group would have been cast before the bronze shutdown. Mr. Dobie knows the situation. Naturally I was not paid for my work. I expected to get that remuneration as the work reached the last stages and largely at the end —

If you will advise me as to what I should do, I will be greatly obliged to you — You know that the group was finished & ready for the bronze casting when I was headed off by Uncle Sam. I am naturally very anxious to be at the unveiling of the group, which some of the big sculptors in N.Y. think is my best work.

I am wondering if Mr. Ogden's fortune had been impaired before his death.

I am wondering if you have a picture of the group. Will send you one if you wish.

Thanking you in advance.

I am cordially yours

Phimister Proctor [23]

Sellards was no help. All he could tell Proctor was that "Ogden's will contained no reference to the completion of this group" and that Mrs. Ogden could not, at least at present, be approached about the matter.[24] The contract called for the heirs to consummate the project if any of the primary parties were, according to Proctor, "to pass out before the finish."[25]

Eventually the estate was settled, Mrs. Ogden enthusiastically renewed support for the project, the war came to a close, and metals were released for domestic use. By the summer of 1946, Proctor gave orders for Gorham to proceed with casting. Dobie began to write text for a didactic plaque on the base, and plans for a spring 1948 unveiling were made. Gorham produced the monument using the sand-cast method. This required fifty-seven separate castings and involved ten molders, five chasers, and two colorers to complete the work. To ship it west, both the colt and the head of the stallion had to be removed so the bronze would fit on a railroad flatcar and still clear bridges and tunnels along the way.[26]

Proctor attended the dedication on Commencement Day, May 31, 1948, in Austin. The occasion was bittersweet since Margaret was no longer alive to share in the formalities. Dobie's remarks about the Texas mustang — "He was small, but he was exceedingly tough, active and enduring. As the Spanish said of him, 'He dies before he quits.'"[27] — might just as easily have referred to the sculptor. A few days later Dobie gave his estimation of Proctor's accomplishment:

The other day there was unveiled in front of the Memorial Museum at Austin the finest and most magnificent work of art representative of Texas life and history to be seen within the boundaries of the state. It is of seven mustang horses — a fierce stallion dominating the group; a two-year-old filly as alert as a buck in September and as ready to bloom as a rosebud in April; a mare guarding her little colt with flaming pride and savage jealousy; and the gleeful and innocent colt itself; then three other mares, each an individual in looks and reaction. Every animal in the group personifies vitality itself. Beyond all doubt, this is one of the very finest sculpture groups in the world.[28]

Proctor had made it clear on numerous occasions that the *Mustangs'* success, despite the agonizing delays, rested mostly on Dobie. "If it hadn't been for Frank Dobie," he mused in a letter to Dobie, the man he considered one of his best friends, "there would have been no mustang group ... and but for Frank Dobie, I would not have been the sculptor."[29] In Proctor's estimation the *Mustangs* was very much a joint effort. Dobie returned the compliment, writing a lengthy essay on the monument, which appeared in *The Cattleman* magazine in September 1948. The part on Proctor was particularly gratifying to the veteran sculptor, who called it quite the "nicest and most accurate story of me that I have had...."[30] But what must have struck the strongest chord with Proctor was Dobie's assessment of the monument's promise of endurance. It had been this hope that had helped Proctor persist through his multitude of travails. Now he could let go, confident in the monument's assured place in history. As Dobie wrote, a few months after the dedication and after watching public response to the thundering herd, "Somehow foreseeing how people will for centuries look at these *Mustangs* and be moved by the beautiful animation inherent in them, I have a better conception of immortality on earth than I have ever had."[31]

Exhibited: None known

Other known versions: A. Phimister Proctor Museum, Poulsbo, Wash. (first plasticene model); Texas Memorial Museum, University of Texas at Austin (plaster maquette, gift of Mrs. Ethel Ogden, 1948)

ALEXANDER PHIMISTER PROCTOR:
A CHRONOLOGY

September 27, 1860: Born in Arkona, a township in Ontario, Canada, to Alexander Proctor and Tirzah Smith-Proctor, the fourth child of eleven, and the last to be born in Canada.

1864–1870: Moves with his family to Clinton, Michigan, by covered wagon, and lives for the following six years in Newton and Des Moines, Iowa.

1871: Crosses the prairies with his family to live in Denver. Is baptized and pledges never to drink alcohol or smoke tobacco (a pledge he keeps his entire life).

1873: Begins art lessons in Denver with J. Harrison Mills (1842–1916), who teaches him wood engraving.

1876: At age sixteen, kills an elk and a bear in the same day.

1879: Receives a commission for twenty illustrations for the book *Hands Up*, written by Sheriff John Cook, the most noted peace officer in Colorado at the time. The book is published in 1882.

1884: Hunts and sketches in Yosemite National Park for six months with Alden Sampson, a friend, patron and fellow artist. After a perilous climb of Half Dome, resolves to dedicate his life to art.

1884–1885: Tries mining to pay for art studies in New York. Ends up selling his Colorado homestead to fund his formal education.

November 1885: Moves to New York and studies (until 1887) at the National Academy of Design and the Art Students League.

Fall 1887: Meets sculptor John Rogers (1829–1904), who takes him on as a pupil and encourages him to start on the model of the *Fawn* in wax. The plaster is shown at the Century Club in New York.

While sketching at the menagerie in New York, cultivates the ability to retain an action picture in his mind by closing his eyes, opening them for a split second, and shutting them again.

Winter 1888–1889: Opens first studio, with Edwin W. Deming (1860–1942), in New York. Learns that the Greeks and Egyptians fashioned their own tools, and decides to make his own tools to increase his modeling control.

Meets noted New York art dealer N. E. Montross who agrees to handle some of his paintings.

Spring 1890: Visits his family in Snohomish, Washington. Hunts and sketches bear and elk in Alberta, Canada.

Summer 1891: Hunts and sketches in the Cascade Mountains. Receives telegram inviting him to participate in the 1893 World's Columbian Exposition in Chicago.

September 1891: Arrives in Chicago to begin his first big commission: over two dozen staff models of American wild animals for the exposition grounds. Meets renowned sculptor Augustus Saint-Gaudens (1848–1907) and Margaret Daisy Gerow (1875–1942), a painter and sculptor working for Lorado Taft (1860–1936).

1892: Meets Theodore Roosevelt and is invited to join the Boone and Crockett Club. Turns down lunch with Roosevelt to dine with his future bride, Margaret.

September 27, 1893: Marries Margaret.

October 1893: Sails for Paris to study French methods of sculpture at the Académie Julian. Studies under Denys Pierre Puech and Jean-Antoine Injalbert. Wins first prize for the *Boxer-Pug* at the Académie Julian's annual sculpture competition.

Spring 1894: Receives a telegram from Augustus Saint-Gaudens asking him to model the horse for a statue of General John A. Logan to be sited in Chicago.

Autumn 1894: Returns to New York to work with Saint-Gaudens.

August 1895: Creates another horse for Saint-Gaudens, this time for the *Sherman Monument* in Central Park, New York.

August–September 1895: Travels to Montana with Henry Stimson (later to become U.S. secretary of state) to sketch, hunt, and assess the Glacier Park area for a future national park.

1896: Begins work on the *Puma* for Prospect Park in Brooklyn, New York.

Visits the Blackfeet Indian reservation in Montana to sketch and model Indians and animals.

Receives the Rinehart Scholarship, which funds three years of study in Paris. While in France, works on the *Puma* sketches and models the *Indian Warrior* for the Rinehart committee.

Autumn 1898: Returns to New York; is awarded the Prix de Rome, which he turns down because it would mean doing classical statues. A feature article on him appears in the September issue of *Brush and Pencil* magazine.

1898: Receives a commission to do the *Quadriga* for the United States Pavilion at the 1900 Paris Universal Exposition. Returns to Paris. Exhibits more sculptures than any other American. Wins a gold medal for his ensemble of works.

Fall 1900: Returns to New York. Receives a commission for various sculptures at the 1901 Pan-American Exposition in Buffalo, New York.

1901: Exhibits nine small bronzes, mostly animals, and serves on awards jury at the Pan-American Exposition in Buffalo, New York. Is elected an associate member of the National Academy of Design.

1902: Completes *Seated Lions* for the Frick Building, Pittsburgh. Also produces animal sculptures for two New York patrons, Cornelius Vanderbilt Jr. and J. Pierpont Morgan.

1903: Receives a commission for two gilded copper *Griffins* for the 1904 Louisiana Purchase Exposition in Saint Louis. Also creates a sculpture of *Louis Joliet* for the exposition grounds.

Makes a number of models for the Zoological Park, New York (Bronx Zoo).

Late 1903: Receives a commission to create four marble sleeping lions for the base of the McKinley monument in Niagara Square, Buffalo, New York.

1904: Elected a full member of the National Academy of Design.

Establishes studio in New York City's MacDougal Alley. Buys a farm, "Indian Hill," near Bedford, New York.

1906: Completes the *Lions* for the McKinley monument and supplies decorations for the Elephant House at the Bronx Zoo.

Receives a commission for two tigers for the entrance to Nassau Hall at Princeton University.

1907: Receives a commission for four tigers for the 16th Street Bridge in Washington, D.C.

1908: Given a major one-man exhibition of his watercolors and sculptures at the Montross Gallery, New York.

1909: Hunts and sketches in Canada's Banff and Waterton Lakes areas. Meets George Pratt and his brother Herbert Pratt. Herbert commissions two *Tigers* and one four-foot *Buffalo* for his estate at Glen Cove, Long Island, New York.

Works on the *Buffalo Head* for the State Dining Room in the White House.

Serves on Boone and Crockett Club's board as member of executive committee.

Joins and exhibits with Canadian Art Club, Toronto, for next several years.

Fall 1910: Takes an antelope hunting trip to Edmonton with Alden Sampson.

1911: Exhibits at the Portland Art Museum, Portland. Receives a commission for four large bronze *Buffalo* for the Q Street Bridge in Washington, D.C. Visits the 200,000-acre Wainwright game preserve to study and sketch buffalo.

With Alden Sampson, moves into new studio designed by McKim, Mead and White at 168 East 51st Street, New York.

Summer 1912: Goes on a hunting trip with George Pratt to Alberta.

Summer 1913: Takes a big game hunting trip with George Pratt to Fort Steele, British Columbia, to gather specimens for the Smithsonian Institution.

Presents large exhibition of sculpture at Gorham Company galleries in New York and receives broad critical approbation.

1914: Travels to Montana and works on *Pursued* with Chief Little Wolf's son, Robert, a Cheyenne Indian, as his model. Performs a secret ceremony to become a blood brother to Chief Little Wolf. Spends winter in Pendleton, Oregon.

1915: Travels to Portland to work on several bas-relief portraits. Attends Pendleton Round-Up. Starts the *Buckaroo.*

Completes work on a small bronze Indian head called *"Sundown" Nez Perce's Chief.*

Homesteads 120 acres near the ranch of William Hanley, cattle king of eastern Oregon and later a U.S. senator.

Exhibits plaster of Q Street Bridge *Buffalo* at Panama-Pacific Exposition, San Francisco.

Spring 1916: Completes the buffalo portion of *Buffalo Hunt* and selects Jackson Sundown, nephew of Chief Joseph, as the model for the horse's rider.

Moves that summer with Margaret and their seven children to Lapwai, a Nez Perce reservation, to model Sundown. Camps in a tipi on Sundown's ranch.

1917: Receives a commission for a *High Relief of Bison Head* for the Arlington Memorial Bridge, Washington, D.C. Receives commissions for four heroic monuments, *Broncho Buster*, *On the War Trail, Pioneer*, and *Indian Drinking.*

Holds major one-man exhibition at the Art Institute of Chicago.

1918: Moves to Palo Alto, California. Needs a larger studio, so Stanford University leases him a room in the engineering building.

Holds another major one-man exhibition at the Corcoran Gallery of Art, Washington, D.C.

1919: Drives 1,500 miles to Browning, Montana, in search of a new model for *On the War Trail* and *Indian Drinking*. Spends the summer modeling Blackfeet Indians. Returns to California in late fall with Big Beaver, his model, to complete *On the War Trail.*

1920: Receives commissions for *Theodore Roosevelt* and the *Circuit Rider* monuments in Oregon.

1923: Sells Palo Alto home and moves to Hollywood, California. Finds models from movie sets for the Kansas City commission *Pioneer Mother*. Presents a large one-man exhibition at the Stendahl Art Gallery, Los Angeles.

1924: Exhibits eighteen works in a group exhibition at the Los Angeles Museum in Exposition Park.

1925: Accepts a studio at the American Academy in Rome and becomes its Resident Sculptor. Travels to Rome in the fall.

1927: Has the *Pioneer Mother* cast in bronze in Rome and transported to Kansas City, Missouri.

1927–1928: Spends the winter in Brussels, Belgium, where the *Til Taylor* monument is cast.

Returns to the United States that summer and settles in Wilton, Connecticut.

1929: Receives a commission for the *General Robert E. Lee* monument in Dallas.

1936: Attends on June 12 the dedication of *General Robert E. Lee* in Dallas, with President Franklin D. Roosevelt unveiling the statue.

Sells the Wilton home and moves to New York.

On a hunting trip to southeastern Alaska, shoots his limit of four bears.

1936–1938: Works on drypoint etchings of wild animals. Margaret develops heart problems.

1937: Moves to Seattle. Receives a commission for *Mustangs* for the University of Texas at Austin.

1939: Lives for part of the year at Rancho Los Palos, Texas, while modeling a stallion, five mares, and a colt for *Mustangs.*

1940: Moves to North Bend, Washington.

1941: Begins serious work on his autobiography, *Sculptor in Buckskin*, and continues to sketch and paint.

1942: Margaret dies.

1943: Moves back to Palo Alto, California, to stay with his daughter Hester.

1946: Hunts in Alaska in September. Kills a bear seventy years after killing his first bear at age sixteen—two days before his eighty-sixth birthday.

1948: Sees the *Mustangs* (completed in 1939) finally cast, with the easing of the World War II bronze shortage. The monument is dedicated in May.

1949: Starts a new sketch of four Indians on horses at full gallop.

1950: Dies in Palo Alto on September 4 at the age of eighty-nine.

EXHIBITIONS

Solo Exhibitions

A. Phimister Proctor, Montross Gallery,
New York, 20 November–5 December 1908
A. Phimister Proctor, Montross Gallery,
New York, 1912
*Exhibition of Bronzes and Plaster Models by
A. Phimister Proctor*, The Gorham
Company, New York, 6–25 October 1913
Small Bronzes by A. Phimister Proctor,
Art Institute of Chicago, Chicago,
8 March–2 April 1917
Works in Sculpture by A. Phimister Proctor,
Corcoran Gallery of Art, Washington, D.C.,
5–31 March 1918
A. Phimister Proctor, Stendahl Art Gallery,
Los Angeles, March 1923

World Expositions

Sculptors of the United States, World's
Columbian Exposition, Chicago, 1893
(designer medal for special contribution)
Exhibition des Beaux-Arts, Paris Universal
Exposition, Paris, 1900 (gold medal for
sculpture)
Exhibition of Fine Arts, Pan-American
Exposition, Buffalo, New York, 1901
(bronze medal for watercolor)
Louisiana Purchase Exposition, Saint Louis,
1904 (gold medal)
Alaska-Yukon-Pacific Exposition, Seattle,
1909
Panama-Pacific Exposition, San Francisco,
1915 (gold medal)
British Empire Exhibition, Wembley, England,
April 1924

Group Exhibitions

1885–1900

Paris Salon, Paris, 1886
Century Club, New York, 1887
Toronto Art Gallery, Toronto, November 1889
Water Color Society of New York, New York,
1889 (second place)
Annual exhibition, National Academy of
Design, New York, 1889
Annual exhibition, National Academy of
Design, New York, 1890
Annual exhibition, National Academy of
Design, New York, 1895
*Seventeenth Annual Exhibition of the Society of
American Artists*, New York, 1895
Paris Salon, Paris, 1897
Paris Salon, Paris, 1898
*Third Exhibition of the National Sculpture
Society*, New York, 1898
Paris Salon, Paris, 1899

1901–1905

Century Club, New York, 1901
Annual exhibition, National Academy of
Design, New York, 1901
Annual exhibition, National Academy of
Design, New York, 1902
Century Club, New York, 1902
Century Club, New York, 1903

Annual exhibition, National Academy of
Design, New York, 1904
Annual exhibition, National Academy of
Design, New York, 1905
Century Club, New York, 1905

1906–1910

Annual exhibition, National Academy of
Design, New York, 1906
*Annual Exhibition of Pictures in Water Color
and Pastel by American Artists*, Montross
Gallery, New York, 1907
Century Club, New York, 1907
Winter exhibition, National Academy of
Design, New York, 1908
Century Club, New York, 1908
Montross Gallery, New York, 21 November–
5 December 1908
Canadian Art Club Exhibition, Art Museum of
Toronto, Toronto, 1909
*A Collection of Small Bronzes Lent by the
National Sculpture Society*, Buffalo Fine Arts
Academy, Albright Art Gallery, Buffalo,
New York, 1909
Century Club, New York, 1909
Second Annual Exhibition, Canadian Art Club,
Toronto, 1–20 March 1909
Canadian Art Club Exhibition, Art Association
of Montreal, Montreal, 1910
Third Annual Exhibition, Canadian Art Club,
Toronto, 7–27 January 1910

1911–1915

Fourth Annual Exhibition, Canadian Art Club,
Toronto, 3–25 March 1911
Century Club, New York, 1911
*Sculptures by Olin Warner and A. Phimister
Proctor*, Portland Art Association, Portland,
Oregon, 1911
*Seventh Annual Exhibition of Selected
Watercolors by American Artists*, Albright
Art Gallery, Buffalo, New York,
14 September–15 October 1911
Winter exhibition, National Academy of
Design, New York, 1912
Exhibition of Sculpture, Montross Gallery,
New York, 27 February–12 March 1912
Fifth Annual Exhibition, Canadian Art Club,
Toronto, 8–27 February 1912
*Exhibition of Bronzes and Plaster Models by
A. Phimister Proctor*, The Gorham Company,
New York, 1913
Century Club, New York, 1913
Sixth Annual Exhibition, Canadian Art Club,
Toronto, 9–31 May 1913
*Twenty-second Annual Exhibition of the Society
of Washington Artists*, Seattle, 12–28 April
1913
American Museum of Natural History,
New York, 22–29 April 1914
Annual exhibition, National Academy of
Design, New York, 1914
Seventh Annual Exhibition, Canadian Art Club,
Toronto, May 1914

*Twenty-ninth Annual Exhibition of American
Oil Paintings and Sculpture*, Art Institute of
Chicago, Chicago, 2 November–
7 December 1914
Frazier Book Store, Pendleton, Oregon,
November 1914, July 1915
Washington State Art Association, Seattle,
July 1915
American Industrial Art, Columbia University,
New York, 1 December 1915–31 January 1916

1916–1920

Beard Galleries, Minneapolis, 1916
Contemporary American Sculpture, Buffalo
Fine Arts Academy, Albright Art Gallery,
Buffalo, New York, 1916
*An Exhibition of Small Bronzes by American
Sculptors*, Buffalo Fine Arts Academy,
Albright Art Gallery, Buffalo, New York,
1918
Annual exhibition, National Academy of
Design, New York, 1918
Winter exhibition, National Academy of
Design, New York, 1919
Paintings and Sculpture by Four Artists of Taos,
Art Institute of Chicago, Chicago, 1919
Painters and Sculptors of Animal Life, Babcock
Gallery, New York, 1920

1921–1925

Annual exhibition, National Academy of
Design, New York, 1921
MacDowell Club of Allied Arts, Ansonia,
Connecticut, 1921
Sixth Annual Exhibition, Greenwich Society of
Artists, Greenwich, Connecticut, 1922
Annual exhibition, National Academy of
Design, New York, 1922
Bohemian Club, San Francisco, 27 November
1920, 1922
National Sculpture Society, New York, 1923
Second Annual Exhibition, Palo Alto Art Club,
Palo Alto, California, 1923
*Sculpture by A. Phimister Proctor [and] Harold
Swartz, Paintings by Conrad Buff [and] Shiyei
Y. Kotoku*, Los Angeles Museum, 1924

1926–1930

Bronzes from the Collection of Simon Casady,
Des Moines Association of Fine Arts,
Des Moines, Iowa, 1929
Wilton Public Library, Wilton, Connecticut,
9–19 August 1929
Winter exhibition, National Academy of
Design, New York, 1930

1931–1936

Grand Central Art Galleries, New York, 1931
Inaugural exhibition, Whitney Museum of
American Art, New York, 1931
Annual exhibition, National Academy of
Design, New York, 1932
Dallas Public Art Gallery, Dallas, 1932
Grand Central Art Galleries, New York, June
1935

Corcoran Gallery of Art, Washington, D.C.,
1935
Exhibition of Paintings and Sculpture, Fort
Worth Frontier Centennial Exposition,
Fort Worth, Texas, 18 July–30 November
1936

After 1936

Army Air Forces Convalescent Center and
Station Hospital, Pawling, New York, 1944
Palo Alto Art Club, Palo Alto, California, 1947

PUBLIC COLLECTIONS, PUBLIC MONUMENTS, AND ORNAMENTAL WORKS

Public Collections

A. Phimister Proctor Museum, Poulsbo, Washington

Agnes Etherington Art Center, Queen's University, Toronto

American Airlines, Dallas

Amon Carter Museum, Fort Worth

Art Institute of Chicago, Chicago

Brookgreen Gardens, Pawleys Island, South Carolina

Brooklyn Botanic Garden, Brooklyn, New York

Brooklyn Museum of Art, Brooklyn, New York

Buffalo Bill Historical Center, Cody, Wyoming

C. M. Russell Museum, Great Falls, Montana

Cleveland Museum of Art, Cleveland

Corcoran Gallery of Art, Washington, D.C.

Dayton Art Institute, Dayton, Ohio

Denver Public Library, Denver

Eiteljorg Museum of Art, Indianapolis, Indiana

George F. Harding Museum, Chicago

George Gund Collection of Western Art, Cleveland

Gilcrease Museum, Tulsa, Oklahoma

Glenbow Museum, Calgary, Alberta

Grey Towers National Historic Landmark, Milford, Pennsylvania

Harry Ransom Humanities Research Center, University of Texas, Austin

Harry S. Truman Library Museum, Independence, Missouri

Jasper County Historical Society, Newton, Iowa

John L. Wehle Gallery of Sporting Art, Genesee Country Village and Museum, Mumford, New York

Kansas City Art Institute, Kansas City, Missouri

Lee Chapel and Museum, Washington and Lee University, Lexington, Virginia

Los Angeles Chamber of Commerce, Los Angeles

Los Angeles County Museum of Art, Los Angeles

Mead Museum of Art, Amherst College, Amherst, Massachusetts

Metropolitan Museum of Art, New York

Montreal Museum of Fine Arts, Montreal

National Academy of Design, New York

National Gallery of Canada, Ottawa

National Museum of Wildlife Art, Jackson, Wyoming

North Carolina Museum of Art, Raleigh

Oakland Museum of Art, Oakland, California

Oregon Historical Society, Portland

Paine Art Center & Gardens, Oshkosh, Wisconsin

Parrish Art Museum, Southampton, New York

Pratt Institute, Brooklyn, New York

Portland Art Museum, Portland, Oregon

R. W. Norton Art Gallery, Shreveport, Louisiana

Rockwell Museum, Corning, New York

Sagamore Hill National Historic Site, National Park Service, Oyster Bay, New York

Saint Louis Art Museum, Saint Louis

Saint Louis County Historical Society, Duluth, Minnesota

San Diego Museum of Art, San Diego

Smithsonian American Art Museum, Washington, D.C.

Third Cavalry Museum, Fort Carson, Colorado

Toledo Museum of Art, Toledo, Ohio

University Gallery, University of Delaware, Newark, Delaware

University of Oregon, Eugene

University of Texas, Austin

Walters Art Museum, Baltimore

William S. Hart Ranch and Museum, Newhall, California

Wilton Public Library, Wilton, Connecticut

Woolaroc Museum, Bartlesville, Oklahoma

Sites of Monumental Works

Buffalo, Dumbarton (Q Street) Bridge, Washington, D.C.

Broncho Buster, Civic Center, Denver

Circuit Rider, State Capitol Building, Salem, Oregon

General Robert E. Lee, Lee Park, Dallas

High Relief of Bison Head, Arlington Memorial Bridge, Washington, D.C.

Indian Fountain, Lake George, New York

Lions, McKinley Monument, Niagara Square, Buffalo, New York

Logan Monument, Grant Park, Chicago

McKnight Memorial Fountain, Wichita High School East, Wichita, Kansas

Mustangs, University of Texas, Austin

On the War Trail, Civic Center, Denver

Oregon Pioneer Mother, University of Oregon, Eugene

Piney Branch Tigers, Piney Branch Bridge (also known as Sixteenth Street Bridge), Washington, D.C.

Pioneer Mother, Penn Valley Park, Kansas City, Missouri

Pioneer, University of Oregon, Eugene

Pumas, Prospect Park, Brooklyn, New York

Seated Lions, Frick Building, Pittsburgh

Sherman Monument, Grand Army Plaza, New York

Theodore Roosevelt, City of Portland, Oregon; City of Mandan, North Dakota; City of Minot, North Dakota; Theodore Roosevelt Birthplace, New York; A. Phimister Proctor Museum

Tiger Couchant, Nassau Hall, Princeton University

Til Taylor, City of Pendleton, Oregon

Sites of Ornamental Works
Various decorations, New York Zoological Society, Bronx, New York

Griffins, Saint Louis Art Museum, Saint Louis

Lion Heads, New York Public Library, New York

Owl, Russel Sage Foundation Building, New York

Irving Hale Plaque, State Capitol Building, Denver; United States Military Academy, West Point, New York

NOTES

Chapter 1

1 J. Harrison Mills, "Concerning Early Art in Colorado," typescript letter, 1916, Western History Collection, Denver Public Library, Denver.

2 Alexander Phimister Proctor, *Sculptor in Buckskin* (Norman, Okla.: University of Oklahoma Press, 1971), p. 12.

3 The date and place of Proctor's birth have been in question for many years. Proctor himself created the problem. First of all, he was not exactly certain where he had been born, but when he submitted accounts of his life and accomplishments, he always claimed his birthplace as Bozanquit in Ontario. There is no such town, but a Bozanquet township exists in Lambton County. The family Bible belonging to Proctor's aunt, Mary E. Proctor, who maintained the family's genealogical records, identifies Arkona as the artist's birthplace. It also notes that he was born on September 27, 1860. Proctor changed that date to 1862 when he married Margaret Gerow in 1893. She was eighteen at the time, and he evidently wanted to be seen as closer to her age. The error, though eventually corrected in the autobiography published after his death, persisted in literature throughout his life and is found in standard sources today.

4 "Former Newsboy of Denver Now World Famous Sculptor," *Denver Post*, 19 December 1909.

5 A.P. Proctor to Edmund Morris, 14 December 1909, letter with handwritten biographical sketch for the Canadian Art Club, Edmund Morris Papers, Art Gallery of Ontario, Toronto.

6 John William Rogers, "Sculptor of Lee Statue Has Had Colorful Career," *Dallas Times Herald*, 24 May 1936.

7 Proctor, *Sculptor in Buckskin*, p. 82.

8 Mills, "Concerning Early Art in Colorado," pp. 7–8.

9 Proctor, *Sculptor in Buckskin*, pp. 20–21. Proctor could not recall the artist's name at the time he wrote his autobiography, but it may have been a painter named H. A. Streight, known as the "Professor," who settled in Denver in 1870 and accepted students; see Mary Lou Martorano, "Artists and Art Organizations in Colorado" (MA thesis, University of Denver, 1962), pp. 35–36.

10 A 1938 typescript notebook, "Denver Artists," Denver, in the collections of the Colorado Historical Society, Denver, says that through the sixth grade Proctor attended the Arapahoe School at Arapahoe and 17th Streets, and for the seventh and eighth grades, the Broadway School at 14th and Broadway.

11 Proctor, *Sculptor in Buckskin*, p. 22.

12 Harrison Mills, "Hunting the Mule-Deer in Colorado," *Scribner's Monthly*, 17, no. 5 (September 1878): 622.

13 Ibid., 613.

14 Mills, "Concerning Early Art in Colorado," p. 8.

15 Proctor, *Sculptor in Buckskin*, p. 22.

16 One of the earliest known accounts of this hunting story appeared in "To Fame In a Year," *Denver Rocky Mountain News*, 15 October 1893.

17 Different sources record different lengths of time the Proctor family actually spent at Grand Lake. Proctor, in his autobiography, suggests that they first vacationed in the area in 1873, two years after arriving in Colorado, and returned over the next twelve years (*Sculptor in Buckskin*, pp. 12, 18). In other accounts the artist says they went there first in 1876 and continued to frequent the area over the next ten years; see Muriel E. Ringstad, "Memoirs of Phimister Proctor," *Frontier Times* (September 1964): 13, 15. Mary Lyons Cairns, in her history of the region, says that Proctor and his brother George arrived to summer with Wescott in 1875, and that the full family, "the first one really to spend much time at Grand Lake," arrived in 1877; see *Grand Lake: The Pioneers* (Denver: The World Press, 1946), p. 113.

18 For discussion on this point, see Peter Hassrick, *The Way West: Art of the American Frontier* (New York: Harry N. Abrams, 1977), p. 16, and Barbara Novak, *Nature and Culture: American Landscape and Painting, 1825–1875* (New York: Oxford University Press, 1980), p. 137.

19 Mills, "Concerning Early Art in Colorado," pp. 1, 4.

20 "Grand Lake," *Denver Rocky Mountain News*, 5 November 1881.

21 "Grand Lake," *Denver Rocky Mountain News*, 25 November 1881.

22 "Academy of Fine Arts," *Denver Tribune*, 13 August 1882.

23 For information on Chain, see Martorano, "Artists and Art Organizations in Colorado," p. 37; Joe Henderson Lundbeck to the Denver Public Library, 6 November 1967, Western History Collection, Denver Public Library; and Patricia Trenton, ed., *Independent Spirits: Women Painters of the American West, 1890–1945* (Berkeley, Calif.: Autry Museum of Western Heritage in association with University of California Press, 1995), p. 213. On the Proctor/Adams studio, see "To Fame In a Year."

24 "Another Successful Day," *Denver Rocky Mountain News*, 10 August 1882.

25 "Helen Henderson Chain," in *Glory That Was Gold* (1934), Western History Collection, Denver Public Library.

26 See "Exhibition at the National Mining Exposition," *Denver Rocky Mountain News*, 18 July 1883, and "Fine Arts in Colorado," *Denver Rocky Mountain News*, 27 July 1883.

27 Roberta Balfour, "Proctor's Inspiration Was Born in the West," *Denver Post*, 29 March 1903.

28 Quoted in Cairns, *Grand Lake: The Pioneers*, p. 119.

29 Ibid.

30 Proctor, *Sculptor in Buckskin*, p. 81.

31 Ibid., 23–25. On Dellenbaugh, see Maria Naylor, *The National Academy of Design Exhibition Record, 1861–1900*, vol. 2 (New York: Kennedy Galleries, 1973), pp. 227–28.

32 Mills, "Concerning Early Art in Colorado, p.11, and Proctor, *Sculptor in Buckskin*, p. 84.

33 Proctor's autobiography dates this trip as 1887 though the photograph is inscribed 1885 (*Sculptor in Buckskin*, pp. 89–93).

34 "To Fame In a Year."

Chapter 2

1 Mills says that Proctor came east in March 1886, but Proctor indicates that he arrived in New York in November 1885: *Sculptor in Buckskin* (Norman, Okla.: University of Oklahoma Press, 1971), p. 84. The school register in the archives of the National Academy of Design lists Proctor as enrolled in the antique class during the academic year 1885–1886.

2 Alexander Phimister Proctor, "Early Days in New York," handwritten account, c. 1943, Proctor Papers.

3 William C. Brownell, "The Art-Schools of New York," *Scribner's Monthly* 16, no. 6 (October 1878): 779.

4 See Proctor, *Sculptor in Buckskin*, p. 85, and Alexander Phimister Proctor, "New York, First Years—Academy," handwritten account, c. 1943, Proctor Papers.

5 Mary Lyons Cairns, *Grand Lake: The Pioneers* (Denver: The World Press, 1946), p. 119.

6 Proctor, *Sculptor in Buckskin*, p. 85.

7 Ibid., 86.

8 Proctor, "Early Days in New York."

9 J. Harrison Mills, "Concerning Early Art in Colorado," typescript letter, 1916, Western History Collection, Denver Public Library, Denver, pp. 9, 12. See *Works of Antoine-Louis Barye Exhibited at the American Art Galleries* (New York: J. J. Little, 1889).

10 Theodore Child, "Antoine-Louis Barye," *Harper's Monthly* 71, no. 424 (September 1885): 594, 590.

11 John William Rogers, "Sculptor of Lee Statue Has Had Colorful Career," *Dallas Times Herald*, 24 May 1936, and Proctor, *Sculptor in Buckskin*, pp. 82–83.

12 David H. Wallace, *John Rogers: The People's Sculptor* (Middletown, Conn.: Wesleyan University Press, 1967), pp. 119–20, and "A. Phimister Proctor, World Famous Sculptor Working on Heroic Statue of Gen. R. E. Lee," *Ridgefield (Conn.) Press*, 9 August 1934. The latter source points out that from Rogers Proctor "gained some of his first material knowledge about sculpting."

13 Proctor, *Sculptor in Buckskin*, p. 94.

14 "To Fame In a Year," *Denver Rocky Mountain News*, 15 October 1893.

15 See Maria Naylor, *The National Academy of Design Exhibition Record 1861–1900*, p. 763. His watercolors included *Young Elk Resting* and *Elk—A Solitary*; see *Exhibition of the American Water Color Society of New York City* (Buffalo, N.Y.: Buffalo Fine Arts Academy, 1890). Proctor showed in traveling exhibitions in Buffalo in 1905, 1907, 1910, and 1911.

16 Proctor, *Sculptor in Buckskin*, p. 109.

17 "About the Studios, Phimister Proctor is a True Natural Sculptor," *Chicago Sunday Inter Ocean*, 1 January 1893. See also Proctor, *Sculptor in Buckskin*, pp. 89–93, 99–103, for discussion of these trips.

18 Rufus Zogbaum, "A Day's 'Drive' with Montana Cow-Boys," *Harper's Monthly* 71, no. 422 (July 1885): 190; Frederic Remington, "A Scout With the Buffalo-Soldiers," *Century Magazine* 37, no. 6 (April 1889): 899–912; and Theodore Roosevelt, "Ranch Life in the Far West," *Century Magazine* 35, no. 4 (February 1888): 495–510.

19 "An Art Student in Ecouen," *Harper's Monthly* 70, no. 417 (February 1885): 398.

20 Julian Hawthorne, "American Wild Animals in Art," *Century Magazine* 27, no. 2 (June 1884): 214.

21 The drawings are in the Proctor Museum, Poulsbo, Washington.

22 For further discussion of gender issues, see Michael S. Kimmel, "Men's Response to Feminism at the Turn of the Century," *Gender & Society* (September 1987): 262.

23 Rogers, "Sculptor of Lee Statue."

24 Proctor, *Sculptor in Buckskin*, p. 113. For slightly different interpretations of that story, see "To Fame In a Year" and Rogers, "Sculptor of Lee Statue."

25 Ibid. See also "About the Studios."

26 Ibid.

27 George Parsons Lathrop, "The Progress of Art in New York," *Harper's Monthly* 87, no. 515 (April 1893): 741.

28 Ibid., 742.

29 See Donald Martin Reynolds, *Masters of American Sculpture* (New York: Abbeville Press, 1993), p. 25.

30 "About the Studios." Taft was quoted in "Portland's Art Tastes Commended by One of Great Animal Sculptors," *Portland Sunday Oregonian*, 17 December 1911.

31 See "To Fame In a Year."

32 "Objected to the Pose," *Chicago Inter Ocean*, 26 May 1893.

33 Halsey C. Ives, *The Dream City, A Portfolio of Photographic Views of the World's Columbian Exposition* (Saint Louis: N. D. Thompson Publishing, 1893). Ives was quoting from a writer for the *Chicago Record*.

34 William A. Coffin, "The Columbian Exposition—I. Fine Arts: French and American Sculpture," *The Nation* 57 (3 August 1893): 81, and an unidentified newspaper clipping, c. 1898, from the Proctor Museum Archives.

35 Ibid.

36 Theodore Roosevelt, *The Wilderness Hunter* (New York: G. P. Putnam's Sons, 1900), p. 11. For a history of the club, see George B. Ward, *Boone and Crockett, National Collection of Heads and Horns* (Cody, Wyo.: Buffalo Bill Historical Center, 1993); for a further explication of the club's mantra of "manly sport" and "large game preservation," see George Bird Grinnell, *American Big-Game Hunting: The Book of the Boone and Crockett Club* (New York: Forest and Stream Publishing, 1893), p. 10.

37 J. H. Gest, "Sculptors of the World's Fair," *Engineer Magazine* 5, no. 4 (July 1893): 427.

38 Proctor, *Sculptor in Buckskin*, p. 116.

39 William Howe Downes, "The Work of Bela L. Pratt, Sculptor," *New England Magazine* 27 (February 1903): 763. See also Reynolds, *Masters of American Sculpture*, p. 28, and James L. Riedy, *Chicago Sculpture* (Urbana, Ill.: University of Illinois Press, 1981), pp. 23–24.

40 Quoted in Thomas Beer, *The Mauve Decade* (New York: Alfred A. Knopf, 1926), p. 43.

41 Gest, "Sculptors of the World's Fair," p. 432.

42 Quoted in Elizabeth Broun, "American Paintings and Sculpture in the Fine Arts Building of the World's Columbian Exposition, Chicago, 1893" (Ph.D. diss., University of Kansas, 1976), p. 6.

43 Proctor, *Sculptor in Buckskin*, pp. 122, 124.

44 Roberta Balfour, "Proctor's Inspiration Was Born in the West," *Denver Post*, 29 March 1903.

Chapter 3

1 George Parsons Lathrop, "The Progress of Art in New York," *Harper's Monthly* 87, no. 515 (April 1893): 741.

2 Alexander Phimister Proctor, *Sculptor in Buckskin* (Norman, Okla.: University of Oklahoma Press, 1971), p. 125. Michael A. Jacobsen, "Some Visual Sources for the Sculpture of Alexander Phimister Proctor," *Apelles* 1, no. 2 (Spring 1980): 16–23 discusses the impact of these European lessons on Proctor's art.

3 Robert Rosenblum and H. W. Janson, *19th-Century Art* (New York: Harry N. Abrams, 1984), p. 499.

4 Ledger book for 1893–1895, Proctor Museum Archives, and Proctor, *Sculptor in Buckskin*, p. 125.

5 Quoted in Hugh O'Neill, "Alexander P. Proctor," *Denver Post*, 29 May 1917.

6 "A. Phimister Proctor," *The News* 1, no. 14 (26 July 1912): 14. For Proctor's relationship with Saint-Gaudens, see Burke Wilkinson, *Uncommon Clay: The Life and Works of Augustus Saint-Gaudens* (New York: Harcourt Brace Jovanovich, 1985), pp. 261–69.

7 Sadakichi Hartmann, "How an American Art Could Be Developed," *The Art Critic* 1, no. 1 (November 1893): 61. See also Lathrop, "The Progress of Art," p. 751.

8 William Sener Rusk, *William Henry Rinehart, Sculptor* (Baltimore: Norman T. A. Munder, 1939), pp. 83–87.

9 Quoted in J. Walker McSpadden, *Famous Sculptors of America* (New York: Dodd, Mead, 1924), p. 311.

10 Homer Saint-Gaudens, *The Reminiscences of Augustus Saint-Gaudens*, vol. 2 (London: Andrew Melrose, 1913), p. 37.

11 Mary Mears, "What the Masters Knew," *Christian Science Monitor*, 1 April 1938. For a discussion of Proctor's French connections with Brush, Borglum, and Pratt, see Nancy Douglas Bowditch, *George de Forest Brush: Recollections of a Joyous Painter* (Peterborough, N.H.: William L. Bauhan, 1970), pp. 48–51; A. Mervyn Davies, *Solon H. Borglum, A Man Who Stands Alone* (Chester, Conn.: Pequot Press, 1974), pp. 60–61; and Proctor, *Sculptor in Buckskin*, p. 137.

12 Quoted in Arthur Goodrich, "The Frontier in Sculpture," *The World's Work* (March 1902): 1873.

13 For a discussion of this point by Michele Bogart, see Kathleen Pyne, et al., *The Quest for Unity: American Art Between World's Fairs*

1876–1893 (Detroit: Detroit Institute of Arts, 1983), p. 258.

14 W. H. de B. Nelson, "Phimister Proctor: Canadian Sculptor," *The Canadian Magazine* 44, no. 6 (April 1915): 499, and Rosenblum and Janson, *19th-Century Art*, pp. 273–74.

15 John James Audubon and John Bachman, *The Quadrupeds of North America*, vol. 2 (New York: V. G. Audubon, 1851), p. 307.

16 See Nelson, "Phimister Proctor: Canadian Sculptor," p. 495.

17 Reproduced in *Third Exhibition of the National Sculpture Society* (New York: National Sculpture Society, 1898), no. 169.

18 Lorado Taft, "A. Phimister Proctor," *Brush and Pencil* 2, no. 6 (September 1898): 240–48.

19 For a discussion of the pavilion, see Diane P. Fischer, et al., *Paris 1900: The "American School" at the Universal Exposition* (Montclair, N.J.: Montclair Art Museum, 1999), pp. 11–12. Saint-Gaudens' letter is quoted in Charlotte Streifer Rubinstein, *American Women Sculptors* (Boston: G. K. Hall, 1990), p. 134.

20 Vance Thompson, "The Narrow Escape of the Clay Horses," *Saturday Evening Post* (24 March 1900).

21 Bowditch, *George de Forest Brush*, p. 50.

22 Sadakichi Hartmann, "A Chat on New York Sculptors," *The Criterion* (15 January 1898): 14.

23 Georgia Fraser, "The Sculptors of the United States Pavilion at the Paris Exposition," *Brush and Pencil* 5, no. 5 (February 1900): 234.

24 Theodore Roosevelt to A.P. Proctor, 2 August 1897, Theodore Roosevelt Collection, Harvard College Library, Harvard University.

25 Lorado Taft, "American Sculpture at the Exposition—I," *Brush and Pencil* 6, no. 4 (July 1900): 172.

26 Quoted in "Sculptor Proctor's Colorado Bear Story," *New York Times*, 24 June 1900.

Chapter 4

1 See Isabelle K. Savell, *The Tonetti Years of Sneden's Landing* (New York: Historical Society of Rockland County, 1977), pp. 168–72, and Alexander Phimister Proctor, *Sculptor in Buckskin* (Norman, Okla.: University of Oklahoma Press, 1971), p. 141.

2 A.P. Proctor to Gifford Pinchot, 6 December 1900, Pinchot Papers.

3 Charles H. Caffin, *American Masters of Sculpture* (Garden City, N.Y.: Doubleday, Page, 1918), p. 198.

4 Charles H. Caffin, "Brief Appreciation of Some American Painters, XII: Horatio Walker," *New York Sun*, 5 January 1902.

5 For a discussion of this, see David Karel, *Horatio Walker* (Quebec: Musée du Québec, 1987), pp. 155–57. For quote, see M. I. Fairbairn, "Horatio Walker and His Art," *The Canadian Magazine* 18, no. 6 (April 1902): 496. Proctor had befriended Walker in 1894 in New York. See Proctor, *Sculptor in Buckskin*, p. 130.

6 William A. Coffin, *Pan-American Exposition: Catalogue of the Exhibition of Fine Arts* (Buffalo, N.Y.: David Gray, 1901), nos. 833–35, 1634–41a.

7 Adeline Adams, *Daniel Chester French, Sculptor* (Boston: Houghton Mifflin, 1932), p. 33.

8 *Seattle Post-Intelligencer*, 30 October 1901.

9 Forrest Crissy, "Edward Kemeys, American Sculptor," *Carter's Monthly* 13, no. 2 (February 1898): 115. See also Hamlin Garland, "Edward Kemeys, A Sculptor of Frontier Life and Wild Animals," *McClure's Magazine* 5 (July 1895): 120–31.

10 Alexander Phimister Proctor, "World's Fair Chicago," handwritten account, c. 1943, Proctor Papers. For further discussion of Kemeys' bitter feelings toward Proctor, see Michael Tingley Richman, "Edward Kemeys (1843–1907): American Animal Sculptor" (MA thesis, George Washington University, 1970), p. 1.

11 *Seattle Post-Intelligencer*, 30 October 1901.

12 "Henry J. Allen Sees the Pioneer Mother," *Kansas City Star*, 18 March 1927.

13 "Largest Bull Moose Killed in Canada By a Sculptor," *New York World*, 26 May 1902. The Proctor family still owns the moose rack. The details of the Vanderbilt and Morgan commissions are not known today.

14 "Zoological Park Opens," *New York Evening Post*, 8 November 1899.

15 William Bridges, *Gathering of Animals: An Unconventional History of the New York Zoological Society* (New York: Harper & Row, 1974), pp. 143–44.

16 Harrison N. Howard, "National Academy of Design Exhibition," *Brush and Pencil* 9, no. 5 (February 1902): 289. Charles de Kay wrote of the pediment study in "The National Academy Exposition," *New York Sun*, 8 January 1902, that "it seems to be a very successful solution of the problem of treating the animals realistically and at the same time of making them contribute to an ornamental design."

17 See "Largest Bull Moose Killed in Canada."

18 Bridges, *Gathering of Animals*, p. 142.

19 "When Leo Poses: Wild Animals at the Zoo Are Patient Models," *New York Herald*, 25 May 1902.

20 Ibid.

21 Lorado Taft, "Sculptors of the World's Fair," *Brush and Pencil* 13, no. 3 (December 1903): 223.

22 Roberta Balfour, "Proctor's Inspiration Was Born in the West," *Denver Post*, 29 March 1903.

23 Taft, "Sculptors of the World's Fair," p. 199.

24 Emily Grant Hutchings, *The Art Gallery of the Universal Exposition* (Saint Louis: Universal Exposition Publishing, 1905), p. 74.

25 George McCue, *Sculpture City, St. Louis: Public Sculpture in the "Gateway to the West"* (New York: Hudson Hills Press, 1988), p. 179.

26 A. A. Howard, "Sculpture at the World's Fair," *Brush and Pencil* 15, no. 1 (January 1905): 40.

27 "Model of McKinley Monument Lion," unidentified clipping, c. 1906, Proctor Museum Archives.

28 Proctor to Pinchot, 25 April 1903, Pinchot Papers.

29 Augustus Saint-Gaudens to Proctor, 27 May 1906, quoted in Homer Saint-Gaudens, *The Reminiscences of Augustus Saint-Gaudens* (London: Andrew Melrose, 1913), pp. 212–14.

30 Proctor to Augustus Saint-Gaudens, 5 June 1906, Saint-Gaudens Papers.

31 Proctor to Homer Saint-Gaudens, 10 December 1907, Saint-Gaudens Papers.

32 For a lengthy description of that stay, see Nancy Douglas Bowditch, *George de Forest Brush: Recollections of a Joyous Painter* (Peterborough, N.H.: William L. Bauhan, 1970), pp. 99–101.

33 Proctor to Pinchot, 7 April 1902, Pinchot Papers.

34 Proctor to Pinchot, 23 April 1907, Pinchot Papers.

35 Pinchot to Elizabeth Custer, 19 December 1907, Frost Collection, Monroe County Historical Museum Archives, Monroe, Michigan.

36 Loyall Farragut to Custer, 16 and 24 November 1907, Frost Collection.

37 Henry L. Stimpson to Custer, 8 January 1908, Frost Collection.

38 Proctor to Custer, 2 December 1907, Frost Collection.

39 Col. George G. Briggs to Custer, 21 December 1907, Frost Collection.

40 A perceptive and thorough account of this commission can be found in Shirley A. Leckie, *Elizabeth Bacon Custer and the Making of a Myth* (Norman, Okla.: University of Oklahoma Press, 1993), pp. 277–81.

41 Proctor to Pinchot, 23 March 1908, Pinchot Papers.

42 Ernest Knaufft, "Saint-Gaudens and American Sculpture," *Review of Reviews, American Monthly* 36 (May 1907): pp. 298–99.

43 Proctor to Pinchot, 10 October 1908, Pinchot Papers.

44 *New York Evening Telegram*, 28 November 1909, and "Music: Drama: Art: Reviews," *The Craftsman* 15, no. 4 (January 1909): 501.

45 Giles Edgerton, "Bronze Sculpture in America: Its Value to the Art History of the Nation," *The Craftsman* 8, no. 6 (March 1908): 617.

46 Royal Cortissoz, "Some Wild Beasts Sculpted by A. Phimister Proctor," *Scribner's* 48, no. 6 (November 1909): 637–40.

Chapter 5

1 A. P. Proctor to Gifford Pinchot, 20 November 1908, Pinchot Papers.

2 "A Successful Canadian Sculptor," *Toronto Saturday Night*, 8 January 1910.

3 See Jean S. McGill, *Edmund Morris: Frontier Artist* (Toronto: Dundurn Press, 1984), p. 117.

4 See Robert J. Lamb, *The Canadian Art Club, 1907–1915* (Edmonton: Edmonton Art Gallery, 1988).

5 Giles Edgerton, "Bronze Sculpture in America: Its Value to the Art History of the Nation," *The Craftsman* 8, no. 4: 628.

6 Irving Hale to Proctor, September 1909, Proctor Museum Archives.

7 Marshall Sprague, *Newport in the Rockies* (Athens, Ohio: Swallow Press, 1961), p. 342.

8 "Former Newsboy of Denver Now World Famous Sculptor," *Denver Post*, 19 December 1909.

9 "Noted Sculptor Here," *Everett (Wash.) Daily Herald*, 12 November 1910, announced Proctor's visit for a week with his mother and two of his sisters, Mrs. J. L. Boyle and Mrs. G. C. Howard.

10 "Seattle Museum's Catalogue Grows … Sculptor Makes Gift," *Seattle Post-Intelligencer*, 28 October 1909. The Seattle Art Museum has no record of such a gift, nor does it currently own the three Proctor works.

11 See Prudence F. Roberts, *Shaping the Collection: C. E. S. Wood and Portland's Early Art Scene* (Portland, Ore.: Portland Art Museum, n.d.), pp. 9–12; Edwin R. Bingham, *Charles Erskine Scott Wood* (Boise, Idaho: Boise State University Press, 1990), pp. 7, 45, 48–49; and Robert Hamburger, *Two Rooms: The Life of Charles Erskine Scott Wood* (Lincoln, Neb.: University of Nebraska Press, 1998), pp. 73, 87.

12 "Portland's Art Tastes Commended by One of Great Animal Sculptors," *Portland Sunday Oregonian*, 17 December 1911.

13 Alexander Phimister Proctor, *Sculptor in Buckskin* (Norman, Okla.: University of Oklahoma Press, 1971), pp. 153–57.

14 Walter Winans, *Animal Sculpture* (New York: G. P. Putnam's Sons, 1913), p. 18.

15 *Harper's Weekly* 51, no. 2955, (9 August 1913): 7.

16 William B. McCormick, "Gallery View of Sculptor's Art Takes One on Journey Through World's Wilds," *New York Press*, 19 October 1913.

17 Charles H. Caffin, "Fine Animal Sculpture by Proctor," *New York American*, 27 October 1913.

18 "Groups of African Animals Exhibited," *New York Press*, 23 April 1914.

19 See William Watson, "Some Recent Small Sculptures," *Scribner's* 40, no. 71 (May 1914): 666.

20 Proctor to Pinchot, 28 April 1914, Pinchot Papers.

21 W. Herbert Dunton, "The Fair in the Cow Country," *Scribner's* 55, no. 4 (April 1914): 454–65.

22 Ibid., 465.

23 "The Buckaroo in Bronze for Park at Depot," *Pendleton (Ore.) Tribune*, 23 July 1915.

24 Proctor to Pinchot, 7 December 1916, Pinchot Papers.

25 "Fine Buffalo, Proctor Hears," *San Francisco Examiner*, 20 November 1915.

26 Lillian Tingle, "Noted Sculptor, Now in Portland, Is Putting Cowboy on 'Art Map,'" *Portland Oregonian*, 25 July 1915.

27 Quoted in Don Russell, *The Lives and Legends of Buffalo Bill* (Norman, Okla.: University of Oklahoma Press, 1960), p. 469.

28 "Museum of Early West, Cody Memorial Plan: Statues to Symbolize Types of Frontier Days," *Denver Rocky Mountain News*, 27 May 1917, and "'Alec' Proctor Comes Here To Discuss Cody Memorial," *Denver Post*, 25 May 1917.

29 "All Tastes Suited in Seven Exhibits at Art Institute," *Chicago Tribune*, 11 March 1917.

30 "Chicago Institute of Art Has Seven One-Man Shows," *Christian Science Monitor*, 6 April 1917.

31 Ibid.

32 See Rick Stewart, *Charles M. Russell, Sculptor* (Fort Worth: Amon Carter Museum, 1994), pp. 75–76.

33 Proctor to Pinchot, 22 January 1916, Pinchot Papers.

34 Proctor to Pinchot, 21 January 1917, Pinchot Papers.

35 See "Bronze to Perpetuate Pioneer: University to Have Sculpture," *Portland Oregon Daily*, 3 January 1917.

36 Francis Parkman, *The Oregon Trail* (Boston: Little, Brown, 1892), pp. 113–15.

37 Frederick V. Holman, *Qualities of the Oregon Pioneers* (Portland: Oregon Historical Society, 1919), pp. 13–14.

38 "Celebrated Sculptor Views Civic Center," *Denver Rocky Mountain News*, 21 September 1917.

39 For an example of Speer's campaign promotion, see "Give While You Live," *Municipal Facts* 1, no. 8 (October 1918): 3.

40 "'Broncho Buster,' Gift of J. K. Mullen, and 'The Indian,' Gift of Stephen Knight, Being Done in Bronze by A. P. Proctor for Civic Center," *Denver Post*, 30 June 1918.

41 Proctor to Pinchot, 29 October 1917, Pinchot Papers. Proctor's timing was propitious.

In 1918 Remington's student and promoter Sally Farnham initiated an effort in Denver and San Francisco to have a heroic enlargement of Remington's *Broncho Buster* or one of his Indian groups erected. Proctor's hometown connections, in this case, paid off. The Remington effort is discussed in Michael Greenbaum, *Icons of the West* (Ogdensburg, N.Y.: Frederic Remington Art Museum, 1996), p. 21.

42 "Denver Sculptor Leaves for East to Ship Indian Equestrian Statue for Civic Center," *Denver Rocky Mountain News*, 5 January 1922.

43 "The Bucking Broncho," *Municipal Facts* 9, no. 5 (May–July 1926): 20.

44 "Carries His Indian Model with Him," *The Spectator* (December 1919).

45 George de Forest Brush to Proctor, 18 January 1920, Proctor Museum Archives. Brush acknowledged that visit and a continuing friendship between the two artists.

46 For a discussion of this work, see A. Seaton-Schmidt, "An American Sculptor: Cyrus E. Dallin," *International Studio* 58, no. 230 (April 1916): 112, and Kent Ahrens, *Cyrus E. Dallin: His Small Bronzes and Plaster* (Corning, N.Y.: Rockwell Museum, 1995), p. 62.

47 "An Indian Fountain," *New York Times*, 20 May 1920.

48 "George D. Pratt Presents Costly Statue to Lake George," *Glen Falls (N.Y.) Times*, 6 May 1921.

Chapter 6

1 Reginald Poland, "Artistic Impression in Denver," *Municipal Facts* 3, no. 9 (September 1920): 3.

2 Ernest Peixotto, "A Sculptor of the West," *Scribner's Monthly* 68, no. 18 (September 1920): 271, 277.

3 Carl E. Akeley to A. P. Proctor, 9 April 1920, Proctor Museum Archives.

4 W. H. de B. Nelson, "Phimister Proctor: Canadian Sculptor," *The Canadian Magazine* 44, no. 66 (April 1915): 500.

5 Proctor to Pinchot, 14 December 1920, Pinchot Papers. An article, "Proctor to Exhibit at Bohemian Club," in the *Palo Alto Times*, 3 November 1920, suggests he had been working on concepts for the piece for at least six weeks before writing Pinchot.

6 Fred Lockley, "Observations and Impressions of the Journal Man," *Portland (Ore.) Journal*, 6 November 1921.

7 A. Phimister Proctor, "The Sculptor and the Subject," *The Spectator*, 11 November 1922.

8 Adeline Adams, *The Spirit of American Sculpture* (New York: National Sculpture Society, 1923), pp. 133–36.

9 See "Palo Alto Sculptor Given Double Honor," *Palo Alto Times*, 26 January 1921.

10 Lockley, "Observations and Impressions," 4 February 1921.

11 Ibid.

12 Ibid. These included portraits of Col. C. E. S. Wood and his daughter Lisa; Walter Burrell; Mr. and Mrs. Theodore B. Wilcox, their daughter Mrs. Squires, and their son T. B. Wilcox Jr.; H. W. Goode; Mrs. Burns; Mrs. Lewis and her daughter Mrs. Hall; Mrs. T. B. Honeyman's daughter; the children of Charles F. Adams; Jack Edwards; Raymond Wilcox's children; and the daughters of A. L. Mills and A. E. Doyle.

13 "A. Phimister Proctor and His Theodore Roosevelt Statue," *Christian Science Monitor*, 10 April 1922.

14 See "William Hanley Succumbs Here," *Pendleton East Oregonian*, 15 September 1933, obituary in Proctor Museum Archives.

15 See "Proctor, A Sculptor of Unusual Power," *Los Angeles Times*, 1 April 1923.

16 *Exhibition of Painters and Sculptors of Animal Life* (New York: Babcock Gallery, 1920).

17 "Statues by Proctor Mark Club Exhibit," *San Francisco Chronicle*, 25 January 1922.

18 "Penwomen Are Entertained Here," *Palo Alto Times*, 4 December 1922.

19 For a notice of the Russell and Proctor exhibitions, see "Out of the West," *Los Angeles Sunday Times*, 8 April 1923. The Russell show was reviewed in "Home Artist Appreciated," *Los Angeles Sunday Times*, 18 March 1923.

20 Proctor to Pinchot, 29 February 1923, Pinchot Papers.

21 "Proctor, A Sculptor of Unusual Power." Although Proctor claimed that the Stendahl Gallery exhibition "was not unduly profitable," from the perspective of others in town, it was termed "the most successful art event of this kind the Pacific Coast has known." See Alexander Phimister Proctor, *Sculptor in Buckskin* (Norman, Okla.: University of Oklahoma Press, 1971), p. 185, and Roy L. McCardell, "A. Phimister Proctor—Sculptor, Artist, Big Game Hunter," *Los Angeles Morning Telegraph*, 12 August 1923.

22 "Noted Artist Visitor Here," *Los Angeles Times*, 25 March 1923.

23 Unidentified clipping, *Los Angeles Telegraph*, c. April 1923, Proctor Museum Archives. Other patrons listed in other sources included Douglas Fairbanks and Mary Pickford, Theodore Robert, William D. Crane, and William P. Carleton. See McCardell, "A. Phimister Proctor—Sculptor, Artist, Big Game Hunter."

24 "Proctor, A Sculptor of Unusual Power."

25 "Famous Sculptor Says L.A. Is Second Athens for Art," *Los Angeles Evening Herald*, 16 October 1923.

26 Proctor to Pinchot, 29 February 1923, Pinchot Papers.

27 Arthur Miller, "Sculptor Finds City Aids Work," *Los Angeles Times*, 31 November 1931.

28 Proctor, *Sculptor in Buckskin*, p. 184.

29 Proctor to Pinchot, 7 June 1923, Pinchot Papers.

30 For the most complete and thoughtful discussion of the Bingham and Leutze paintings, see J. Gray Sweeney, *The Columbus of the Woods* (Saint Louis: Washington University Gallery of Art, 1992), pp. 41–51, 60–77. For insights into Borglum's *The American Pioneer, A Reverie*, see A. Mervyn Davies, *Solon H. Borglum, A Man Who Stands Alone* (Chester, Conn.: Pequot Press, 1974), p. 169.

31 Taft to Proctor, 26 May 1926, Proctor Museum Archives.

32 Quoted in Margaret Whittemore, "The Pioneer Mother Is Subject of Many Memorials In Bronze, Stone and Marble," *Kansas City Star*, 9 May 1954.

33 Mary Briggs to Edwin C. Shaw, 9 May and 8 August 1923, Edwin Coupland Shaw Papers, Archives of American Art, Smithsonian Institution, Washington, D.C., reels 1124–1125 and 4597.

34 Proctor to Pinchot, 14 December 1920, Pinchot Papers, and Proctor, *Sculptor in Buckskin*, p. 188.

35 See *Exhibition of American Sculpture* (New York: Hispanic Society of America, 1923) and *Sculpture by A. Phimister Proctor, Harold Swartz, Paintings by Conrad Buff, Shiyei Y. Kotoku* (Los Angeles: Los Angeles Museum, 1923).

36 "A. Phimister Proctor to Aid Plan to Erect Statues in City Parks," *Los Angeles Evening Herald*, 20 March 1923.

37 Proctor, *Sculptor in Buckskin*, p. 188. In a letter to Pinchot of late 1924, Proctor said of Los Angeles that "there is little here in my line," suggesting that more than balmy climate and a few exhibitions was required for him to remain in southern California. Proctor to Pinchot, 30 December 1924, Pinchot Papers.

38 Royal Cortissoz, *American Artists* (New York: Charles Scribner's Sons, 1923), pp. 307–12.

39 Royal Cortissoz, "Some Wild Beasts Sculpted by A. Phimister Proctor," *Scribner's* 48, no. 6 (November 1909): 640, and "Phimister Proctor Shows at Museum," unidentified clipping, c. December 1924, Proctor Papers.

40 Cortissoz, *American Artists*, pp. 3, 18.

41 Proctor to Pinchot, 10 October 1925, Pinchot Papers.

42 Proctor to Pinchot, 3 April 1926, Pinchot Papers.

43 Ibid. For further reference to the children's art studies, see "Sculptor Who Did Roosevelt, Now Working on 'Pioneer Mother' in Rome," *New York Herald* (Paris), 14 July 1926.

44 "As Those of the Blood," *Kansas City Star*, 13 November 1927.

45 "Noted American Sculptor Says U.S. Art Is Best, But Calls Modern Work Hideous," *Saint Louis Post Dispatch*, 19 November 1927.

46 See "Art in New York," *Christian Science Monitor*, 6 November 1931, and "Mrs. Whitney Is Host at New Museum to Editors and Critics," *New York Herald Tribune*, 17 November 1931.

47 W. C. Brown to Proctor, 19 January 1931, Oregon Historical Society Library.

48 "Famous Sculptor Returns Home to Make Memorial," *Denver Post*, 22 August 1931.

49 J. Henry Scattergood to Proctor, 21 March 1931, Proctor Museum Archives.

50 See Robert M. Utley, *The Last Days of the Sioux Nation* (New Haven: Yale University Press, 1963), p. 69.

51 "Will Celebrate Gift of McKnight Memorial Friday," *Wichita Evening Eagle*, 17 September 1931.

52 "Noted Sculptor Here," *Franklin (Seattle) Tolo*, 28 October 1931.

Chapter 7

1 S. Clarke Keeler, "Wilton and the Arts," *New Canaan (Conn.) Advertiser*, 2 August 1934.

2 Ibid.

3 See the comment of the sculptor Hermon MacNeil, published in 1934 by the Dallas Southern Women's Memorial Association in their fund-raising brochure that "it is quite a unique thing to make any group of two equestrians." Dallas Public Library, Dallas.

4 Lorado Taft to A. P. Proctor, 20 April 1935, Proctor Museum Archives.

5 Ibid.

6 "New York Sculptor to Visit Dallas for Lee Statue Bid," *Dallas Daily News*, 17 April 1932.

7 Proctor to Pinchot, 4 May 1933, Pinchot Papers.

8 Proctor to Pinchot, 29 September 1933, Pinchot Papers.

9 "Magnificent Obsession," *Dallas News*, 1 July 1937.

10 A letter from Proctor to his son Gifford notes that he had let the contract to Gorham for $18,000 by that date: "Now if O. Ogden comes across with the money he was $4,000 behind, we'll be able to get out without loss, perhaps a little profit." Proctor to Gifford Proctor, 20 November 1940, Proctor Papers.

11 Proctor to J. Frank Dobie, 8 July 1942, Dobie Papers.

12 Ibid.

13 Proctor to Dobie, 24 October 1947, Dobie Papers.

14 Frank Langston, "Texas Mustangs In Bronze," *Dallas Daily Times Herald*, 16 May 1948.

15 John Young-Hunter to Proctor, 16 June 1948, and Malvina Hoffman to Proctor, 20 March 1948, Proctor Museum Archives.

16 Proctor to Dobie, 24 October 1947, Dobie Papers.

17 "Painter Accepts Mustang Statue Given by Ogden," *Austin American*, 1 June 1948.

18 Dobie to Proctor, 22 June 1948, Dobie Papers.

19 Proctor to Dobie, 31 July 1948, Dobie Papers.

20 Proctor to Dobie, 27 September 1947, Dobie Papers.

21 Proctor to Dobie, 27 December 1949, Dobie Papers.

22 "A. Phimister Proctor, World-famous Sculptor, Dies Here at Age of 90," *Palo Alto Times*, 5 September 1950.

Plates

3 Fawn (first model)

1 Alexander Phimister Proctor, *Sculptor in Buckskin* (Norman, Okla.: University of Oklahoma Press, 1971), p. 95.

2 A careful review of *Harper's Weekly* for the years surrounding the creation of the *Fawn* has not revealed the illustration. Nor do the Century Club records indicate that the plaster was shown in 1887 or 1888. Nonetheless, Dellenbaugh could have brought his influence to bear and had the plaster displayed in a venue separate from the club's normal scheduled exhibition program. I am grateful to Jonathan Harding, curator of the Century Club, for his helpful research in this matter.

3 Proctor, *Sculptor in Buckskin*, p. 96. See also "To Fame in a Year," *Denver Rocky Mountain News*, 15 October 1893, p. 10, which corroborates Proctor's interpretation but suggests that the Century Club exhibition and Millet's notice of the piece occurred in the early 1890s.

4 "About the Studios: Phimister Proctor Is a True Natural Sculptor," *Chicago Sunday Inter Ocean*, 1 January 1893.

5 An example appeared in "Sculptor Is Famous as Big Game Hunter; Depicts Animal Life," *Daily Palo Alto Times*, 30 June 1922.

4 Polar Bear

1 Alexander Phimister Proctor, *Sculptor in Buckskin* (Norman, Okla.: University of Oklahoma Press, 1971), p. 114.

2 "About the Studios: Phimister Proctor is a True Natural Sculptor," *Chicago Sunday Inter Ocean*, 1 January 1893.

3 Proctor, *Sculptor in Buckskin*, p. 115.

4 *Art Treasures from the World's Fair* (Chicago: Werner, 1895), pp. 59, 61.

5 Ibid., 61.

6 Halsey C. Ives, *World's Columbian Exposition, 1893. Official Catalogue: Part X. Department K. Fine Arts* (Chicago: W. B. Gonkey, 1893), p. 13.

7 Augustus Saint-Gaudens to A. P. Proctor, 9 June 1900, Saint-Gaudens Papers.

5 Panther

1 A. P. Proctor to Edmund Morris, 14 December 1909, Edmund Morris Papers, Art Gallery of Ontario, Toronto.

2 *Palo Alto Times*, 22 November 1922.

3 Details of this gift were recounted over and over in the press in subsequent years. Roosevelt's account appears in Theodore Roosevelt, *Theodore Roosevelt, An Autobiography* (New York: Macmillan, 1913), p. 54. The illustration is found on p. 32.

4 Alexander Phimister Proctor, *Sculptor in Buckskin* (Norman, Okla.: University of Oklahoma Press, 1971), pp. 92–93.

5 Ibid., 96.

6 Ibid., 98.

7 "About the Studios: Phimister Proctor is a True Natural Sculptor," *Chicago Sunday Inter Ocean*, 1 January 1893.

8 John James Audubon and John Bachman, *The Quadrupeds of North America*, vol. 2 (New York: V. G. Audubon, 1851), p. 311.

9 "Portland's Art Tastes Commended by One of Great Animal Sculptors," *Portland Sunday Oregonian*, 17 December 1911.

10 *Palo Alto Times*, 22 November 1922.

11 See "Proctor, A Sculptor of Unusual Power," *Los Angeles Times*, 1 April 1923.

6 Fawn (second model)

1 "Snohomish Boy a Leader in Art: A. Phimister Proctor Makes His Mark as a Sculptor of Animal Life," *Snohomish Daily Herald*, 18 May 1907, relates this story but ascribes it to 1892, which is unlikely since Proctor was working that summer in Chicago. Alexander Phimister Proctor, *Sculptor in Buckskin* (Norman, Okla.: University of Oklahoma Press, 1971), p. 113, discusses a Snohomish visit in 1891.

2 "About the Studios: Phimister Proctor Is a True Natural Sculptor," *Chicago Sunday Inter Ocean*, 1 January 1893.

3 "To Fame in a Year," *Denver Rocky Mountain News*, 15 October 1893, p. 10.

4 Proctor, *Sculptor in Buckskin*, p. 126.

5 Thayer Tolles, ed., *American Sculpture in the Metropolitan Museum of Art*, vol. 1 (New York: Metropolitan Museum of Art, 1999), p. 413.

7 Logan Monument

1 Quoted in Alexander Phimister Proctor, *Sculptor in Buckskin* (Norman, Okla.: University of Oklahoma Press, 1971), p. 127.

2 Ibid., 116.

3 Ira J. Back and Mary Lackvitz Gray, *A Guide to Chicago's Public Sculpture* (Chicago: University of Chicago Press, 1983), p. 8. See also "A Monument to General John A. Logan," clipping, Proctor Museum Archives.

4 Augustus Saint-Gaudens to Logan's son, 2 April 1895, Saint-Gaudens Papers.

5 John R. Walsh to Saint-Gaudens, 31 May 1895, quoted in Homer Saint-Gaudens, *The Reminiscences of Augustus Saint-Gaudens*, vol. 2 (London: Andrew Melrose, 1913), p. 105.

6 Ibid., 102.

7 Ibid., 101.

8 For the foundry's commitment to cast the work, see Arthur Merritt, Secretary, Henry-Bonnard Bronze Company, to Saint-Gaudens, 3 February 1897, Saint-Gaudens Papers.

9 Mary Logan to Saint-Gaudens, 14 August 1897, Saint-Gaudens Papers.

10 Saint-Gaudens to Dewitt Miller, 26 December 1904, Saint-Gaudens Papers.

11 Robert Rosenblum and H. W. Janson, *19th-Century Art* (New York: Harry N. Abrams, 1984), p. 467. See also Burke Wilkinson, *Uncommon Clay: The Life and Works of Augustus Saint-Gaudens* (New York: Harcourt Brace Jovanovich, 1985), p. 152.

8 Sherman Monument

1 For a full list, see John H. Dryfhout, *The Work of Augustus Saint-Gaudens* (Hanover, N.H.: University Press of New England, 1982), p. 254.

2 Homer Saint-Gaudens suggests that the studio was at the boarding stables on 59th Street. See Homer Saint-Gaudens, *The Reminiscences of Augustus Saint-Gaudens*, vol. 2 (London: Andrew Melrose, 1913), p. 77.

3 Alexander Phimister Proctor, *Sculptor in Buckskin* (Norman, Okla.: University of Oklahoma Press, 1971), p. 131.

4 Ibid., 129.

5 Frederic Remington, "Getting Horses in Horse-Show Form," *Harper's Weekly* 39, no. 2030 (16 November 1895): 1088.

6 "The Sherman Statue," *New York Tribune*, 31 May 1903.

7 Proctor, *Sculptor in Buckskin*, pp. 178, 187.

8 Ernest Knaufft, "Saint Gaudens and American Sculpture," *The American Review of Reviews* (1906).

9 *Philadelphia Inquirer*, 9 May 1908.

10 "Rally to Sherman Horse," *New York Evening Post*, 11 May 1908.

11 "No Man Did More to Remove the Slur on Commemorative Sculpture … His Many Bas-Reliefs," *New York Times*, 1 March 1908.

12 "The Sherman Statue."

13 *The Century-Association Year-Book* (New York: Century-Association, 1952), p. 71.

9 Dog with Bone

1 Alexander Phimister Proctor, *Sculptor in Buckskin* (Norman, Okla.: University of Oklahoma Press, 1971), p. 126.

2 Quoted in Francis Ribemont, *Rosa Bonheur (1822–1899)* (Bordeaux: Musée des Beaux-Arts de Bordeaux, 1997), p. 97.

10 Cub Bear and Rabbit

1 Two of the three known castings of this statuette are marked with the date 1894.

2 See Edwin Willard and Therese O. Deming, *Animal Folk of Wood and Plain* (New York: Frederick A. Stokes, 1916). Proctor mentions Deming in *Sculptor in Buckskin* (Norman, Okla.: University of Oklahoma Press, 1971), p. 97.

3 James Jackson Jarves, *The Art-Idea* (1864; reprint, edited by Benjamin Rowland Jr., Cambridge, Mass.: Belknap Press of Harvard University Press, 1960), p. 183.

11 Arab Stallion

1 "To Fame in a Year," *Denver Rocky Mountain News*, 15 October 1893, p. 10.

2 Alexander Phimister Proctor, *Sculptor in Buckskin* (Norman, Okla.: University of Oklahoma Press, 1971), p. 131.

3 See Frederic Remington, "Horses of the Plains," *Century Magazine* 37, no. 3 (January 1889): 332–43.

4 The drawing appeared in William C. Gulliver, "Types of Saddle-Horses," *Harper's Weekly*, (19 November 1892) :112. See also Remington's depiction of an Arabian horse from the Czar's stables, *Ruban Cossack, Imperial Guard Corps*, in Poultney Bigelow, "In the Barracks of the Czar," *Harper's Monthly* (April 1893): 783. The original is in the collection of the Mead Art Museum, Amherst College, Amherst, Massachusetts.

5 Robert Evren, et al., *Charles Cary Rumsey: 1879–1922* (Buffalo, N.Y.: Burchfield Center for Western New York Art, 1983), pp. 13–14.

12 Indian Warrior

1 Quoted in Halsey C. Ives, *The Dream City: A Portfolio of Photographic Views of the World's Columbian Exposition* (Saint Louis: N. D. Thompson Publishing, 1893).

2 David B. Dearinger, ed., *Paintings and Sculptures in the Collection of the National Academy of Design*, vol. 1 (New York: Hudson Hills Press, 2003).

3 Alexander Phimister Proctor, *Sculptor in Buckskin* (Norman, Okla.: University of Oklahoma Press, 1971), p. 134.

4 Ibid.

5 Ibid., 137–38.

6 *Chicago Evening Post*, 24 June 1899.

7 Quoted in Marvin C. Ross, *The West of Alfred Jacob Miller* (Norman, Okla.: University of Oklahoma Press, 1968), p. 64.

8 George de Forest Brush, "An Artist Among the Indians," *Century* 30, no. 1 (May 1885): 55.

9 "Portland's Art Tastes Commended By One of Great Animal Sculptors," *Portland Sunday Oregonian*, 17 December 1911. This had been suggested a dozen years earlier by Lorado Taft, who wrote of the *Indian Warrior* that it "shows us … Mr. Proctor is fully equal to the difficult problems of the human figure." See "A. Phimister Proctor," *Brush and Pencil* 2, no. 6 (September 1898): 244.

10 "Indian Chief on Horseback," unidentified clipping, Proctor Museum Archives.

13 American Horse

1 Frederic Remington, "Getting Horses in Horse-Show Form," *Harper's Weekly* 39, no. 2030 (16 November 1895): 1088.

2 It is unclear why the horse in Remington's painting is identified as Transport rather than Ontario. Nowhere in the *Harper's Weekly* article is there any discussion of a horse by that name, nor does the Art Institute of Chicago (where Remington's painting of the jumping horse resides) possess any known source that connects the picture with a horse named Transport.

3 Ibid.

4 Ibid.

5 Alexander Phimister Proctor, *Sculptor in Buckskin* (Norman, Okla.: University of Oklahoma Press, 1971), p. 129. Proctor recounts several anecdotes about Ontario on p. 130.

14, 15 Puma (Nos. 1 and 2)

1 Alexander Phimister Proctor, *Sculptor in Buckskin* (Norman, Okla.: University of Oklahoma Press, 1971), p. 137.

2 Ibid., 108.

3 Hamlin Garland, "Edward Kemeys, A Sculptor of Frontier Life and Wild Animals," *McClure's Magazine* 5 (July 1895): 120–31. The illustration appears on p. 128. Proctor is also known to have painted at least one watercolor of a

puma (perhaps using the New York menagerie) before leaving America in 1896. The painting was purchased by American art collector William T. Evans and its current whereabouts is unknown. See William H. Truettner, "William T. Evans, Collector of American Paintings," *The American Art Journal* 3, no. 2 (fall 1971): 77. This may be the painting *Jaguar*, which Proctor exhibited at the National Academy of Design in New York in 1895.

4 *The World's Columbian Exposition Reproduced* (Chicago: Rand, McNally, 1894) gives full credit to Kemeys, while Halsey C. Ives, *The Dream City, A Portfolio of Photographic Views of the World's Columbian Exposition* (Saint Louis: N. D. Thompson Publishing, 1893) suggests that both artists were involved in creating the *Jaguars*, as they were sometimes called. "About the Studios, Phimister Proctor is a True Natural Sculptor," *Chicago Sunday Inter Ocean*, 1 January 1893, describes Proctor as the sole author of the "two Jaguars in full action."

5 "About the Studios."

6 *Art Treasures from the World's Fair* (Chicago: Werner, 1895).

7 Charles H. Caffin, "Fine Animal Sculpture by Proctor," *New York American* (October 1913).

8 For reference to the defiant nature of the two pumas, see *Arts and Decoration* (August 1911): 393.

9 Except when both versions are exhibited together, there is no indication which one was shown in these venues.

16 Buffalo

1 Alexander Phimister Proctor, *Sculptor in Buckskin* (Norman, Okla.: University of Oklahoma Press, 1971), p. 137.

2 E. Bénézit, *Dictionnaire critique et documentaire des peintres, sculpteurs...*, vol. 4 (Paris, France: Librairie Grund, 1976), p. 615.

3 Lorado Taft, "A. Phimister Proctor," *Brush and Pencil* 2, no. 6 (September 1898): 241, 243. The illustration appears on p. 247.

4 Proctor, *Sculptor in Buckskin*, p. 115.

5 Ibid., 153.

17 Elk

1 Known castings of this bronze are marked with a copyright date of 1899, but the first records of the Copyright Office date from 1909.

2 *The World's Columbian Exposition Reproduced* (Chicago: Rand, McNally, 1894).

3 Ibid.

4 *Art Treasures from the World's Fair* (Chicago: Werner, 1895), p. 19.

5 "A. Phimister Proctor and His Theodore Roosevelt Statue," *Christian Science Monitor*, 19 April 1922.

6 John William Rogers, "Sculptor of Lee Statue Has Had Colorful Career," *Dallas Times Herald*, 24 May 1936, p. 12.

7 Georgia Fraser, "The Sculptors of the United States Pavilion at the Paris Exposition," *Brush and Pencil* 5, no. 5 (February 1900): 234.

8 Peter Hastings Falk and Andrea Ansell Bien, *The Annual Exhibition Record for the National Academy of Design, 1901–1950* (Madison, Conn.: Sound View Press, 1990), p. 460.

9 *Pan-American Exposition: Catalogue of the Exhibition of Fine Arts* (Buffalo, N.Y.: David Gray, 1901), p. 70.

18 Charging Elephant

1 Alexander Phimister Proctor, *Sculptor in Buckskin* (Norman, Okla.: University of Oklahoma Press, 1971), p. 98.

2 Ibid.

3 See Royal Cortissoz, "Some Wild Beasts Sculpted by A. Phimister Proctor," *Scribner's* 48, no. 6 (November 1909): 640.

4 "Jungle Portraits," *Vanity Fair* (December 1913): 42.

5 "When Leo Poses: Wild Animals at the Zoo Are Patient Models," *New York Herald*, 25 May 1902, p. 16.

6 Account book for 1893–1894, Proctor Museum Archives. The "Elephant" was purchased for fifty dollars on December 5.

7 *Buffalo Commercial*, 3 August 1916.

19 Moose Family

1 A. P. Proctor to Gifford Pinchot, 8 January 1902, Pinchot Papers.

2 "Mounted, It Now Ornaments Niche in Natural History Collection," *New York World*, 26 May 1902.

3 Proctor to Pinchot, 7 April 1902, Pinchot Papers.

4 Pinchot to Proctor, 9 May 1902, Pinchot Papers.

5 Proctor to Pinchot, 25 April 1903, Pinchot Papers.

6 Proctor to Pinchot, 7 June 1903, Pinchot Papers.

7 Proctor to Pinchot, 14 September 1904, Pinchot Papers.

8 Proctor to Pinchot, 9 November 1904, Pinchot Papers. The *Moose Family* was exhibited at both the Century Club and the National Academy of Design in early 1905. In at least the former showing, if not both, the plaster rather than a bronze cast was exhibited.

9 See Pinchot to Proctor, 21 November 1906, and Proctor to Pinchot, 26 November 1906, Pinchot Papers.

20 Griffins

1 Roberta Balfour, "Proctor's Inspiration Was Born in the West," *Denver Post*, 29 March 1903.

2 Ibid. See also Alexander Phimister Proctor, *Sculptor in Buckskin* (Norman, Okla.: University of Oklahoma Press, 1971), p. 143, regarding the commission.

3 Quoted in Osmund Overby, *The Saint Louis Art Museum: An Architectural History* (Saint Louis: Saint Louis Art Museum, 1987), p. 6.

4 Ibid., 10, and C. W. Benjamin, "Alexander Phimister Proctor," 1988, an information sheet distributed by the Saint Louis Art Museum's Resource Center, p. 17.

21 Caribou

1 Alexander Phimister Proctor, *Sculptor in Buckskin* (Norman, Okla.: University of Oklahoma Press, 1971), p. 109.

2 I am grateful to the New York Zoological Society's archivist, Steve Johnson, for reviewing those minutes for me.

22 Morgan Stallion

1 Mark Bennitt, ed., *History of the Louisiana Purchase Exposition* (Saint Louis: Universal Exposition Publishing, 1905), p. 31.

2 Alexander Phimister Proctor, *Sculptor in Buckskin* (Norman, Okla.: University of Oklahoma Press, 1971), p. 143.

3 Ibid.

23 Lions (McKinley Monument)

1 "Memorial Fund Grows with the People's Favor," *Buffalo Evening News*, 18 September 1901.

2 Ibid.

3 See J. N. Mathews to Augustus Saint-Gaudens, 20 August and 3 September 1902, Saint-Gaudens Papers.

4 As late as 1905, interested parties were still trying to engage Saint-Gaudens in the project, wanting him to produce a portrait of McKinley for the monument. Because of Saint-Gaudens' ill health and overcommitted schedule, this idea did not come to fruition. See Theodore Roosevelt to Saint-Gaudens, 17 May 1905, and H. Van Buren Magonigle to Saint-Gaudens, 19 June 1905, Saint-Gaudens Papers.

5 "Model of McKinley Monument Lion," unidentified clipping, c. 1906, Proctor Museum Archives.

6 Ibid.

7 Ibid.

8 Alexander Phimister Proctor, *Sculptor in Buckskin* (Norman, Okla.: University of Oklahoma Press, 1971), p. 145.

9 A. P. Proctor to Saint-Gaudens, 5 June 1906, Saint-Gaudens Papers.

10 Ibid.

11 Proctor, *Sculptor in Buckskin*, p. 146, gives the weight of the lions as twelve tons each. Another source suggests their weight at fifteen tons. See "Facts About the McKinley Monument," *Buffalo Evening News* clipping, June 1907, Buffalo and Erie County Historical Society, Buffalo, N.Y.

12 Proctor, *Sculptor in Buckskin*, pp. 146, 148.

13 Paul MacClennan, "McKinley Monument Was Created With Care, Concern, Deliberation," *Buffalo Evening News*, 16 September 1976.

14 *Palo Alto Times*, 22 November 1922.

24 Panther with Kill

1 For information on Pitcher, see Aubrey L. Haynes, *The Yellowstone Story: A History of Our First National Park*, vol. 2 (Yellowstone National Park: Yellowstone Library and Museum Association, 1977), p. 457.

2 Quoted in George Bird Grinnell, ed., *American Big Game in Its Haunts* (New York: Forest and Stream Publishing, 1904), p. 36.

3 Frederic Remington, "Mountain Lions in Yellowstone Park," *Collier's* 24, no. 4 (17 March 1900): 14.

4 "Snohomish Boy Leader in Art," unidentified clipping attributed to *New York World*, 18 May 1909, Proctor Museum Archives.

5 Ibid.

6 Ibid. Vivian A. Paladin somehow confused this story with one that we have been unable to corroborate in which William F. Cody lassoed the cougar in Yellowstone Park and gave it to Roosevelt, who in turn donated it to the Bronx Zoo where Proctor used it to model his *Panther*, first cast, in the late 1890s. Vivian A. Paladin, "A. Phimister Proctor: Master Sculptor of Horses," *Montana* 14, no. 1 (January 1964): 15–16.

7 "Snohomish Boy Leader in Art."

8 Alexander Phimister Proctor, *Sculptor in Buckskin* (Norman, Okla.: University of Oklahoma Press, 1971), p. 148.

9 Glenn F. Benge, *Antoine-Louis Barye: Sculptor of Romantic Realism* (University Park, Pa.: Pennsylvania State University Press, 1984), pp. 6–7.

10 See John Elderfield, *Henri Matisse: A Retrospective* (New York: Museum of Modern Art, 1992), pp. 46, 85.

25 Silver King

1 Gifford Pinchot to A. P. Proctor, 13 October 1906, Pinchot Papers.

2 Pinchot to Margaret Proctor, 25 March 1907, Pinchot Papers.

3 Proctor to Pinchot, 14 November 1907, Pinchot Papers.

4 Proctor to Pinchot, 13 December 1907, Pinchot Papers.

5 Pinchot to Proctor, 30 December 1907, Pinchot Papers.

6 "Animal Life Shown in Proctor Exhibit," unidentified clipping, c. 1908, Proctor Museum Archives.

7 Quoted in "Portland's Art Tastes Commended by One of Great Animal Sculptors," *Portland Sunday Oregonian*, 17 December 1911.

26 Moose

1 Although the inscription "COPY RT.-07" suggests that Proctor had a copyright taken out on this work in 1907, neither the Copyright Office nor the Proctor Museum Archives have records of such a transaction.

2 William B. McCormick, "Gallery View of Sculptor's Art Takes One on Journey Through World's Wilds," *New York Press*, 19 October 1913, p. 8. The Pinchot estate does not own one of these bronzes.

3 Halsey C. Ives, *The Dream City: A Portfolio of Photographic Views of the World's Columbian Exposition* (Saint Louis: N. D. Thompson Publishing, 1893).

4 Quoted in *Art Treasures From the World's Fair* (Chicago: Werner, 1895), p. 45.

5 Ibid.

6 "Will Celebrate Gift of McKnight Memorial Friday," *Wichita Evening Eagle*, 17 September 1931, p. 2.

27 Head of Brown Bear

1 *Catalogue of Sculpture, Bronzes, Water Colors, and Sketches ... by A. Phimister Proctor, N.A.* (New York: Montross Gallery, 1908), p. 3, no. 34a.

2 Alexander Phimister Proctor, *Sculptor in Buckskin* (Norman, Okla.: University of Oklahoma Press, 1971), p. 118.

3 This information comes from Jack Renault, executive director of the Boone and Crockett Club, as it was related to him by a member of the Merriam family. For reference to the little bear as the club's "mascot," see note 2.

4 *New York Evening Telegram*, 28 November 1908.

5 For information on Bierstadt's moose, see George Bird Grinnell, *American Big Game in Its Haunts* (New York: Forest and Stream Publishing, 1904), pp. 384–85, and Samuel Merrill, *The Moose Book* (New York: E. P. Dutton, 1916), p. 189. For the bear illustration, see A. Pendarves Vivian, *Wanderings in the Western Land* (London: Sampson Low, Marston, Searle, and Rivington, 1879), title page.

28 Bear Cub

1 Alexander Phimister Proctor, *Sculptor in Buckskin*, (Norman, Okla.: University of Oklahoma Press, 1971), p. 27.

2 *A. Phimister Proctor* (New York: Montross Gallery, 1908), no. 23.

3 William Lyman Underwood, *Wild Brothers: Strangest of True Stories from the North Woods* (Boston: Atlantic Monthly Press, 1921), pp. 90–91.

4 Ernest Thompson Seton, *Wild Animals at Home* (New York: Grosset & Dunlap, 1913), pp. 204–09.

5 See *The West That Has Passed* (New York: Folsom Galleries, 1916), nos. 9, 12.

29 Wolf

1 A. P. Proctor to Bertha Dobie, 30 March 1944, Dobie Papers.

2 J. Frank Dobie, *The Voice of the Coyote* (Boston: Little Brown, 1949), p. 33.

3 Ibid., 47.

4 The story appeared in the April 1952 issue of *Outdoor Magazine* and has recently been reprinted in Neil B. Carmony, ed., *Afield with J. Frank Dobie* (Silver City, N.Mex.: High-Lonesome Books, 1992), pp. 221–29.

5 Ibid., 228.

6 Proctor to J. Frank Dobie, 27 December 1949, Dobie Papers.

7 Proctor to Dobie, 22 January 1950, Dobie Papers.

8 Carmony, *Afield with J. Frank Dobie*, p. 229.

9 *A. Phimister Proctor* (New York: Montross Gallery, 1908).

30 Piney Branch Tigers

1 James M. Goode, *The Outdoor Sculpture of Washington, D.C.: A Comprehensive Historical Guide*, (Washington, D.C.: Smithsonian Press, 1974), p. 427.

2 Gifford Pinchot to A. P. Proctor, 2 August 1909, Pinchot Papers.

3 Proctor to Pinchot, 4 August 1909, Pinchot Papers.

4 Proctor to Pinchot, 28 July 1909, Pinchot Papers.

5 Proctor to Pinchot, 30 July 1909, Pinchot Papers.

6 Proctor to Pinchot, 20 September 1909, Pinchot Papers.

7 "Big Tigers For Bridge at National Capital," *Everett (Wash.) Daily Herald*, c. 1909, Proctor Museum Archives.

8 "Tale of the Tigers," *Evening Star*, Washington, D.C., c. 1911, courtesy Jeff Nelson.

9 *New York Herald*, 11 June 1910.

10 Letter to Proctor from Jno. Williams & Co. Founders, 17 June 1910, Proctor Museum Archives.

11 "Tale of the Tigers."

12 Ibid.

13 R. W. Shufeldt, "Zoological Statuary at the National Capital," *Natural History* 19, nos. 4–5 (1919): 470–477. Shufeldt was a champion of Proctor's and held unfavorable opinions of other outdoor animal sculptures, such as the *Connecticut Bridge Lions*, which he described as "sickly."

31 Buffalo Head

1 See Valerie Jablow, "Presidential Designs," *Smithsonian* 31, no. 8 (November 2000): 48–50.

2 James M. Goode, "White House Album: The Theodore Roosevelt Years," *White House History* 2, no. 1 (June 1997): 58.

3 I am grateful to Clay R. Bauske, curator of the Harry S. Truman Library Museum, for providing me with much of the history of the Buffalo Mantel.

4 Alexander Phimister Proctor, *Sculptor in Buckskin* (Norman, Okla.: University of

Oklahoma Press, 1971), p. 182. Roosevelt's "Council of Fine Arts," National Art Commission, was appointed in January 1909.

5 William Loeb Jr. to A. P. Proctor, 1 February 1909, Proctor Museum Archives, and Theodore Roosevelt to Proctor, 28 February 1909, Theodore Roosevelt Collection, Harvard College Library, Cambridge, Massachusetts.

6 See Sue Gentry, "Mantel, Once in State Dining Room of White House, Placed at Truman Library," *Independence (Mo.) Examiner*, 18 April 1957, p. 1.

7 Harry S. Truman to Leslie M. Beals, 6 December 1962, Collection of the Harry S. Truman Library Museum, Independence, Mo.

8 Daisy Cleland, *Washington Evening Star*, 3 July 1962, p. B7.

32 Tiger Couchant

1 "Tigers by a Denver Sculptor Ordered by Princeton '79ers to Guard Old Nassau's Steps," *Denver Rocky Mountain News*, 14 April 1909.

2 Contract agreement, 1 February 1909, Proctor Museum Archives.

3 "Circus Tiger for Princeton," unidentified clipping, 1909, Proctor Museum Archives.

4 Royal Cortissoz, "Some Wild Beasts Sculpted by A. Phimister Proctor," *Scribner's* 48, no. 6 (November 1909): 638–39.

5 Alexander Phimister Proctor, *Sculptor in Buckskin* (Norman, Okla.: University of Oklahoma Press, 1971), pp. 150–51.

6 "Princeton to Have Two Bronze Tigers," *New York Herald*, 11 June 1910, and William A. Day to Proctor, 17 June 1910, Proctor Museum Archives. See also "Canadian Sculptor's Work," *Toronto Saturday Night* 23, no. 38 (2 July 1910).

7 Charles H. Caffin, "Fine Animal Sculpture by Proctor," *New York America* (October 1913).

8 "Sculptor Proctor Tells of Hunting the Tiger in Many Civilized Jungles," *New York World*, 14 June 1914, and "The Princeton Tiger," *Laguna Life*, Laguna Beach, Calif., 23 March 1923.

33 Lions

1 A. P. Proctor to Edmund Morris, 11 November 1911, Edmund Morris Papers, Art Gallery of Ontario, Toronto.

2 Ibid. As it turned out, Proctor did not send the bronze to Toronto in 1912. It was included in the Canadian Art Club's May 1913 show as *Lions of the Desert* (relief), no. 74.

3 "Portland's Art Tastes Commended by One of Great Animal Sculptors," *Portland Sunday Oregonian*, 17 December 1911.

4 William B. McCormick, "Gallery View of Sculptor's Art Takes One on Journey Through World's Wilds," *New York Press*, 19 October 1913, p. 8.

5 Charles H. Caffin, "Fine Animal Sculpture by Proctor," *New York American*, October 1913, from a partially identified clipping in the Proctor Museum Archives.

6 "Zoo Unveils Lion Frieze," *Portland Oregonian*, 10 May 1962.

34 Buffalo

1 Letter from W. Silas Sheetz to the Honorable Commissioners of the District of Columbia, from the Washington, D.C., Archives, 8 October 1898. I am grateful to

Jeff Nelson for generously providing me with a copy of this letter and sharing his important research on the history of the bridge.

2 Minutes from hearing relative to H.R. Bill 16639, "For the construction of a bridge over Rock Creek at Q Street," 25 January 1905, from the Washington, D.C., Archives, courtesy of Jeff Nelson.

3 See letters from Virginia C. Moore and Louisa Rittenhouse to the commissioners' office from 1903, 1904, 1905, 1911; from the Washington, D.C., Archives, courtesy of Jeff Nelson.

4 Copy of petition came from the Washington, D.C., Archives, 20 January 1905, and is addressed to the Senate and House of Representatives; courtesy of Jeff Nelson.

5 Glen Brown and Bedford Brown IV, Architects, "The Q Street Bridge, Washington, D.C.," *The American Architect*, CVIII, no. 2079 (27 October 1915): 273–79.

6 Ibid.

7 John Joseph Earley information was obtained from Symposium Program & Abstracts titled: "John Joseph Earley: Expanding the Art and Science of Concrete" from the Fourth Biennial Symposium on the Historic Development of Metropolitan Washington, D.C., organized by the Latrobe Chapter Society of Architectural Historians, March 31 and April 1, 2001, abstract courtesy of Jeff Nelson.

8 Alexander Phimister Proctor, *Sculptor in Buckskin* (Norman, Okla.: University of Oklahoma Press, 1971), p. 154.

9 Unidentified clipping, 1915, Proctor Museum Archives.

10 A. P. Proctor to a Captain Mark Brooke, Acting Engineer Commissioner for the District of Columbia, February 1913, Proctor Museum Archives. Proctor moved from his MacDougal Alley studio uptown to a new, vastly enlarged studio at 168 East 51st Street in November 1911 in order to accommodate this new work. See letter from Proctor to Gifford Pinchot, 9 November 1911, Pinchot Papers.

11 Proctor to Brooke, 9 August 1913, Proctor Museum Archives.

12 Proctor to Col. Chester Harding, Engineer Commissioner, District Commissioner for the District of Columbia, 19 January 1914, Proctor Museum Archives.

13 See for example William Walton, "Some Recent Small Sculptures," *Scribner's* 40, no. 71 (May 1914): 666.

14 Anton Kunst Art and Architectural Bronze Foundry to Proctor, 9 April 1925, Proctor Museum Archives.

15 R. W. Shufeldt, "Zoological Statuary at the National Capital," *Natural History* 19, nos. 4–5 (1919): 470–77.

35 Buckaroo

1 Alexander Phimister Proctor, *Sculptor in Buckskin* (Norman, Okla.: University of Oklahoma Press, 1971), p. 167. For a discussion of the term "buckaroo," see Philip Ashton Rollins, *The Cowboy* (1922; reprint, Norman, Okla.: University of Oklahoma Press, 1997), p. 39.

2 W. Herbert Dunton, "The Fair in the Cow Country," *Scribner's* 55, no. 4 (April 1914): 455.

3 Charles Wellington Furlong, *Let 'Er Buck: A Story of the Passing of the West* (New York: G. P. Putnam's Sons, 1921), p. 7.

4 Ibid., 88.

5 Ibid., 88–89.

6 "Cowboys Live in Clay Under Skillful Hands of A. Phimister Proctor," *Portland Evening Telegram*, 24 July 1915. Other accounts suggest that Angel served as the prime model. See Rex Lampman, "Suggestion Is Made That Pendleton Take Steps to Acquire Work of Art," *Portland Oregon Journal*, 22 July 1915.

7 Furlong, *Let 'Er Buck*, p. 88.

8 "Cowboys Live in Clay." For reference to Red Parker, see Virgil Rupp, *Let 'Er Buck: A History of the Pendleton Round-Up* (Pendleton, Ore.: Pendleton Round-Up Association, 1985), p. 19. In his autobiography, Proctor says he hired a cowboy named Red to model for the *Buckaroo* (see note 1). However, all contemporary newspaper accounts suggest Bill Ridings as the man.

9 Proctor, *Sculptor in Buckskin*, p. 163.

10 See Brian W. Dippie, *Charles M. Russell, Word Painter* (Fort Worth, Tex.: Amon Carter Museum, 1993), p. 173.

11 "Oregon Sculptor Is Seen in Public," *Pendleton East Oregonian*, 12 November 1914.

12 "Sculpture on Exhibition," *Pendleton East Oregonian*, 16 November 1914.

13 "Sculptor's Tools Damaged in Early Morning Blaze," *Pendleton East Oregonian*, 12 November 1914.

14 Announcement of the Seattle showing appeared in "Sculptor to Exhibit Small Bronzes Here," *Seattle Post-Intelligencer*, 16 July 1915; the Lillian Tingle review appeared in "Sculptor Is Guest," *Portland Morning Oregonian*, 23 July 1915.

15 "Famous Statue to Be Exhibited Today," *Pendleton East Oregonian*, 29 July 1915. See also Lampman, "Suggestion Is Made."

16 "To Exhibit 'Buckaroo,'" *Pendleton (Ore.) Tribune*, 29 July 1915.

17 Anne Shannon Monroe, "Oregon Sculpture Is Seen by Public," *Portland Oregonian*, 12 November 1915.

18 "Buckaroo in Oregon Room Is Unveiled," *Pendleton (Ore.) Tribune*, 18 November 1915.

19 I am grateful to Vern Milligan for sharing with me a Gorham foundry casting report on the *Buckaroo* compiled by Samuel J. Hough. The *Buckaroo* was exhibited in *Small Bronzes by A. Phimister Proctor* at the Art Institute from March 8 through April 2, 1917. It is thought that the Art Institute acquired the casting at that time. It was deaccessioned along with two other Proctor bronzes by the museum in 1990. See *Important American Paintings, Drawings and Sculpture of the 18th, 19th and 20th Centuries* (New York: Christie's, 23 May 1990).

20 Ledger 2, p. 67, and ledger 5, p. 308, Roman Bronze Works Archives, Amon Carter Museum, Fort Worth, Tex.

21 Proctor ledger book for 1930s, Proctor Museum Archives.

36 Bust of Iron Tail

1 See Frederick J. Dockstader, *Great North American Indians: Profiles in Life and Leadership* (New York: Van Nostrand Reinhold, 1977), pp. 122–23. Wild West Show Archives, Buffalo Bill Historical Center, Cody, Wyoming.

2 "Cowboys Live in Clay Under Skillful Hands of A. Phimister Proctor," *Portland (Ore.) Evening Telegram*, 24 July 1915.

3 *Gotham Weekly Gazette*, 31 May 1914.

4 I am grateful to Laila Williamson of the American Museum of Natural History, New York, for sharing information with me regarding the loan and the subsequent acquisition of the Proctor collection.

37 Little Wolf

1 Tom Weist, *A History of the Cheyenne People* (Billings, Mont.: Montana Council for Indian Education, 1977), p. 164.

2 "'Alec' Proctor Comes Here to Discuss Cody Memorial," *Denver Post*, 25 May 1917, p. 16.

38 Pursued

1 William Walton, "Some Recent Small Sculptures," *Scribner's* 60, no. 5 (May 1914): 665.

2 W. Herbert Dunton, "The Fair in the Cow Country," *Scribner's* 55, no. 4 (April 1914): 454–65.

3 Ibid., 457.

4 Ibid.

5 George Bird Grinnell, *The Fighting Cheyennes* (New York: Charles Scribner's Sons, 1915).

6 Laban Little Wolf was the nephew of the famous Chief Little Wolf, who led the historic return of the Cheyenne back to Montana from Oklahoma in 1879. Robert would have been in his mid-twenties when the Proctors visited Lame Deer. This is discussed in a letter to Proctor's daughter Hester from John Artichoker Jr., superintendent of the Northern Cheyenne Agency in 1965, in the Proctor Museum Archives. Proctor relates his experiences with the Cheyenne in *Sculptor in Buckskin* (Norman, Okla.: University of Oklahoma Press, 1971), pp. 158–62. He does not mention Robert and therefore, by inference, suggests that Laban was the model for *Pursued*. Proctor does tell how, as the summer ended, he was forced to retain another model, Rolling Bull, to complete his work.

7 Ibid., 159.

8 "Sculptor A. Phimister Proctor and His Work," *Portland (Ore.) Evening Telegram*, 24 July 1915, p. 2.

39 Slim

1 Alexander Phimister Proctor, *Sculptor in Buckskin* (Norman, Okla.: University of Oklahoma Press, 1971), p. 166.

2 Rex Lampman, "Suggestion Is Made That Pendleton Take Steps to Acquire Works of Art," *Portland Oregon Journal*, 22 July 1915.

3 Charles Wellington Furlong, *Let 'Er Buck: A Story of the Passing of the West* (New York: G. P. Putnam's Sons, 1921), pp. 88–89.

4 "Sculptures of the Western Frontier," *New York Herald*, 12 March 1916.

5 Lillian Tingle, "Sculptor Is Guest," *Portland Morning Oregonian*, 23 July 1915.

6 "Cowboys Live in Clay Under Skillful Hands of A. Phimister Proctor," *Portland (Ore.) Evening Telegram*, 24 July 1915.

7 "'The Buckaroo' Is Now in Jail," *Pendleton East Oregonian*, 28 July 1915.

8 "Bill Ridings in Jail as a Horse Thief," *Pendleton (Ore.) Tribune*, 28 July 1915.

9 "Bill Ridings Sent to Prison to Serve From 1 to 10 Years," *Pendleton East Oregonian*, 28 January 1916.

40 Buffalo Hunt

1 "Proctor Boosts for the Round-Up Among Friends," *Pendleton East Oregonian*, 23 March 1916.

2 "Noted Men Will View Round-Up," *Pendleton East Oregonian*, 15 August 1916.

3 Dan Smith, "Sculptures of the Western Frontier," *New York Herald*, 12 March 1916, section 3, p. 1.

4 See *American Art News* 9 (15 April 1911): 2; "Cowboy Artist, Self Taught, Will Show in New York," *New York World*, 9 April 1911; and Arthur Hoeber, "The Painter of the West That Has Passed: The Work of Charles M. Russell, Hunter, Cowboy, and Artist, The Painter of the Cattle and Indian Days," *World's Work* 22 (July 1911).

5 Lorado Taft, "Sculptors of the World's Fair," *Brush and Pencil* 13, no. 3 (December 1903): 229, 223.

6 Quoted in Rowena L. and Gordon D. Alcorn, "Jackson Sundown: Nez Perce Horseman," *Montana* 23, no. 4 (Autumn 1983): 49. This source has provided most of the biographical information used here; see pp. 446–51.

7 Alexander Phimister Proctor, *Sculptor in Buckskin* (Norman, Okla.: University of Oklahoma Press, 1971), p. 169.

8 Alcorn, "Jackson Sundown," p. 49.

9 "Statue of Indian Is Nearly Finished," *Pendleton (Ore.) Evening Tribune*, 19 September 1916.

10 "Real Indian Is New Champion Buckaroo of the Wide World," *Portland (Ore.) Journal*, 24 September 1916.

11 See "'Me Catch Um' Says Sundown Referring to Champion Title," *Pendleton (Ore.) Tribune*, 25 September 1916.

12 "Jackson Sundown First Indian to Win World's Broncho Busting Championship," *Pendleton East Oregonian*, 25 September 1916.

13 Frank Owen Payne, "Two New Bronzes by A. Phimister Proctor," unidentified clipping, c. 1917, Proctor Museum Archives.

41 Broncho Buster

1 Quoted in Roberta Balfour, "Proctor's Inspiration Was Born in the West," *Denver Post*, 29 March 1903.

2 Ibid.

3 "Putting Finishing Touches to Art Work," *Pendleton (Ore.) Evening Tribune*, 3 July 1915.

4 Rex Lampman, "Suggestion is Made That Pendleton Take Steps to Acquire Work of Art," *Portland Oregon Journal*, 22 July 1915.

5 Ibid.

6 "Portland Men Are Eager to See City Have Proctor Work," unidentified clipping, Proctor Museum Archives.

7 "Bill Ridings in Jail as a Horse Thief," *Pendleton (Ore.) Tribune*, 28 July 1915. See also "'The Buckaroo' is Now in Jail," *Pendleton East Oregonian*, 28 July 1915, and "'Buckaroo' Model in Jail," *Portland Oregonian*, 29 July 1915.

8 "Fine Buffalo, Proctor Hears," *San Francisco Examiner*, 20 November 1915.

9 "Noted Sculptor Is Nearing Finish On Model of a Bucker," *Pendleton East Oregonian*, 29 June 1915.

10 Hugh O'Neill, "'Alec' Proctor Comes Here to Discuss Cody Memorial," *Denver Post*, 25 May 1917.

11 Mrs. James Albert Helen Henderson Chain, "Alexander Phimister Proctor: Sculptor & Painter," Denver Artists, notebook,

Colorado Historical Society, Denver. Chain claims this happened in 1915, but Speer was not mayor that year, nor were the Proctors in Denver.

12 David Kent Ballast, *The Denver Chronicle: From a Golden Past to a Mile-High Future* (Houston: Gulf Publishing, 1995), pp. 54–63, and Charles A. Johnson, *Denver's Mayor Speer* (Denver: Green Mountain Press, 1969), pp. xix–xxi, 38–47.

13 William H. Wilson, *The City Beautiful Movement* (Baltimore: Johns Hopkins University Press, 1989), p. 252.

14 "Celebrated Sculptor Views Civic Center," *Denver Rocky Mountain News*, 21 September 1917.

15 "Two New Statues to Add to City's Art Possessions," *Denver Post*, 30 June 1918.

16 Alexander Phimister Proctor, *Sculptor in Buckskin* (Norman, Okla.: University of Oklahoma Press, 1971), pp. 177–79.

17 Roy Myers, "Statuary Worth Hundred Thousand Made in Los Altos Barn," *San Jose Mercury Herald*, 21 July 1918.

18 See "Denver's Civic Center Takes Form," *Municipal Facts* (April 1919): 3–7; "Some Recent Civic Benefactions," *Municipal Facts* (September–October 1919): 3–5; and Samuel Sergeant Newbury, *Art in Denver* (Denver: City Club of Denver, 1928), p. 18.

19 On Seattle's failed efforts, see Wilson, *The City Beautiful Movement*, p. 234. On Proctor in Seattle, see "Noted Sculptor Visits Seattle, Urges More Statues for City," *Seattle Daily Times*, 11 August 1919.

20 Arthur Frenzel, "A. Phimister Proctor, One of Early-Day Westerners, Will Put Up Monuments Where Once He Played Ball—Art Works to Cost $30,000," *Denver Post*, 26 December 1919.

21 "The Bucking Broncho," *Municipal Facts* (May–July 1926): 20.

42 "Sundown" Nez Perce's Chief

1 "Jackson Sundown Home with Spoils of Roundup [*sic*]," *Seattle Post-Intelligencer*, unidentified clipping, Proctor Museum Archives.

2 "Proctor's Sculpture Will Make Immortal Winner of Round-Up," *Portland Oregon Sunday Journal*, 11 February 1917.

3 "Pendleton Gets Back to Normal After a Whirlwind Round-Up," *Portland Oregon Journal*, 26 September 1916. The caption above an accompanying photograph read "Real Indian Is Happy and Popular Champion."

4 "Proctor A Sculptor of Unusual Power," *Los Angeles Times*, 1 April 1923.

5 "All Tastes Suited in Seven Exhibits at Art Institute," *Chicago Tribune*, 11 March 1917. The exhibition was titled *Small Bronzes by A. Phimister Proctor* and ran from 8 March through 12 April, 1917.

6 "Chicago Institute of Art Has Seven One-Man Shows," *Christian Science Monitor*, 26 April 1917.

7 Frank Owen Payne, "Two New Bronzes by A. Phimister Proctor," unidentified clipping, c. 1917, Proctor Museum Archives.

8 *Idaho County Free Press*, 27 December 1923.

43 On the War Trail

1 David Kent Ballast, *Denver's Civic Center: A Walking Tour* (Denver: David Kent Ballast, 1977).

2 A. W. Steele to A. P. Proctor, 23 May 1922, Colorado Historical Society, Denver.

3 "Sculptor Here on Auto Tour Seeking Jackson Sundown to Pose Again," *Pendleton East Oregonian*, 4 June 1918.

4 Roy Myers, "Statuary Worth Hundred Thousand Made in Los Altos Barn," *San Jose Mercury Herald*, 21 July 1918.

5 "Two New Statues to Add to City's Art Possessions," *Denver Post*, 30 June 1918.

6 Two unidentified clippings, Proctor Museum Archives. The reference to the rodeos says Sundown "lost interest in his work and returned to Idaho, after failing to ride Coyote, a noted outlaw horse, on two occasions, at San Francisco and San Jose roundups." The "Foghorn" Murphy story comes from syndicated columnist Edwin C. Hill, who wrote an article, "Indian Love," about Proctor and Sundown in 1939. See also Alexander Phimister Proctor, *Sculptor in Buckskin* (Norman, Okla.: University of Oklahoma Press, 1971), pp. 179–80.

7 One article stated that Red Belt, the model's real name, was Big Beaver's son. See "Artist Takes Indian Model East With Him," *San Francisco Chronicle*, 30 November 1919.

8 See "'Red Belt,' Indian Model of Sculptor, Discovers Pacific," *Daily Palo Alto Times*, 27 October 1919.

9 "Artist Takes Indian Model East With Him."

10 Ernest Peixotto, "A Sculptor of the West," *Scribner's Monthly* 68, no. 18 (September 1920): 274.

11 "Denver Sculptor Leaves for East to Ship Indian Equestrian Statue for Civic Center," *Denver Rocky Mountain News*, 5 January 1922.

12 "New Indian Statue Goes Up in Civic Center," *Denver Rocky Mountain News*, 10 May 1922.

44 Theodore Roosevelt

1 "Equestrian Statue of Roosevelt to be Commenced Soon," unidentified clipping, 30 June 1920, Proctor Museum Archives.

2 *Christian Science Monitor*, 16 August 1920.

3 A. Phimister Proctor, "The Sculptor and the Subject," *The Spectator*, 11 November 1922.

4 Carl E. Akeley to A. P. Proctor, 13 January 1921, Proctor Museum Archives.

5 "Model Wears T.R.'s Uniform," *Portland Oregon Journal*, 5 June 1921.

6 Proctor, "The Sculptor and the Subject."

7 "Coe Statue Lauded by Mrs. Roosevelt," *Portland (Ore.) Telegram*, 5 May 1926.

8 Kermit visited the New York studio in February 1922 (see Kermit Roosevelt to Proctor, 23 February 1922, Proctor Museum Archives). For a letter from the president's sister, Corinne Roosevelt Robinson, after she viewed the plaster maquette, see "Statue Site in Doubt," *Portland Oregonian*, 19 June 1922.

9 Ibid.

10 "Site Selected For Memorial," *Portland (Ore.) Telegram*, 6 March 1922.

11 "Statue by Proctor Is Declared to be Virile Record of Theodore Roosevelt," *Portland Oregonian*, 12 November 1922.

12 Royal Cortissoz, "Roosevelt: An Equestrian Monument Destined for Oregon," *New York Tribune*, 16 April 1922. Proctor sent the Cortissoz review to friends in Portland who saw to it that the critic's words found their way into print in the Oregon press. See, for example, "Roosevelt Statue Wins Praise of Famous Critics," *Portland Oregon Journal*, 30 April 1922.

13 See "Our Park's Heroic Bronzes," *The Spectator*, 19 December 1925, and "Dr. Henry Waldo Coe Visits Minot and Selects Site for Roosevelt Statue Which He Has Presented to City," *Ward County Independent*, 25 October 1923.

14 Lewis F. Crawford, "Oregon Critic Not Able to Appreciate Sculptor's Conception of Roosevelt Equestrian Statue," unidentified clipping, Proctor Museum Archives.

15 "Some Hind Legs," *The Spectator*, 9 January 1926.

16 "Famous Bronze Horses—Pick the Winner," *Portland Oregonian*, 10 January 1926.

17 "T. Roosevelt's Statue Authentic," *Portland Oregonian*, 29 October 1948.

18 "Coe Statue Lauded by Mrs. Roosevelt."

19 Ibid.

45 Circuit Rider

1 "Heroic Circuit Riders To Be Well Honored," *Portland (Ore.) Telegram*, 8 January 1921.

2 Ibid.

3 Booth family stories and genealogy records were supplied by Harriet Wittlie.

4 Unidentified clipping, c. 1921, Proctor Museum Archives. See also "Statue to Commemorate Heroism and Self-Sacrifice of Early-Day Pastors Created By Noted Westerner," *Portland Oregonian*, 9 January 1921.

5 Judge Charles H. Carey, "Circuit Rider Memorial Declared Fine Conception," *Portland Oregonian*, 9 January 1921.

6 Ibid.

7 "Palo Alto Sculptor Given Double Honor," *Palo Alto Times*, 26 January 1921; "Statue to Honor Pioneer of Oregon," *San Francisco Bulletin*, 4 February 1921; and "Sculptor Finishes Working Models of Theodore Roosevelt and 'Circuit Rider,'" *Portland Oregonian*, 25 September 1921.

8 Unidentified clipping, c. 1921, Proctor Museum Archives.

9 "Roosevelt Statue Forms Feature at A. P. Proctor Studio," *Daily Palo Alto*, 2 November 1921.

10 "Sculptor to Open Studio to Public," *Palo Alto Times*, 29 November 1922.

11 Louise M. O'Hara, "Completes Statue of 'The Circuit Rider,'" *San Francisco Call*, 27 December 1922; and "Honor the Pioneer," *San Francisco Journal*, 19 August 1922.

12 Gertrude Robinson Ross, "The Sculptor of The West," *Oregon Magazine*, 30 January 1923.

13 A. M. Simpson to Proctor, telegram, 28 February 1923, Proctor Museum Archives. See *Exhibition of American Sculptures* (New York: National Sculpture Society, 1923) for reference to Proctor's participation.

14 Joseph N. Teal, "The American Pioneer" (speech delivered at the unveiling and dedication of the *Circuit Rider*, Salem, Oregon, 1924).

15 "History in Bronze," *Seattle Post-Intelligencer*, 9 February 1924, and Charles J. Lisle, "Statue of 'Circuit Rider' Is Received by State in Presence of Thousands Who Pay Tribute to Robert Booth, Minister," unidentified clipping, 30 April 1924, Proctor Museum Archives.

16 William Swing, "Capitol's Bronze Circuit Rider Statue Suffers Split Seams In Storm Tumble," *Portland Oregonian*, 26 October 1962, and Tony Bacon, "Capitol Statue Repaired By Vancouver Sculptor," *Portland Oregonian*, 8 August 1963.

46 Indian Girl

1 Alexander Phimister Proctor, *Sculptor in Buckskin* (Norman, Okla.: University of Oklahoma Press, 1971), p. 183. This is corroborated in a letter to the sculpture's first patron, Ora Maytag of Newton, Iowa, in which Proctor, as he makes plans to ship the bronze from Rome to Newton, said, "It will be a long journey for her. California to Rome, then back to Iowa." A. P. Proctor to Ora Maytag, 3 April 1926, Collection of the Jasper County Historical Society, Newton, Iowa.

2 See Virgil Rupp, *Let 'Er Buck: A History of the Pendleton Round-Up* (Pendleton, Ore.: Pendleton Round-Up Association, 1985), pp. 181–88.

3 See Charles Wellington Furlong, *Let 'Er Buck: A Story of the Passing of the West* (New York: G. P. Putnam's Sons, 1921), p. 82.

4 Proctor to Maytag, 1 June 1926, Jasper County Historical Society.

5 "Of Art and Italy's Sovereigns," unidentified clipping from an Oregon newspaper, 1926, Proctor Museum Archives.

6 James D. Phelan to Proctor, 13 October 1926, Proctor Museum Archives.

7 Loring Holmes Dodd, *The Golden Age of American Sculpture* (Boston: Chapman & Grimes, 1936).

8 "At 80 Starts His Masterpiece," *New York Sun*, 21 April 1930.

9 See Michael A. Jacobsen, "Some Visual Sources for the Sculpture of Alexander Phimister Proctor," *Apelles* 1, no. 2 (spring 1980): 21.

47 Pioneer Mother (Equestrian)

1 Alexander Phimister Proctor, *Sculptor in Buckskin* (Norman, Okla.: University of Oklahoma Press, 1971), p. 184. Hough is quoted in W. H. Hutchinson, *The World, the Work and the West of W. H. D. Koerner* (Norman, Okla.: University of Oklahoma Press, 1978), p. 143.

2 Proctor, *Sculptor in Buckskin*, p. 184.

3 Giles Carroll Mitchell, *There Is No Limit: Architecture and Sculpture in Kansas City* (Kansas City, Mo.: Brown-White, 1934), p. 77. See also Proctor, *Sculptor in Buckskin*, p. 185. Vanderslice was president of Vanderslice-Lynds Mercantile Co., a grain brokerage house, and the Eagle Elevator Co. He was months old when his parents migrated from Kentucky to Kansas. Although the model for the monument was Margaret Proctor, the primary tribute paid here was to the patron's mother, Sarah J. Vanderslice, and his mother-in-law, Martha A. Flinn, a Kansas pioneer from Virginia. See "A Grain Merchant's Tribute to Pioneer Mothers," *The Southwest Miller* 6, no. 38 (15 November 1927): 1–2.

4 Proctor, *Sculptor in Buckskin*, p. 185.

5 "Agreement," Proctor Museum Archives. The final cost of the project as borne by Vanderslice, which included the pedestal and site preparation, was reported as $100,000. See *Kansas City Star*, 21 October 1927.

6 "The Pioneer Mother," *New York Herald Tribune*, 25 March 1925.

7 See Proctor, *Sculptor in Buckskin*, p. 187. Letters and telegrams from the three foundries to Proctor provided the prices that they would charge. Roman Bronze Works telegrammed on February 6, 1925, that a bronze measuring twelve feet to the top of the

woman's head would cost $21,000. The Gorham Company wrote on April 3, 1925, with an equivalent quote. All three documents are in the Proctor Museum Archives.

8 "Seek Site for Gift Statue," *Kansas City Star*, 5 April 1925, and "Western Spirit Shown," *Portland Oregonian*, 14 April 1925.

9 Henry Cavendish, "Royalty Sees American Art Show in Rome," *New York American*, 3 June 1928.

10 "Henry J. Allen Sees the Pioneer Mother," *Kansas City Star*, 18 March 1927.

11 See especially "Sculptor Who Did Roosevelt, Now Working on 'Pioneer Mother' in Rome," *New York Herald (Paris)*, 14 July 1926, and "I Sovrani Visitano l'Accademia Americana, al Gianicolo," *Il Piccolo*, 22–23 May 1926.

12 Mitchell, *There Is No Limit*, pp. 79–80.

13 "K.C. Worships at Mother Shrine," *Kansas City Journal*, 12 November 1927.

14 "As Those of Their Blood," *Kansas City Star*, 13 November 1927. See also "30,000 Trek to Pioneer Statue," *Kansas City Journal*, 14 November 1927.

15 See Margaret Whitemore, "Phimister Proctor's Statue of a Pioneer Mother," *The American Magazine of Art* 19, no. 7 (July 1928): 376–77.

16 "Agreement," Proctor Museum Archives.

17 Ibid.

18 Proctor, *Sculptor in Buckskin*, p. 188. The Santa Barbara Art Museum records indicate that the Cleggs acquired their cast directly from the artist in 1927. Information was provided by the museum's assistant director for curatorial affairs, Robert Henning.

19 Quoted in Mitchell, *There Is No Limit*, p. 83. Borglum's assessment is corroborated by art historian Donald Martin Reynolds, who refers to the *Pioneer Mother* as "the most powerful monument to the pioneer mother." See *Masters of American Sculpture: The Figurative Tradition from the American Renaissance to the Millennium* (New York: Abbeville Press, 1993), p. 220.

48 High Relief of Bison Head

1 James M. Goode, *The Outdoor Sculptures of Washington, D.C.* (Washington: Smithsonian Press, 1974), p. 193.

2 From an inscription on the reverse of a photograph titled *Bison Head*, Proctor Museum Archives.

3 A photograph shows one of the *Bison Head* reliefs clearly dated 1927 over the artist's signature. See Proctor Museum Archives.

4 See Wayne Craven, *Sculpture in America* (New York: Thomas Y. Crowell, 1968), p. 569.

5 See note 2.

49 U.S. Cavalryman

1 Voorheis Richeson, "Troop 'G' of the Second Wins Goodrich Trophy," *U.S. Army Recruiting News* 10, no. 7 (1 April 1928): 4. See also "To the Best Cavalry Unit in the U.S. Army," *New York Sun*, 8 February 1928.

2 A. P. Proctor to Major General H. B. Crosby, 5 August 1926, Proctor Museum Archives.

3 Ibid.

4 Richeson, "'Troop G' of the Second Wins."

5 I am grateful to Scott Hamric of the Third Cavalry Museum, Fort Carson, Colorado, for supplying this and much other information concerning the history of the Goodrich Riding Trophy.

6 "Noted Sculptor Pines for Oregon," *The Spectator*, unidentified clipping, 1926, Proctor Museum Archives.

7 Hester Proctor, "Phimister Proctor," undated typescript of a speech, National Cowboy and Western Heritage Museum, Oklahoma City.

8 See First Lieutenant Joseph T. Martin, "The Armor Leadership Award," *Armor* (Sept.–Oct. 1976): 27–28, and "Draper Trophy," *Armor* (July–August 1977): 74.

50 Til Taylor

1 Unidentified clipping, *Pendleton East Oregonian*, c. 1926, Proctor Museum Archives.

2 Alexander Phimister Proctor, *Sculptor in Buckskin* (Norman, Okla.: University of Oklahoma Press, 1971), p. 164.

3 Benjamin W. Olcott to A. P. Proctor, 31 August 1920, Proctor Museum Archives.

4 See "Sentiment Is Being Sounded Out on Use of Til Taylor Fund," *Pendleton (Ore.) Tribune*, 1 October 1921.

5 "Umatilla Dream of Statue Honoring Memory of Tillman Taylor Realized…," *Pendleton East Oregonian*, 19 September 1929.

6 Fred Lockley, "Observations and Impressions of the Journal Man," *Portland (Ore.) Journal*, 6 November 1921.

7 Ibid.

8 "Sculptor Who Did Roosevelt, Now Working on 'Pioneer Mother' in Rome," *New York Herald (Paris)*, 14 July 1926.

9 "Pendleton Prepares for Unveiling of Til Taylor Memorial Statue in Park…," *Pendleton East Oregonian*, 22 September 1928.

10 "Un Statuaire du Far-West," *L'Etoile Belge*, 21 May 1928.

11 "He Modeled, Threw Lasso for Royalty," *Seattle Daily Times*, 7 November 1928.

12 "Likeness of Til Taylor Is Work of Beauty," *Pendleton East Oregonian*, 6 August 1929.

13 Ibid.

14 "Proctor Praises Color of Til Taylor Statue in Pioneer Park…," unidentified clipping, c. 1932, Proctor Museum Archives.

51 McKnight Memorial Fountain

1 "Pass Up Wichita in Selecting Sculptor," *Wichita Eagle*, 14 June 1929.

2 Ibid. There is no evidence that this approval process was followed.

3 Ibid.

4 "Beautiful Work of Art Presented to School By Victor Murdock," *Wichita Eagle*, 20 September 1931.

5 "Famous Sculptor Here to Help Dedicate Memorial Fountain," *Wichita Beacon*, 17 September 1931.

6 This history has been graciously provided me by Dr. Chris Polk and extracted from *Report to the Historic Wichita Board*, 12 November 1975.

7 "Famous Sculptor Here."

52 Oregon Pioneer Mother

1 Burt Brown Barker to A. P. Proctor, 3 November 1927, quoted in the dedication program for the *Oregon Pioneer Mother*, 7 May 1932, Proctor Museum Archives.

2 "Statue to Picture Sunset of Pioneer's Life," *Portland Oregonian*, 25 May 1930.

3 See note 1. On Barker's debt to his wife's art inspiration, see "Donor of Statue Dedicated to

Pioneer Mothers Tells of Inspiration for Project," *Portland Oregonian*, 1 May 1932.

4 Alexander Phimister Proctor, *Sculptor in Buckskin* (Norman, Okla.: University of Oklahoma Press, 1971), p. 192.

5 "Statue to Picture Sunset of Pioneer's Life."

6 Roman Bronze Works records for job # RB 1025, 12/9/29, Amon Carter Museum Archives, Fort Worth, Texas. Even as late as May 1930, however, it had not been decided whether the final monument would be made of bronze or marble. See "Pioneer Mother Memorial May Be Given to University," *Eugene (Ore.) Guardian*, 24 May 1930.

7 E. C. Sherburne, "A Tribute to Pioneer Women," *Christian Science Monitor*, 10 May 1930.

8 President Herbert Hoover to Barker, quoted in the dedication program for the *Oregon Pioneer Mother*, 7 May 1932, Proctor Museum Archives.

9 "Pioneer Mother Memorial May Be Given to University."

10 Proctor to Gifford Proctor, 22 January 1946, Papers of Gifford Proctor, Wilton, Conn. Proctor thought he recalled casting three bronzes of this work, each three feet high, but none has been found.

53 Pony Express

1 Howard R. Driggs, *Covered-Wagon Centennial and Ox-Team Days* (New York: World Book, 1931), pp. 117, 120.

2 William Henry Jackson, *Time Exposure* (New York: G. P. Putnam's Sons, 1940), p. 332.

3 Driggs, *Covered-Wagon Centennial*, p. 118.

4 Ibid., 120.

5 *Newark (N.J.) Evening News*, 18 April 1931.

54 General Robert E. Lee

1 Mildred Young, "Dallasite Perpetuates Tradition of Old South," *Dallas Herald*, 14 June 1963. According to association records, Elizabeth Rogers died in 1967 at age ninety-one. I am grateful to the association historian, Mrs. Dewey D. Johnston, for sharing this and many other insights about the Lee monument with me.

2 Alexander Phimister Proctor, *Sculptor in Buckskin* (Norman, Okla.: University of Oklahoma Press, 1971), p. 192. Some sources suggest that this was a competition, but association records make no mention of other artists being involved. An article in the *Dallas Morning News*, "Gen. R. E. Lee and Young Aide Riding Together Selected as Memorial to Go in One of City Parks," 19 May 1932, suggests that several sculptors "bid for the commission."

3 See Proctor, *Sculptor in Buckskin*, p. 192.

4 "New York Sculptor to Visit Dallas for Lee Statue Bid," *Dallas Daily News*, 17 April 1932, and "New York Sculptor to Lecture Wednesday," *Dallas Herald*, 17 April 1932.

5 Proctor, *Sculptor in Buckskin*, p. 192.

6 *Dallas Times Herald*, undated clipping, Proctor Museum Archives. Proctor (*Sculptor in Buckskin*, p. 193) says this took place in August 1933, but the article mentions that he planned to spend the summer working on the project in his Wilton, Connecticut, studio.

7 *The Dallas Southern Memorial Association*, flyer, 22 January 1934, Texas/Dallas History and Archives Division, Club and Organisation Yearbook Files–Dallas Southern Memorial Association–Misc.

8 "Lee Memorial To Be Erected in Oak Lawn," unidentified clipping, Proctor Museum Archives. A brochure, "History of General Robert E. Lee and Confederate Soldier Monument" in the files of the Dallas Southern Memorial Association indicates that the park was not officially renamed until May 5, 1936, and then as "Robert E. Lee Park."

9 "A. Phimister Proctor, World-Famous Sculptor Working on Heroic Statue of Gen. R. E. Lee," *Ridgefield (Conn.) Press*, 9 August 1934.

10 "Group to Seek Pledged Money for Lee Statue," *Dallas Morning News*, 7 January 1935, and "Washingtonians' Art Interest at the Corcoran Gallery," *Washington Post*, 5 May 1935.

11 Leila Mechlin, "New Statue of Gen. Lee," *Washington Sunday Star*, 12 May 1935.

12 Sherwood Trask to A.P. Proctor, 2 February 1936, Proctor Museum Archives. The *New York Times* photograph appeared in the paper that same day.

13 "Dallas Gives Roosevelt Greatest Welcome of Tour," *Dallas Morning News*, 13 June 1936, and Proctor, *Sculptor in Buckskin*, p. 197.

14 "President Unveils Statue of R. E. Lee in Brief Ceremony," unidentified clipping, Proctor Museum Archives.

15 Mrs. Russell V. Rogers, introductory remarks, dedication of Lee monument, 1936, in "The Dallas Southern Memorial Association," brochure, 1939–1940, Dallas Southern Memorial Association files.

16 "Mr. Proctor Replies," unidentified clipping, Proctor Museum Archives.

55 Mustangs

1 J. Frank Dobie, *The Mustangs* (Boston: Little, Brown, 1934).

2 J. Frank Dobie, "The Monument of the Seven Mustangs," *The Cattleman* 35, no. 4 (September 1948): 194.

3 Ibid.; also Howard and Audrey Karl Shaff, *Six Wars at a Time: The Life and Times of Gutzon Borglum, Sculptor of Mount Rushmore* (Sioux Falls, S. Dak.: Augustana College, 1985), pp. 233–34. Borglum's model was completed in 1926. He helped the association raise funds, and the bronze monument was eventually set in place in 1942.

4 Proctor, *Sculptor in Buckskin* (Norman, Okla.: University of Oklahoma Press, 1971), p. 198.

5 "Mustang Statue Lifelong Dream of Man Who Grew Up On One," *Austin American-Statesman*, 30 May 1948. Exactly who the other aspirants were is not known. Dobie was friends with Joe DeYong of Santa Barbara and correspondence suggests that he may have submitted a model for consideration. See J. Frank Dobie to Joe DeYong, 27 October and 11 November 1938, DeYong Papers, National Cowboy and Western Heritage Museum, Oklahoma City.

6 See Lon Tinkle, *An American Original: The Life of J. Frank Dobie* (Boston: Little, Brown, 1978), p. 159.

7 Charles B. Driscoll, "New York Day By Day," quoted in *Minneapolis Evening Journal*, 25 April 1939.

8 Proctor, *Sculptor in Buckskin*, p. 199.

9 "Mustang Memorial Will Be Erected," *The Cattleman* 25, no. 12 (May 1939): 7.

10 "Memorial to Mustang Given U.T. by Austin Man," *Austin American-Statesman*, 9 March 1939.

11 Ibid.

12 See E. H. Sellards to Dobie, 6 December 1938, Dobie Papers.

13 "Memorial to Mustang Given U.T. by Austin Man."

14 "Sculptor Casts Texas Cowhorses in Epic Bronze for University of Texas Campus," *Corpus Christi Caller*, 20 November 1940.

15 "Mustang Group to Be Erected at University," *Dallas Times Herald Daily*, 27 October 1939.

16 "New York Sculptor Completes Model for Museum Statuary," *Daily Texan*, 21 May 1940.

17 "New Proctor Statue to Texas U. Campus," *Wilton Bulletin*, 3 July 1941.

18 William S. Drake to A. P. Proctor, 9 June 1941, Collections of the Texas Memorial Museum. A subsequent letter in the same collection from Drake to Ogden, dated January 2, 1942, explains the dire impact of delays: "The Office of Production Management issued orders that no bronze castings for civilian purposes would be permitted after December 31st, 1941, which means that no work of this character can be cast during the duration of the existing emergencies."

19 Proctor to Dobie, November 1941, Dobie Papers.

20 Proctor to Dobie, 1 February 1942, Dobie Papers.

21 Proctor to Dobie, 8 July 1942, Dobie Papers.

22 Proctor to Dobie, 29 July 1943, Dobie Papers.

23 Proctor to Sellards, 2 June 1944, Collections of the Texas Memorial Museum. Dobie echoed Proctor's sentiments when he wrote Sellards on June 8, 1944, suggesting that the matter be promptly placed in the hands of competent, sympathetic lawyers. "It is only fair to Mr. Proctor, who has already been wronged. It is only fair to the people that Ogden had in mind and to his own memory" (Collections of the Texas Memorial Museum).

24 Sellards to Proctor, 2 June 1944, Collections of the Texas Memorial Museum.

25 Proctor to Dobie's wife, Bertha, 3 June 1944, Dobie Papers.

26 "Sculptor Sees His Mustangs," *Providence (R.I.) Evening Bulletin*, 24 April 1948.

27 "$60,000 U.T. Mustang Monument Is Unveiled," *Houston Post*, 1 June 1948.

28 J. Frank Dobie, "Will Longhorn Monument Join the Mustangs," *Sunday American-Statesman*, 6 June 1948.

29 Proctor to Dobie, 24 October 1947, Dobie Papers.

30 Dobie, "The Monument of the Seven Mustangs," and Proctor to Dobie, 30 October 1948, Dobie Papers.

31 Dobie to Proctor, 13 August 1948, Dobie Papers.

BIBLIOGRAPHY

Manuscripts

Custer, Elizabeth, Personal Papers, Frost Collection, Monroe County Historical Museum, Monroe, Mich.

Dobie, J. Frank, Personal Papers, Collections of the Harry Ransom Humanities Research Center, University of Texas at Austin (abbreviated to "Dobie Papers")

Gorham Company Papers, Archives of American Art, Washington, D.C.

Pinchot, Gifford, Personal Papers, Manuscript Division, Library of Congress, Washington, D.C. (abbreviated to "Pinchot Papers")

Proctor, Alexander Phimister, Biographical Sketches, Typescript, Proctor Papers, Colorado Historical Society, Denver (abbreviated to "Proctor Papers")

_____, Personal Papers, A. Phimister Proctor Museum, Poulsbo, Wash. (abbreviated to "Proctor Museum Archives")

_____, Personal Papers, Archives of American Art, Washington, DC.

Roman Bronze Works Archives, Amon Carter Museum, Fort Worth, Tex.

Saint-Gaudens, Augustus, Personal Papers, Rauner Special Collections Library, Dartmouth College Library, Hanover, N.H. (abbreviated to "Saint-Gaudens Papers")

Shaw, Edwin Coupland, Personal Papers, Archives of American Art, Washington, D.C.

Unpublished Materials

Broun, Elizabeth, "American Paintings and Sculpture in the Fine Arts Building of the World's Columbian Exposition, Chicago, 1893" (Ph.D. dissertation, University of Kansas, 1976).

Martorano, Mary Lou, "Artists and Art Organizations in Colorado" (MA thesis, University of Denver, 1962).

Mills, J. Harrison, "Concerning Early Art in Colorado" (typescript letter, 1916, Western History Collection, Denver Public Library, Denver).

National Museum of American Art, "Inventory of American Sculpture" (National Museum of American Art, Smithsonian Institution, Washington, D.C., 1988).

Proctor, Hester, "Alexander Phimister Proctor, Sculptor" (typescript, Research Center, National Cowboy and Western Heritage Museum, Oklahoma City).

Richman, Michael Tingley, "Edward Kemeys (1843–1907), American Animal Sculptor" (MA thesis, George Washington University, 1970).

Shapiro, Michael E., "The Development of American Bronze Foundries" (Ph. D. dissertation, Harvard University, 1980).

Books

Ahrens, Kent, *Cyrus E. Dallin: His Small Bronzes and Plasters* (Corning, N.Y.: Rockwell Museum, 1995).

Armstrong, Tom, et al., *200 Years of American Sculpture* (New York: David R. Godine, 1976).

Art Institute of Chicago, *Small Bronzes by A. Phimister Proctor* (Chicago: Art Institute of Chicago, 1917).

Bowditch, Nancy Douglas, *George de Forest Brush: Recollections of a Joyous Painter* (Peterborough, N.H.: William L. Bauhan, 1970).

Bridges, William, *Gathering of Animals: An Unconventional History of the New York Zoological Society* (New York: Harper & Row, 1974).

Broder, Patricia Janis, *Bronzes of the American West* (New York: Harry N. Abrams, 1973).

Caffin, Charles H., *American Masters of Sculpture* (Garden City, N.Y.: Doubleday, Page, 1913).

Cairns, Mary Lyons, *Grand Lake: The Pioneers* (Denver: The World Press, 1946).

Cook, General D. J., *Hands Up* (Denver: Republican Publishing Company, 1882).

Corcoran Gallery of Art, *Works in Sculpture by A. Phimister Proctor* (Washington, D.C: Corcoran Gallery of Art, 1918).

Craven, Wayne, *Sculpture in America* (New York: Thomas Y. Crowell, 1968).

Davies, A. Mervyn, *Solon H. Borglum, A Man Who Stands Alone* (Chester, Conn.: Pequot Press, 1974).

Dryfhout, John H., *The Work of Augustus Saint-Gaudens* (Hanover, N.H.: University Press of New England, 1982)

Falk, Peter Hastings and Andrea Ansell Bien, *The Annual Exhibition Record of the National Academy of Design*, 1901–1950 (Madison, Conn.: Sound View Press, 1990).

Fischer, Diane P., et al., *Paris 1900: The "American School" at the Universal Exposition* (Montclair, N.J.: Montclair Art Museum, 1999).

Furlong, Charles Wellington, *Let 'Er Buck: A Story of the Passing of the West* (New York: G. P. Putnam's Sons, 1921).

Gardner, Albert Ten Eyck, *American Sculpture: A Catalogue of the Collection of the Metropolitan Museum of Art* (Greenwich, Conn.: New York Graphic Society, 1965).

Gorham Company, *A. Phimister Proctor* (New York: Gorham Company, 1913).

Greenthal, Kathryn, *Augustus Saint-Gaudens* (New York: Metropolitan Museum of Art, 1985).

Jackman, Rilla Evelyn, *American Arts* (New York: Rand McNally & Co., 1940).

Lamb, Robert J., *The Canadian Art Club*, 1907–1915 (Edmonton: Edmonton Art Gallery, 1988).

Leckie, Shirley A., *Elizabeth Bacon Custer and the Making of a Myth* (Norman, Okla.: University of Oklahoma Press, 1993).

MacKay, James, *The Animaliers: A Collector's Guide to the Animal Sculptors of the Nineteenth & Twentieth Centuries* (New York: E. P. Dutton Co., 1975).

McGill, Jean S., *Edmund Morris: Frontier Artist* (Toronto: Dundurn Press, 1984).

McSpadden, J. Walker, *Famous Sculptors of America* (New York: Dodd, Mead, 1924).

Montross Gallery, *Sculpture, Bronzes, Water Colors, and Sketches Exhibited by A. Phimister Proctor, N. A.* (New York: Montross Gallery, 1908).

Naylor, Maria, *The National Academy of Design Exhibition Record, 1861–1900* (New York: Kennedy Galleries, 1973).

Proctor, Alexander Phimister, *Sculptor in Buckskin* (Norman, Okla.: University of Oklahoma Press, 1971).

Proske, Beatrice Gilman, *Brookgreen Gardens: Catalogue of Sculpture* (Brookgreen, S.C.: Brookgreen Gardens, 1936).

Pyne, Kathleen, et al., *The Quest for Unity: American Art Between World's Fairs 1876–1893* (Detroit: Detroit Institute of Arts, 1983).

Reynolds, Donald Martin, *Masters of American Sculpture* (New York: Abbeyville Press, 1993).

Rusk, William Sener, *William Henry Rinehart* (Baltimore: Norman T. A. Munder, 1939).

Saint-Gaudens, Homer, *The Reminiscences of Augustus Saint-Gaudens* (London: Andrew Melrose, 1913).

Savell, Isabelle K., *The Tonetti Years of Sneden's Landing* (New York: Historical Society of Rockland County , 1977).

Shapiro, Michael E., *Bronze Casting and American Sculpture 1850–1900* (Newark, Del.: University of Delaware Press, 1985).

Stewart, Rick, *Charles M. Russell, Sculptor* (Fort Worth, Tex.: Amon Carter Museum, 1994).

Taft, Lorado, *The History of American Sculpture* (New York: Macmillan, 1924).

Tolles, Thayer, Lauretta Dimmick and Donna J. Hassler, *American Sculpture in the Metropolitan Museum of Art* (New York: Metropolitan Museum of Art, 1999–2001).

Wallace, David H., *John Rogers: The People's Sculptor* (Middletown, Conn.: Wesleyan University Press, 1967).

Wilkinson, Burke, *Uncommon Clay: The Life and Works of Augustus Saint-Gaudens* (New York: Harcourt Brace Javonovich, 1985).

Winans, Walter, *Animal Sculpture* (New York: G. P. Putnam's Sons, 1913).

Periodicals

"A. Phimister Proctor," *The News*, Vol. 1, No. 14 (July 26, 1912).

"About the Studios, Phimister Proctor Is a True Natural Sculptor," *Chicago Sunday Inter Ocean* (January 1, 1893).

"Animal Life Shown in Proctor Exhibition," *New York Tribune* (November 20, 1908).

"A Successful Canadian Sculptor," *Toronto Saturday Night* (January 8, 1910).

Balfour, Roberta, "Proctor's Inspiration Was Born in the West," *Denver Post* (March 29, 1903).

Brush, Edward Hale, "An Animal Sculptor," *Arts and Decoration*, Vol. 1 (August 1911).

Caffin, Charles H., "Fine Animal Sculpture by Proctor," *New York American* (October 27, 1913).

Cortissoz, Royal, "Roosevelt: An Equestrian Monument Destined for Oregon," *New York Tribune* (April 16, 1922).

_____, "Some Wild Beasts Sculpted by A. Phimister Proctor," *Scribner's*, Vol. 48, No. 6 (November 1909).

Dallin, Cyrus E., "American Sculpture—Its Present Aspects and Tendencies," *Brush and Pencil*, Vol. 11, No. 6 (March 1903).

Dial, Scott, "Alexander Phimister Proctor," *Southwest Art*, Vol. 5, No. 11 (May 1976).

"Former Newsboy of Denver Now World Famous Sculptor," *Denver Post* (December 19, 1909).

Edgerton, Giles, "Bronze Sculpture in America: Its Value to the Art History of the Nation," *The Craftsman*, Vol. 8, No.4 (1908).

Garland, Hamlin, "Edward Kemeys, A Sculptor of Frontier Life and Animals," *McClure's Magazine*, Vol. 5 (July 1895).

Hawthorne, Julian, "American Wild Animals in Art," *Century Magazine*, Vol. 27, No. 2 (June 1884).

Howard, A. A., "Sculpture at the World's Fair," *Brush and Pencil*, Vol. 15, No. 1 (January 1905).

Jacobsen, Michael A., "Some Visual Sources for the Sculpture of Alexander Phimister Proctor," *Apelles*, Vol. 1, No. 2 (Spring 1980).

McCardell, Roy L., "A. Phimister Proctor—Sculptor, Artist, Big Game Hunter," *Los Angeles Morning Telegraph* (August 12, 1923).

McVey, William M., "Animals, Animal Sculpture and Animal Sculptors," *National Sculpture Review*, Vol. 19, No.2 (Summer 1970).

Nelson, W. H. de B., "Phimister Proctor: Canadian Sculptor," *The Canadian Magazine*, Vol. 44, No. 6 (April 1915).

Paladin, Vivian A., "A. Phimister Proctor: Master Sculptor of Horses," *Montana*, Vol. 14, No. 1 (Winter 1964).

Payne, Frank Owen, "Two New Bronzes by A. Phimister Proctor," *International Studio*, Vol. 85 (March 1926).

Peixotto, Ernest, "A Sculptor of the West," *Scribner's Monthly*, Vol. 68, No. 18 (September 1920).

Poland, Reginald, "Artistic Expression in Denver," *Municipal Facts*, Vol. 3, No. 9 (September 1920).

"Portland's Art Tastes Commended by One of Great Animal Sculptors," *Portland Sunday Oregonian* (December 17, 1911).

Proctor, A. Phimister, "A Quiet Morning in a Goose Pit," *Recreation* (February 1916).

_____, "Never Too Old," *The Alaska Sportsman*, Vol. 11, No. 9 (September 1945).

_____, "The Sculptor and the Subject," *The Spectator* (November 11, 1922).

"Proctor: A Sculptor of Unusual Power," *Los Angeles Times* (April 1, 1923).

Riggall, F. H., "A Record Twice Lost," *Outdoor Life* (December 1957).

Ringstad, Muriel E., "Memoirs of Phimister Proctor," *Frontier Times* (September 1964).

Rogers, John William, "Sculptor of Lee Statue Has Had Colorful Career," *Dallas Times Herald*, Dallas (May 24, 1936).

Ross, Gertrude Robison, "The Sculptor of the West," *Oregon Magazine* (January 30, 1923).

Shufeldt, R. W., "Zoological Statuary at the National Capital," *Natural History*, Vol. 19, Nos. 4–5 (April–May 1919).

Smith, Dan, "Sculptures of the Western Frontier," *New York Herald* (March 12, 1916).

Stickley, Gustav, "Music: Drama: Art: Reviews," *The Craftsman*, Vol. 15, No. 4 (January 1909).

Taft, Lorado, "A. Phimister Proctor, " *Brush and Pencil*, Vol. 2, No. 6 (September 1898).

_____, "American Sculpture at the Exposition—I," *Brush and Pencil*, Vol. 6, No. 4 (July 1900).

_____, "Sculptors of the World's Fair—A Chapter of Appreciations," *Brush and Pencil*, Vol. 13, No. 3 (December 1903).

"To Fame In a Year," *Denver Rocky Mountain News* (October 15, 1893).

Watson, William, "Some Recent Small Sculptures," *Scribner's*, Vol. 40, No. 71 (May 1914).

"When Leo Poses: Wild Animals at the Zoo Are Patient Models," *New York Herald* (May 25, 1902).